AROUND THE WORLD
ON A PENNY-FARTHING

Thomas Stevens was born in 1855 at Berkhamsted in Hertfordshire. He moved with his parents to the USA in 1871, working for a time on their farm in Missouri before moving to Laramie, Wyoming, to work in the Union Pacific Rolling Mills. After two years he travelled the West, and it was in Denver in 1883 that he conceived the idea of travelling the world on a bicycle. As a newspaper correspondent, he was later to achieve brief fame as the first journalist to meet Sir Henry Stanley on his long trek to the coast of East Africa.

Nick Crane is a freelance journalist and author specializing in cycling. His books include *The CTC Route Guide to Cycling in Britain and Ireland*, *Cycling in Europe*, *Bicycles Up Kilimanjaro*, *Journey to the Centre of the Earth* and *The Great Bicycle Adventure* co-written with his cousin Richard Crane.

4/12

CENTURY TRAVELLERS

AROUND THE WORLD ON A PENNY-FARTHING

From San Francisco to Yokohama

Thomas Stevens

Introduction by Nick Crane

ARROW BOOKS

Century Travellers

Published by Arrow Books Limited
20 Vauxhall Bridge Road, London SW1V 2SA

An imprint of the Random Century Group

London Melbourne Sydney Auckland Johannesburg
and agencies throughout the world

First published by Sampson, Low, Marston, Searle & Rivington Ltd
as *Around the World on a Bicycle* 1888
Century edition 1988
First published in this edition as
Around the World on a Penny-Farthing by Arrow 1991

© Thomas Stevens

Printed and bound in Great Britain by
The Guernsey Press Co. Ltd
Guernsey, C.I.

ISBN 0 09 973920 8

CONTENTS

FROM SAN FRANCISCO TO TEHERAN

FROM TEHERAN TO YOKOHAMA

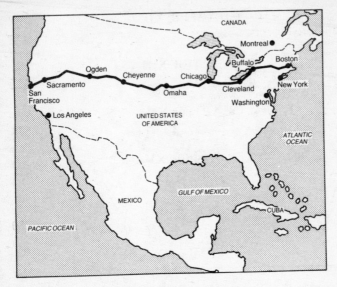

Stevens' route across the United States

Stevens' route through Europe, using the modern names of countries

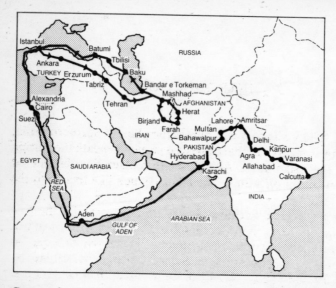

Stevens' route through the Middle East and the Indian sub-continent, using the modern names of countries

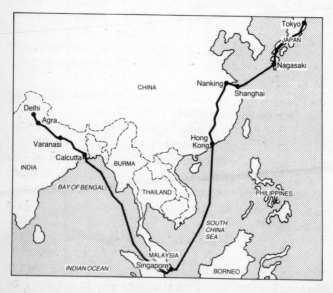

Stevens' route through Asia

INTRODUCTION

In May 1986 I was part way across the plain of northern India, pedalling along a road that appeared to melt beneath the wilting heat of the Asian noon. Ahead, the thin black line shimmered like a reflection on water. The tarmac stuck like treacle to the tyres.

With my cousin Richard, I was hoping to make the first journey to the point in the world most distant from the open sea, an abstract grid-reference in the deserts of north-west China. To make the journey more interesting, we were travelling by bicycle. From the Bay of Bengal, we would cycle through India and Nepal, and then over the Himalayas and across the Tibetan Plateau to China.

A solitary rock as big as a bus drifted by, and then some tiny paddy-fields puddled with shade cast by the nodding heads of a clump of palms. At a cluster of brushwood huts, we stopped and bought *chapatis* and hot sweet tea from a leathery old man wrapped in an off-white *dhoti*. High-pitched wailing music rattled from a radio hanging on a nail by the hut entrance. A dog rolled in the dust.

I looked around. We were in hills. The Rajmahal Hills. One hundred years ago, in September 1886, Thomas Stevens had come this way. But he had been going in the opposite direction, heading towards the Bay of Bengal and Calcutta, and the boat to Hong Kong. His journey was nearly finished; ours had just begun. Except for the tarmac and the transistor, nothing much in the Rajmahal Hills would have changed since Stevens clattered by perched on his penny farthing. The *chapatis* and tea tasted just as good.

Initially, Stevens had planned to travel overland to the Orient, a bold route which had already been interrupted in Afghanistan and now again in India where he allowed himself to bend before the weight of local advice: 'To cross overland from India to China with a bicycle,' he noted, 'is not to be thought of'. For Stevens not to attempt the unthinkable was uncharacteristic, but in the circumstances his rarely-observed caution was understandable. There were no roads across the high plateau of Tibet, and a thousand miles of yak tracks would have been – even by Stevens' extraordinary standards – a trifle trying. Richard and I had no such problems. Today, the road that leads from India, through Tibet to China is the kind of highway along which Stevens would have flown with little more worry than the wear he would inflict upon the brake-spoon of his high-wheeler.

For a man who made the first self-propelled journey around the world, Thomas Stevens has received remarkably little notice. As a journalist he had the skill of observation, description and wit; as a traveller he had curiosity and a dogged sense of purpose. But he had something else too: he was an adventurer. By combining the latest trend in travel – the bicycle – with a journey so completely fanciful that most dismissed him as an impractical visionary, he guaranteed himelf a place in the public eye. At a time when nobody had even cycled across America, Stevens planned to ride across his own continent, then Europe and Asia too. It was an outrageous challenge. Here was an opportunity to achieve something that would be noted in history books. He would be famous. The ride would be more than a record, for records can be broken; this was a 'first', and it would be his for ever.

Unlike so many of today's expeditions, Stevens was not sponsored up to the hilt, he had no support team and had fairly hypothetical maps. He would ride, or fall, by his own wits. For moral support he had the spirit of his fellow 'Wheelmen', while *Outing* magazine, for whom he was special correspondent, would bring the silent support of thousands of readers.

Let us reflect for a moment upon the bicycle of the time. When the tensioned wheel was invented in the early 1870s, it became possible to build large, lightweight wheels, and hence the penny-farthing, or 'Ordinary' as it was properly known. This new form of fast, fashionable personal transport swept through Britain and by the mid 'seventies an estimated 50,000 were on the roads. In 1878 the Cyclists' Touring Club was formed, followed two years later by the League of American Wheelmen. Even the gentry adopted pedal transport after

Queen Victoria was found in 1881 to have ordered two tricycles for her personal use. By 1883 membership of the Cyclists' Touring Club (CTC membership figures have always been a good indicator of the nation's cycling health) had swelled to an astonishing 10,627. Yet cycling in both Britain and the USA was still a local affair, with the exception perhaps of the early Land's End to John o' Groats record attempts which were taking place at this time. Surprisingly, nobody had cycled across America.

Stevens' bicycle was an 1883-pattern 50 inch Columbia Expert. It was little more than a giant wheel that trailed a tiny 'castor' to prevent it rolling over and it was twice as heavy as a modern bicycle. The rider had to sit too far back in relation to the pedals, while the handlebars were too close to the saddle. The result was a bolt-upright riding position which created the maximum wind-resistance and which failed to make best use of the rider's muscles. The rider sat balanced precariously at a height equivalent to a tall man's shoulders. The centre of gravity of both bike and rider was both high and horribly far forward. Too sharp a touch of the brake, particularly going down hill, or even a collision with a stone, could pitch the rider over the handlebars. There was a *very* long way to fall should you take a dreaded 'header'. Headers were often fatal.

When Thomas Stevens left San Francisco in 1884 he was probably unaware that the penny-farthing had all but run its course. Later that year James Humber announced the invention of his diamond-framed chain-driven bicycle, the ancestor of which runs on our roads today. The penny-farthing's fifteen-year life had been short but flamboyant. On the eve of its extinction it was Thomas Stevens who gave this grand old bike its finest ride.

The world in 1884, the year Stevens started his ride, was a fast-changing place. America was quietening down: the Civil War had ended nineteen years earlier and Geronimo, the last of the Indian chiefs to run free, would surrender before Stevens reached Yokohama. Meanwhile Mark Twain (an avid cyclist himself) was bringing the great outdoors indoors with *The Adventures of Huckleberry Finn*. Abroad, the great empires were still twitching their flanks: in 1884 General Gordon was on a one-way march to Khartoum and the Russians were making tentative encroachments into Afghanistan. In London, the first deep tube underground railway was completed, and the first part of the *Oxford English Dictionary* was published. Beneath the Alps, the St Gotthard Tunnel was opened. And in this year too a technological development took place that would change the sound, sight and smell of cities and roads for the next century: Karl Benz managed to build the world's first petrol-driven motor car. For cyclists the honeymoon was over.

In an age when no Grand Tour was complete without its porters and trunks full of spare suits, apothecary cases and iron locks for inadequate hotel rooms, it is remarkable to discover in these pages just how *little* luggage Stevens travelled with. He had no coat, or tent, or sleeping bag, and seldom carried food or drink. If he needed shelter, his sheet of thin, oiled cambric could be used as a poncho, or draped over his upturned bicycle to form a tent, or wrapped tightly round his body to insulate him from the cold of night. In a leather case he carried a few medicines, matches, map, a notebook, fountain pen, travellers' ink-pot and League of American Wheelman badge. His Waterbury fob watch (with its chain removed) ticked loudly in a special pocket in his pantaloons. Stevens' extra clothing was limited to a second riding shirt. He set himself the goal of achieving 40 miles a day, though regularly exceeded this.

With such a simple machine and solid tyres to boot, Stevens needed few tools and no puncture repair kit. Instead he carried a .38 Smith & Wesson, which proved a handy companion in the wilder recesses of central Asia. Initially his revolver seems to have functioned as a toy with which he could occupy himself in moments of boyish abandon; romping across America like a kid with a new catapult, he admits that on most days he found *something* to fire at. Fortunately for the wildlife he was a hopeless shot. It is in these early stages of the ride that we see a Stevens busting with carefree *joie de vivre*, relishing the excitement and danger and loving the attention bestowed upon his dashing 'Wheel'. One of my favourite scenes is of the exuberant Stevens pedalling acrobatically around the tables of the pool-room bar in Carlin, Nevada.

To find humour in any situation, however uncomfortable, is a gift to be treasured by any traveller. Stevens has an endearing knack of understating horrendous predicaments: soaked to the skin by English rain, he writes charitably of 'superabundant moisture' and having waded naked through a neck-deep lake of Persian mud he emerges uttering 'sundry theological remarks'; *Stevenspeak* for what no doubt was a stream of indelicate oaths. It takes a lynch mob in China to make him declare that 'Things begin to look pretty desperate'. His descriptions of the foodstuffs he has to face, from hairy butter to buffalo milk, produces the shrinking of palate he intended, while one cannot help but feel that the description of the Chinese picnic of fricasseed kitten is richly tongue in cheek. Horses he races as equals, wheel against hoof, while with mules and donkeys he treads common ground as a fellow beast of burden. And in a boat off the coast of Constantinople a scraggy half-grown chicken tended by two Armenians elicits an hilarious rhetorical discourse upon the plight of 'chickendom'.

Neither should this book be overlooked as a kaleidoscopic source of historical minutiae. Travelling on his own, under his own steam on a route of his own choice, at a time when the world's more colourful cultures were more or less intact, Stevens sampled every stratum of life from impoverished peasant to prince. His journalistic instinct means that we are treated to almost photographic accounts of dress and countenance. The bloodcurdling officers of Mahmoud Yusuph Khan seem ready to leap right from the page.

In England, Stevens marvels at the solid roads, comparing them to the sandy tracts of America and commenting that it is the first time he has ridden 300 miles without taking a 'header'. We cycle into a Paris that has no cars and pass by Persian camel caravans. New technology like the iron telegraph, the steam trains of Turkey and the arrival of gas and electric lighting in Teheran (toys for the Shah! cried Stevens with undisguised indignation, not 'improvements made with any idea of benefitting the condition of the city as a whole').

For most of us the ride alone would be challenge enough, but for Stevens every day had to have its quota of drama, not least because he wanted to 'stir' his readers. When the excitement drops off, we find him almost wishing for a bit of mild 'devilment' in the form of an attack on his person in order to make the narrative 'more stirring'. It is fair to say that Stevens, like any adventurous travel-writer, went out of his way at times to create the kind of incidents that spawn a good story. One has the sneaking suspicion that he longed now and again to be provoked into creating a bit of mayhem with his Smith & Wesson, but one of his great discoveries was that people everywhere treated him with the greatest consideration.

Around the World on a Bicycle is a great read for those who know the thrill of independent travel – and for those who wonder what they are missing. So often in these pages I have found myself yelping with familiarity: the pounding heart when discovered sleeping rough at night; the enormous view across the Great Plains as one rides out of the Rockies beyond Laramie (the road down which Stevens span as free as a bird is now Interstate 80, heavy with the grunting diesel engines); the sapping heat of northern India. And the incongruities: 'I am struck with the novelty of the situation,' he wrote as he crossed by bicycle the burning alkali flats of Nevada's Forty Mile Desert. That novelty I too have felt: riding a bicycle across the Gobi Desert, cycling on the ice of Lapland in winter and pedalling around the summit cone of Kilimanjaro. Cyclists – practical and slightly eccentric by nature – are able more than most to derive pleasure from the absurd.

Unlike many other manifestations of modern travel and tourism, cycling has done nothing to harm the environment. Yet it is perhaps surprising how little some things have changed since Stevens' journey: foreign cyclists in China still get chased; the skylarks still soar above the English grasslands; and the humble bicycle still opens doors in every country. But what I wonder would Stevens say now if he saw what cars have done to his native Chilterns, how trucks have changed India's Grand Trunk Road and what the factories spew into the air above Canton?

In an age when the bicycle shares the highway with altogether less appealing companions than the four-legged travellers with whom Stevens mixed, it is hard not to look back longingly on those purer days. Equally the overland route to the Far East is less accessible to travellers now than it was in Stevens' day. We can hope for the future that the political complexion of central Asia will mellow sufficiently for it to be possible to replicate Stevens' journey, but I doubt whether the story would be as stirring nor as well told as the original.

Nick Crane
1988

FROM SAN FRANCISCO TO TEHERAN

Thomas Stevens

CHAPTER 1

OVER THE SIERRAS NEVADAS

Various attempts have been made from time to time, by ambitious cyclers, to wheel across America from ocean to ocean; but – 'Around the World!'

'The impracticable scheme of a visionary,' was the most charitable verdict one could reasonably have expected.

The first essential element of success, however, is to have sufficient confidence in one's self to brave the criticisms – to say nothing of the witticisms – of a sceptical public. So eight o'clock on the morning of April 22, 1884, finds me and my fifty-inch machine on the deck of the Alameda, one of the splendid ferry-boats plying between San Francisco and Oakland, and a ride of four miles over the sparkling waters of the bay lands us, twenty-eight minutes later, on the Oakland pier, that juts far enough out to allow the big ferries to enter the slip in deep water. On the beauties of San Francisco Bay it is, perhaps, needless to dwell, as everybody has heard or read of this magnificent sheet of water, its surface flecked with snowy sails, and surrounded by a beautiful framework of evergreen hills; its only outlet to the ocean the famous Golden Gate – a narrow channel through which come and go the ships of all nations.

With the hearty well-wishing of a small group of Oakland and 'Frisco cyclers who have come, out of curiosity, to see the start, I mount and ride away to the east, down San Pablo Avenue, toward the village of the same Spanish name, some sixteen miles distant. The first seven miles are a sort of half-macadamized road, and I bowl briskly along.

The next morning I start off in a drizzling rain, and, after going sixteen miles, I have to remain for the day at Elmira. Here, among other items of interest, I learn that twenty miles farther ahead the Sacramento River is flooding the country, and the only way I can hope to get through is to take to the

The Start.

Central Pacific track and cross over the six miles of open trestle-work that spans the Sacramento River and its broad bottom-lands, that are subject to the annual spring overflow. From Elmira my way leads through a fruit and farming country that is called second to none in the world. Magnificent farms line the road; at short intervals appear large well-kept vineyards, in which gangs of Chinese coolies are hoeing and pulling weeds, and otherwise keeping trim. A profusion of peach, pear, and almond orchards enlivens the landscape with a wealth of pink and white blossoms, and fills the balmy spring air with a subtle sensuous perfume that savors of a tropical clime.

Already I realize that there is going to be as much 'foot-riding' as anything for the first part of my journey; so, while halting for dinner at the village of Davisville, I deliver my rather slight shoes over to the tender mercies of an Irish cobbler of the old school, with *carte blanche* instructions to fit them out for hard service. While diligently hammering away at the shoes, the old cobbler grows communicative, and in almost unintelligible brogue tells a complicated tale of Irish life, out of which I can make neither head, tail, nor tale; though nodding and assenting to it all, to the great satisfaction of the loquacious manipulator of the last, who in an hour hands over the shoes with the proud assertion, 'They'll last yez, be jabbers, to Omaha.'

*   *   *

That night I stay in Sacramento, the beautiful capital of the Golden State, whose well-shaded streets and blooming, almost tropical gardens combine to form a city of quiet, dignified beauty, of which Californians feel justly proud. Three and a half miles east of Sacramento, the high trestle bridge spanning the main stream of the American River has to be crossed, and from this bridge is obtained a remarkably fine view of the snow-capped Sierras, the great barrier that separates the fertile valleys and glorious climate of California, from the bleak and barren sage-brush plains, rugged mountains, and forbidding wastes of sand and alkali, that, from the summit of the Sierras, stretch away to the eastward for over a thousand miles. The view from the American River bridge is grand and imposing, encompass-ing the whole foot-hill country, which rolls in broken, irregular billows of forest-crowned hill and charming vale, upward and onward to the east, gradually getting more rugged, rocky, and immense, the hills changing to mountains, the vales to cañons, until they terminate in bald, hoary peaks whose white rugged pinnacles seem to penetrate the sky, and stand out in ghostly, shadowy outline against the azure depths of space beyond.

Rougher and more hilly become the roads as we gradually penetrate farther and farther into the foot-hills. We are now in far-famed Placer County, and the evidences of the hardy gold diggers' work in pioneer days are all about us. In every gulch and ravine are to be seen broken and decaying sluice-boxes. Bare, whitish-looking patches of washed-out gravel show where a 'claim' has been worked over and abandoned. In every direction are old water-ditches, heaps of gravel, and abandoned shafts – all telling, in language more eloquent than word or pen, of the palmy days of '49, and succeeding years; when, in these deep gulches, and on these yellow hills, thousands of bronzed, red-shirted miners dug and delved, and 'rocked the cradle' for the precious yellow dust and nuggets. But all is now changed, and where were hundreds before, now only a few 'old timers' roam the foot-hills, prospecting, and working over the old claims; but 'dust,' 'nuggets,' and 'pockets' still form the burden of conversation in the village bar-room or the cross-roads saloon. Now and then a 'strike' is made by some lucky – or perhaps it turns out, unlucky – prospector. This for a few days kindles anew the slumbering spark of 'gold fever' that lingers in the veins of the people here, ever ready to kindle into a flame at every bit of exciting news, in the way of a lucky 'find' near home, or new gold-fields in some distant land.

To day is Sunday, and it rains and snows with little interruption, so that I am compelled to stay over till Monday morning. While it is raining at Clipper Gap, it is snowing higher up in the mountains, and a railway employee volunteers the cheering information that, during the winter, the snow has drifted and accumulated in the sheds, so that a train can barely squeeze through, leaving no room for a person to stand to one side. I have my own ideas of whether this state of affairs is probable or not, however, and determine to pay no heed to any of these rumors, but to push ahead. So I pull out on Monday morning and take to the railway track again, which is the only passable road since the tremendous downpour of the last two days.

The first thing I come across is a tunnel burrowing through a hill. This tunnel was originally built the proper size, but, after being walled up, there were indications of a general cave-in; so the company had to go to work and build another thick rock-wall inside the other, which leaves barely room for the trains to pass through without touching the sides. It is anything but an inviting path around the hill; but it is far the safer of the two. Once my foot slips, and I unceremoniously sit down and slide around in the soft yellow clay, in my frantic endeavors to keep from slipping down the hill. This hardly enhances my personal appearance; but it doesn't matter much, as I am where no one can see, and a clay-besmeared individual is worth a dozen dead ones. Soon I am on the track again, briskly trudging up the steep grade toward the snow-line, which I can plainly see, at no great distance ahead, through the windings around the mountains.

Crossing the Sierra Nevadas.

This morning I follow the railway track around the famous 'Cape Horn,' a place that never fails to photograph itself permanently upon the memory of all who once see it. For scenery that is magnificently grand and picturesque, the view from where the railroad track curves around Cape Horn is probably without a peer on the American continent.

When the Central Pacific Railway company started to grade their road-bed around here, men were first swung over this precipice from above with ropes, until they made standing room for themselves; and then a narrow ledge was cut on the almost perpendicular side of the rocky mountain, around which the railway now winds.

Standing on this ledge, the rocks tower skyward on one side of the track so close as almost to touch the passing train; and on the other is a sheer precipice of two thousand five hundred feet, where one can stand on the edge and see, far below, the north fork of the American River, which looks like a thread of silver laid along the narrow valley, and sends up a far-away, scarcely perceptible roar, as it rushes and rumbles along over its rocky bed. The railroad track is carefully looked after at this point, and I was able, by turning round and taking the down grade, to experience the novelty of a short ride, the memory of which will be ever welcome should one live to be as old as 'the oldest inhabitant.' The scenery for the next few miles is glorious; the grand and imposing mountains are partially covered with stately pines down to their bases, around which winds the turbulent American River, receiving on its boisterous march down the mountains tribute from hundreds of smaller streams and rivulets, which come splashing and dashing out of the dark cañons and crevasses of the mighty hills.

This afternoon I pass a small camp of Digger Indians, to whom my bicycle is as much a mystery as was the first locomotive; yet they scarcely turn their uncovered heads to look; and my cheery greeting of 'How' scarce elicits a grunt and a stare in reply. Long years of chronic hunger and wretchedness have well-nigh eradicated what little energy these Diggers ever possessed. The discovery of gold among their native mountains has been their bane; the only antidote the rude grave beneath the pine and the happy hunting-grounds beyond.

The next morning finds me briskly trundling through the great, gloomy snow-sheds that extend with but few breaks for the next forty miles. When I emerge from them on the other end

I shall be over the summit and well down the eastern slope of the mountains. These huge sheds have been built at great expense to protect the track from the vast quantities of snow that fall every winter on these mountains. They wind around the mountain-sides, their roofs built so slanting that the mighty avalanche of rock and snow that comes thundering down from above glides harmlessly over, and down the chasm on the other side, while the train glides along unharmed beneath them. The section-houses, the water-tanks, stations, and everything along here are all under the gloomy but friendly shelter of the great protecting sheds.

In the Central Pacific Snow-sheds.

Fortunately I find the difficulties of getting through much less than I had been led by rumors to anticipate: and although no riding can be done in the sheds, I make very good progress, and trudge merrily along, thankful of a chance to get over the mountains without having to wait a month or six weeks for the snow outside to disappear. At intervals short breaks occur in the sheds, where the track runs over deep gulch or ravine, and at one of these openings the sinuous structure can be traced for quite a long distance, winding its tortuous way around the rugged mountain sides, and through the gloomy pine forest, all but buried under the snow. It requires no great effort of the mind to imagine it to be some wonderful relic of a past civilization, when a venturesome race of men thus dared to invade these vast wintry solitudes and burrow their way through the deep snow, like moles burrowing through the loose earth. Not a living thing is in sight, and the only sounds the occasional roar of a distant snow-slide, and the mournful sighing of the breeze as it plays a weird, melancholy dirge through the gently swaying branches of the tall, sombre pines, whose stately trunks are half buried in the omnipresent snow.

To-night I stay at the Summit Hotel, seven thousand and seventeen feet above the level of the sea. The 'Summit' is nothing if not snowy, and I am told that thirty feet on the level is no unusual thing up here. Indeed, it looks as if snow-balling on the 'Glorious Fourth' were no great luxury at the Summit House; yet notwithstanding the decidedly wintry aspect of the Sierras, the low temperature of the Rockies farther east is unknown; and although there is snow to the right, snow to the left, snow all around, and ice under foot, I travel all through the gloomy sheds in my shirt-sleeves, with but a gossamer rubber coat thrown over my shoulders to keep off the snow-water which is constantly melting and dripping through the roof, making it almost like going through a shower of rain. Often, when it is warm and balmy outside, it is cold and frosty under the sheds, and the dripping water, falling among the rocks and timbers, freezes into all manner of fantastic shapes. Whole menageries of ice animals, birds and all imaginable objects, are here reproduced in clear crystal ice, while in many places the ground is covered with an irregular coating of the same, that often has to be chipped away from the rails.

East of the summit is a succession of short tunnels, the space between being covered with snow-shed; and when I came through, the openings and crevices through which smoke from the engines is wont to make its escape, and through which a few rays of light penetrate the gloomy interior, are blocked up with snow, so that it is both dark and smoky; and groping one's way with a bicycle over the rough surface is anything but pleasant going. But there is nothing so bad, it seems, but that it can get a great deal worse; and before getting far, I hear an approaching train and forthwith proceed to occupy as small an amount of space as possible against the side, while three laboriously puffing engines, tugging a long, heavy freight train up the steep grade, go past. These three puffing, smoke-emitting monsters fill every nook and corner of the tunnel with dense smoke, which creates a darkness by the side of which the natural darkness of the tunnel is daylight in comparison. Here is a darkness that can be felt; I have to grope my way forward, inch by inch; afraid to set my foot down until I have felt the place, for fear of blundering into a culvert; at the same time never knowing whether there is room, just where I am, to get out of the way of a train. A cyclometer wouldn't have to exert itself much through here to keep tally of the revolutions; for, besides advancing with extreme caution, I pause every few steps to listen; as in the oppressive darkness and equally oppressive silence the senses are so keenly on the alert that the gentle rattle of the bicycle over the uneven surface seems to make a noise that would prevent me hearing an approaching train.

This finally comes to an end; and at the opening in the sheds I climb up into a pine-tree to obtain a view of Donner Lake, called the 'Gem of the Sierras.' It is a lovely little lake, and amid the pines, and on its shores occurred one of the most pathetically tragic events of the old emigrant days. Briefly related: A small party of emigrants became snowed in while camped at the lake, and when, toward spring, a rescuing party reached the spot, the last survivor of the party, crazed with the fearful suffering he had undergone, was sitting on a log, savagely gnawing away at a human arm, the last remnant of his companions in misery, off whose emaciated carcasses he had for some time being living!

My road now follows the course of the Truckee River down

the eastern slope of the Sierras, and across the boundary line into Nevada. The Truckee is a rapid, rollicking stream from one end to the other, and affords dam-sites and mill-sites without limit.

There is little ridable road down the Truckee cañon; but before reaching Verdi, a station a few miles over the Nevada line, I find good road, and ride up and dismount at the door of the little hotel as coolly as if I had rode without a dismount all the way from 'Frisco. Here at Verdi is a camp of Washoe Indians, who at once showed their superiority to the Diggers by clustering around and examining the bicycle with great curiosity. Verdi is less than forty miles from the summit of the Sierras, and from the porch of the hotel I can see the snow-storm still fiercely raging up in the place where I stood a few hours ago; yet one can feel that he is already in a dryer and altogether different climate. The great masses of clouds, travelling inward from the coast with their burdens of moisture, like messengers of peace with presents to a far country, being unable to surmount the great mountain barrier that towers skyward across their path, unload their precious cargoes on the mountains; and the parched plains of Nevada open their thirsty mouths in vain. At Verdi I bid good-by to the Golden State and follow the course of the sparkling Truckee toward the Forty-mile Desert.

CHAPTER II

OVER THE DESERTS OF NEVADA

Gradually I leave the pine-clad slopes of the Sierras behind, and every revolution of my wheel reveals scenes that constantly remind me that I am in the great 'Sage-brush State.' How appropriate indeed is the name! Sage-brush is the first thing seen on entering Nevada, almost the only vegetation seen while passing through it, and the last thing seen on leaving it. Clear down to the edge of the rippling waters of the Truckee, on the otherwise barren plain, covering the elevated table-lands, up the hills, even to the mountain-tops – everywhere, everywhere, nothing but sage-brush. In plain view to the right, as I roll on toward Reno, are the mountains on which the world-renowned Comstock lode is situated, and Reno was formerly the point from which this celebrated mining-camp was reached.

For a short distance, next morning, the road is ridable, but nearing Wadsworth it gets sandy, and 'sandy,' in Nevada means deep, loose sand, in which one sinks almost to his ankles at every step, and where the possession of a bicycle fails to awaken that degree of enthusiasm that it does on a smooth, hard road. At Wadsworth I have to bid farewell to the Truckee River, and start across the Forty-mile Desert, which lies between the Truckee and Humboldt Rivers. Standing on a sand-hill and looking eastward across the dreary, desolate waste of sand, rocks, and alkali, it is with positive regret that I think of leaving the cool, sparkling stream that has been my almost constant companion for nearly a hundred miles. It has always been at hand to quench my thirst or furnish a refreshing bath. More than once have I beguiled the tedium of some uninteresting part of the journey by racing with some trifling object hurried along on its rippling surface. I shall miss the murmuring music of its dancing waters as one would miss the conversation of a companion.

This Forty-mile Desert is the place that was so much dreaded by the emigrants *en route* to the gold-fields of California, there being not a blade of grass nor drop of water for the whole forty miles; nothing but a dreary waste of sand and rocks that reflects the heat of the sun, and renders the desert a veritable furnace in midsummer; and the stock of the emigrants, worn out by the long journey from the States, would succumb by the score in crossing. Though much of the trail is totally unfit for cycling, there are occasional alkali flats that are smooth and hard enough to play croquet on; and this afternoon, while riding with careless ease across one of these places, I am struck with the novelty of the situation. I am in the midst of the dreariest, deadest-looking country imaginable. Whirlwinds of sand, looking at a distance like huge columns of smoke, are wandering erratically over the plains in all directions. The blazing sun casts, with startling vividness on the smooth white alkali, that awful scraggy, straggling shadow that, like a vengeful fate, always accompanies the cycler on a sunny day, and which is the bane of a sensitive wheelman's life! The only representative of animated nature hereabouts is a species of small gray lizard that scuttles over the bare ground with astonishing rapidity. Not even a bird is seen in the air. All living things seem instinctively to avoid this dread spot save the lizard. A desert forty miles wide is not a particularly large one; but when one is in the middle of it, it might as well be as extensive as Sahara itself, for anything he can see to the contrary, and away off to the right I behold as perfect a mirage as one could wish to see. A person can scarce help believe his own eyes, and did one not have some knowledge of these strange and wondrous phenomena, one's orbs of vision would indeed open with astonishment; for seemingly but a few miles away is a beautiful lake, whose shores are fringed with wavy foliage, and whose cool waters seem to lave the burning desert sands at its edge.

Sunday, May 4th, finds me anchored for the day at the village of Lovelocks, on the Humboldt River, where I spend quite a remarkable day. Never before did such a strangely assorted crowd gather to see the first bicycle ride they ever saw, as the crowd that gathers behind the station at Lovelocks to-day to see me. There are perhaps one hundred and fifty people, of whom a hundred are Piute and Shoshone Indians, and the remainder a

The "Forty-mile Desert."

mingled company of whites and Chinese railroaders; and among them all it is difficult to say who are the most taken with the novelty of the exhibition – the red, the yellow, or the white. Later in the evening I accept the invitation of a Piute brave to come out to their camp, behind the village, and witness rival teams of Shoshone and Piute squaws play a match-game of 'Fi-re-fla,' the national game of both the Shoshone and Piute tribes. The principle of the game is similar to polo. The squaws are armed with long sticks, with which they endeavor to carry a shorter one to the goal. It is a picturesque and novel sight to see the squaws, dressed in costumes in which the garb of savagery and civilization is strangely mingled and the many colors of the rainbow are promiscuously blended, flitting about the field with the agility of a team of professional polo-players; while the bucks and old squaws, with their pappooses, sit around and watch the game with unmistakable enthusiasm. The Shoshone team wins and looks pleased.

Alkali flats abound, and some splendid riding is to be obtained east of Iron Point. Just before darkness closes down over the surrounding area of plain and mountain I reach Stone-House section-house.

'Yes, I guess we can get you a bite of something; but it will be cold,' is the answer vouchsafed in reply to my query about supper.

Being more concerned these days about the quantity of provisions I can command than the quality, the prospect of a cold supper arouses no ungrateful emotions. I would rather have a four-pound loaf and a shoulder of mutton for supper now than a smaller quantity of extra choice viands; and I manage to satisfy the cravings of my inner man before leaving the table. But what about a place to sleep? For some inexplicable reason these people refuse to grant me even the shelter of their roof for the night. They are not keeping hotel, they say, which is quite true; they have a right to refuse, even if it *is* twenty miles to the next place; and they *do* refuse.

'There's the empty Chinese bunk-house over there. You can crawl in there, if you arn't afeered of ghosts,' is the parting remark, as the door closes and leaves me standing, like an outcast, on the dark, barren plain.

A week ago this bunk-house was occupied by a gang of

Chinese railroaders, who got to quarrelling among themselves, and the quarrel wound up in quite a tragic poisoning affair, that resulted in the death of two, and nearly killed a third. The Chinese are nothing, if not superstitious, and since this affair no Chinaman would sleep in the bunk-house or work on this section; consequently the building remains empty. The 'spooks' of murdered Chinese are everything but agreeable company; nevertheless they are preferable to inhospitable whites, and I walk over to the house and stretch my weary frame in – for aught I know – the same bunk in which, but a few days ago, reposed the ghastly corpses of the poisoned Celestials. Despite the unsavory memories clinging around the place, and my pillowless and blanketless couch, I am soon in the land of dreams. It is scarcely presumable that one would be blessed with rosy-hued visions of pleasure under such conditions, however, and near midnight I awake in a cold shiver. The snowy mountains rear their white heads up in the silent night, grim and ghostly all around, and make the midnight air chilly, even in midsummer. I lie there, trying in vain to doze off again, for it grows perceptibly cooler. At two o'clock I can stand it no longer, and so get up and strike out for Battle Mountain, twenty miles ahead.

The moon has risen; it is two-thirds full, and a more beautiful sight than the one that now greets my exit from the bunk-house it is scarcely possible to conceive. Only those who have been in this inter-mountain country can have any idea of a glorious moonlight night in the clear atmosphere of this dry, elevated region. It is almost as light as day, and one can see to ride quite well wherever the road is ridable. The pale moon seems to fill the whole broad valley with a flood of soft, silvery light; the peaks of many snowy mountains loom up white and spectral; the stilly air is broken by the excited yelping of a pack of coyotes noisily baying the pale-yellow author of all this loveliness, and the wild, unearthly scream of an unknown bird or animal coming from some mysterious, undefinable quarter completes an ideal Western picture, a poem, a dream, that fully compensates for the discomforts of the preceding hour.

From Battle Mountain my route leads across a low alkali bottom, through which dozens of small streams are flowing to the Humboldt. Many of them are narrow enough to be jumped, but not with a bicycle on one's shoulder, for under such conditions there is always a disagreeable uncertainty that one may disastrously alight before he gets ready. But I am getting tired of partially undressing to ford streams that are little more than ditches, every little way, and so I hit upon the novel plan of using the machine for a vaulting-pole. Reaching it out into the centre of the stream, I place one hand on the head and the other on the saddle, and vault over, retaining my hold as I alight on the opposite shore. Pulling the bicycle out after me, the thing is done.

It grows pitchy dark ere I leave the cañon on my way to Carlin. Farther on, the gorge widens, and thick underbrush intervenes between the road and the river. From out the brush I see peering two little round phosphorescent balls, like two miniature moons, turned in my direction. I wonder what kind of an animal it is, as I trundle along through the darkness, revolver in hand, ready to defend myself, should it make an attack. I think it is a mountain-lion, as they seem to be plentiful in this part of Nevada. Late as it is when I reach Carlin, the 'boys' must see how a bicycle is ridden, and, as there is no other place suitable, I manage to circle around the pool-table in the hotel bar-room a few times, nearly scalping myself against the bronze chandelier in the operation. I hasten, however, to explain that these proceedings took place immediately after my arrival, lest some worldly wise, over-sagacious person should be led to suspect them to be the riotous undertakings of one who had 'smiled with the boys once too often.' Little riding is possible all through this section of Nevada, and, in order to complete the forty miles a day that I have rigorously imposed upon myself, I sometimes get up and pull out at daylight. It is scarce more than sunrise when, following the railroad through Five-mile Cañon – another rift through one of the many mountain chains that cross this part of Nevada in all directions under the general name of the Humboldt Mountains – I meet with a startling adventure. I am trundling through the cañon alongside the river, when, rounding the sharp curve of a projecting mountain, a tawny mountain lion is perceived trotting leisurely along ahead of me, not over a hundred yards in advance. He hasn't seen me yet; he is perfectly oblivious of the fact that he is in 'the presence.' A person of ordinary discretion would simply have revealed his presence by a gentlemanly sneeze, or a slight noise of any kind, when the lion would have immediately bolted back into the underbrush. Unable to resist the temptation, I fired at him, and of course missed him, as a person naturally would at a hundred yards with a bull-dog revolver. The bullet must have singed him a little though, for, instead of wildly scooting for the brush, as I anticipated, he turns savagely round and comes bounding rapidly toward me, and at twenty paces crouches for a spring. Laying his cat-like head almost on the ground, his round eyes flashing fire, and his tail angrily waving to and fro, he looks savage and dangerous. Crouching behind the bicycle, I fire at him again. Nine times out of ten a person will overshoot the mark with a revolver under such circumstances, and, being anxious to avoid this, I do the reverse, and fire too low. The ball strikes the ground just in front of his head, and throws the sand and gravel in his face, and perhaps in his wicked round eyes; for he shakes his head, springs up, and makes off into the brush. I shall shed blood of some sort yet before I leave Nevada! There isn't a day that I don't shoot at something or other; and all I ask of any animal is to come within two hundred yards and I will squander a cartridge on him, and I never fail to hit – the ground.

The next day, when nearing the entrance to Montella Pass, over the Goose Creek Range, I happen to look across the mingled sage-brush and juniper-spruce brush to the right, and a sight greets my eyes that causes me to instinctively look around for a tall tree, though well knowing that there is nothing of the kind for miles; neither is there any ridable road near, or I might try my hand at breaking the record for a few miles. Standing bolt upright on their hind legs, by the side of a clump of juniper-spruce bushes and intently watching my movements, are a pair of full-grown cinnamon bears. When a bear sees a man before the man happens to descry him, and fails to betake himself off immediately, it signifies that he is either spoiling for a fight or doesn't care a continental password whether war is declared or not. Moreover, animals recognize the peculiar advantages of two to one in a fight equally with their human inferi–superiors; and those two over there are apparently in no particular hurry to move on. They don't seem awed at my presence. On the contrary, they look suspiciously like being undecided and hesitative about whether to let me proceed peacefully on my

Encounter with a Mountain Lion.

way or not. Their behavior is outrageous; they stare and stare and stare, and look quite ready for a fight. I don't intend one to come off, though, if I can avoid it. I prefer to have it settled by arbitration. I haven't lost these bears; they aren't mine, and I don't want anything that doesn't belong to me. I am not covetous; so, lest I should be tempted to shoot at them if I come within the regulation two hundred yards, I 'edge off' a few hundred yards in the other direction, and soon have the intense satisfaction of seeing them stroll off toward the mountains. I wonder if I don't owe my escape on this occasion to my bicycle?

CHAPTER III

THROUGH MORMON-LAND AND OVER THE ROCKIES

A DREARY-LOOKING country is the 'Great American Desert,' in Utah, the northern boundary line of which I traverse next morning. To the left of the road is a low chain of barren hills; to the right, the uninviting plain, over which one's eye wanders in vain for some green object that might raise hopes of a less desolate region beyond; and over all hangs an oppressive silence – the silence of a dead country – a country destitute of both animal and vegetable life. Over the great desert hangs a smoky haze, out of which Pilot Peak, thirty-eight miles away, rears its conical head 2,500 feet above the level plain at its base.

Some riding is obtained at intervals along this unattractive stretch of country, but there are no continuously ridable stretches, and the principal incentive to mount at all is a feeling of disgust at so much compulsory walking. A noticeable feature through the desert is the almost unquenchable thirst that the dry saline air inflicts upon one. Reaching a railway section-house, I find no one at home; but there is a small underground cistern of imported water, in which 'wrigglers' innumerable wriggle, but which is otherwise good and cool. There is nothing to drink out of, and the water is three feet from the surface; while leaning down to try and drink, the wooden framework at the top gives way and precipitates me head first into the water. Luckily, the tank is large enough to enable me to turn round and reappear at the surface, head first, and with considerable difficulty I scramble out again, with, of course, not a dry thread on me.

At three in the afternoon I roll into Terrace, a small Mormon town. Here a rather tough-looking citizen, noticing that my garments are damp, suggests that 'cycling must be hard work to make a person perspire like that in this dry climate. At the Matlin section-house I find accommodation for the night with a whole-souled section-house foreman, who is keeping bachelor's hall temporarily, as his wife is away on a visit at Ogden. From this house, which is situated on the table-land of the Red Dome Mountains, can be obtained a more comprehensive view of the Great American Desert than when we last beheld it. It has all the appearance of being the dry bed of an ancient salt lake or inland sea. A broad, level plain of white alkali, which is easily mistaken in the dim distance for smooth, still water, stretches away like a dead, motionless sea as far as human vision can penetrate, until lost in the haze; while, here and there, isolated rocks lift their rugged heads above the dreary level, like islets out of the sea. It is said there are many evidences that go to prove this desert to have once been covered by the waters of the great inland sea that still, in places, laves its eastern borders with its briny flood. I am informed there are many miles of smooth, hard, salt-flats, over which a 'cycler could skim like a bird; but I scarcely think enough of bird-like skimming to go searching for it on the American Desert. A few miles east of Matlin the road leads over a spur of the Red Dome Range, from whence I obtain my first view of the Great Salt Lake, and soon I am enjoying a long-anticipated bath in its briny waters. It is disagreeably cold, but otherwise an enjoyable bath. One can scarce sink beneath the surface, so strongly is the water impregnated with salt.

Ten miles farther on, from the vantage-ground of a pass over another spur of the same range, is obtained a widely extended view of the country to the east. For nearly thirty miles from the base of the mountains, low, level mud-flats extend eastward, bordered on the south by the marshy, sinuous shores of the lake, and on the north by the Blue Creek Mountains. Thirty miles to the east – looking from this distance strangely like flocks of sheep grazing at the base of the mountains – can be seen the white-painted houses of the Mormon settlements, that thickly dot the narrow but fertile strip of agricultural land between Bear River and the mighty Wahsatch Mountains, that, rearing their snowy crest skyward, shut out all view of what lies beyond. From this height the level mud-flats appear as if one could mount his wheel and bowl across at a ten-mile pace; but I shall be agreeably surprised if I am able to aggregate ten miles of riding out of the thirty. Immediately after getting down into the bottom I make the acquaintance of the tiny black gnats that one of our whiskey-bereaved friends at Tacoma had warned me against. One's head is constantly enveloped in a black cloud of these little wretches. They are of infinitesimal proportions, and get into a person's ears, eyes, and nostrils, and if one so far forgets himself as to open his mouth, they swarm in as though they think it the 'pearly gates ajar,' and this their last chance of effecting an entrance. Mingled with them, and apparently on the best of terms, are swarms of mosquitoes, which appear perfect Jumbos in comparison with their disreputable associates.

After crossing Bear River I find myself on a somewhat superior road leading through the Mormon settlements to Ogden. No greater contrast can well be imagined than that presented by this strip of country lying between the lake and the Wahsatch Mountains, and the desert country to the westward. One can almost fancy himself suddenly transported by some good genii to a quiet farming community in an Eastern State. Instead of untamed broncos and wild-eyed cattle, roaming at their own free will over unlimited territory, are seen staid work-horses ploughing in the field, and the sleek milch-cow peacefully cropping tame grass in enclosed meadows. Birds are singing merrily in the willow hedges and the shade-trees; green fields of alfalfa and ripening grain line the road and spread themselves over the surrounding country in alternate squares, like those of a vast checker-board. Farms, on the average, are small, and, consequently, houses are thick; and not a farm-house among them all but is embowered in an orchard of fruit and shade-trees that mingle their green leaves and white blossoms harmoniously. At noon I roll into a forest of fruit-trees, among which, I am informed, Willard City is situated; but one can see nothing of any city. Nothing but thickets of peach, plum, and apple trees, all in full bloom, surround the spot where I alight and begin to look around for some indications of the city. 'Where is Willard City?' I inquire of a boy who comes out from one of the orchards carrying a can of kerosene in his hand, suggestive of having just come from a grocery, and so he has. 'This is Willard City, right here,' replies the boy; and then, in response to my inquiry for the hotel, he points to a small gate leading into an orchard, and tells me the hotel is in there.

The hotel – like every other house and store here – is embowered amid an orchard of blooming fruit-trees, and looks like anything but a public eating-house. No sign up, nothing to distinguish it from a private dwelling; and I am ushered into a nicely furnished parlor, on the neatly papered walls of which hang enlarged portraits of Brigham Young and other Mormon celebrities, while a large-sized Mormon bible, expensively bound in morocco, reposes on the centre-table. A charming Miss of –teen summers presides over a private table, on which is spread for my material benefit the finest meal I have eaten since leaving California. Such snow-white bread! Such delicious butter! And the exquisite flavor of 'spiced peach-butter' lingers in my fancy even now; and as if this were not enough for 'two bits' (a fifty per cent come-down from usual rates in the mountains), a splendid bouquet of flowers is set on the table to round off the repast with their grateful perfume.

Passing through two tunnels that burrow through rocky spurs stretching across the cañon, as though to obstruct farther progress, across the river, to the right, is the 'Devil's Slide' – two perpendicular walls of rock, looking strangely like man's handiwork, stretching in parallel lines almost from base to summit of a sloping, grass-covered mountain. The walls are but a dozen feet apart. It is a curious phenomenon, but only one among many that are scattered at intervals all through here. A short distance farther, and I pass the famous 'Thousand-mile Tree' – a rugged pine, that stands between the railroad and the river, and which has won renown by springing up just one thousand miles from Omaha. This tree is having a tough struggle for its life these days; one side of its honored trunk is smitten as with the leprosy. The fate of the Thousand-mile Tree is plainly sealed. It is unfortunate in being the most conspicuous target on the line for the fe-ro-ci-ous youth who comes West with a revolver in his pocket and shoots at things from the car-window. Judging from the amount of cold lead contained in that side of its venerable trunk next the railway few of these thoughtless marksmen go past without honoring it with a shot.

The next day at noon finds me 'tucked in my little bed' at Carter, decidedly the worse for wear, having experienced the toughest twenty-four hours of the entire journey. I have to ford no less than nine streams of ice-cold water; get benighted on a rain-soaked adobe plain, where I have to sleep out all night in an abandoned freight-wagon; and, after carrying the bicycle across seven miles of deep, sticky clay, I finally arrive at Carter, looking like the last sad remnant of a dire calamity – having had nothing to eat for twenty-four hours. From Carter my route leads through the Bad-Lands, amid buttes of mingled clay and rock, which the elements have worn into all conceivable shapes, and conspicuous among them can be seen, to the south, 'Church Buttes,' so called from having been chiselled by the dexterous hand of nature into a group of domes and pinnacles, that, from a distance, strikingly resembles some magnificent cathedral. High-water marks are observable on these buttes, showing that Noah's flood, or some other aqueous calamity once happened around here; and one can easily imagine droves of miserable, half-clad Indians, perched on top, looking with doleful, melancholy expression on the surrounding wilderness of water.

Stopping for the night at Lookout, I make an early start, in order to reach Laramie City for dinner. These Laramie Plains 'can smile and look pretty' when they choose, and, as I bowl along over a fairly good road this sunny Sunday morning, they certainly choose. The Laramie River on my left, the Medicine Bow and Snowy ranges – black and white respectively – towering aloft to the right, and the intervening plains dotted with herds of antelope, complete a picture that can be seen nowhere save on the Laramie Plains. Reaching a swell of the plains, that almost rises to the dignity of a hill, I can see the nickel-plated wheels of the Laramie wheelmen glistening in the sunlight on the opposite side of the river several miles from where I stand. They have come out a few miles to meet me, but have taken the wrong side of the river, thinking I had crossed below Rock Creek. The members of the Laramie Bicycle Club are the first wheelmen I have seen since leaving California; and, as I am personally acquainted at Laramie, it is needless to dwell on my reception at their hands. The rambles of the Laramie Club are well known to the cycling world from the many interesting letters from the graphic pen of their captain, Mr. Owen, who, with two other members, once took a tour on their wheels to the Yellowstone National Park. They have some very good natural roads around Laramie, but in their rambles over the mountains these 'rough riders of the Rockies' necessarily take risks that are unknown to their fraternal brethren farther east.

Tuesday morning I pull out to scale the last range that separates me from 'the plains' – popularly known as such – and, upon arriving at the summit, I pause to take a farewell view of the great and wonderful inter-mountain country, across whose mountains, plains, and deserts I have been travelling in so novel a manner for the last month. The view from where I stand is magnificent – ay, sublime beyond human power to describe – and well calculated to make an indelible impression on the mind of one gazing upon it, perhaps for the last time. The Laramie Plains extend northward and westward, like a billowy green sea. Emerging from a black cañon behind Jelm Mountain, the Laramie River winds its serpentine course in a northeast direction until lost to view behind the abutting mountains of the range, on which I now stand, receiving tributes in its course from the Little Laramie and numbers of smaller streams that emerge from the mountainous bulwarks forming the western border of the marvellous picture now before me. The unusual rains have filled the numberless depressions of the plains with ponds and lakelets that in their green setting glisten and glimmer in the bright morning sunshine like gems. A train is coming from the west, winding around among them as if searching out the most beautiful, and finally halts at Laramie City, which nestles in their midst – the fairest gem of them all – the 'Gem of the Rockies.'

As I lean on my bicycle on this mountain-top, drinking in the glorious scene, and inhaling the ozone-laden air, looking through the loop-holes of recent experiences in crossing the great wonderland to the west; its strange intermingling of forest-clad hills and grassy valleys; its barren, rocky mountains and dreary, desolate plains; its vast, snowy solitudes and its sunny, sylvan nooks; the no less strange intermingling of people; the wandering red-skin with his pathetic history; the feverishly hopeful prospector, toiling and searching for precious metals locked in the eternal hills; and the wild and free cow-boy who, mounted on his wiry bronco, roams these plains and mountains, free as the Arab of the desert – I heave a sigh as I realize that no tongue or pen of mine can hope to do the subject justice.

Gradually the Rockies have receded from my range of vision, and I am alone on the boundless prairie. There is a feeling of utter isolation at finding one's self alone on the plains that is not experienced in the mountain country. There is something tangible and companionable about a mountain; but here, where there is no object in view anywhere – nothing but the boundless, level plains, stretching away on every hand as far as the eye can reach, and all around, whichever way one looks, nothing but the green carpet below and the cerulean arch above – one feels that he is the sole occupant of a vast region of otherwise unoccupied space. This evening, while fording Pole Creek with the bicycle, my clothes, and shoes – all at the same time – the latter fall in the river; and in my wild scramble after the shoes I drop some of the

Fishing out my Clothes.

clothes; then I drop the machine in my effort to save the clothes, and wind up by falling in the water with everything. Everything is fished out again all right, but a sad change has come over the clothes and shoes. This morning I was mistaken for a homeless, friendless wanderer; this evening as I stand on the bank of Pole Creek with nothing over me but a thin mantle of native modesty, and ruefully wring the water out of my clothes, I feel considerably like one! Pine Bluffs provides me with shelter for the night, and a few miles' travel next morning takes me across the boundary-line into Nebraska. My route leads down Pole Creek, with ridable roads probably half the distance, and low, rocky bluffs lining both sides of the narrow valley, and leading up to high, rolling prairie beyond. Over those rocky bluffs the Indians were wont to stampede herds of buffalo, which falling over the precipitous bluffs, would be killed by hundreds, thus procuring an abundance of beef for the long winter. There are no buffalo here now – they have departed with the Indians – and I shall never have a chance to add a bison to my game-list on this tour. But they have left plenty of tangible evidence behind, in the shape of numerous deeply worn trails leading from the bluffs to the creek.

The prairie hereabouts is spangled with a wealth of divers-colored flowers that fill the morning air with gratifying perfume. The air is soft and balmy, in striking contrast to the chilly atmosphere of early morning in the mountain country, where the accumulated snows of a thousand winters exert their chilling influence in opposition to the benign rays of old Sol. This evening I pass through 'Prarie-dog City,' the largest congregation of prairie-dog dwellings met with on the tour. The 'city' covers hundreds of acres of ground, and the dogs come out in such multitudes to present their noisy and excitable protests against my intrusion, that I consider myself quite justified in shooting at them. I hit one old fellow fair and square, but he disappears like a flash down his hole, which now becomes his grave. The lightning-like movements of the prairie-dog, and his instinctive inclination toward his home, combine to perform the last sad rites of burial for his body at death. As, toward dark, I near Potter Station, where I expect accommodation for the night, a storm comes howling from the west, and it soon resolves into a race between me and the storm. With a good ridable road I could win the race; but, being handicapped with an unridable trail, nearly obscured beneath tall, rank grass, the storm overtakes me, and comes in at Potter Station a winner by about three hundred lengths.

CHAPTER IV

FROM THE GREAT PLAINS TO THE ATLANTIC

THROUGH the courtesy of the commanding officer at Fort Sidney I am enabled to resume my journey eastward under the grateful shade of a military summer helmet in lieu of the semi-sombrero slouch that has lasted me through from San Francisco. Certainly it is not without feelings of compunction that one discards an old friend, that has gallantly stood by me through thick and thin throughout the eventful journey across the inter-mountain country; but the white helmet gives such a delightfully imposing air to my otherwise forlorn and woe-begone figure that I ride out of Sidney feeling quite vain.

This afternoon is passed the first homestead, as distinguished from a ranch – consisting of a small tent pitched near a few acres

The First Homestead.

of newly upturned prairie – in the picket-line of the great agricultural empire that is gradually creeping westward over the plains, crowding the autocratic cattle-kings and their herds farther west, even as the Indians and their still greater herds – buffaloes – have been crowded out by the latter. At Ogallala – which but a few years ago was *par excellence* the cow-boys' rallying point – 'homesteads,' 'timber claims,' and 'pre-emption' now form the all-absorbing topic.

Homesteads now become more frequent, groves of young cottonwoods, representing timber claims, are occasionally encountered, and section-house accommodation becomes a thing of the past. Near Willow Island I come within a trifle of stepping on a belligerent rattlesnake, and in a moment his deadly fangs are hooked to one of the thick canvas gaiters I am wearing. Were my exquisitely outlined calves encased in cycling stockings only, I should have had a 'heap sick foot' to amuse myself with for the next three weeks, though there is little danger of being 'snuffed out' entirely by a rattlesnake favor these days; an all-potent remedy is to drink plenty of whiskey as quickly as possible after being bitten, and whiskey is one of the easiest things to obtain in the West. Giving his snakeship to understand that I don't appreciate his 'good intentions' by vigorously shaking him off, I turn my 'barker' loose on him, and quickly convert him into a 'goody-good snake;' for if 'the only good Indian is a dead one,' surely the same terse remark applies with much greater force to the vicious and deadly rattler. As I progress eastward, sod-houses and dug-outs become less frequent, and at long intervals frame schoolhouses appear to remind me that I am passing through a civilized country. Stretches of sand alternate with ridable roads all down the Platte. Often I have to ticklishly wobble along a narrow space between two yawning ruts, over ground that is anything but smooth. I consider it a lucky day that passes without adding one or more to my long and eventful list of headers, and to-day I am fairly 'unhorsed' by a squall of wind that – taking me unawares – blows me and the bicycle fairly over.

At Kearney Junction the roads are excellent, and everything is satisfactory; but an hour's ride east of that city I am shocked at the gross misconduct of a vigorous and vociferous young mule who is confined alone in a pasture, presumably to be weaned. He evidently mistakes the picturesque combination of man and machine for his mother, as, on seeing us approach, he assumes a thirsty, anxious expression, raises his unmusical, undignified voice, and endeavors to jump the fence. He follows along the whole length of the pasture, and when he gets to the end, and realizes that I am drawing away from him, perhaps forever, he bawls out in an agony of grief and anxiety, and, recklessly bursting through the fence, comes tearing down the road, filling the air with the unmelodious notes of his soul-harrowing music. The road is excellent for a piece, and I lead him a lively chase, but he finally overtakes me, and, when I slow up, he jogs along behind quite contentedly.

Heretofore I have omitted mentioning the tremendously hot weather I have encountered lately, because of my inability to produce legally tangible evidence; but to-day, while eating dinner at a farm-house, I leave the bicycle standing against the fence, and old Sol ruthlessly unsticks the tire, so that, when I mount, it comes off, and gives me a gymnastic lesson all unnecessary. My first day's experience in the great 'Hawkeye State' speaks volumes for the hospitality of the people, there being quite a rivalry between two neighboring farmers about which should take me in to dinner.

After three days' journey through the great Prairie State my head is fairly turned with kindness and flattery; but the third night, as if to rebuke my vanity, I am bluntly refused shelter at three different farm-houses. I am benighted, and conclude to make the best of it by 'turning in' under a hay-cock; but the Fox River mosquitoes oust me in short order, and compel me to 'mosey' along through the gloomy night to Yorkville. At Yorkville a stout German, on being informed that I am going to ride to Chicago, replies, 'What! Ghigago mit dot? Why, mine dear vellow, Ghigago's more as vorty miles; you gan't ride mit dot to Ghigago;' and the old fellow's eyes fairly bulge with astonishment at the bare idea of riding forty miles 'mit dot.' I considerately refrain from telling him of my already 2,500-mile jaunt 'mit dot,' lest an apoplectic fit should waft his Teutonic soul to realms of sauer-kraut bliss and Limburger happiness forever. On the morning of July 4th I roll into Chicago where, having persuaded myself that I deserve a few days' rest, I remain till the Democratic Convention winds up on the 13th.

At ten o'clock in the morning, July 17th, I bowl across the boundary line into Ohio. Following the Merchants' and Bankers' Telegraph road to Napoleon, I pass through a district where the rain has overlooked them for two months; the rear wheel of the bicycle is half buried in hot dust; the blackberries are dead on the bushes, and the long-suffering corn looks as though afflicted with the yellow jaundice. I sup this same evening with a family of Germans, who have been settled here forty years, and scarcely know a word of English yet. A fat, phlegmatic-looking baby is peacefully reposing in a cradle, which is simply half a monster pumpkin scooped out and dried; it is the most intensely rustic cradle in the world. Surely, this youngster's head ought to be level on agricultural affairs, when he grows up, if anybody's ought!

Twenty-four hours after entering Pennsylvania I make my exit across the boundary into the Empire State. The roads continue good, and after dinner I reach Westfield, six miles from the famous Lake Chautauqua, which beautiful hill and forest embowered sheet of water is popularly believed by many of its numerous local admirers to be the highest navigable lake in the world. If so, however, Lake Tahoe in the Sierra Nevada Mountains comes next, as it is about six thousand feet above the level of the sea, and has three steamers plying on its waters! At Fredonia I am shown through the celebrated watch-movement factory here, by the captain of the Fredonia Club, who accompanies me to Silver Creek, where we call on another enthusiastic wheelman – a physician who uses the wheel in preference to a horse, in making professional calls throughout the surrounding country. Taking supper with the genial 'Doc.,' they both accompany me to the summit of a steep hill leading up out of the creek bottom. No wheelman has ever yet rode up this hill, save the muscular and gritty captain of the Fredonia Club, though several have attempted the feat. From the top my road ahead is plainly visible for miles, leading through the broad and smiling Cattaraugus Valley that is spread out like a vast garden below, through which Cattaraugus Creek slowly winds its tortuous way. Stopping over night at Angola I proceed to Buffalo next morning, catching the first glimpse of that important 'seaport of the lakes,' where, fifteen miles across the bay, the wagon-road is almost licked by the swashing waves;

and entering the city over a 'misfit' plank-road, off which I am almost upset by the most audaciously indifferent woman in the world. A market woman homeward bound with her empty truck-wagon, recognizes my road-rights to the extent of barely room to squeeze past between her wagon and the ditch; and holds her long, stiff buggy-whip so that it 'swipes' me viciously across the face, knocks my helmet off into the mud ditch, and well-nigh upsets me into the same. The woman – a crimson-crested blonde – jogs serenely along without even deigning to turn her head.

Over good roads to Syracuse, and from thence my route leads down the Erie Canal, alternately riding down the canal tow-path, the wagon-roads, and between the tracks of the New York Central Railway. On the former, the greatest drawback to peaceful cycling is the towing-mule and his unwarrantable animosity toward the bicycle, and the awful, unmentionable profanity engendered thereby in the utterances of the boatmen. Sometimes the burden of this sulphurous profanity is aimed at me, sometimes at the inoffensive bicycle, or both of us collectively, but oftener is it directed at the unspeakable mule, who is really the only party to blame. A mule scares, not because he is really afraid, but because he feels skittishly inclined to turn back, or to make trouble between his enemies – the boatmen, his task-master, and the cycler, an intruder on his exclusive domain, the Erie tow-path. A span of mules will pretend to scare, whirl around, and jerk loose from the driver, and go 'scooting' back down the tow-path in a manner indicating that nothing less than a stone wall would stop them; but, exactly in the nick of time to prevent the tow-line jerking them sidewise into the canal, they stop. Trust a mule for never losing his head when he runs away, as does his hot-headed relative, the horse; he never once allows surrounding circumstances to occupy his thoughts to an extent detrimental to his own self-preservative interests.

Crossing the Massachusetts boundary at the village of State Line, I find the roads excellent; and, thinking that the highways of the 'Old Bay State' will be good enough anywhere, I grow careless about the minute directions given me by Albany wheel-men, and, ere long, am laboriously toiling over the heavy roads and steep grades of the Berkshire Hills, endeavoring to get what

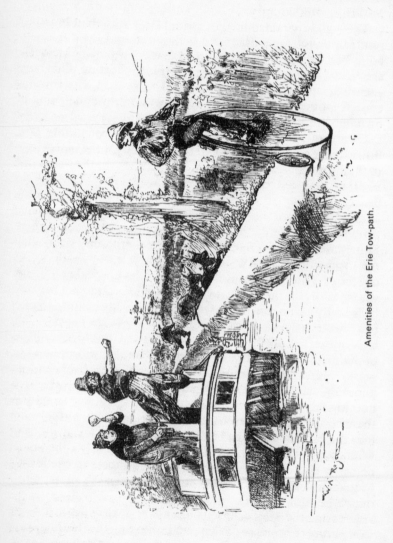

Amenities of the Erie Tow-path.

consolation I can, in return for unridable roads, out of the charming scenery, and the many interesting features of the Berkshire-Hill country.

The widely heralded intellectual superiority of the Massachusetts fair ones asserts itself even in the wildest parts of these wild hills; for at small farms – that, in most States, would be characterized by bare-footed brown-faced housewives – I encounter spectacled ladies whose fair faces reflect the encyclopædia of knowledge within, and whose wise looks naturally fill me with awe. At Westfield I learn that Karl Kron, the author and publisher of the American roadbook, 'Ten Thousand Miles on a Bicycle' – not to be outdone by my exploit of floating the bicycle across the Humboldt – undertook the perilous feat of swimming the Potomac with his bicycle suspended at his waist, and had to be fished up from the bottom with a boat-hook. Since then, however, I have seen the gentleman himself, who assures me that the whole story is a canard. Over good roads to Springfield – and on through to Palmer; from thence riding the whole distance to Worcester between the tracks of the railway, in preference to the variable country roads.

On to Boston next morning, now only forty miles away, I pass venerable weather-worn mile-stones, set up in old colonial days, when the Great West, now trailed across with the rubber hoofmarks of 'the popular steed of to-day,' was a pathless wilderness, and on the maps a blank. Striking the famous 'sand-papered roads' at Framingham – which, by the by, ought to be pumice-stoned a little to make them as good for cycling as stretches of gravelled road near Springfield, Sandwich, and Plano, Ill.; La Porte, and South Bend, Ind.; Mentor, and Willoughby, O.; Girard, Penn.; several places on the ridge road between Erie and Buffalo, and the alkali flats of the Rocky Mountain territories. Soon the blue intellectual haze hovering over 'the Hub' heaves in sight, and, at two o'clock in the afternoon of August 4th, I roll into Boston, and whisper to the wild waves of the sounding Atlantic what the sad sea-waves of the Pacific were saying when I left there, just one hundred and three and a half days ago, having wheeled about 3,700 miles to deliver the message.

Passing the winter of 1884–85 in New York, I became

acquainted with the *Outing Magazine*, contributed to it sketches of my tour across America, and in the Spring of 1885 continued around the world as its special correspondent; embarking April 9th from New York, for Liverpool, aboard the City of Chicago.

CHAPTER V

FROM AMERICA TO THE GERMAN FRONTIER

At noon on the 19th we reach Liverpool, where I find a letter awaiting me from A. J. Wilson (Faed), inviting me to call on him at Powerscroft House, London, and offering to tandem me through the intricate mazes of the West End; likewise asking whether it would be agreeable to have him, with others, accompany me from London down to the South coast – a programme to which, it is needless to say, I entertain no objections. As the custom-house officer wrenches a board off the broad, flat box containing my American bicycle, several fellow-passengers, prompted by their curiosity to obtain a peep at the machine which they have learned is to carry me around the world, gather about; and one sympathetic lady, as she catches a glimpse of the bright nickeled forks, exclaims, 'Oh, what a shame that they should be allowed to wrench the planks off! They might injure it;' but a small tip thoroughly convinces the individual prying off the board that, by removing one section and taking a conscientious squint in the direction of the closed end, his duty to the British government would be performed as faithfully as though everything were laid bare; and the kind-hearted lady's apprehensions of possible injury are thus happily allayed. In two hours after landing, the bicycle is safely stowed away in the underground store-rooms of the Liverpool & Northwestern Railway Company, and in two hours more I am wheeling rapidly toward London, through neatly cultivated fields, and meadows and parks of that intense greenness met with nowhere save in the British Isles, and which causes a couple of native Americans, riding in the same compartment, and who are visiting England for the first time, to express their admiration of it all in the unmeasured language of the genuine Yankee when truly astonished and delighted.

Soon after reaching London I have the pleasure of meeting

'Faed,' a gentleman who carries his cycling enthusiasm almost where some people are said to carry their hearts – on his sleeve; so that a very short acquaintance only is necessary to convince one of being in the company of a person whose interest in whirling wheels is of no ordinary nature. When I present myself at Powerscroft House, Faed is busily wandering around among the curves and angles of no less than three tricycles, apparently endeavoring to encompass the complicated mechanism of all three in one grand comprehensive effort of the mind, and the addition of as many tricycle crates standing around makes the premises so suggestive of a flourishing tricycle agency that an old gentleman, happening to pass by at the moment, is really quite excusable in stopping and inquiring the prices, with a view to purchasing one for himself. Our tandem ride through the West End has to be indefinitely postponed, on account of my time being limited, and our inability to procure readily a suitable machine; and Mr. Wilson's bump of discretion would not permit him to think of allowing me to attempt the feat of manoeuvring a tricycle myself among the bewildering traffic of the metropolis, and risk bringing my 'wheel around the world' to an inglorious conclusion before being fairly begun. While walking down Parliament Street my attention is called to a venerable-looking gentleman wheeling briskly along among the throngs of vehicles of every description, and I am informed that the bold tricycler is none other than Major Knox Holmes, a vigorous youth of some seventy-eight summers, who has recently accomplished the feat of riding one hundred and fourteen miles in ten hours; for a person nearly eighty years of age this is really quite a promising performance, and there is small doubt but that when the gallant Major gets a little older – say when he becomes a centenarian – he will develop into a veritable prodigy on the cinder-path!

Having obtained my passport, and got it *viséd* for the Sultan's dominions at the Turkish consulate, and placed in Faed's possession a bundle of maps, which he generously volunteers to forward to me, as I require them in the various countries it is proposed to traverse, I return on April 30th to Liverpool, from which point the formal start on the wheel across England is to be made. Four o'clock in the afternoon of May 2nd is the time announced, and Edge Hill Church is the appointed place, where Mr. Lawrence Fletcher, of the Anfield Bicycle Club, and a number of other Liverpool wheelmen, have volunteered to meet and accompany me some distance out of the city. Several of the Liverpool daily papers have made mention of the affair. Accordingly, upon arriving at the appointed place and time, I find a crowd of several hundred people gathered to satisfy their curiosity as to what sort of a looking individual it is who has crossed America awheel, and furthermore proposes to accomplish the greater feat of the circumlocution of the globe. A small sea of hats is enthusiastically waved aloft; a ripple of applause escapes from five hundred English throats as I mount my glistening bicycle; and, with the assistance of a few policemen, the twenty-five Liverpool cyclers who have assembled to accompany me out, extricate themselves from the crowd, mount and fall into line two abreast; and merrily we wheel away down Edge Lane and out of Liverpool.

'Think I'll get such roads as this all through England?' I ask of my escort as we wheel joyously southward along smooth, macadamized highways that would make the 'sand-papered roads' around Boston seem almost unfit for cycling in comparison, and that lead through picturesque villages and noble parks; occasionally catching a glimpse of a splendid old manor among venerable trees, that makes one unconsciously begin humming:–

'The ancient homes of England,
How beautiful they stand
Amidst the tall ancestral trees
O'er all the pleasant land!'

'Oh, you'll get much better roads than this in the southern counties,' is the reply; though, fresh from American roads, one can scarce see what shape the improvements can possibly take. Out of Lancashire into Cheshire we wheel, and my escort, after wishing me all manner of good fortune in hearty Lancashire style, wheel about and hie themselves back toward the rumble and roar of the world's greatest sea-port, leaving me to pedal pleasantly southward along the green lanes and amid the quiet rural scenery of Staffordshire to Stone, where I remain Sunday night. The country is favored with another drenching down-pour of rain during the night, and moisture relentlessly descends at short, unreliable intervals on Monday morning, as I proceed toward Birmingham. Notwithstanding the super-abundant moisture the morning ride is a most enjoyable occasion, requiring but a dash of sunshine to make everything perfect. The mystic voice of the cuckoo is heard from many an emerald copse around; songsters that inhabit only the green hedges and woods of 'Merrie England' are carolling their morning vespers in all directions; skylarks are soaring, soaring skyward, warbling their unceasing pæans of praise as they gradually ascend into cloudland's shadowy realms; and occasionally I bowl along beneath an archway of spreading beeches that are colonized by crowds of noisy rooks incessantly 'cawing' their approval or disapproval of things in general. Surely England, with its wellnigh perfect roads, the wonderful greenness of its vegetation, and its roadsters that meet and regard their steel-ribbed rivals with supreme indifference, is the natural paradise of 'cyclers. There is no annoying dismounting for frightened horses on these happy highways, for the English

Resting in an English Village.

horse, though spirited and brimful of fire, has long since accepted the inevitable, and either has made friends with the wheelman and his swift-winged steed, or, what is equally agreeable, maintains a haughty reserve.

It is Sunday evening, May 10th, and my ride through 'Merrie England' is at an end. Among other agreeable things to be ever remembered in connection with it is the fact that it is the first three hundred miles of road I ever remember riding over without scoring a header – a circumstance that impresses itself none the less favorably perhaps when viewed in connection with the solidity of the average English road. It is not a very serious misadventure to take a flying header into a bed of loose sand on an American country road; but the prospect of rooting up a flint-stone with one's nose, or knocking a curb-stone loose with one's bump of cautiousness, is an entirely different affair; consequently, the universal smoothness of the surface of the English highways is appreciated at its full value by at least one wheelman whose experience of roads is nothing if not varied. Comfortable quarters are assigned me on board the Channel steamer, and a few minutes after bidding friends and England farewell, at Newhaven, at 11.30 P.M., I am gently rocked into unconsciousness by the motion of the vessel, and remain happily and restfully oblivious to my surroundings until awakened next morning at Dieppe, where I find myself, in a few minutes, on a foreign shore.

*   *   *

The market-women are arraying their varied wares all along the main streets of Mantes as I wheel down toward the banks of the Seine this morning. I stop to procure a draught of new milk, and, while drinking it, point to sundry long rows of light, flaky-looking cakes strung on strings, and motion that I am desirous of sampling a few at current rates; but the good dame smiles and shakes her head vigorously, as well enough she might, for I learn afterward that the cakes are nothing less than dried yeast-cakes, a breakfast off which would probably have produced spon-taneous combustion. Getting on to the wrong road out of Mantes, I find myself at the river's edge down among the Seine watermen. I am shown the right way, but from Mantes to Paris

The Champs Elysée at 10 P.M.

they are not Normandy roads; from Mantes southward they gradually deteriorate until they are little or no better than the 'sand-papered roads of Boston.' Having determined to taboo *vin ordinaire* altogether I astonish the *restaurateur* of a village where I take lunch by motioning away the bottle of red wine and calling for '*de l'eau*,' and the glances cast in my direction by the other customers indicate plainly enough that they consider the proceeding as something quite extraordinary.

Rolling through Saint Germain, Chalon Pavèy, and Nanterre, the magnificent Arc de Triomphe looms up in the distance ahead, and at about two o'clock, Wednesday, May 13th, I wheel into the gay capital through the Porte Maillott. Asphalt pavement now takes the place of macadam, and but a short distance inside the city limits I notice the 'cycle depot of Renard Frères. Knowing instinctively that the fraternal feelings engendered by the magic wheel reaches to wherever a wheelman lives, I hesitate not to dismount and present my card. Yes, Jean Glinka, apparently an *employé* there, comprehends *Anglais;* they have all heard of my tour, and wish me *bon voyage*, and Jean and his bicycle is forthwith produced and delegated to accompany me into the interior of the city and find me a suitable hotel.

Among other agreeable and sensible arrangements at the Hotel du Loiret, there is no such thing as opening one's room-door from the outside save with the key; and unless one thoroughly understands this handy peculiarity, and has his wits about him continually, he is morally certain, sometime when he is leaving his room, absent-mindedly to shut the door and leave the key inside. This is, of course, among the first things that happen to me, and it costs me half a franc and three hours of wretchedness before I see the interior of my room again. The hotel keeps a rude skeleton-key on hand, presumably for possible emergencies of this nature; but in manipulating this uncouth instrument *le portier* actually locks the door, and as the skeleton-key is expected to manage the catch only, and not the lock, this, of course, makes matters infinitely worse. The keys of every room in the house are next brought into requisition and tried in succession, but not a key among them all is a duplicate of mine. What is to be done? *Le portier* looks as dejected as though Paris was about to be bombarded, as he goes down and breaks the dreadful news to *le propriétaire*. Up comes *le propriétaire* – avoirdupois three hundred pounds – sighing like an exhaust-pipe at every step. For fifteen unhappy minutes the skeleton-key is wriggled and twisted about again in the key-hole, and the fat *propriétaire* rubs his bald head impatiently, but all to no purpose. Each returns to his respective avocation. Impatient to get at my writing materials, I look up at the iron bars across the fifth-story windows above, and motion that if they will procure a rope I will descend from thence and enter the window. They one and all point out into the street; and, thinking they have sent for something or somebody, I sit down and wait with Job-like patience for something to turn up. Nothing, however, turns up, and at the expiration of an hour I naturally begin to feel neglected and impatient, and again suggest the rope; when, at a motion from *le propriétaire*, *le portier* pilots me around a neighboring corner to a locksmith's establishment, where, voluntarily acting the part of interpreter, he engages on my behalf, for half a franc, a man to come with a bunch of at least a hundred skeleton-keys of all possible shapes to attack the refractory key-hole. After trying nearly all the keys, and disburdening himself of whole volumes of impulsive French ejaculations, this man likewise gives it up in despair; but, now everything else has been tried and failed, the countenance of *le portier* suddenly lights up, and he slips quietly around to an adjoining room, and enters mine inside of two minutes by simply lifting a small hook out of a staple with his knife-blade. There appears to be a slight coolness, as it were, between *le propriétaire* and me after this incident, probably owing to the intellectual standard of each becoming somewhat lowered in the other's estimation in consequence of it. *Le propriétaire*, doubtless, thinks a man capable of leaving the key inside of the door must be the worst type of an ignoramus; and certainly my opinion of him for leaving such a diabolical arrangement unchanged in the latter half of the nineteenth century is not far removed from the same.

The roads for thirty miles east of Paris are not Normandy roads, but the country for most of the distance is fairly level, and for mile after mile, and league beyond league, the road is beneath avenues of plane and poplar, which, crossing the plain in every direction like emerald walls of nature's own building, here embellish and beautify an otherwise rather monotonous stretch of country. The villages are little different from the villages of Normandy, but the churches have not the architectural beauty of the Normandy churches, being for the most part massive structures without any pretence to artistic embellishment in their construction. Monkish-looking priests are a characteristic feature of these villages, and when, on passing down the narrow, crooked streets of Fontenay, I wheel beneath a massive stone archway, and looking around, observe cowled priests and everything about the place seemingly in keeping with it, one can readily imagine himself transported back to medieval times. One of these little interior French villages is the most unpromising looking place imaginable for a hungry person to ride into; often one may ride the whole length of the village expectantly looking around for some visible evidence of wherewith to cheer the inner man, and all that greets the hungry vision is a couple of four-foot sticks of bread in one dust-begrimed window, and a few mournful-looking crucifixes and Roman Catholic paraphernalia in another.

It has rained heavily during the night, but the roads around here are composed mainly of gravel, and are rather improved than otherwise by the rain; and from Sezanne, through Champenoise and on to Vitry le François, a distance of about sixty-five kilometres, is one of the most enjoyable stretches of road imaginable. The contour of the country somewhat resembles the swelling prairies of Western Iowa, and the roads are as perfect for most of the distance as an asphalt boulevard. The hills are gradual acclivities, and, owing to the good roads, are mostly ridable, while the declivities make the finest coasting imaginable; the exhilaration of gliding down them in the morning air, fresh after the rain, can be compared only to Canadian tobogganing. Ahead of you stretches a gradual downward slope, perhaps two kilometres long. Knowing full well that from top to bottom there exists not a loose stone or a dangerous spot, you give the ever ready steel-horse the rein; faster and faster whirl the glistening wheels until objects by the road-side become indistinct phantoms as they glide instantaneously by, and to strike a hole or obstruction is to be transformed into a human sky-rocket, and, later on, into a new arrival in another world. A wild yell of warning at a blue-

bloused peasant in the road ahead, shrill screams of dismay
from several females at a cluster of cottages, greet the ear as you
sweep past like a whirlwind, and the next moment reach the
bottom at a rate of speed that would make the engineer of the
Flying Dutchman green with envy.

Vitry le François is a charming old town in the beautiful
valley of the Marne; in the middle ages it was a strongly fortified
city; the moats and earth-works are still perfect. The only
entrance to the town, even now, is over the old draw-bridges,
the massive gates, iron wheels, chains, etc., still being intact, so
that the gates can yet be drawn up and entrance denied to foes,
as of yore; but the moats are now utilized for the boats of the
Marne and Rhine Canal, and its is presumable that the old
draw-bridges are nowadays always left open. To-day is Sunday
– and Sunday in France is equivalent to a holiday –
consequently Vitry le François, being quite an important town,
and one of the business centres of the prosperous and populous
Marne Valley, presents all the appearance of circus-day in an
American agricultural community. Several booths are erected
in the market square, the proprietors and *attachés* of two
peregrinating theatres, several peep-shows, and a dozen various
games of chance, are vying with each other in the noisiness of
their demonstrations to attract the attention and small change
of the crowd to their respective enterprises. Like every other
highway in this part of France the Marne and Rhine Canal is
fringed with an avenue of poplars, that from neighboring
elevations can be seen winding along the beautiful valley for
miles, presenting a most pleasing effect.

Lunéville is a town I pass through, some distance nearer the
border, and the military display here made is perfectly
overshadowing. Even the scarecrows in the fields are military
figures, with wooden swords threateningly waving about in
their hands with every motion of the wind, and the most
frequent sound heard along the route is the sharp bang! bang! of
muskets, where companies of soliders are target-practising in
the woods. There seems to be a bellicose element in the very
atmosphere; for every dog in every village I ride through verily
takes after me, and I run clean over one bumptious cur, which,
miscalculating the speed at which I am coming, fails to get
himself out of the way in time. It is the narrowest escape from a

header I have had since starting from Liverpool; although both man and dog were more scared than hurt. Sixty-five kilometres from Nancy, and I take lunch at the frontier town of Blamont. The road becomes more hilly, and a short distance out of Blamont, behold, it is as though a chalk-line were made across the roadway, on the west side of which it had been swept with scrupulous care, and on the east side not swept at all; and when, upon passing the next roadman, I notice that he bears not upon his cap the brass stencil-plate bearing the inscription, 'Cantonnier,' I know that I have passed over the frontier into the territory of Kaiser Wilhelm.

CHAPTER VI

GERMANY, AUSTRIA, AND HUNGARY

Notwithstanding Alsace was French territory only fourteen years ago (1871) there is a noticeable difference in the inhabitants, to me the most acceptable being their great linguistic superiority over the people on the French side of the border. I linger in Saarburg only about thirty minutes, yet am addressed twice by natives in my own tongue; and at Pfalzburg, a smaller town, where I remain over night, I find the same characteristic. Ere I penetrate thirty kilometres into German territory, however, I have to record what was never encountered in France; an insolent teamster, who, having his horses strung across a narrow road-way in the suburbs of Saarburg, refuses to turn his leaders' heads to enable me to ride past, thus compelling me to dismount. Soldiers drilling, soldiers at target practice, and soldiers in companies marching about in every direction, greet my eyes upon approaching Pfalzburg; and although there appears to be less beating of drums and blare of trumpets than in French garrison towns, one seldom turns a street corner without hearing the measured tramp of a military company receding or approaching. These German troops appear to march briskly and in a business-like manner in comparison with the French, who always seem to carry themselves with a tired and dejected deportment; but the over-ample and rather slouchy-looking pantaloons of the French are probably answerable, in part, for this impression. One cannot watch these sturdy-looking German soldiers without a conviction that for the stern purposes of war they are inferior only to the soldiers of our own country.

The road-beds of this country are hard enough for anything; but a certain proportion of clay in their composition makes a slippery coating in rainy weather. I enter the village of Marlenheim and observe the first stork's nest, built on top of a chimney, that I have yet seen in Europe, though I saw plenty of them afterward. The parent stork is perched solemnly over her youthful brood, which one would naturally think would get smoke-dried. A short distance from Marlenheim I descry in the hazy distance the famous spire of Strasburg cathedral looming conspicuously above everything else in all the broad valley; and at 1.30 P.M. I wheel through the massive arched gateway forming part of the city's fortifications, and down the broad but roughly paved streets, the most mud-bespattered object in all Strasburg. The fortifications surrounding the city are evidently intended strictly for business, and not merely for outward display. The railway station is one of the finest in Europe, and among other conspicuous improvements one notices steam tram-cars. While trundling through the city I am imperatively ordered off the sidewalk by the policeman; and when stopping to inquire of a respectable-looking Strasburger for the Appenweir road, up steps an individual with one eye and a cast off military cap three sizes too small. After querying, '*Appenweir? Englander?*' he wheels 'about face' with military precision – doubtless thus impelled by the magic influence of his headgear – and beckons me to follow. Not knowing what better course to pursue I obey, and after threading the mazes of a dozen streets, composed of buildings ranging in architecture from the much gabled and not unpicturesque structures of mediæval times to the modern brown-stone front, he pilots me outside the fortifications again, points up the Appenweir road, and after the never neglected formality of touching his cap and extending his palm, returns city-ward.

Oberkirch is a pretty village at the entrance to the narrow and charming valley of the River Rench, up which my route leads, into the fir-clad heights of the Black Forest. A few miles farther up the valley I wheel through a small village that nestles amid surroundings the loveliest I have yet seen. Dark, frowning firs intermingled with the lighter green of other vegetation crown the surrounding spurs of the Knibis Mountains; vineyards, small fields of waving rye, and green meadow cover the lower slopes with variegated beauty, at the foot of which huddles the cluster of pretty cottages amid scattered orchards of blossoming fruit-trees. The cheery lute of the herders on the mountains, the carol of birds, and the merry music of dashing mountain-streams fill the fresh morning air with melody. All through this country there are apple-trees, pear-trees, cherry-trees – everywhere. In the fruit season one can scarce open his mouth out-doors without having the goddess Pomona pop in some delicious morsel. The poplar avenues of France have disappeared, but the road is frequently shaded for miles with fruit-trees. I never before saw a spot so lovely – certainly not in combination with a wellnigh perfect road for wheeling. On through Oppenau and Petersthal my way leads – this latter a place of growing importance as a summer resort, several commodious hotels with swimming-baths, mineral waters, etc., being already prepared to receive the anticipated influx of health and pleasure-seeking guests this coming summer – and then up, up, up among the dark pines leading over the Black Forest Mountains. Mile after mile of steep incline has now been trundled, following the Rench River to its source. Ere long the road I have lately traversed is visible far below, winding and twisting up the mountain-slopes. Groups of swarthy peasant women are carrying on their heads baskets of pine cones to the villages below. At a distance the sight of their bright red dresses among the sombre green of the pines is suggestive of the fairies with which legend has peopled the Black Forest.

The strains of instrumental music come floating over the level bottom of the Lech valley as, toward eventide, I approach the beautiful environs of Augsburg, and ride past several beer-gardens, where merry crowds of Augsburgers are congregated, quaffing foaming lager, eating sausages, and drinking inspiration from the music of military bands. 'Where is the headquarters of the Augsburg Velocipede Club?' I inquire of a promising-looking youth as, after covering one hundred and twenty kilometres since ten o'clock, I wheel into the city. The club's headquarters are at a prominent café and beer-garden in the south-eastern suburbs, and repairing thither I find an accommodating individual who can speak English, and who willingly accepts the office of interpreter between me and the proprietor of the garden. Seated amid hundreds of soldiers, Augsburg civilians, and peasants from the surrounding country, and with them extracting genuine enjoyment from a tankard of foaming Augsburg lager, I am informed that most of the members of the club are celebrating the Whitsuntide holidays by touring about the surrounding country, but that I am very welcome to Augsburg, and I am conducted to the Hotel Mohrenkopf (Moor's Head Hotel), and invited to consider myself the guest of the club as long as I care to remain in Augsburg – the Bavarians are nothing if not practical.

Mr. Josef Kling, the president of the club, accompanies me as far out as Friedburg on Monday morning; it is the last day of the holidays, and the Bavarians are apparently bent on making the most of it. The suburban beer-gardens are already filled with people, and for some distance out of the city the roads are thronged with holiday-making Augsburgers repairing to various pleasure resorts in the neighboring country, and the peasantry streaming cityward from the villages, their faces beaming in anticipation of unlimited quantities of beer. About every tenth person among the outgoing Augsburgers is carrying an accordion; some playing merrily as they walk along, others preferring to carry theirs in blissful meditation on the good time in store immediately ahead, while a thoughtful majority have large umbrellas strapped to their backs. Music and song are heard on every hand, and as we wheel along together in silence, enforced by an ignorance of each other's language, whichever way one looks, people in holiday attire and holiday faces are moving hither and thither.

Now my road leads through forests of dark firs; and here I overtake a procession of some fifty peasants, the men and women alternately chanting in weird harmony as they trudge along the road. The men are bareheaded, carrying their hats in hand. Many of the women are barefooted, and the pedal extremities of others are incased in stockings of marvellous pattern; not any are wearing shoes. All the colors of the rainbow are represented in their respective costumes, and each carries a large umbrella strapped at his back; they are trudging along at quite a brisk pace, and altogether there is something weird and fascinating about the whole scene: the chanting and the surroundings. The variegated costumes of the women are the only bright objects amid the gloominess of the dark green pines. As I finally pass ahead, the unmistakable expressions of interest on the faces of the men, and the even rows of ivories displayed by the women, betray a diverted attention.

An hour after noon I am industriously dodging loose flints on

the level road leading across the Isar River Valley toward
Munich; the Tyrolese Alps loom up, shadowy and indistinct, in
the distance to the southward, their snowy peaks recalling
memories of the Rockies through which I was wheeling exactly
a year ago. While wending my way along the streets toward the
central portion of the Bavarian capital the familiar sign,
'American Cigar Store,' looking like a ray of light penetrating
through the gloom and mystery of the multitudinous unread-

Whitsuntide in Bavaria.

able signs that surround it, greets my vision, and I immediately wend my footsteps thitherward. I discover in the proprietor, Mr. Walsch, a native of Munich, who, after residing in America for several years, has returned to dream away declining years amid the smoke of good cigars and the quaffing of the delicious amber beer that the brewers of Munich alone know how to brew. Then who should happen in but Mr. Charles Buscher, a thorough-going American, from Chicago, who is studying art here at the Royal Academy of Fine Arts, and who straightway volunteers to show me Munich.

Munich is visited heavily with rain during the night, and for several kilometres, next morning, the road is a horrible waste of loose flints and mud-filled ruts, along which it is all but impossible to ride; but after leaving the level bottom of the Isar River the road improves sufficiently to enable me to take an occasional, admiring glance at the Bavarian and Tyrolese Alps, towering cloudward on the southern horizon, their shadowy outlines scarcely distinguishable in the hazy distance from the fleecy clouds their peaks aspire to invade. While absent-mindedly taking a more lingering look than is consistent with safety when picking one's way along the narrow edge of the roadway between the stone-strewn centre and the ditch, I run into the latter, and am rewarded with my first Cis-atlantic header, but fortunately both myself and the bicycle come up uninjured. Unlike the Swabish peasantry, the natives east of Munich appear as prosy and unpicturesque in dress as a Kansas homesteader.

Ere long there is noticeable a decided change in the character of the villages, they being no longer clusters of gabled cottages, but usually consist of some three or four huge, rambling buildings, at one of which I call for a drink and observe that brewing and baking are going on as though they were expecting a whole regiment to be quartered on them. Among other things I mentally note this morning is that the men actually seem to be bearing the drudgery of the farm equally with the women; but the favorable impression becomes greatly imperilled upon meeting a woman harnessed to a small cart, heavily laboring along, while her husband – kind man – is walking along-side, holding on to a rope, upon which he considerately pulls to assist her along and lighten her task.

At the town of Simbach I cross the Inn River again on a substantial wooden bridge, and on the opposite side pass under an old stone archway bearing the Austrian coat-of-arms. Here I am conducted into the custom-house by an officer wearing the sombre uniform of Franz Josef, and required, for the first time in Europe, to produce my passport. After a critical and unnecessarily long examination of this document I am graciously permitted to depart. In an adjacent money-changer's office I exchange what German money I have remaining for the paper currency of Austria, and once more pursue my way toward the Orient, finding the roads rather better than the average German ones, the Austrians, hereabouts at least, having had the goodness to omit the loose flints so characteristic of Bavaria. Once out of the valley of the Inn River, however, I find the uplands intervening between it and the valley of the Danube aggravatingly hilly.

The men here seem to be dull, uninteresting mortals, dressed in tight-fitting, and yet, somehow, ill-fitting, pantaloons, usually about three sizes too short, a small apron of blue ducking – an unbecoming garment that can only be described as a cross between a short jacket and a waistcoat – and a narrow-rimmed, prosy-looking billycock hat. The peasant women are the poetry of Austria, as of any other European country, and in their short red dresses and broad-brimmed, gypsy hats, they look picturesque and interesting in spite of homely faces and ungraceful figures.

Spending the night at Neu Lengbach, I climb hills and wabble along, over rough, lumpy roads, toward Vienna, reaching the Austrian capital Sunday morning, and putting up at the *Englischer Hof* about noon. At Vienna I determine to make a halt of two days, and on Tuesday pay a visit to the headquarters of the Vienna Wanderers' Bicycle Club, away out on a suburban street called *Schwimmschulenstrasse*; and the club promises that if I will delay my departure another day they will get up a small party of wheelmen to escort me seventy kilometres, to Presburg.

The Viennese impress themselves upon me as being possessed of more than ordinary individuality. Yonder comes a man, walking languidly along, and carrying his hat in his hand, because it is warm, and just behind him comes a fellow-citizen muffled up in an overcoat because – because of Viennese individuality. The people seem to walk the streets with a swaying, happy-go-anyhow sort of gait, colliding with one another and jostling together on the sidewalk in the happiest manner imaginable.

At five o'clock on Thursday morning I am dressing, when I am notified that two cyclers are awaiting me below. Church-bells are clanging joyously all over Vienna as we meander toward suburbs, and people are already streaming in the direction of the St. Stephen's Church, near the centre of the city, for to-day is *Frohnleichnam* (Corpus Christi), and the Emperor and many of the great ecclesiastical, civil, and military personages of the empire will pass in procession with all pomp and circumstance; and the average Viennese is not the person to miss so important an occasion. Three other wheelmen are awaiting us in the suburbs, and together we ride through the waving barley-fields of the Danube bottom to Schwechat, for the light breakfast customary in Austria, and thence onward to Petronelle, thirty kilometres distant, where we halt a few minutes for a Corpus Christi procession, and drink a glass of white Hungarian wine. Near Petronelle are the remains of an old Roman wall, extending from the Danube to a lake called the *Neusiedler See*. My companions say it was built 2,000 years ago, when the sway of the Romans extended over such parts of Europe as were worth the trouble and expense of swaying. The roads are found rather rough and inferior, on account of loose stones and uneven surface, as we push forward toward Presburg, passing through a dozen villages whose streets are carpeted with fresh-cut grass, and converted into temporary avenues, with branches stuck in the ground, in honor of the day they are celebrating.

My Austrian escort rides out with me to a certain cross-road, to make sure of heading me direct toward Budapest, and as we part they bid me good speed, with a hearty '*Eljen!*' – the Hungarian '*Hip, hip, hurrah*.' After leaving Presburg and crossing over into Hungary the road-bed is of a loose gravel that, during the dry weather this country is now experiencing, is churned up and loosened by every passing vehicle, until one might as well think of riding over a ploughed field. But there is a fair proportion of ridable side-paths, so that I make reasonably good time. Altenburg, my objective point for the night, is the centre of a sixty-thousand-acre estate belonging to the Archduke Albrecht, uncle of the present Emperor of Austro-Hungary, and one of the wealthiest land-owners in the empire.

Gangs of gypsies are now frequently met with; they are dark-skinned, interesting people, and altogether different-looking from those occasionally encountered in England and America, where, although swarthy and dark-skinned, they bear no comparison in that respect to these, whose skin is wellnigh black, and whose gleaming white teeth and brilliant, coal-black eyes stamp them plainly as alien to the race around them. Ragged, unwashed, happy gangs of vagabonds these stragglers appear, and regular droves of partially or wholly naked youngsters come racing after me, calling out 'kreuzer! kreuzer! kreuzer!' and holding out hand or tattered hat in a supplicating manner as they run along-side. Unlike the peasantry, none of these gypsies touch their hats; indeed, yon swarthy-faced vagabond, arrayed mainly in gewgaws, and eyeing me curiously with his piercing black eyes, may be priding himself on having royal blood in his veins; and, unregenerate chicken-lifter though he doubtless be, would scarce condescend to touch his tattered tile even to the Emperor of Austria. The black eyes scintillate as they take notice of what they consider the great wealth of sterling silver about the machine I bestride. Eastward from Altenburg the main portion of the road continues for the most part unridably loose and heavy.

The roads east of Nezmely are variable, flint-strewn ways predominating; otherwise the way would be very agreeable, since the gradients are gentle, and the dust not over two inches deep, as against three in most of Austro-Hungary thus far traversed. The weather is broiling hot; but I worry along perseveringly, through rough and smooth, toward the land of the rising sun. Nearing Budapest the roads become somewhat smoother, but at the same time hillier, the country changing to vine-clad slopes; and all along the undulating ways I meet wagons laden with huge wine-casks. Reaching Budapest in the afternoon, I seek out Mr. Kosztovitz, of the Budapest Bicycle Club, and consul of the Cyclists' Touring Club, who proves a most agreeable gentleman, and who, besides being an enthusiastic cycler, talks English perfectly. There is more of the sporting spirit in Budapest, perhaps, than in any other city of its size on the Continent, and no sooner is my arrival known than I am taken in hand and practically compelled to remain over at least one day. Svetozar Igali, a noted cycle tourist of the village of Duna Szekesö, now visiting the international exhibition at Budapest, volunteers to accompany me to Belgrade, and perhaps to Constantinople.

A noticeable feature of Budapest, besides a predilection for sport among the citizens, is a larger proportion of handsome ladies than one sees in most European cities, and there is, moreover, a certain atmosphere about them that makes them rather agreeable company. If one is travelling around the world with a bicycle, it is not at all inconsistent with Budapest propriety for the wife of the wheelman sitting opposite you to remark that she wishes she were a rose, that you might wear her for a button-hole bouquet on your journey, and to ask whether or not, in that case, you would throw the rose away when it faded. Compliments, pleasant, yet withal as meaningless as the coquettish glances and fan-play that accompany them, are given with a freedom and liberality that put the sterner native of more western countries at his wits' end to return them. But the most delightful thing in all Hungary is its gypsy music. As it is played here beneath its own sunny skies, methinks there is nothing in the wide world to compare with it. The music does not suit the taste of some people, however; it is too wild and thrilling. Budapest is a place of many languages, one of the waiters in the exhibition café claiming the ability to speak and understand no less than fourteen different languages and dialects.

My companion is what in England or America would be considered a 'character;' he dresses in the thinnest of racing costumes through which the broiling sun readily penetrates, wears racing-shoes, and a small jockey-cap with an enormous poke, beneath which glints a pair of 'specs;' he has rat-trap pedals to his wheel, and winds a long blue girdle several times around his waist, consumes raw eggs, wine, milk, a certain Hungarian mineral water, and otherwise excites the awe and admiration of his sport-admiring countrymen. Igali's only fault as a road companion is his utter lack of speed, six or eight kilometres an hour being his natural pace on average roads, besides footing it up the gentlest of gradients and over all rough stretches. Except for this little drawback, he is an excellent man to take the lead, for he is a genuine Magyar, and orders the peasantry about with the authoritative manner of one born to rule and tyrannize; sometimes, when the surface is uneven for wheeling, making them drive their clumsy ox-wagons almost into the road-side ditch in order to avoid any possible chance of difficulty in getting past. Igali knows four languages: French, German, Hungarian, and Slavonian, but *Anglaise nicht*, though with what little French and German I have picked up while crossing those countries we manage to converse and understand each other quite readily, especially as I am, from constant practice, getting to be an accomplished pantomimist, and Igali is also a pantomimist by nature, and gifted with a versatility that would make a Frenchman envious.

Notwithstanding music until 11.30 P.M., yesterday, we are on the road before six o'clock this morning – for genuine, unadulterated Hungarian music does not prevent one getting up bright and fresh next day – and about noon we roll into Duna Szekeso, Igali's native town, where we have decided to halt for the remainder of the day to get our clothing washed, one of my shoes repaired, and otherwise prepare for our journey to the Servian capital. Duna Szekeso is a calling-place for the Danube steamers, and this afternoon I have the opportunity of taking observations of a gang of Danubian roustabouts at their noontide meal. They are a swarthy, wild-looking crowd, wearing long hair parted in the middle, or not parted at all; to their national costume are added the jaunty trappings affected by river men in all countries. Their food is coarse black bread and meat, and they take turns in drinking wine from a wooden tube protruding from a two-gallon watch-shaped cask, the body of which is composed of a section of hollow log instead of staves, lifting the cask up and drinking from the tube, as they would from the bung-hole of a beer-keg. Their black bread would hardly suit the palate of the Western world; but there are doubtless a few individuals on both sides of the Atlantic who would willingly be transformed into a Danubian roustabout long enough to make the acquaintance of yonder rude cask.

After bathing in the river we call on several of Igali's friends, among them the Greek priest and his motherly-looking wife,

Igali being of the Greek religion. There appears to be the greatest familiarity between the priests of these Greek churches and their people, and during our brief visit the priest, languid-eyed, fat, and jolly, his equally fat and jolly wife, and Igali, caress playfully, and cut up as many antics as three kittens in a bay window. The farther one travels southward the more amiable and affectionate in disposition the people seem to become.

Five o'clock next morning finds us wheeling out of Duna Szekeso, and during the forenoon we pass through Baranyavär, a colony of Greek Hovacs, where the women are robed in white drapery as scant as the statuary which the name of their religion calls to memory. The roads to-day are variable; there is little but what is ridable, but much that is rough and stony enough to compel slow and careful wheeling. Early in the evening, as we wheel over the bridge spanning the River Drave, an important tributary of the Danube, into Eszek, the capital of Slavonia, unmistakable rain-signs appear above the southern horizon.

CHAPTER VII

THROUGH SLAVONIA AND SERVIA

Eszek is a fortified city, and has been in time past an important fortress. It has lost much of its importance since the introduction of modern arms, for it occupies perfectly level ground, and the fortifications consist merely of large trenches that have been excavated and walled, with a view of preventing the city from being taken by storm – not a very overshadowing consideration in these days, when the usual mode of procedure is to stand off and bombard a city into the conviction that further resistance is useless. After dinner the assistant editor of *Der Drau* comes around and pilots us about the city and its pleasant environments. The worthy assistant editor is a sprightly, versatile Slav, and, as together we promenade the parks and avenues, the number and extent of which appear to be the chief glory of Eszek, the ceaseless flow of language and wellnigh continuous interchange of gesticulations between himself and Igali are quite wonderful, and both of them certainly ought to retire to-night far more enlightened individuals than they found themselves this morning.

We have been worrying along at some sort of pace, with the exception of the usual noontide halt, since six o'clock this morning, and the busy mosquito is making life interesting for belated wayfarers, when we ride into Sarengrad and put up at the only *gasthaus* in the village. Our bedroom is situated on the ground floor, the only floor in fact the *gasthaus* boasts, and we are in a fair way of either being lulled to sleep or kept awake, as the case may be, by a howling chorus of wine-bibbers in the public room adjoining; but here, again, Igali shows up to good advantage by peremptorily ordering the singers to stop, and stop instanter. The amiably disposed peasants, notwithstanding the wine they have been drinking, cease their singing and become silent and circumspect, in deference to the wishes of the two strangers with the wonderful machines. We now make a practice of taking our bicycles into our bedroom with us at night, otherwise every right hand in the whole village would busy itself pinching the 'gum-elastic' tires and pedal-rubbers, twirling the pedals, feeling spokes, backbone, and forks, and critically examining and commenting upon every visible portion of the mechanism; and who knows but that the latent cupidity of some easy-conscienced villager might be aroused at the unusual sight of so much 'silver' standing around loose (the natives hereabout don't even ask whether the nickelled parts of the bicycle are silver or not; they take it for granted to be so), and surreptitiously attempt to chisel off enough to purchase an embroidered coat for Sundays? From what I can understand of their comments among themselves, it is perfectly consistent with their ideas of the average Englishman that he should bestride a bicycle of solid silver, and if their vocabulary embraced no word corresponding to our 'millionnaire,' and they desired to use one, they would probably pick upon the word 'Englander' as the most appropriate. While we are making our toilets in the morning eager faces are peering inquisitively through the bedroom windows; a murmur of voices, criticizing us and our strange vehicles, greets our waking moments, and our privacy is often invaded, in spite of Igali's inconsiderate treatment of them whenever they happen to cross his path.

This afternoon my bicycle causes the first runaway since the trifling affair at Lembach, Austria. A brown-faced peasant woman and a little girl, driving a small, shaggy pony harnessed to a basket-work, four-wheeled vehicle, are approaching; their humble-looking steed betrays no evidence of restiveness until just as I am turning out to pass him, when, without warning, he gives a swift, sudden bound to the right, nearly upsetting the vehicle, and without more ado bolts down a considerable embankment and goes helter-skelter across a field of standing grain.

The old lady pluckily hangs on to the reins, and finally succeeds in bringing the runaway around into the road again without damaging anything save the corn. It might have ended much less satisfactorily, however, and the incident illustrates one possible source of trouble to a 'cycler travelling alone through countries where the people neither understand, nor can be expected to understand, a wheelman's position; the situation would, of course, be aggravated in a country village where, not speaking the language, one could not make himself understood in his own defence.

Such is the reverie into which I fall while reclining beneath a spreading mulberry-tree waiting for Igali to catch up; for he has promised that I shall see the Slavonian national dance sometime to-day, and a village is now visible in the distance. At the Danube-side village of Hamenitz an hour's halt is decided upon to give me the promised opportunity of witnessing the dance in its native land. It is a novel and interesting sight. A round hundred young gallants and maidens are rigged out in finery such as no other people save the Croatian and Slavonian peasants ever wear – the young men braided and embroidered, and the damsels having their hair entwined with a profusion of natural flowers in addition to their costumes of all possible hues. Forming themselves into a large ring, distributed so that the sexes alternate, the young men extend and join their hands in front of the maidens, and the latter join hands behind their partners; the steel-strung tamboricas strike up a lively twanging air, to which the circle of dancers endeavor to shuffle time with their feet, while at the same time moving around in a circle. Livelier and faster twang the tamboricas, and more and more animated becomes the scene as the dancing, shuffling ring endeavors to keep pace with it. As the fun progresses into the fast and furious stages the youths' hats have a knack of getting into a jaunty position on the side of their heads, and the wearers' faces assume a reckless, flushed appearance, like men half intoxicated, while the maidens' bright eyes and beaming faces betoken unutterable happiness; finally the music and the shuffling of feet terminate with a rapid flourish, everybody kisses everybody – save, of course, mere luckless onlookers like Igali and myself – and the Slavonian national dance is ended.

Unmistakable evidence that one is approaching the Orient appears in the semi-Oriental costumes of the peasantry and roving gypsy bands, as we gradually near the Servian capital. An Oriental costume in Eszek is sufficiently exceptional to be a novelty, and so it is until one gets south of Peterwardein, when the national costumes of Slavonia and Croatia are gradually merged into the tasselled fez, the many-folded waistband, and the loose, flowing pantaloons of Eastern lands. Here at Batainitz the feet are encased in rude raw-hide moccasins, bound on with leathern thongs, and the ankle and calf are bandaged with many folds of heavy red material, also similarly bound. The scene around our *gasthaus*, after our arrival, resembles a popular meeting; for, although a few of the villagers have been to Belgrade and seen a bicycle, it is only within the last six months that Belgrade itself has boasted one, and the great majority of the Batainitz people have simply heard enough about them to whet their curiosity for a closer acquaintance. Moreover, from the interest taken in my tour at Belgrade on account of the bicycle's recent introduction in that capital, these villagers, but a dozen kilometres away, have heard more of my journey than people in villages farther north, and their curiosity is roused in proportion.

We are astir by five o'clock next morning; but the same curious crowd is making the stone corridors of the rambling old *gasthaus* impassable, and filling the space in front, gazing curiously at us, and commenting on our appearance whenever we happen to become visible, while waiting with commendable patience to obtain a glimpse of our wonderful machines. They are a motley, and withal a ragged assembly; old women devoutly cross themselves as, after a slight repast of bread and milk, we sally forth with our wheels, prepared to start; and the spontaneous murmur of admiration which breaks forth as we mount becomes louder and more pronounced as I turn in the saddle and doff my helmet in deference to the homage paid us by hearts which are none the less warm because hidden beneath the rags of honest poverty and semi-civilization. It takes but little to win the hearts of these rude, unsophisticated people. A two hours' ride from Batainitz, over level and reasonably smooth roads, brings us into Semlin, quite an important Slavonian city on the Danube, nearly opposite Belgrade, which is on the same side, but separated from it by a large tributary called the Save. Ferry-boats ply regularly between the two cities, and, after an hour spent in hunting up different officials to gain permission for Igali to cross over into Servian territory without having a regular traveller's passport, we escape from the madding crowds of Semlinites by boarding the ferry-boat, and ten minutes later are exchanging signals with three Servian wheelmen, who have come down to the landing in full uniform to meet and welcome us to Belgrade.

Many readers will doubtless be as surprised as I was to learn that at Belgrade, the capital of the little Kingdom of Servia, independent only since the Treaty of Berlin, a bicycle club was organized in January, 1855, and that now, in June of the same year, they have a promising club of thirty members, twelve of whom are riders owning their own wheels. Their club is named, in French, *La Société Velocipédique Serbe*; in the Servian language it is unpronounceable to an Anglo-Saxon, and printable only with Slav type. The president, Milorade M. Nicolitch Terzibachitch, is the Cyclists' Touring Club Consul for Servia, and is the southeastern picket of that organization, their club being the extreme 'cycle outpost in this direction. Our approach has been announced beforehand, and the club has thoughtfully 'seen' the Servian authorities, and so far smoothed the way for our entrance into their country that the officials do not even make a pretence of examining my passport or packages – an almost unprecedented occurrence, I should say, since they are more particular about passports here than perhaps in any other European country, save Russia and Turkey.

Here at Belgrade I am to part company with Igali, who, by the way, has applied for, and just received, his certificate of appointment to the Cyclists' Touring Club Consulship of Duna Szekesö and Mohacs, an honor of which he feels quite proud. True, there is no other 'cycler in his whole district, and hardly likely to be for some time to come; but I can heartily recommend him to any wandering wheelman happening down the Danube Valley on a tour; he knows the best wine-cellars in all the country round, and, besides being an agreeable and accommodating road companion, will prove a salutary check upon the headlong career of anyone disposed to over-exertion.

By the famous Treaty of Berlin the Servians gained their complete independence, and their country, from a principality, paying tribute to the Sultan, changed to an independent kingdom with a Servian on the throne, owing allegiance to nobody, and the people have not yet ceased to show, in a thousand little ways, their thorough appreciation of the change; besides filling the picture-galleries of their museum with portraits of Servian heroes, battle-flags, and other gentle reminders of their past history, they have, among other practical methods of manifesting how they feel about the departure of the dominating crescent from among them, turned the leading Turkish mosque into a gas-house. One of the most interesting relics in the Servian capital is an old Roman well, dug from the brow of the fortress hill to below the level of the Danube, for furnishing water to the city when cut off from the river by a besieging army. It is an enormous affair, a tubular brick wall about forty feet in circumference and two hundred and fifty feet deep, outside of which a stone stairway, winding round and round the shaft, leads from top to bottom. Openings through the wall, six feet high and three wide, occur at regular intervals all the way down, and, as we follow our ragged guide down, down into the damp and darkness by the feeble light of a tallow candle in a broken lantern, I cannot help thinking that these o'erhandy openings leading into the dark, watery depths have, in the tragic history of Belgrade, doubtless been responsible for the mysterious disappearance of more than one objectionable person. It is not without certain involuntary misgivings that I take the lantern from the guide – whose general appearance is, by the way, hardly calculated to be reassuring – and, standing in one of the openings, peer down into the darksome depths, with him hanging on to my coat as an act of precaution.

Three carriages with cyclers and their friends accompany us a dozen kilometres out to a wayside *mehana* (the Oriental name hereabouts for hotels, wayside inns, etc.); Douchan Popovitz, and Hugo Tichy, the captain of the club, will ride forty-five kilometres with me to Semendria, and at 4 o'clock we mount our wheels and ride away southward into Servia. Arriving at the *mehana*, wine is brought, and then the two Servians accompanying me, and those returning, kiss each other, after the manner and custom of their country; then a general hand-shaking and well-wishes all around, and the carriages turn toward Belgrade, while we wheelmen alternately ride and trundle over a muddy – for it has rained since noon – and mountainous road till 7.30, when relatives of Douchan Popovitz, in the village of Grotzka, kindly offer us the hospitality of their house till morning, which we hesitate not to avail ourselves of. When about to part at the *mehana,* the immortal Igali unwinds from around his waist that long blue girdle, the arranging and rearranging of which has been a familiar feature of the last week's experiences, and presents it to me for a *souvenir* of himself, a courtesy which I return by presenting him with several of the Byzantine coins given to me by the Belgrade antiquary as before mentioned.

Beyond Semendria, where the captain leaves us for the return journey, we leave the course of the Danube, which I have been following in a general way for over two weeks, and strike due southward up the smaller, but not less beautiful, valley of the Morava River, where we have the intense satisfaction of finding roads that are both dry and level, enabling us, in spite of the broiling heat, to bowl along at a sixteen-kilometre pace to the village, where we halt for dinner and the usual three hours noontide siesta. Seeing me jotting down my notes with a short piece of lead-pencil, the proprietor of the *mehana* at Semendria, where we take a parting glass of wine with the captain, and who admires America and the Americans, steps in-doors for a minute, and returns with a telescopic pencil-case, attached to a silken cord of the Servian national colors, which he places around my neck, requesting me to wear it around the world, and, when I arrive at my journey's end, sometimes to think of Servia.

With Igali's sky-blue girdle encompassing my waist, and the Servian national colors fondly encircling my neck, I begin to feel quite a heraldic tremor creeping over me, and actually surprise myself casting wistful glances at the huge antiquated horse pistol stuck in yonder bull-whacker's ample waistband; moreover, I really think that a pair of these Servian moccasins would not be bad foot-gear for riding the bicycle! All up the Morava Valley the roads continue far better than I have expected to find in Servia, and we wheel meerily along, the Resara Mountains covered with dark pine forests, skirting the valley on the right, sometimes rising into peaks of quite respectable proportions. The sun sinks behind the receding hills, it grows dusk, and finally dark, save the feeble light vouchsafed by the new moon, and our destination still lies several kilometres ahead. But at about nine we roll safely into Jagodina, well-satisfied with the consciousness of having covered one hundred and forty-five kilometres to-day, in spite of delaying our start in the morning until eight o'clock, and the twenty kilometres of indifferent road between Grotzka and Semendria. There has been no reclining under road-side mulberry-trees for my companion to catch up to-day, however; the Servian wheelman is altogether a speedier man than Igali, and, whether the road is rough or smooth, level or hilly, he is found close behind my rear wheel; my own shadow follows not more faithfully than does the 'best rider in Servia.'

The roads to-day average even better than yesterday, and at six o'clock we roll into Nisch, one hundred and twenty kilometres from our starting-point this morning, and two hundred and eighty from Belgrade. As we enter the city a gang of convicts working on the fortifications forget their clanking shackles and chains, and the miseries of their state, long enough to greet us with a boisterous howl of approval, and the guards who are standing over them for once, at least, fail to check them, for their attention, too, is wholly engrossed in the same wondrous subject. Nisch appears to be a thoroughly Oriental city, and here I see the first Turkish ladies, with their features hidden behind their white *yashmaks*.

Riding out of Nisch this morning we stop just beyond the suburbs to take a curious look at a grim monument of Turkish prowess, in the shape of a square stone structure which the Turks built in 1840, and then faced the whole exterior with grinning rows of Servian skulls partially embedded in mortar. The Servians, naturally objecting to having the skulls of their comrades thus exposed to the gaze of everybody, have since removed and buried them; but the rows of indentations in the thick mortared surface still bear unmistakable evidence of the nature of their former occupants.

Men on horseback are encountered, the long guns of the Orient slung at their backs, and knife and pistols in sash, looking altogether ferocious. Not only are these people perfectly harmless, however, but I verily think it would take a good deal of aggravation to make them even think of fighting. The fellow whose horse we frightened down a rocky embankment, at the imminent risk of breaking the neck of both horse and rider, had both gun, knife, and pistols; yet, though he probably thinks us emissaries of the evil one, he is in no sense a dangerous character, his weapons being merely gewgaws to adorn his person. Finally, the summit of this range is gained, and the long, grateful descent into the valley of the Nissava River begins. The surface during this descent, though averaging very good, is not always of the smoothest; several dismounts are found to be necessary, and many places ridden over require a quick hand and ready eye to pass. The Servians have made a capital point in fixing their new boundary-line south of this mountain-range.

Mountaineers are said to be 'always freemen;' one can with equal truthfulness add that the costumes of mountaineers' wives and daughters are always more picturesque than those of their sisters in the valleys. In these Balkan Mountains their costumes are a truly wonderful blending of colors, to say nothing of fantastic patterns, apparently a medley of ideas borrowed from Occident and Orient. One woman we have just passed is wearing the loose, flowing pantaloons of the Orient, of a bright-yellow color, a tight-fitting jacket of equally bright blue; around her waist is folded many times a red and blue striped waistband, while both head and feet are bare. This is no holiday attire; it is plainly the ordinary everyday costume.

The rain ceased soon after noon on Sunday, and, although the roads are all but impassable, I pull out southward at five o'clock on Monday morning, trundling up the mountain-roads through mud that frequently compels me to stop and use the scraper. After the summit of the hills between Bela Palanka and Pirot is gained, the road descending into the valley beyond becomes better, enabling me to make quite good time into Pirot, where my passport undergoes an examination, and is favored with a *visé* by the Servian officials preparatory to crossing the Servian and Bulgarian frontier about twenty kilometres to the southward. Pirot is quite a large and important village, and my appearance is the signal for more excitement than the Piroters have experienced for many a day.

While I am partaking of bread and coffee in the hotel, the main street becomes crowded as on some festive occasion, the grown-up people's faces beaming with as much joyous anticipation of what they expect to behold when I emerge from the hotel as the unwashed countenances of the ragged youngsters around them. Leading citizens who have been to

Paris or Vienna, and have learned something about what sort of road a 'cycler needs, have imparted the secret to many of their fellow-townsmen, and there is a general stampede to the highway leading out of town to the southward. This road is found to be most excellent, and the enterprising people who have walked, ridden, or driven out there, in order to see me ride past to the best possible advantage, are rewarded by witnessing what they never saw before – a cycler speeding along past them at ten miles an hour. This gives such general satisfaction that for some considerable distance I ride between a double row of lifted hats and general salutations, and a swelling murmur of applause runs all along the line.

Two citizens, more enterprising even than the others, have determined to follow me with team and light wagon to a road-side office ten kilometres ahead, where passports have again to be examined. The road for the whole distance is level and fairly smooth; the Servian horses are, like the Indian ponies of the West, small, but wiry and tough, and although I press forward quite energetically, the whip is applied without stint, and when the passport office is reached we pull up alongside it together, but their ponies' sides are white with lather. The passport officer is so delighted at the story of the race, as narrated to him by the others, that he fetches me out a piece of lump sugar and a glass of water, a common refreshment partaken of in this country.

Yet a third time I am halted by a roadside official and required to produce my passport, and again at the village of Zaribrod, just over the Bulgarian frontier, which I reach about ten o'clock. To the Bulgarian official I present a small stamped card-board check, which was given me for that purpose at the last Servian examination, but he doesn't seem to understand it, and demands to see the original passport. When my English passport is produced he examines it, and straightway assures me of the Bulgarian official respect for an Englishman by grasping me warmly by the hand. The passport office is in the second story of a mud hovel, and is reached by a dilapidated flight of out-door stairs. My bicycle is left leaning against the building, and during my brief interview with the officer a noisy crowd of semi-civilized Bulgarians have collected about, examining it and commenting unreservedly concerning it and myself. The officer, ashamed of the rudeness of his countrymen

The Zaribrod Passport Office.

and their evidently untutored minds, leans out of the window, and in a chiding voice explains to the crowd that I am a private individual, and not a travelling mountebank going about the country giving exhibitions, and advises them to uphold the dignity of the Bulgarian character by scattering forthwith. But the crowd doesn't scatter to any appreciable extent; they don't care whether I am public or private; they have never seen anything like me and the bicycle before, and the one opportunity of a lifetime is not to be lightly passed over. They are a wild, untamed lot, these Bulgarians here at Zaribrod, little given to self-restraint.

When I emerge, the silence of eager anticipation takes entire possession of the crowd, only to break forth into a spontaneous howl of delight from three hundred bared throats when I mount into the saddle and ride away into – Bulgaria.

CHAPTER VIII

BULGARIA, ROUMELIA, AND INTO TURKEY

Bulgaria – at least by the route I am crossing it – is a land of mountains and elevated plateaus, and the inhabitants I should call the 'ranchers of the Orient,' in their general appearance and demeanor bearing the same relation to the plodding corn-hoer and scythe-swinger of the Morava Valley as the Niobrara cowboy does to the Nebraska homesteader. On the mountains are encountered herds of goats in charge of men who reck little for civilization, and the upland plains are dotted over with herds of ponies that require constant watching in the interest of scattered fields of grain. For lunch I halt at an unlikely-looking *mehana*, near a cluster of mud hovels, which, I suppose, the Bulgarians consider a village, and am rewarded by the blackest of black bread, in the composition of which sand plays no inconsiderable part, and the remnants of a chicken killed and stewed at some uncertain period of the past. Of all places invented in the world to disgust a hungry, expectant wayfarer, the Bulgarian *mehana* is the most abominable. Black bread and mastic (a composition of gum-mastic and Boston rum, so I am informed) seem to be about the only things habitually kept in stock, and everything about the place plainly shows the proprietor to be ignorant of the crudest notions of cleanliness.

At 4.30 P.M. I wheel into Sofia, the Bulgarian Capital, having covered one hundred and ten kilometres to-day, in spite of mud, mountains, and roads that have been none of the best. Here again I have to patronize the money-changers, for a few Servian francs which I have are not current in Bulgaria; and the Israelite, who reserved unto himself a profit of two francs on the pound at Nisch, now seems the spirit of fairness itself along-side a hook-nosed wizen-faced relative of his here at Sofia, who wants two Servian francs in exchange for each Bulgarian coin of the same intrinsic value; and the best I am able to get by going to several different money-changers is five francs in exchange for seven; yet the Servian frontier is but sixty kilometres distant, with stages running to it daily; and the two coins are identical in intrinsic value. At the Hotel Concordia, in Sofia, in lieu of plates, the meat is served on round, flat blocks of wood about the circumference of a saucer – the 'trenchers' of the time of Henry VIII – and two respectable citizens seated opposite me are supping off black bread and a sliced cucumber, both fishing slices of the cucumber out of a wooden bowl with their fingers.

The road southward from Sofia is abominable, being originally constructed of earth and large unbroken bowlders; it has not been repaired for years, and the pack-trains and ox-wagons forever crawling along have, during the wet weather of many seasons, tramped the dirt away, and left the surface a wretched waste of ruts, holes, and thickly protruding stones. It is the worst piece of road I have encountered in all Europe; and although it is ridable this morning by a cautious person, one risks and invites disaster at every turn of the wheel. 'Old Boreas' comes howling from the mountains of the north, and hustles me briskly along over ruts, holes, and bowlders, however, in a most reckless fashion, furnishing all the propelling power needful, and leaving me nothing to do but keep a sharp lookout for breakneck places immediately ahead.

Mud is the principal element of the road leading out of Ichtiman and over the Kodja Balkans this morning. The curious crowd of Ichtimanites that follow me through the mud-holes and filth of their native streets, to see what is going to happen when I get clear of them, are rewarded but poorly for their trouble; the best I can possibly do being to make a spasmodic run of a hundred yards through the mud, which I do purely out of consideration for their inquisitiveness, since it seems rather disagreeable to disappoint a crowd of villagers who are expectantly following and watching one's every movement, wondering, in their ignorance, why you don't ride instead of walk. It is a long, wearisome trundle up the muddy slopes of the Kodja Balkans, but, after the descent into the Maritza Valley begins, some little ridable surface is encountered, though many loose stones are lying about, and pitch-holes innumerable, make riding somewhat risky, considering that the road frequently leads immediately alongside precipices. Pack-donkeys are met on these mountain-roads, sometimes filling the way, and coming doggedly and indifferently forward, even in places where I have little choice between scrambling up a rock on one side of the road or jumping down a precipice on the other. I can generally manage to pass them, however, by placing the bicycle on one side, and, standing guard over it, push them off one by one as they pass. Some of these Roumelian donkeys are the most diminutive creatures I ever saw; but they seem capable of toiling up these steep mountain-roads with enormous loads. I met one this morning carrying bales of something far bigger than himself, and a big Roumelian, whose feet actually came in contact with the ground occasionally, perched on his rump; the man looked quite capable of carrying both the donkey and his load.

It is after crossing the Kodja Balkans and descending into the Maritza Valley that one finds among the people a peculiarity that, until a person becomes used to it, causes no little mystification and many ludicrous mistakes. A shake of the head, which with us means a negative answer, means exactly the reverse with the people of the Maritza Valley; and it puzzled me not a little more than once yesterday afternoon when inquiring whether I was on the right road, and when patronizing fruit-stalls in Tatar Bazardjik. One never feels quite certain about being right when, after inquiring of a native if this is the correct road to Mustapha Pasha or Philippopolis he replies with a vigorous shake of the head; and although one soon gets accustomed to this peculiarity in others, and accepts it as it is intended, it is not quite so easy to get into the habit yourself. This queer custom seems to prevail only among the inhabitants of this particular valley, for after leaving it at Adrianople I see nothing more of it. Another peculiarity all through Oriental, and indeed through a good part of Central Europe, is that, instead of the 'whoa' which we use to a horse, the driver hisses like a goose.

Yesterday evening's downpour has little injured the road between the *mehana* and Philippopolis, the capital of Roumelia, and I wheel to the confines of that city in something over two hours. Philippopolis is most beautifully situated, being built on and around a cluster of several rocky hills; a situation which, together with a plenitude of waving trees, imparts a

Meeting the "Bulgarian Express."

pleasing and picturesque effect. With a score of tapering minarets pointing skyward among the green foliage, the scene is thoroughly Oriental; but, like all Eastern cities, 'distance lends enchantment to the view.'

All through Roumelia the gradual decay of the Crescent and the corresponding elevation of the Cross is everywhere evident; the Christian element is now predominant, and the Turkish authorities play but an unimportant part in the government of internal affairs. Naturally enough, it does not suit the Mussulman to live among people whom his religion and time-honored custom have taught him to regard as inferiors, the consequence being that there has of late years been a general folding of tents and silently stealing away; and to-day it is no very infrequent occurrence for a whole Mussulman village to pack up, bag and baggage, and move bodily to Asia Minor, where the Sultan gives them tracts of land for settlement.

As though in wilful aggravation of the case, a village of gypsies have their tents pitched and their donkeys grazing in the last Mohammedan cemetery I see ere passing over the Roumelian border into Turkey proper, where, at the very first village, the general aspect of religious affairs changes, as though its proximity to the border should render rigid distinctions desirable. Instead of the crumbling walls and tottering minarets, a group of closely veiled women are observed praying outside a well-preserved mosque, and praying sincerely too, since not even my never-before-seen presence and the attention-commanding bicycle are sufficient to win their attention for a moment from their devotions, albeit those I meet on the road peer curiously enough from between the folds of their muslin *yashmaks*.

It begins to rain soon after I leave Mustapha Pasha, forcing me to take refuge in a convenient culvert beneath the road. I have been under this shelter but a few minutes when I am favored with the company of three swarthy Turks, who, riding toward Mustapha Pasha on horseback, have sought the same shelter. These people straightway express their astonishment at finding me and the bicycle under the culvert, by first commenting among themselves; then they turn a battery of Turkish interrogations upon my devoted head, nearly driving me out of my senses ere I escape. They are, of course, quite unintelligible to me; for if one of them asks a question a shrug of the shoulders only causes him to repeat the same over and over again, each time a little louder and a little more deliberate. Sometimes they are all three propounding questions and emphasizing them at the same time, until I begin to think that there is a plot to talk me to death and confiscate whatever valuables I have about me. They all three have long knives in their waistbands, and, instead of pointing out the mechanism of

Turkish Amenities.

the bicycle to each other with the finger, like civilized people, they use these long, wicked-looking knives for the purpose. They may be a coterie of heavy villains for anything I know to the contrary, or am able to judge from their general appearance, and in view of the apparent disadvantage of one against three in such cramped quarters, I avoid their immediate society as much as possible by edging off to one end of the culvert. They are probably honest enough, but as their stock of interrogations seems inexhaustible, at the end of half an hour I conclude to face the elements and take my chances of finding some other shelter farther ahead rather than endure their vociferous onslaughts any longer. They all three come out to see what is going to happen, and I not ashamed to admit that I stand tinkering around the bicycle in the pelting rain longer than is necessary before mounting, in order to keep them out in it and get them wet through, if possible, in revenge for having practically ousted me from the culvert, and since I have a water-proof, and they have nothing of the sort, I partially succeed in my plans.

A few miles wheeling over very fair roads, next morning, brings me into Adrianople, where, at the Hotel Constantinople, I obtain an excellent breakfast of roast lamb, this being the only well-cooked piece of meat I have eaten since leaving Nisch. It has rained every day without exception since it delayed me over Sunday at Bela Palanka, and this morning it begins while I am eating breakfast, and continues a drenching downpour for over an hour. While waiting to see what the weather is coming to, I wander around the crooked and mystifying streets, watching the animated scenes about the bazaars, and try my best to pick up some knowledge of the value of the different coins, for I have had to deal with a bewildering mixture of late, and once again there is a complete change. Medjidis, cheriks, piastres, and paras now take the place of Serb francs, Bulgar francs, and a bewildering list of nickel and copper pieces, down to one that I should think would scarcely purchase a wooden toothpick.

At eleven o'clock I decide to make a start, I and the bicycle being the focus of attraction for a most undignified mob as I trundle through the muddy streets toward the suburbs. Arriving at a street where it is possible to mount and ride for a short distance, I do this in the hope of satisfying the curiosity of the crowd, and being permitted to leave the city in comparative peace and privacy; but the hope proves a vain one, for only the respectable portion of the crowd disperses, leaving me, solitary and alone, among a howling mob of the rag, tag, and bobtail of Adrianople, who follow noisily along, vociferously yelling for me to '*bin! bin!*' (mount, mount), and '*chu! chu!*' (ride, ride) along the really unridable streets. This is the worst crowd I have encountered on the entire journey across two continents, and, arriving at a street where the prospect ahead looks comparatively promising, I mount, and wheel forward with a view of outdistancing them if possible; but a ride of over a hundred yards without dismounting would be an exceptional performance in Adrianople after a rain, and I soon find that I have made a mistake in attempting it, for, as I mount, the mob grows fairly wild and riotous with excitement, flinging their red fezes at the wheels, rushing up behind and giving the bicycle smart pushes forward, in their eagerness to see it go faster, and more than one stone comes bounding along the street, wantonly flung by some young savage unable to contain himself. I quickly decide upon allaying the excitement by dismounting, and trundling until the mobs gets tired of following, whatever the distance.

Once well out of the city the road is quite good for several kilometres, and I am favored with a unanimous outburst of approval from a rough crowd at a suburban *mehana,* because of outdistancing a horseman who rides out from among them to overtake me. At Adrianople my road leaves the Maritza Valley and leads across the undulating uplands of the Adrianople Plains, hilly, and for most of the way of inferior surface.

Several showers occur during the afternoon, and the distance travelled has been short and unsatisfactory, when just before dark I arrive at Eski Baba, where I am agreeably surprised to find a *mehana,* the proprietor of which is a reasonably mannered individual. Since getting into Turkey proper, reasonably mannered people have seemed wonderfully scarce, the majority seeming to be most boisterous and headstrong. Next to the bicycle the Turks of these interior villages seems to exercise their minds the most concerning whether I have a passport; as I enter Eski Baba; a *gendarme* standing at the police-barrack gates shouts after me to halt and produce 'passaporte.' Exhibiting my passport at almost every village is getting monotonous, and, as I am going to remain here at least overnight, I ignore the *gendarme's* challenge and wheel on to the *mehana*. Two *gendarmes* are soon on the spot, inquiring if I have a 'passaporte;' but, upon learning that I am going no farther to-day, they do not take the trouble to examine it, the average Turkish official religiously believing in never doing anything to-day that can be put off till to-morrow.

It is raining heavily again on Sunday morning – in fact, the last week has been about the rainiest that I ever saw outside of England – and considering the state of the roads south of Eski Baba, the prospects look favorable for a Sunday's experience in an interior Turkish village. Men are solemnly squatting around the benches of the *mehana*, smoking nargilehs and sipping tiny cups of thick black coffee, and they look on in wonder while I devour a substantial breakfast; but whether it is the novelty of seeing a 'cycler feed, or the novelty of seeing *anybody* eat as I am doing, thus early in the morning, I am unable to say; for no one else seems to partake of much solid food until about noontide. All the morning long, people swarming around are importuning me with, '*Bin, bin, bin, monsieur!*' The bicycle is locked up in a rear chamber, and thrice I accommodatingly fetch it out and endeavor to appease their curiosity by riding along a hundred-yard stretch of smooth road in the rear of the *mehana*; but their importunities never for a moment cease.

Once during the afternoon I attempt to write, but I might as well attempt to fly, for the *mehana* is crowded with people who plainly have not the slightest conception of the proprieties. Finally a fez is wantonly flung, by an extra-enterprising youth, at my ink-bottle, knocking it over, and but for its being a handy contrivance, out of which the ink will not spill, it would have made a mess of my notes. Seeing the uselessness of trying to write, I meander forth, and into the leading mosque, and without removing my shoes, tread its sacred floor for several minutes, and stand listening to several devout Mussulmans reciting the Koran aloud, for, be it known, the great fast of Ramadan has begun, and fasting and prayer is now the faithful Mussulman's daily lot for thirty days, his religion forbidding him either eating or drinking from early morn till close of day. After looking about the interior, I ascend the steep spiral stairway up to the minaret balcony whence the *muezzin* calls the faithful to prayer five times a day. As I pop my head out through the little opening leading to the balcony, I am slightly taken aback by finding that small footway already occupied by the *muezzin*, and it is a fair question as to whether the *muezzin's* astonishment at seeing my white helmet appear through the opening is greater, or mine at finding him already in possession. However, I brazen it out by joining him, and he, like a sensible man, goes about his business just the same as if nobody were about. The people down in the streets look curiously up and call

On the Minaret with the Muezzin.

one another's attention to the unaccustomed sight of a white-helmeted 'cycler and a *muezzin* upon the minaret together; but the fact that I am not interfered with in any way goes far to prove that the Mussulman fanaticism, that we have all heard and read about so often, has wellnigh flickered out in European Turkey; moreover, I think the Eski Babans would allow me to do anything, in order to place me under obligations to '*bin! bin!*' whenever they ask me.

CHAPTER IX

THROUGH EUROPEAN TURKEY

On Monday morning I am again awakened by the *muezzin* calling the Mussulmans to their early morning devotions, and, arising from my mat at five o'clock, I mount and speed away southward from Eski Baba. Not less than a hundred people have collected to see the wonderful performance again.

I am now approaching pretty close to the Sea of Marmora, and next morning I am agreeably surprised to find sandy roads, which the rains have rather improved than otherwise; and although much is unridably heavy, it is immeasurably superior to yesterday's mud. I pass the country residence of a wealthy pasha, and see the ladies of his harem seated in the meadow hard by, enjoying the fresh morning air. They form a circle, facing inward, and the swarthy eunuch in charge stands keeping watch at a respectful distance. I carry a pocketful of bread with me this morning, and about nine o'clock, upon coming to a ruined mosque and a few deserted buildings, I approach one at which signs of occupation are visible, for some water. This place is simply a deserted Mussulman village, from which the inhabitants probably decamped in a body during the last Russo-Turkish war; the mosque is in a tumble-down condition, the few dwelling-houses remaining are in the last stages of dilapidation, and the one I call at is temporarily occupied by some shepherds, two of whom are regaling themselves with food of some kind out of an earthenware vessel.

Obtaining the water, I sit down on some projecting boards to eat my frugal lunch, fully conscious of being an object of much furtive speculation on the part of the two occupants of the deserted house, which, however, fails to strike me as anything extraordinary, since these attentions have long since become an ordinary every-day affair. Not even the sulky and rather hand-dog expression of the men, which failed not to escape my observation at my first approach, awakened any shadow of suspicion in my mind of their being possibly dangerous characters, although the appearance of the place itself is really sufficient to make one hesitate about venturing near; and upon sober after-thought I am fully satisfied that this is a resort of a certain class of disreputable characters, half shepherds, half brigands, who are only kept from turning full-fledged free-booters by a wholesome fear of retributive justice. While I am discussing my bread and water one of these worthies saunters with assumed carelessness up behind me and makes a grab for my revolver, the butt of which he sees protruding from the holster. Although I am not exactly anticipating this movement,

"And makes a grab for my Revolver."

travelling alone among strange people makes one's faculties of self-preservation almost mechanically on the alert, and my hand reaches the revolver before his does. Springing up, I turn round and confront him and his companion, who is standing in the doorway. A full exposition of their character is plainly stamped on their faces, and for a moment I am almost tempted to use the revolver on them. Whether they become afraid of this or whether they have urgent business of some nature will never be known to me, but they both disappear inside the door; and, in view of my uncertainty of their future intentions, I consider it advisable to meander on toward the coast.

An hour after, I am gratified at obtaining my first glimpse of the Sea of Marmora off to the right, and in another hour I am disporting in the warm clear surf, a luxury that has not been within my reach since leaving Diep,pe, and which is a thrice welcome privilege in this land, where the usual ablutions at *mehanas* consist of pouring water on the hands from a tin cup. The beach is composed of sand and tiny shells, the warm surf-waves are clear as crystal, and my first plunge in the Marmora, after a two months' cycle tour across a continent, is the most thoroughly enjoyable bath I ever had; notwithstanding, I feel it my duty to keep a loose eye on some shepherds perched on a handy knoll, who look as if half inclined to slip down and examine my clothes. The clothes, with, of course, the revolver and every penny I have with me, are almost as near to them as to me, and always, after ducking my head under water, my first care is to take a precautionary glance in their direction.

En route into Stamboul, on the following morning, I meet the first train of camels I have yet encountered; in the gray of the morning, with the scenes around so thoroughly Oriental, it seems like an appropriate introduction to Asiatic life. Eight o'clock finds me inside the line of earthworks thrown up by Baker Pasha when the Russians were last knocking at the gates of Constantinople, and ere long I am trundling through the crooked streets of the Turkish Capital toward the bridge which connects Stamboul with Galata and Pera. Even here my ears are assailed with the eternal importunities to '*bin! bin!*' the officers collecting the bridge-toll even joining in the request. To accommodate them I mount, and ride part way across the bridge, and at 9 o'clock on July 2nd, just two calendar months from the start at Liverpool, I am eating my breakfast in a Constantinople restaurant.

I am not long in finding English-speaking friends, to whom my journey across the two continents is not unknown, and who kindly direct me to the Chamber of Commerce Hotel, Rue Omar, Galata, a home-like establishment, kept by an English lady. I have been purposing of late to remain in Constantinople during the heated term of July and August, thinking to shape my course southward through Asia Minor and down the Euphrates Valley to Bagdad, and by taking a south-easterly direction as far as circumstances would permit into India, keep pace with the seasons, thus avoiding the necessity of remaining over anywhere for the winter. At the same time I have been reckoning upon meeting Englishmen in Constantinople who, having travelled extensively in Asia, could further enlighten me regarding the best route to India. As I house my bicycle and am shown to my room I take a retrospective glance across Europe and America, and feel almost as if I have arrived at the half-way house of my journey. The distance from Liverpool to Constantinople is fully 2,500 miles, which brings the wheeling distance from San Francisco up to something over 6,000.

Someone has said that to see Constantinople is to see the entire East; and judging from the different costumes and peoples one meets on the streets and in the bazaars, the saying is certainly not far amiss. From its geographical situation, as well as from its history, Constantinople naturally takes the front rank among the cosmopolitan cities of the world, and the crowds thronging its busy thoroughfares embrace every condition of man between the kid-gloved exquisite without a wrinkle in his clothes and the representative of half-savage Central Asian States incased in sheepskin garments of rudest pattern. The great fast of Ramadan is under full headway, and all true Mussulmans neither eat nor drink a particle of anything throughout the day until the booming of cannon at eight in the evening announces that the fast is ended, when the scene quickly changes into a general rush for eatables and drink. Between eight and nine o'clock in the evening, during Ramadan, certain streets and bazaars present their liveliest appearance, and from the highest-classed restaurant patronized by bey and pasha to the venders of eatables on the streets, all do a rushing business; even the *sujees* (water-venders), who with leather water-bottles and a couple of tumblers wait on thirty pedestrians with pure drinking water, at five paras a glass, dodge about among the crowds, announcing themselves with lusty lung, fully alive to the opportunities of the moment.

One of the most inconvenient things about Constantinople is the great scarcity of small change. Everybody seems to be short of fractional money save the money-changers – people who are here a genuine necessity, since one often has to patronize them before making the most trifling purchase. Ofttimes the storekeeper will refuse point-blank to sell an article when change is required, solely on account of his inability or unwillingness to supply it. After drinking a cup of coffee, I have had the *kahvajee* refuse to take any payment rather than change a cherik. Inquiring the reason for this scarcity, I am informed that whenever there is any new output of this money the noble army of money-changers, by a liberal and judicious application of backsheesh, manage to get a corner on the lot and compel the general public, for whose benefit it is ostensibly issued, to obtain what they require through them. However this may be, they manage to control its circulation to a great extent; for while their glass cases display an overflowing plenitude, even the fruit-vender, whose transactions are mainly of ten and twenty paras, is not infrequently compelled to lose a customer because of his inability to make change. There are not less than twenty money-changers' offices within a hundred yards of the Galata end of the principal bridge spanning the Golden Horn, and certainly not a less number on the Stamboul side.

Even the principal streets of Constantinople are but indifferently lighted at night, and, save for the feeble glimmer of kerosene lamps in front of stores and coffee-houses, the by-streets are in darkness. Small parties of Turkish women are encountered picking their way along the streets of Galata in charge of a male attendant, who walks a little way behind, if of the better class, or without the attendant in the case of poorer people, carrying small Japanese lanterns. Sometimes a lantern will go out, or doesn't burn satisfactorily, and the whole party halts in the middle of the, perhaps, crowded thoroughfare, and clusters around until the lantern is readjusted. The Turkish lady walks with a slouchy gait, her shroud-like *abbas* adding not a little to the ungracefulness.

Pointing skyward from the summit of the hill back of

Seraglio Point are the four tapering minarets of the world-renowned St. Sophia mosque, and a little farther to the left is the Sultana Achmet mosque, the only mosque in all Mohammedanism with six minarets. Near by is the old Seraglio Palace, or rather what is left of it, built by Mohammed II in 1467, out of materials from the ancient Byzantine palaces, and in a department of which the *sanjiak shereef* (holy standard), *boorda-y shereef* (holy mantle), and other venerated relics of the prophet Mohammed are preserved. To this place, on the 15th of Ramadan, the Sultan and leading dignitaries of the Empire repair to do homage to the holy relics, upon which it would be the highest sacrilege for Christian eyes to gaze. The hem of this holy mantle is reverently kissed by the Sultan and the few leading personages present, after which the spot thus brought in contact with human lips is carefully wiped with an embroidered napkin dipped in a golden basin of water; the water used in this ceremony is then supposed to be of priceless value as a purifier of sin, and is carefully preserved, and, corked up in tiny phials, is distributed among the sultanas, grand dignitaries, and prominent people of the realm, who in return make valuable presents to the lucky messengers and Mussulman ecclesiastics employed in its distribution. This precious liquid is doled out drop by drop, as though it were nectar of eternal life received direct from heaven, and, mixed with other water, is drunk immediately upon breaking fast each evening during the remaining fifteen days of Ramadan.

On Saturday morning, July 18th, the sound of martial music announces the arrival of the soldiers from Stamboul, to guard the streets through which the Sultan will pass on his way to a certain mosque to perform some ceremony in connection with the feast just over. At the designated place I find the streets already lined with Circassian cavalry and Ethiopian zouaves; the latter in red and blue zouave costumes and immense turbans. Mounted *gendarmes* are driving civilians about, first in one direction and then in another, to try and get the streets cleared, occasionally fetching some unlucky wight in the threadbare shirt of the Galata plebe a stinging cut across the shoulders with short raw-hide whips – a glaring injustice that elicits not the slightest adverse criticism from the spectators, and nothing but silent contortions of face and body from the individual receiving the attention. I finally obtain a good place, where nothing but an open plank fence and a narrow plot of ground thinly set with shrubbery intervenes between me and the street leading from the palace. In a few minutes the approach of the Sultan is announced by the appearance of half a dozen Circassian outriders, who dash wildly down the streets, one behind the other, mounted on splendid dapple-gray chargers; then come four close carriages, containing the Sultan's mother and leading ladies of the imperial harem, and a minute later appears a mounted guard, two abreast, keen-eyed fellows, riding slowly, and critically eyeing everybody and everything as they proceed; behind them comes a gorgeously arrayed individual in a perfect blaze of gold braid and decorations, and close behind him follows the Sultan's carriage, surrounded by a small crowd of pedestrians and horsemen, who buzz around the imperial carriage like bees near a hive, the pedestrians especially dodging about hither and thither, hopping nimbly over fences, crossing gardens, etc., keeping pace with the carriage meanwhile, as though determined upon ferreting out and destroying anything in the shape of danger that may possibly be lurking along the route.

Ere I am in the Ottoman capital a week, I have the opportunity of witnessing a fire, and the workings of the Constantinople Fire Department. While walking along Tramway Street, a hue and cry of '*yangoon var! yangoon var!*' (there is fire! there is fire!) is raised, and three barefooted men, dressed in the scantiest linen clothes, come charging pell-mell through the crowded streets, flourishing long brass hose-nozzles to clear the way; behind them comes a crowd of about twenty others, similarly dressed, four of whom are bearing on their shoulders a primitive wooden pump, while others are carrying leathern water-buckets. They are trotting along at quite a lively pace, shouting and making much unnecessary commotion, and lastly comes their chief on horseback, cantering close at their heels, as though to keep the men well up to their pace. The crowds of pedestrians, who refrain from following after the firemen, and who scurried for the sidewalks at their approach, now resume their place in the middle of the street; but again the wild cry of '*yangoon var!*' resounds along the narrow street, and the same scene of citizens scuttling to the sidewalks, and a hurrying fire

Constantinople Fire Laddies.

brigade followed by a noisy crowd of *gamins*, is enacted over
again, as another and yet another of these primitive organ-
izations go scooting swiftly past. It is said that these nimble-
footed firemen do almost miraculous work, considering the
material they have at command – an assertion which I think is
not at all unlikely; but the wonder is that destructive fires are not
much more frequent, when the fire department is evidently so
inefficient. In addition to the regular police force and fire
department, there is a system of night watchmen, called *bekjees*,
who walk their respective beats throughout the night, carrying
staves heavily shod with iron, with which they pound the
flagstones with a resounding 'thwack!'

Occasionally one notices among the busy throngs a person
wearing a turban of dark green; this distinguishing mark being
the sole privilege of persons who have made the pilgrimage to
Mecca. All true Mussulmans are supposed to make this
pilgrimage some time during their lives, either in person or by
employing a substitute to go in their stead, wealthy pashas
sometimes paying quite large sums to some *imam* or other holy

person to go as their proxy, for the holier the substitute the greater is supposed to be the benefit to the person sending him. Other persons are seen with turbans of a lighter shade of green than the returned Mecca pilgrims. These are people related in some way to the reigning sovereign.

An afternoon ramble with a guide through Stamboul embraces the Museum of Antiquities, the St. Sophia Mosque, the Costume Museum, the thousand and one columns, the Tomb of Sultan Mahmoud, the world-renowned Stamboul Bazaar, the Pigeon Mosque, the Saraka Tower, and the Tomb of Sultan Suliman I. Passing over the Museum of Antiquities, which to the average observer is very similar to a dozen other institutions of the kind, the visitor very naturally approaches the portals of the St. Sophia Mosque with expectations enlivened by having already read wondrous accounts of its magnificence and unapproachable grandeur. But, let one's fancy riot as it will, there is small fear of being disappointed in the 'finest mosque in Constantinople.'

The Stamboul Bazaar well deserves its renown, since there is nothing else of its kind in the whole world to compare with it. Its labyrinth of little stalls and shops if joined together in one straight line would extend for miles; and a whole day might be spent quite profitably in wandering around, watching the busy scenes of bargaining and manufacturing. Here, in this bewildering maze of buying and selling, the peculiar life of the Orient can be seen to perfection; the 'mysterious veiled lady' of the East is seen thronging the narrow traffic-ways and seated in every stall; water-venders and venders of *carpooses* (water-melons) and a score of different eatables are meandering through. Here, if your guide be an honest fellow, he can pilot you into stuffy little holes full of antique articles of every description, where genuine bargains can be picked up; or, if he be dishonest, and in league with equally dishonest tricksters, whose places are antiquaries only in name, he can lead you where everything is basest imitation. In the former case, if anything is purchased he comes in for a small and not undeserved commission from the shopkeeper, and in the latter for perhaps as much as thirty per cent. I am told that one of these guides, when escorting a party of tourists with plenty of money to spend and no knowledge whatever of the real value or genuineness of antique articles, often makes as much as ten or fifteen pounds sterling a day commission.

No fairer site ever greeted human vision than the prospect from the Tower of Saraka. Stamboul, Galata, Pera, and Scutari, with every suburban village and resort for many a mile around, can be seen to perfection from the commanding height of Saraka Tower. The guide can here point out every building of interest in Stamboul – the broad area of roof beneath which the busy scenes of Stamboul Bazaar are enacted from day to day, the great Persian khan, the different mosques, the Sultan's palaces at Pera, the Imperial kiosks up the Bosphorus, the old Grecian aqueduct, along which the water for supplying the great reservoir of the thousand and one columns used to be conducted, the old city walls, and scores of other interesting objects too numerous to mention here. On the opposite hill, across the Golden Horn, Galata Watch-tower points skyward above the mosques and houses of Galata and Pera. The two bridges connecting Stamboul and Galata are seen thronged with busy traffic; a forest of masts and spars is ranged all along the Golden Horn; steamboats are plying hither and thither across the Bosphorus; the American cruiser Quinnebaug rides at anchor opposite the Imperial water-side palace; the blue waters of the Sea of Marmora and the Gulf of Ismidt are dotted here and there with snowy sails or lined with the smoke of steamships; all combined to make the most lovely panorama imaginable, and to which the coastwise hills and more lofty mountains of Asia Minor in the distance form a most appropriate background.

Not being able to spare the time for visiting all the objects of interest enumerated by the guide, I elect to see the howling dervishes as the most interesting among them. Accordingly we take the ferry-boat across to Scutari on Thursday afternoon in time to visit the English cemetery before the dervishes begin their peculiar services. We pass through one of the largest Mussulman cemeteries of Constantinople, a bewildering area of tombstones beneath a grove of dark cypresses, so crowded and disorderly that the oldest gravestones seem to have been pushed down, or on one side, to make room for others of a later generation, and these again for still others. In happy comparison to the disordered area of crowded tombstones in the Mohammedan graveyard is the English cemetery, where the soldiers who died at the Scutari hospital during the Crimean war were buried, and the English residents of Constantinople now bury their dead. The situation of the English cemetery is a charming spot, on a sloping bluff, washed by the waters of the Bosphorus, where the requiem of the murmuring waves is perpetually sung for the brave fellows interred there. An Englishman has charge; and after being in Turkey a month it is really quite refreshing to visit this cemetery, and note the scrupulous neatness of the grounds. The keeper must be industry personified, for he scarcely permits a dead leaf to escape his notice; and the four angels beaming down upon the grounds from the national monument erected by England, in memory of the Crimean heroes, were they real visitors from the better land, could doubtless give a good account of his stewardship.

The howling dervishes have already begun to howl as we open the portals leading into their place of worship by the influence of a cherik placed in the open palm of a sable eunuch at the door; but it is only the overture, for it is half an hour later when the interesting part of the programme begins. The first hour seems to be devoted to preliminary meditations and comparatively quiet ceremonies; but the cruel-looking instruments of self-flagellation hanging on the wall, and a choice and complete assortment of drums and other noise-producing but unmelodious instruments, remind the visitor that he is in the presence of a peculiar people. Sheepskin mats almost cover the floor of the room, which is kept scrupulously clean, presumably to guard against the worshippers soiling their lips whenever they kiss the floor, a ceremony which they perform quite frequently during the first hour; and everyone who presumes to tread within that holy precinct removes his over-shoes, if he is wearing any, otherwise he enters in his stockings.

At five o'clock the excitement begins; thirty or forty men are ranged around one end of the room, bowing themselves about most violently, and keeping time to the movements of their bodies with shouts of '*Allah! Allah!*' and then branching off into a howling chorus of Mussulman supplications, that, unintelligible as they are to the infidel ear, are not altogether devoid of melody in the expression, the Turkish language abounding in words in which there is a world of mellifluousness. A dancing dervish, who has been patiently awaiting at the inner gate, now receives a nod of permission from the priest, and, after laying aside an outer garment, waltzes nimbly into the room, and straightway begins spinning round like a ballet-dancer in Italian opera, his arms extended, his long skirt forming a complete circle around him as he revolves, and his eyes fixed with a determined gaze into vacancy. Among the howlers is a negro, who is six feet three at least, not in his socks, but in the finest pair of under-shoes in the room, and whether it be in the ceremony of kissing the floor, knocking foreheads against the same, kissing the hand of the priest, or in the howling and bodily contortions, this towering son of Ham performs his part with a grace that brings him conspicuously to the fore in this respect. But as the contortions gradually become more violent, and the cry of 'Allah akbar! Allah hai!' degenerates into violent grunts of 'h-o-o-o-o-a-hoo-hoo,' the half-exhausted devotees fling aside everything but a white shroud, and the perspiration fairly streams off them, from such violent exercise in the hot weather and close atmosphere of the small room. The exercises make rapid inroads upon the tall negro's powers of endurance, and he steps to one side and takes a breathing-spell of five minutes, after which he resumes his place again, and, in spite of the ever-increasing violence of both lung and muscular exercise, and the extra exertion imposed by his great height, he keeps it up heroically to the end.

For twenty-five minutes by my watch, the one lone dancing dervish – who appears to be a visitor merely, but is accorded the brotherly privilege of whirling round in silence while the others howl – spins round and round like a tireless top, making not the slightest sound, spinning in a long, persevering, continuous whirl, as though determined to prove himself holier than the howlers, by spinning longer than they can keep up their howling – a fair test of fanatical endurance, so to speak. One cannot help admiring the religious fervor and determination of purpose that impel this lone figure silently around on his axis for twenty-five minutes, at a speed that would upset the equilibrium of anybody but a dancing dervish in thirty seconds; and there is something really heroic in the manner in which he at last suddenly stops, and, without uttering a sound or betraying any sense of dizziness whatever from the exercise, puts on his coat again and departs in silence, conscious, no doubt, of being a holier person than all the howlers put together, even though they are still keeping it up. As unmistakable signals of distress are involuntarily hoisted by the violently exercising devotees, and the weaker ones quietly fall out of line, and the military precision of the twists of body and bobbing and jerking of head begins to lose something of its regularity, the six 'encouragers,' ranged on sheep-skins before the line of howling men, like non-commissioned officers before a squad of new recruits, increase their encouraging cries of 'Allah! Allah akbar!' as though fearful that the din might subside, on account of the several already exhausted organs of articulation, unless they chimed in more lustily and helped to swell the volume.

Little children now come trooping in, seeking with eager anticipation the happy privilege of being ranged along the floor like sardines in a tin box, and having the priest walk along their bodies, stepping from one to the other along the row, and returning the same way, while two assistants steady him by holding his hands. In the case of the smaller children, the priest considerately steps on their thighs, to avoid throwing their internal apparatus out of gear; but if the recipient of his holy attentions is, in his estimation, strong enough to run the risk, he steps square on their backs. The little things jump up as sprightly as may be, kiss the priest's hand fervently, and go trooping out of the door, apparently well pleased with the novel performance. Finally human nature can endure it no longer, and the performance terminates in a long, despairing wail of 'Allah! Allah! Allah!' The exhausted devotees, soaked wet with perspiration, step forward, and receive what I take to be rather an inadequate reward for what they have been subjecting themselves to – viz., the privilege of kissing the priest's already much-kissed hand, and at 5.45 P.M. the performance is over. I take my departure in time to catch the six o'clock boat for Galata, well satisfied with the finest show I ever saw for a cherik.

I have already made mention of there being many beautiful sea-side places to which Constantinopolitans resort on Sundays and holidays, and among them all there is no lovelier spot than the island of Prinkipo, one of the Prince's Islands group, situated some twelve miles from Constantinople, down the Gulf of Ismidt. Shelton Bey (Colonel Shelton), an English gentleman, who superintends the Sultan's cannon-foundry at Tophana, and the well-known author of Shelton's 'Mechanic's Guide,' owns the finest steam-yacht on the Bosphorus, and three Sundays out of the five I remain here, this gentleman and his excellent lady kindly invite me to visit Prinkipo with them for the day.

While here at Constantinople I received by mail from America a Butcher spoke cyclometer, and on the second visit to Prinkipo I measured the road which has been made around half the island; the distance is four English miles and a fraction. The road was built by refugees employed by the Sultan during the last Russo-Turkish war, and is a very good one; for part of the distance it leads between splendid villas, on the verandas of which are seen groups of the wealth and beauty of the Osmanli capital, Armenians, Greeks, and Turks – the latter ladies sometimes take the privilege of dispensing with the *yashmak* during their visits to the comparative seclusion of Prinkipo villas – with quite a sprinkling of English and Europeans. The sort of impression made upon the imaginations of Prinkipo young ladies by the bicycle is apparent from the following comment made by a bevy of them confidentially to Shelton Bey, and kindly written out by him, together with the English interpretation thereof. The Prinkipo ladies' compliment to the first bicycle rider visiting their beautiful island is: '*O Bizdan kayáore ghyurulduzug em nezaketli sadi bir dakika utchum ghyuriorus nazaman bir dah backiorus O bittum gitmush.*' (He glides noiselessly and gracefully past; we see him only for a moment; when we look again he is quite gone.) The men are of course less poetical, their ideas running more to the practical side of the possibilities of the new arrival, and they comment as follows: '*Onum beyghir hich-bir-shèy yemiore hich-bir-shèy ichmiore hich yorumliore ma sheitan gibi ghitiore.*' (His horse, he eats nothing, drinks nothing, never gets tired, and goes like the very devil.)

The bull-dog revolver, under the protecting presence of which I have travelled thus far, has to be abandoned here at Constantinople, having proved itself quite a wayward weapon since it came from the gunsmith's hands in Vienna, who seemed to have upset the internal mechanism in some mysterious

Prinkipo the Beautiful.

manner while boring out the chambers a trifle to accommodate European cartridges. My experience thus far is that a revolver has been more ornamental than useful; but I am now about penetrating far different countries to any I have yet traversed. Plenty of excellently finished German imitations of the Smith & Wesson revolver are found in the magazines of Constantinople; but, apart from it being the duty of every Englishman or American to discourage, as far as his power goes, the unscrupulousness of German manufacturers in placing upon foreign markets what are, as far as outward appearance goes, the exact counterparts of our own goods, for half the money, a genuine American revolver is a different weapon from its would-be imitators, and I hesitate not to pay the price for the genuine article. Remembering the narrow escape on several occasions of having the bull-dog confiscated by the Turkish *gendarmerie*, and having heard, moreover, in Constantinople, that the same class of officials in Turkey in Asia will most assuredly want to confiscate the Smith & Wesson as a matter of private speculation and enterprise, I obtain through the British consul a *teskéré* giving me special permission to carry a revolver. Subsequent events, however, proved this precaution to be unnecessary, for a more courteous, obliging, and gentlemanly set of fellows, according to their enlightenment, I never met anywhere, than the government officials of Asiatic Turkey.

CHAPTER X

THE START THROUGH ASIA

Accordingly nine o'clock on Monday morning, August 10th, finds me aboard the little Turkish steamer that plies semi-weekly between Ismidt and the Ottoman capital, my bicycle, as usual, the centre of a crowd of wondering Orientals. This Ismidt steamer, with its motley crowd of passengers, presents a scene that upholds with more eloquence than words Constantinople's claim of being the most cosmopolitan city in the world; and a casual observer, judging only from the evidence aboard the boat, would pronounce it also the most democratic. There appears to be no first, second, or third class; everybody pays the same fare, and everybody wanders at his own sweet will into every nook and corner of the upper deck, perches himself on top of the paddle-boxes, loafs on the pilot's bridge, or reclines among the miscellaneous assortment of freight piled up in a confused heap on the fore-deck; in short, everybody seems perfectly free to follow the bent of his inclinations, except to penetrate behind the scenes of the aftmost deck, where, carefully hidden from the rude gaze of the male passengers by a canvas partition, the Moslem ladies have their little world of gossip and coffee, and fragrant cigarettes. Every public conveyance in the Orient has this walled-off retreat, in which Osmanli fair ones can remove their *yashmaks*, smoke cigarettes, and comport themselves with as much freedom as though in the seclusion of their apartments at home.

Greek and Armenian ladies mingle with the main-deck passengers, however, the picturesque costumes of the former contributing not a little to the general Oriental effect of the scene. The dress of the Armenian ladies differs but little from Western costumes, and their deportment would wreathe the benign countenance of the Lord Chamberlain with a serene smile of approval; but the minds and inclinations of the gentle

Hellenic dames seem to run in rather a contrary channel. Singly, in twos, or in cosey, confidential coteries, arm in arm, they promenade here and there, saying little to each other or to anybody else. By the picturesqueness of their apparel and their seemingly bold demeanor they attract to themselves more than their just share of attention; but with well-feigned ignorance of this they divide most of their time and attention between rolling cigarettes and smoking them.

The deck of a Constantinople steamer affords splendid opportunity for character study, and the Ismidt packet is no exception. Nearly every person aboard has some characteristic, peculiar and distinct from any of the others. At intervals of about fifteen minutes a couple of Armenians, bare-footed, bare-legged, and ragged, clamber with much difficulty and scraping of shins over a large pile of empty chicken-crates to visit one particular crate. Their collective baggage consists of a thin, half-grown chicken tied by both feet to a small bag of barley, which is to prepare it for the useful but inglorious end of all chickendom. They have imprisoned their unhappy charge in a crate that is most difficult to get at. Why they didn't put it in one of the nearer crates, what their object is in climbing up to visit it so frequently, and why they always go together, are problems of the knottiest kind.

A far less difficult riddle is the case of a middle-aged man, whose costume and avocation explain nothing, save that he is not an Osmanli. He is a passenger homeward bound to one of the coast villages, and he constantly circulates among the crowd with a basket of water-melons, which he has brought aboard 'on spec,' to vend among his fellow-passengers, hoping thereby to gain sufficient to defray the cost of his passage. Seated on whatever they can find to perch upon, near the canvas partition, all unmoved by the gay and stirring scenes before them, is a group of Mussulman pilgrims from some interior town, returning from a pilgrimage to Stamboul – fine-looking Osmanli graybeards, whose haughty reserve not even the bicycle is able to completely overcome, although it proves more efficacious in subduing it and waking them out of their habitual contemplative attitude than anything else aboard. Two of these men are of magnificent physique; their black eyes, rather full lips, and swarthy skins betraying Arab blood. In addition to the long daggers and antiquated pistols so universally worn in the Orient, they are armed with fine, large, pearl-handled revolvers, and they sit cross-legged, smoking cigarette after cigarette in silent meditation, paying no heed even to the merry music and the dancing of the Greeks.

Osmanli Pilgrims.

At Jelova, the first village the steamer halts at, a couple of *zaptiehs* come aboard with two prisoners whom they are conveying to Ismidt. These men are lower-class criminals, and their wretched appearance betrays the utter absence of hygienic considerations on the part of the Turkish prison authorities; they evidently have had no cause to complain of any harsh measures for the enforcement of personal cleanliness. Their foot-gear consists of pieces of rawhide, fastened on with odds and ends of string; and pieces of coarse sacking tacked on to what were once clothes barely suffice to cover their nakedness; bare-headed – their bushy hair has not for months felt the smoothing influence of a comb, and their hands and faces look as if they had just endured a seven-years' famine of soap and water. This latter feature is a sure sign that they are not Turks, for prisoners are most likely allowed full liberty to keep themselves clean, and a Turk would at least have come out into the world with a clean face.

The *zaptiehs* squat down together and smoke cigarettes, and allow their charges full liberty to roam wheresoever they will while on board, and the two prisoners, to all appearances perfectly oblivious of their rags, filth, and the degradation of their position, mingle freely with the passengers; and, as they move about, asking and answering questions, I look in vain among the latter for any sign of the spirit of social Pharisaism that in a Western crowd would have kept them at a distance. Both these men have every appearance of being the lowest of criminals – men capable of any deed in the calendar within their mental and physical capacities; they may even be members of the very gang I am taking this steamer to avoid; but nobody seems to either pity or condemn them; everybody acts toward them precisely as they act toward each other. Perhaps in no other country in the world does this social and moral apathy obtain among the masses to such a degree as in Turkey.

Impatient at consuming a whole day in reaching Ismidt, I have been thinking of taking to the road immediately upon landing, and continuing till dark, taking my chances of reaching some suitable stopping-place for the night. But the good people of Ismidt raise their voices in protest against what they professedly regard as a rash and dangerous proposition.

Having decided to remain here over-night, I seek the accommodation of a rudely comfortable hotel, kept by an Armenian, where, at the supper-table, I am first made acquainted with the Asiatic dish called '*pillau*,' that is destined to form no inconsiderable part of my daily bill of fare for several weeks. *Pillau* is a dish that is met with in one disguise or another all over Asia. With a foundation of boiled rice, it receives a variety of other compounds, the nature of which will appear as they enter into my daily experiences. In deference to the limited knowledge of each other's language possessed by myself and the proprietor, I am invited into the cookhouse and permitted to take a peep at the contents of several different pots and kettles simmering over a slow fire in a sort of brick trench, to point out to the waiter such dishes as I think I shall like. Failing to find among the assortment any familiar acquaintances, I try the *pillau*, and find it quite palatable, preferring it to anything else the house affords.

CHAPTER XI

ON THROUGH ASIA

Early dawn on Tuesday morning finds me already astir and groping about the hotel in search of some of the slumbering employees to let me out. Pocketing a cold lunch in lieu of eating breakfast, I mount and wheel down the long street leading out of the eastern end of town. On the way out I pass a party of caravan-teamsters who have just arrived with a cargo of mohair from Angora; their pack-mules are fairly festooned with strings of bells of all sizes, from a tiny sleigh-bell to a solemn-voiced sheet-iron affair the size of a two-gallon jar. These bells make an awful din; the men are unpacking the weary animals, shouting both at the mules and at each other, as if their chief object were to create as much noise as possible; but as I wheel noiselessly past, they cease their unpacking and their shouting, as if by common consent, and greet me with that silent stare of wonder that men might be supposed to accord to an apparition from another world. For some few miles a rough macadam road affords a somewhat choppy but nevertheless ridable surface, and further inland it develops into a fairly good roadway, where a dismount is unnecessary for several miles.

A foretaste of what awaits me farther in the interior is obtained even within the first few hours of the morning, when a couple of horsemen canter at my heels for miles; they seem delighted beyond measure, and their solicitude for my health and general welfare is quite affecting. When I halt to pluck some blackberries, they solemnly pat their stomachs and shake their heads in chorus, to make me understand that blackberries are not good things to eat; and by gestures they notify me of bad places in the road which are yet out of sight ahead. Rude *mehanas*, now called *khans*, occupy little clearings by the road-side, at intervals of a few miles; and among the *habitués* congregated there I notice several of the Circassian refugees on whose account friends at Ismidt and Constantinople have shown themselves so concerned for my safety.

A Circassian Refugee.

They are dressed in the long Cossack coats of dark cloth peculiar to the inhabitants of the Caucasus; two rows of bone or metal cartridge-cases adorn their breast, being fitted into flutes or pockets made for them; they wear either top boots or top boot-legs, and the counterpart of my own moccasins; and their head-dress is a tall black lamb's-wool turban, similar to the national headgear of the Persians. They are by far the best-dressed and most respectable-looking men one sees among the groups; for while the majority of the natives are both ragged and barefooted, I don't remember ever seeing Circassians either. To all outward appearances they are the most trustworthy men of them all; but there is really more deviltry concealed beneath the smiling exterior of one of these homeless mountaineers from Circassia than in a whole village of the less likely-looking natives here, whose general cut-throat appearance – an effect produced, more than anything else, by the universal custom of wearing all the old swords, knives, and pistols they can get hold of – really counts for nothing. In picturesqueness of attire some of these *khan* loafers leave nothing to be desired; and although I am this morning wearing Igali's cerulean scarf as a sash, the tri-colored pencil string of Servia around my neck, and a handsome pair of Circassian moccasins, I am absolutely nowhere by the side of many a native whose entire wardrobe wouldn't fetch half a medjedie in a Galata auction-room.

At Sabanja the wagon-road terminates, and my way becomes execrable beyond anything I ever encountered; it leads over a low mountain-pass, following the track of the ancient roadway, that on the acclivity of the mountain has been torn up and washed about, and the stone blocks scattered here and piled up there by the torrents of centuries, until it would seem to have been the sport and plaything of a hundred Kansas cyclones. Round about and among this disorganized mass, caravans have picked their way over the pass from the first dawn of commercial intercourse; following the same trail year after year, the stepping-places have come to resemble the steps of a rude stairway. From the summit of the pass is obtained a comprehensive view of the verdure-clad valley; here and there white minarets are seen protruding above the verdant area, like lighthouses from a green sea; villages dot the lower slopes of the mountains, while a lake, covering half the width of the valley for a dozen miles, glimmers in the mid-day sun, making altogether a scene that in some countries would long since have been immortalized on canvas or in verse. The descent is even rougher, if anything, than the western side, but it leads down into a tiny valley that, if situated near a large city, would resound with the voices of merry-makers the whole summer long. The undergrowth of this morning's observations has entirely disappeared; wide-spreading chestnut and grand old sycamore trees shade a circumscribed area of velvety green-sward and isolated rocks; a tiny stream, a tributary of the Sackaria, meanders along its rocky bed, and forest-clad mountains tower almost perpendicularly around the charming little vale save one narrow outlet to the east. There is not a human being in sight, nor a sound to break the silence save the murmuring of the brook, as I fairly clamber down into this little sylvan retreat; but a wreath of smoke curling above the trees some distance from the road betrays the presence of man. The whole scene vividly calls to mind one of those marvellous mountain-retreats in which writers of banditti stories are wont to pitch their heroes' silken tent – no more appropriate rendezvous for a band of story-book free-booters could well be imagined.

Following the course of the little tributary for several miles, crossing and recrossing it a number of times, I finally emerge with it into the valley of Sackaria. There are some very good roads down this valley, which is narrow, and in places contracts to but little more than a mere neck between the mountains. At one of the narrowest points the mountains present an almost perpendicular face of rock, and here are the remnants of an ancient stone wall reputed to have been built by the Greeks, somewhere about the twelfth century, in anticipation of an invasion of the Turks from the south. The wall stretches across the valley from mountain to river, and is quite a massive affair; an archway has been cut through it for the passage of caravans. Soon after passing through this opening I am favored with the company of a horseman, who follows me for three or four miles, and thoughtfully takes upon himself the office of telling me when to *bin* and when not to *bin*, according as he thinks the road suitable for 'cycling or not, until he discovers that his gratuitous advice produces no visible effect on my movements, when he desists and follows along behind in silence like a sensible fellow. About five o'clock in the afternoon I cross the Sackaria on an old stone bridge, and half an hour later roll into Geiveh, a large village situated in the middle of a triangular valley about seven miles in width. My cyclometer shows a trifle over forty miles from Ismidt; it has been a variable forty miles; I shall never forget the pass over the old causeway, the view of the Sabanja Valley from the summit, nor the lovely little retreat on the eastern side.

It rains quite heavily during the night, and while waiting for it to dry up a little in the morning, the Geivehites voluntarily tender me much advice concerning the state of the road ahead, being governed in their ideas according to their knowledge of a 'cycler's mountain-climbing ability. By a round dozen of men, who penetrate into my room in a body ere I am fairly dressed, and who, after solemnly salaaming in chorus, commence delivering themselves of expressive pantomime and gesticulations, I am led to understand that the road from Geiveh to Tereklu is something fearful for a bicycle. One fat old Turk, undertaking to explain it more fully, after the others have exhausted their knowledge of sign language, swells himself up like an inflated toad and imitates the labored respiration of a broken-winded horse in order to duly impress upon my mind the physical exertion I may expect to put forth in 'riding' – he also paws the air with his right foot – over the mountain-range that looms up like an impassable barrier three miles east of the town. The Turks as a nation have the reputation of being solemn-visaged, imperturbable people, yet one occasionally finds them quite animated and 'Frenchy' in their behavior – the bicycle may, however, be in a measure responsible for this.

The next two hours find me engaged in the laborious task of climbing a mere bridle-path up the rugged mountain slope, along which no wheeled vehicle has certainly ever been before. There is in some places barely room for pack animals to pass between the masses of rocks, and at others, but a narrow ledge between a perpendicular rock and a sheer precipice. The steepest portions are worn into rude stone stairways by the feet of pack animals that toiled over this pass just as they toiled before America was discovered and have been toiling ever since; and for hundreds of yards at a stretch I am compelled to push the bicycle ahead, rear wheel aloft, in the well-known manner of going up-stairs. While climbing up a rather awkward place, I meet a lone Arab youth, leading his horse by the bridle, and come near causing a serious accident. It was at the turning of a sharp corner that I met this swarthy-faced youth face to face, and the sudden appearance of what both he and the horse thought was a being from a far more distant sphere than the western half of our own so frightened them both that I expected every minute to see them go toppling over the precipice. Reassuring the boy by speaking a word or two of Turkish, and seeing the impossibility of either passing him or of his horse being able to turn around, I turn about and retreat a short distance, to where there is more room. He is not quite assured of my terrestrial character even yet; he is too frightened to speak, and he trembles visibly as he goes past, greeting me with a leer of mingled fear and suspicion; at the same time making a brave but very sickly effort to ward off any evil designs I might be meditating against him by a pitiful propitiatory smile which will haunt my memory for weeks; though I hope by plenty of exercise to escape an attack of the nightmare.

This is the worst mountain climbing I have done with a bicycle; all the way across the Rockies there is nothing approaching this pass for steepness; although on foot or horseback it would of course not appear so formidable. When part way up, a bank of low hanging clouds come rolling down to meet me, enveloping the mountain in fog, and bringing on a disagreeable drizzle which scarcely improves the situation.

Five miles from the bottom of the pass and three hours from Geiveh I reach a small *postaya-khan,* occupied by one *zaptieh* and the station-keeper, where I halt for a half hour and get the *zaptieh* to brew me a cup of coffee, feeling the need of a little refreshment after the stiff tugging of the last two hours. Coffee is the only refreshment obtainable here, and, though the weather looks anything but propitious, I push ahead toward a regular roadside *khan*, which I am told I shall come to at the distance of another hour – the natives of Asia Minor know nothing of miles or kilometres, but reckon the distance from point to point by the number of hours it usually takes to go on horseback. Reaching this *khan* at three o'clock, I call for something to satisfy the cravings of hunger, and am forthwith confronted with a loaf of black bread, villanously heavy, and given a preliminary peep into a large jar of a crumbly white substance as villanously odoriferous as the bread is heavy, and which I think the proprietor expects me to look upon as cheese.

While engaged in the discussion of this delectable meal, a

caravan of mules arrives in charge of seven rough-looking Turks, who halt to procure a feed of barley for their animals, the supplying of which appears to be the chief business of the *khan-jee*. No sooner have these men alighted and ascertained the use of the bicycle, than I am assailed with the usual importunities to ride for their further edification. It would be quite as reasonable to ask a man to fly as to ride a bicycle anywhere near the *khan*; but in the innocence of their hearts and the dulness of their Oriental understandings they think differently. They regard my objections as the result of a perverse and contrary disposition, and my explanation of '*mimkin deyil*' as but a groundless excuse born of my unwillingness to oblige. One old gray-beard, after examining the bicycle, eyes me meditatively for a moment, and then comes forward with a humorous twinkle in his eye, and pokes me playfully in the ribs, and makes a peculiar noise with the mouth: 'q-u-e-e-k,' in an effort to tickle me into good-humor and compliance with their wishes; in addition to which, the artful old dodger, thinking thus to work on my vanity, calls me 'Pasha Effendi.' Finding that toward their entreaties I give but the same reply, one of the younger men coolly advocates the use of force to coerce me into giving them an exhibition of my skill on the *araba*. As far as I am able to interpret, this bold visionary's argument is: 'Behold, we are seven; Effendi is only one; we are good Mussulmans – peace be with us – he is but a Frank – ashes on his head – let us make him *bin*.'

CHAPTER XII

THROUGH THE ANGORA GOAT COUNTRY

The other members of the caravan company, while equally anxious to see the performance, and no doubt thinking me quite an unreasonable person, disapprove of the young man's proposition; and the *khan-jee* severely reprimands him for talking about resorting to force, and turning to the others, he lays his forefingers together and says something about Franks, Mussulmans, Turks, and Ingilis; meaning that even if we are Franks and Mussulmans, we are not prevented from being at the same time allies and brothers.

From the *khan* the ascent is more gradual, though in places muddy and disagreeable from the drizzling rain which still falls, and about 4 P.M. I arrive at the summit. The descent is smoother, and shorter than the western slope, but is even more abrupt; the composition is a slaty, blue clay, in which the caravans have worn trails so deep in places that a mule is hidden completely from view. There is no room for animals to pass each other in these deep trench-like trails, and were any to meet, the only possible plan is for the ascending animals to be backed down until a wider place is reached. There is little danger of the larger caravans being thus caught in these 'traps for the unwary,' since each can hear the other's approach and take precautions; but single horsemen and small parties must sometimes find themselves obliged to either give or take, in the depths of these queer highways of commerce. It is quite an awkward task to descend with the bicycle, as for much of the way the trail is not even wide enough to admit of trundling in the ordinary manner, and I have to adopt the same tactics in going down as in coming up the mountain, with the difference, that on the eastern slope I have to pull back quite as stoutly as I had to push forward on the western. In going down I meet a man with three donkeys, but fortunately I am able to scramble up the bank sufficiently to let him pass. His donkeys are loaded with half-ripe grapes, which he is perhaps taking all the way to Constantinople in this slow and laborious manner, and he offers me some as an inducement for me to ride for his benefit. Some wheelmen, being possessed of a sensitive nature, would undoubtedly think they had a right to feel aggrieved or insulted if offered a bunch of unripe grapes as an inducement to go ahead and break their necks; but these people here in Asia Minor are but simple-hearted, overgrown children; they will go straight to heaven when they die, every one of them.

Not long after my arrival at Tereklu I am introduced to another peculiar and not unknown phase of the character of these people, one that I have sometimes read of, but was scarcely prepared to encounter before being on Asian soil three days. From some of them having received medical favors from the medicine chest of travellers and missionaries, the Asiatics have come to regard every Frank who passes through their country as a skilful physician, capable of all sorts of wonderful things in the way of curing their ailments; and immediately after supper I am waited upon by my first patient, the *mulazim* of the Tereklu *zaptiehs*. He is a tall, pleasant-faced fellow, whom I remember as having been wonderfully courteous and considerate while I was riding for the people before supper, and he is suffering with neuralgia in his lower jaw. He comes and seats himself beside me, rolls a cigarette in silence, lights it, and hands it to me, and then, with the confident assurance of a child approaching its mother to be soothed and cured of some ailment, he requests me to cure his aching jaw, seemingly having not the slightest doubt of my ability to afford him instant relief. I ask him why he don't apply to the *hakim* (doctor) of his native town. He rolls another cigarette, makes me throw the half-consumed one away, and having thus ingratiated himself a trifle deeper into my affections, he tells me that the Tereklu *hakim* is '*fenna;*' in other words, no good, adding that there is a *duz hakim* at Gieveh, but Gieveh is over the Kara Su *dagh*. At this juncture he seems to arrive at the conclusion that perhaps I require a good deal of coaxing and good treatment, and, taking me by the hand, he leads me in that affectionate, brotherly manner down the street and into a coffee-*khan*, and spends the next hour in pressing upon me coffee and cigarettes, and referring occasionally to his aching jaw. The poor fellow tries so hard to make himself agreeable and awaken my sympathies, that I really begin to feel myself quite an ingrate in not being able to afford him any relief, and slightly embarrassed by my inability to convince him that my failure to cure him is not the result of indifference to his sufferings.

Casting about for some way of escape without sacrificing his good-will, and having in mind a box of pills I have brought along, I give him to understand that I am at the top of the medical profession as a stomach-ache *hakim*, but as for the jaw-ache I am, unfortunately, even worse than his compatriot over the way. Had I attempted to persuade him that I was not a doctor at all, he would not have believed me; his mind being unable to grasp the idea of a Frank totally unacquainted with the noble Æsculapian art; but he seems quite aware of the existence of specialists in the profession, and notwithstanding my inability to deal with his particular affliction, my modest confession of being unexcelled in another branch of medicine seems to satisfy him. My profound knowledge of stomachic disorders and their treatment excuses my ignorance of neuralgic remedies.

Mussulman women are the most gossipy and inquisitive creatures imaginable; a very natural result, I suppose, of having had their feminine rights divine under constant restraint and suppression by the peculiar social position women occupy in Mohammedan countries. When I have arrived in town and am surrounded and hidden from outside view by a solid wall of men, it is really quite painful to see the women standing in small groups at a distance trying to make out what all the excitement is about. Nobody seems to have a particle of sympathy for their very natural inquisitiveness, or even to take any notice of their presence. It is quite surprising to see how rapidly the arrival of the Frank with the wonderful *araba* becomes known among these women from one end of town to another; in an incredibly short space of time, groups of shrouded forms begin to appear on the housetops and other vantage-points, craning their necks to obtain a glimpse of whatever is going on.

It is hardly six o'clock when I issue forth next morning, but there are at least fifty women congregated in the cemetery, alongside which my route leads. During the night they seem to have made up their minds to grasp the only opportunity of 'seeing the elephant' by witnessing my departure; and as, 'when a woman will she will,' etc., applies to Turkish ladies as well as to any others, in their laudable determination not to be disappointed they have been patiently squatting among the gray tombstones since early dawn. The roadway is anything but smooth, nevertheless one could scarce be so dead to all feelings of commiseration as to remain unmoved by the sight of that patiently waiting crowd of shrouded females; accordingly I mount and pick my way along the street and out of town. Modest as is this performance, it is the most marvellous thing they have seen for many a day; not a sound escapes them as I wheel by, they remain as silent as though they were the ghostly population of the graveyard they occupy, for which, indeed, shrouded as they are in white from head to foot, they might easily be mistaken by the superstitious.

Descending into a narrow valley, I reach a road-side *khan*, adjoining a thrifty-looking melon-garden – this latter a welcome sight, since the day is warm and sultry; and a few minutes' quiet, soulful communion with a good ripe water-melon, I think to myself, will be just about the proper caper to indulge in after being worried with dogs, people, small streams, and unridable hills since six o'clock.

'*Carpoose?*' I inquire, addressing the proprietor of the *khan*, who issues forth from the stable.

'*Peeki, effendi,*' he answers, and goes off to the garden for the melon. Smiling sweetly at vacancy, in joyous anticipation of the coming feast and the soothing influence I feel sure of its exerting upon my feelings, somewhat ruffled by the many annoyances of the morning, I seek a quiet, shady corner, thoughtfully loosening my revolver-belt a couple of notches ere sitting down. In a minute the *khan-jee* returns, and hands me a 'cucumber' about the size of a man's forearm.

'That isn't a *carpoose*; I want a *carpoose* – *a su carpoose!*' I explain.

'*Su carpoose, yoke!*' he replies; and as I have not yet reached that reckless disregard of possible consequences to which I afterward attain, I shrink from tempting Providence by trying conclusions with the overgrown and untrustworthy cucumber; so bidding the *khan-jee* adieu, I wheel off down the valley. I find a fair proportion of good road along this valley; the land is rich, and though but rudely tilled, it produces wonderfully heavy crops of grain when irrigated. Small villages, surrounded by neglected-looking orchards and vineyards, abound at frequent intervals. Wherever one finds an orchard, vineyard, or melon-patch, there is also almost certain to be seen a human being evidently doing nothing but sauntering about, or perhaps eating an unripe melon.

This naturally creates an unfavorable impression upon a traveller's mind; it means either that the kleptomaniac tendencies of the people necessitate standing guard over all portable property, or that the Asiatic follows the practice of hovering around all summer, watching and waiting for nature to bestow her blessings upon his undeserving head. Along this valley I meet a Turk and his wife bestriding the same diminutive donkey, the woman riding in front and steering their long-eared craft by the terror of her tongue in lieu of a bridle. The fearless lady halts her steed as I approach, trundling my wheel, the ground being such that riding is possible but undesirable. 'What is that for, effendi?' inquires the man, who seems to be the more inquisitive of the two. 'Why, to *bin*, of course! don't you see the saddle?' says the woman, without a moment's hesitation; and she bestows a glance of reproach upon her worse half for thus betraying his ignorance, twisting her neck round in order to send the glance straight at his unoffending head. This woman, I mentally conclude, is an extraordinary specimen of her race; I never saw a quicker-witted person anywhere; and I am not at all surprised to find her proving herself a phenomenon in other things. When a Turkish female meets a stranger on the road, and more especially a Frank, her first thought and most natural impulse is to make sure that no part of her features is visible – about other parts of her person she is less particular. This remarkable woman, however, flings custom to the winds, and instead of drawing the ample folds of her *abbas* about her, uncovers her face entirely, in order to obtain a better view; and, being unaware of my limited understanding, she begins discussing bicycle in quite a chatty manner. I fancy her poor husband looks a trifle shocked at this outrageous conduct of the partner of his joys and sorrows; but he remains quietly and discreetly in the background; whereupon I register a silent vow never more to be surprised at anything, for that long-suffering and submissive being, the hen-pecked husband, is evidently not unknown even in Asiatic Turkey.

A couple of miles down grade brings me to Torbali, a place of several thousand inhabitants with a small covered bazaar and every appearance of a thriving interior town, as thrift goes in Asia Minor. It is high noon, and I immediately set about finding the wherewithal to make a substantial meal. I find that upon arriving at one of these towns, the best possible disposition to make of the bicycle is to deliver it into the hands of some respectable Turk, request him to preserve it from the meddle-

A Faithful Guardian.

some crowd, and then pay no further attention to it until ready to start. Attempting to keep watch over it oneself is sure to result in a dismal failure, whereas an Osmanli gray-beard becomes an ever-willing custodian, regards its safe-keeping as appealing to his honor, and will stand guard over it for hours if necessary, keeping the noisy and curious crowds of his townspeople at a respectful distance by brandishing a thick stick at anyone who ventures to approach too near. These men will never accept payment for this highly appreciated service, it seems to appeal to the Osmanli's spirit of hospitality; they seem happy as clams at high tide while gratuitously protecting my property, and I have known them to unhesitatingly incur the displeasure of their own neighbors by officiously carrying the bicycle off into an inner room, not even granting the assembled people the harmless privilege of looking at it from a distance – for there might be some among the crowd possessed of the *fenna ghuz* (evil eye), and rather than have them fix their baleful gaze upon the important piece of property left under his charge by a stranger, he chivalrously braves the displeasure of his own people; smiling complacently at their shouts of disapproval, he triumphantly bears it out of their sight and from the fell influence of the possible *fenna ghuz*.

Unfortunately, the streets and environments of Torbali are in a most wretched condition; to escape sprained ankles it is necessary to walk with a great deal of caution, and the idea of bicycling through them is simply absurd. Nevertheless the populace turns out in high glee, and their expectations run riot as I relieve the *kahvay-jee* of his faithful vigil and bring forth my wheel. They want me to *bin* in their stuffy little bazaar, crowded with people and donkeys; mere alley-ways with scarcely a twenty yard stretch from one angle to another; the surface is a disorganized mass of holes and stones over which the wary and hesitative donkey picks his way with the greatest care; and yet the popular clamor is '*Bin, bin; bazaar, bazaar!*' The people who have been showing me how courteously and considerately it is possible for Turks to treat a stranger, now seem to have become filled with a determination not to be convinced by anything I say to the contrary; and one of the most importunate and headstrong among them sticks his bearded face almost up against my own placid countenance (I have already learned to wear an unruffled, martyr-like expression on these howling occasions) and fairly shrieks out, '*Bin! bin!*' as though determined to hoist me into the saddle, whether or no, by sheer force of his own desire to see me there. This person ought to know better, for he wears the green turban of holiness, proving him to have made a pilgrimage to Mecca, but the universal desire to see the bicycle ridden seems to level all distinctions.

All this tumult, it must not be forgotten, is carried on in perfect good humour; but it is, nevertheless, very annoying to have it seem that I am too boorish to repay their kindness by letting them see me ride; even walking out of town to avoid gratifying them, as some of them doubtless think. These little embarrassments are some of the penalties of not knowing enough of the language to be able to enter into explanations. Learning that there is a piece of wagon-road immediately outside the town, I succeed in silencing the clamor to some extent by promising to ride when the *araba yole* is reached; whereupon hundreds come flocking out of town, following expectantly at my heels. Consoling myself with the thought that perhaps I will be able to mount and shake the clamorous multitude off by a spurt, the promised *araba yole* is announced; but the fates are plainly against me to-day, for I find this road leading up a mountain slope from the very beginning. The people cluster expectantly around, while I endeavor to explain that they are doomed to disappointment – that to be disappointed in their expectations to see the *araba* ridden is plainly their *kismet,* for the hill is too steep to be ridden. They laugh knowingly and give me to understand that they are not quite such simpletons as to think that an *araba* cannot be ridden along an *araba yole.* 'This is an *araba yole,*' they argue, 'you are riding an *araba;* we have seen even our own clumsily-made *arabas* go up here time and again, therefore it is evident that you are not sincere,' and they gather closer around and spend another ten minutes in coaxing. It is a ridiculous position to be in; these people use the most endearing terms imaginable; some of them kiss the bicycle and would get down and kiss my dust-begrimed moccasins if I would permit it; at coaxing they are the most persevering people I ever saw.

For a full mile up the mountain road, and with a patient insistence quite commendable in itself, they persist in their aggravating attentions; aggravating, notwithstanding that they remain in the best of humor, and treat me with the greatest consideration in every other respect, promptly and severely checking any unruly conduct among the youngsters, which once or twice reveals itself in the shape of a stone pitched into the wheel, or some other pleasantry peculiar to the immature Turkish mind. At length one enterprising young man, with wild visions of a flying wheelman descending the mountain road with lightning-like velocity, comes prominently to the fore, and unblushingly announces that they have been bringing me along the wrong road; and, with something akin to exultation in his gestures, motions for me to turn about and ride back. Had the others seconded this brilliant idea there was nothing to prevent me from being misled by the statement; but his conduct is at once condemned; for though pig-headed, they are honest of heart, and have no idea of resorting to trickery to gain their object. It now occurs to me that perhaps if I turn round and ride down hill a short distance they will see that my trundling up hill is really a matter of necessity instead of choice, and thus rid me of their undesirable presence.

Hitherto the slope has been too abrupt to admit of any such thought, but now it becomes more gradual. As I expected, the proposition is heralded with unanimous shouts of approval, and I take particular care to stipulate that after this they are to follow me no farther; any condition is acceptable to them as long as it includes seeing how the thing is ridden. It is not without certain misgivings that I mount and start cautiously down the declivity between two rows of turbaned and fez-bedecked heads, for I have not yet forgotten the disagreeable actions of the mob at Adrianople in running up behind and giving the bicycle vigorous forward pushes, a proceeding that would be not altogether devoid of danger here, for besides the gradient, one side of the road is a yawning chasm. These people, however, confine themselves solely to howling with delight, proving themselves to be well-meaning and comparatively well-behaved after all. Having performed my part of the compact, a few of the leading men shake hands, and express their gratitude and well-wishes; and after calling back several youngsters who seem unwilling to abide by the agreement forbidding them to follow any farther, the whole noisy company proceed along footpaths leading down the cliffs to town, which is in plain view almost immediately below.

In view of the nature of the country and the distance to Keshtobek, I have no idea of being able to reach that place to-night, and when I arrive at the ruins of an old mud-built *khan*, at dusk, I conclude to sup off the memories of my excellent dinner and a piece of bread I have in my pocket, and avail myself of its shelter for the night. While eating my frugal repast, up ride three muleteers, who, after consulting among themselves some minutes, finally picket their animals and prepare to join my company; whether for all night or only to give their animals a feed of grass, I am unable to say. Anyhow, not liking the idea of spending the whole night, or any part of it, in these unfrequented hills with three ruffianly-looking natives, I again take up my line of march along mountain mule-paths for some three miles farther, when I descend into a small valley, and it being too dark to undertake the task of pitching my tent, I roll myself up in it instead. Soothed by the music of a babbling brook, I am almost asleep, when a glorious meteor shoots athwart the sky, lighting up the valley with startling vividness for one brief moment, and then the dusky pall of night descends, and I am gathered into the arms of Morpheus.

* * *

The little *khan* I stop at is, of course, besieged by the usual crowd, but they a happy-hearted, contented people, bent on lionizing me the best they know how; for have they not witnessed by marvellous performance of riding an *araba*, a beautiful web-like *araba*, more beautiful than any *makina* they ever saw before, and in a manner that upsets all their previous ideas of equilibrium? Have I not proved how much I esteem them by riding over and over again for fresh batches of new arrivals, until the whole population has seen the performance? And am I not hobnobbing and making myself accessible to the people, instead of being exclusive and going straightway to the pasha's, shutting myself up and permitting none but a few privileged persons to intrude upon my privacy? All these things appeal strongly to the better nature of the imaginative Turks, and not a moment during the whole evening am I suffered to be unconscious of their great appreciation of it all. A bountiful supper of scrambled eggs fried in butter, and then the *mulazim* of *zaptiehs* takes me under his special protection and shows me around the town.

When it grows dark the *mulazim* takes me to the public coffee-garden, near the burned bazaar, a place which is really no garden at all, only some broad, rude benches encircling a round water-tank or fountain, and which is fenced in with a low, wabbly picket-fence. Seated crossed-legged on the benches are a score of sober-sided Turks, smoking *nargilehs* and cigarettes, and sipping coffee; the feeble light dispensed by a lantern on top of a pole in the centre of the tank makes the darkness of the 'garden' barely visible; a continuous splashing of water, the result of the overflow from a pipe projecting three feet above the surface, furnishes the only music; the sole auricular indication of the presence of patrons is when some customer orders '*kahvay*' or '*nargileh*' in a scarcely audible tone of voice, and this is the Turk's idea of an evening's enjoyment.

Returning to the *khan*, I find it full of happy people looking at the bicycle; commenting on the wonderful *marifet* (skill) apparent in its mechanism, and the no less marvellous *marifet* required in riding it. They ask me if I made it myself and *katchlira?* (how many liras?) and then requesting the privilege of looking at my *teskeri* they find rare amusement in comparing my personal charms with the description of my form and features as interpreted by the passport officer in Galata.

Quilts are provided for me, and I spend the night on the divan of the *khan*; a few roving mosquitoes wander in at the open window and sing their siren songs around my couch, a few entomological specimens sally forth from their permanent abode in the lining of the quilts to attack me and disturb my slumbers; but later experience teaches me to regard my slumbers to-night as comparatively peaceful and undisturbed. In the early morning I am awakened by the murmuring voices of visitors gathering to see me off; coffee is handed to me ere my eyes are fairly open, and the savory odor of eggs already sizzling in the pan assail my olfactory nerves. The *khan-jee* is an Osmanli and a good Mussulman, and when ready to depart I carelessly toss him my purse and motion for him to help himself – a thing I would not care to do with the keeper of a small tavern in any other country or of any other nation. Were he entertaining me in a private capacity he would feel injured at any hint of payment; but being a *khan-jee*, he opens the purse and extracts a cherik – twenty cents.

CHAPTER XIII

BEY BAZAAR, ANGORA, AND EASTWARD

Another scary youth takes to his heels as I descend into the valley and halt at the village of Charkhan, a mere shapeless cluster of mud-hovels. Before one of these a ragged agriculturist solemnly presides over a small heap of what I unfortunately mistake at the time for pumpkins. I say 'unfortunately,' because after-knowledge makes it highly probable that they were the celebrated Charkhan musk-melons, famous far and wide for their exquisite flavor; the variety can be grown elsewhere, but, strange to say, the peculiar, delicate flavor which makes them so celebrated is absent when they vegetate anywhere outside this particular locality. It is supposed to be owing to some peculiar mineral properties of the soil.

Ascending from this interesting locality my road now traverses a dreary, monotonous district of whitish, sun-blistered hills, waterless and verdureless for fourteen miles. The cool, refreshing breezes of early morning have been dissipated by the growing heat of the sun; the road continues fairly good, and while riding I am unconscious of oppressive heat; but the fierce rays of the sun blisters my neck and the backs of my hands, turning them red and causing the skin to peel off a few days afterward, besides ruining a section of my gossamer coat exposed on top of the Lamson carrier. The air is dry and thirst-creating, there is considerable hill-climbing to be done, and long ere the fourteen miles are covered I become sufficiently warm and thirsty to have little thought of anything else but reaching the means of quenching thirst. Away off in the distance ahead is observed a dark object, whose character is indistinct through the shimmering radiation from the heated hills, but which, upon a nearer approach, proves to be a jujube-tree, a welcome sentinel in those arid regions, beckoning the thirsty traveller to a never-failing supply of water. At the jujube-tree I find a most magnificent fountain, pouring forth at least twenty gallons of delicious cold water to the minute. The spring has been walled up and a marble spout inserted, which gushes forth a round, crystal column, as though endeavoring to compensate for the prevailing aridness and to apologize to the thirsty wayfarer for the inhospitableness of its surroundings.

The heat becomes almost unbearable; the region of treeless, shelterless hills continues to characterize my way, and when, at two o'clock P.M., I reach the town of Bey Bazaar, I conclude that the thirty-nine miles already covered is the limit of discretion to-day, considering the oppressive heat, and seek the friendly accommodation of a *khan*. There I find that while shelter from the fierce heat of the sun is obtainable, peace and quiet are altogether out of the question. Bey Bazaar is a place of eight thousand inhabitants, and the *khan* at once becomes the objective point of, it seems to me, half the population. I put the machine up on a barricaded *yattack*-divan, and climb up after it; here I am out of the meddlesome reach of the 'madding crowd,' but there is no escaping from the bedlam-like clamor of their voices, and not a few, yielding to their uncontrollable curiosity, undertake to invade my retreat; these invariably 'skedaddle' respectfully at my request, but new-comers are continually intruding. The tumult is quite deafening, and I should certainly not be surprised to have the *khan-jee* request me to leave the place, on the reasonable ground that my presence is, under the circumstances, detrimental to his interests, since the crush is so great that transacting business is out of the question. The *khan-jee*, however, proves to be a speculative individual, and quite contrary thoughts are occupying his mind. His subordinate, the *kahvay-jee*, presents himself with mournful countenance and humble attitude, points with a perplexed air to the surging mass of fezzes, turbans, and upturned Turkish faces, and explains – what needs no explanation other than the evidence of one's own eyes – that he cannot transact his business of making coffee.

'This is your *khan*,' I reply; 'why not turn them out?'

'*Mashallah, effendi!* I would, but for everyone I turned out, two others would come in – the sons of burnt fathers!' he says, casting a reproachful look down at the struggling crowd of his fellow-countrymen.

'What do you propose doing, then?' I inquire.

'*Katch para, effendi,*' he answers, smiling approvingly at his own suggestion.

The enterprising *kahvay-jee* advocates charging them an admission fee of five paras (half a cent) each as a measure of protection, both for himself and me, proposing to make a 'divvy' of the proceeds. Naturally enough the idea of making a farthing show of either myself or the bicycle is anything but an agreeable proposition, but it is plainly the only way of protecting the *kahvay-jee* and his *khan* from being mobbed all the afternoon and far into the night by a surging mass of inquisitive people; so I reluctantly give him permission to do whatever he pleases to protect himself. I have no idea of the financial outcome of the speculative *khan-jee*'s expedient, but the arrangement secures me to some extent from the rabble, though not to any appreciable extent from being worried. The people nearly drive me out of my seven senses with their peculiar ideas of making themselves agreeable, and honoring me; they offer me cigarettes, coffee, mastic, cognac, fruit, raw cucumbers, melons, everything, in fact, but the one thing I should really appreciate – a few minutes quiet, undisturbed, enjoyment of my own company; this is not to be secured by locking one's self in a room, nor by any other expedient I have yet tried in Asia.

The last party of sight-seers for the day call around near midnight, some time after I have retired to sleep; they awaken me with their garrulous observations concerning the bicycle, which they are critically examining close to my head with a classic lamp; but I readily forgive them their nocturnal intrusion, since they awaken me to the first opportunity of hearing women wailing for the dead. A dozen or so of women are wailing forth their lamentations in the silent night but a short distance from the *khan*; I can look out of a small opening in the wall near my shake-down, and see them moving about the house and premises by the flickering glare of torches. I could never have believed the female form divine capable of producing such doleful, unearthly music; but there is no telling what these shrouded forms are really capable of doing, since the opportunity of passing one's judgment upon their accomplishments is confined solely to an occasional glimpse of a languishing eye. The *kahvay-jee*, who is acting the part of explanatory lecturer to these nocturnal visitors, explains the meaning of the wailing by pantomimically describing a corpse, and then goes on to explain that the smallest imaginable proportion of the lamentations that are making night hideous is genuine grief for the departed, most of the uproar being made by a body of professional mourners hired for the occasion. When I awake in the morning the unearthly wailing is still going vigorously forward, from which I infer they have been keeping it up all night. Though gradually becoming inured to all sorts of strange scenes and customs, the united wailing and lamentations of a houseful of women, awakening the echoes of the silent night, savor too much of things supernatural and unearthly not to jar unpleasantly on the senses; the custom is, however, on the eve of being relegated to the musty past by the Ottoman Government.

In the larger cities where there are corpses to be wailed over every night, it has been found so objectionable to the expanding intellects of the more enlightened Turks that it has been prohibited as a public nuisance, and these days it is only in such conservative interior towns as Bey Bazaar that the custom still obtains.

Continuing on my way I am next halted by a young man of the better class, who, together with the *zaptieh*, endeavors to prevail upon me to stop, going through the pantomime of writing and reading, to express some idea that our mutual ignorance of each other's language prevents being expressed in words. The result is a rather curious *intermezzo*. Thinking they want to examine my *teskeri* merely to gratify their idle curiosity, I refuse to be thus bothered, and, dismissing them quite brusquely, hurry along over the rough cobble-stones in hopes of reaching ridable ground and escaping from the place ere the inevitable 'madding crowd' become generally aware of my arrival. The young man disappears, while the *zaptieh* trots smilingly but determinedly by my side, several times endeavoring to coax me into making a halt; which is, however, promptly interpreted by myself into a paternal plea on behalf of the villagers – a desire to have me stop until they could be generally notified and collected – the very thing I am hurrying along to avoid. I am already clear of the village and trundling up the inevitable acclivity, the *zaptieh* and a small gathering still doggedly hanging on, when the young man reappears, hurriedly approaching from the rear, followed by half the village. The *zaptieh* pats me on the shoulder and points back with a triumphant smile; thinking he is referring to the rabble, I am rather inclined to be angry with him and chide him for dogging my footsteps, when I observe the young man waving aloft a letter, and at once understand that I have been guilty of an ungenerous misinterpretation of their determined attentions. The letter is from Mr. Binns, an English gentleman at Angora, engaged in the exportation of mohair, and contains an invitation to become his guest while at Angora. A well-deserved backsheesh to the good-natured *zaptieh* and a penitential shake of the young man's hand silence the self-accusations of a guilty conscience, and, after riding a short distance down the hill for the satisfaction of the people, I continue on my way, trundling up the varying gradations of a general acclivity for two miles.

The tortuous windings of the *chemin de fer* finally bring me to a *cul-de-sac* in the hills, terminating on the summit of a ridge overlooking a broad plain; and a horseman I meet informs me that I am now midway between Bey Bazaar and Angora. While ascending this ridge I become thoroughly convinced of what has frequently occurred to me between here and Nalikhan – that if the road I am traversing is, as the people keep calling it, a *chemin de fer*, then the engineer who graded it must have been a youth of tender age, and inexperienced in railway matters, to imagine that trains can ever round his curve or climb his grades. There is something about this broad, artificial highway, and the tremendous amount of labor that has been expended upon it, when compared with the glaring poverty of the country it traverses, together with the wellnigh total absence of wheeled vehicles, that seem to preclude the possibility of its having been made for a wagon-road; and yet, notwithstanding the belief of the natives, it is evident that it can never be the road-bed of a railway. We must inquire about it at Angora.

Descending into the Angora Plain, I enjoy the luxury of a continuous coast for nearly a mile, over a road that is simply perfect for the occasion, after which comes the less desirable performance of ploughing through a stretch of loose sand and gravel. While engaged in this latter occupation I overtake a *zaptieh*, also *en route* to Angora, who is letting his horse crawl leisurely along while he concentrates his energies upon a watermelon, evidently the spoils of a recent visitation to a melon-garden somwhere not far off; he hands me a portion of the booty, and then requests me to *bin*, and keeps on requesting me to *bin* at regular three-minute intervals for the next half-hour. At the end of that time the loose gravel terminates, and I find myself on a level and reasonably smooth dirt-road, making a shorter cut across the plain to Angora than the *chemin de fer*. The *zaptieh* is, of course, delighted at seeing me thus mount, and not doubting but that I will appreciate his company, gives me to understand that he will ride alongside to Angora. For nearly two miles that sanguine but unsuspecting minion of the Turkish Government spurs his noble steed alongside the bicycle in spite of my determined pedalling to shake him off; but the road improves; faster spins the whirling wheels; the *zaptieh* begins to lag behind a little, though still spurring his panting horse into keeping reasonably close behind; a bend now occurs in the road, and an intervening knoll hides us from each other; I put on more steam, and at the same time the *zaptieh* evidently gives it up and relapses into his normal crawling pace, for when three miles or thereabout are covered I look back and perceive him leisurely heaving in sight from behind the knoll.

Five P.M., August 16, 1885, finds me seated on a rude stone slab, one of those ancient tombstones whose serried ranks constitute the suburban scenery of Angora, ruefully disburdening my nether garments of mud and water, the results of a slight miscalculation of my abilities at leaping irrigating ditches with the bicycle for a vaulting-pole. While engaged in this absorbing occupation several inquisitives mysteriously collect from somewhere, as they invariably do whenever I happen to halt for a minute, and following the instructions of the Ayash letter I inquire the way to the 'Ingilisin Adam' (Englishman's man). They pilot me through a number of narrow, ill-paved streets leading up the sloping hill which Angora occupies – a situation that gives the supposed ancient capital of Galatia a striking appearance from a distance – and into the premises of an Armenian whom I find able to make himself intelligible in English, if allowed several minutes undisturbed possession of his own faculties of recollection between each word – the

Racing with the Zaptieh.

gentleman is slow but not quite sure. From him I learn that Mr.
Binns and family reside during the summer months at a
vineyard five miles out, and that Mr. Binns will not be in town
before to-morrow morning; also that, 'You are welcome to the
humble hospitality of our poor family.'

This latter way of expressing it is a revelation to me, and the
leaden-heeled and labored utterance, together with the general
bearing of my volunteer host, is not less striking; if meekness,

lowliness, and humbleness, permeating a person's every look, word, and action, constitute worthiness, then is our Armenian friend beyond a doubt the worthiest of men. Laboring under the impression that he is Mr. Binns' 'Ingilisin Adam,' I have no hesitation about accepting his proffered hospitality for the night; and storing the bicycle away, I proceed to make myself quite at home, in that easy manner peculiar to one accustomed to constant change. Later in the evening imagine my astonishment at learning that I have thus nonchalantly quartered myself, so to speak, not on Mr. Binns' man, but on an Armenian pastor who has acquired his slight acquaintance with my own language from being connected with the American Mission having headquarters at Kaisarieh!

About ten o'clock Mr. Binns arrives, and is highly amused at the ludicrous mistake that brought me to the Armenian pastor's instead of to his man, with whom he had left instructions concerning me, should I arrive after his departure in the evening for the vineyard; in return he has an amusing story to tell of the people waylaying him on his way to his office, telling him that an Englishman had arrived with a wonderful *araba*, which he had immediately locked up in a dark room and would allow nobody to look at it, and begging him to ask me if they might come and see it. We spend the remainder of the forenoon looking over the town and the bazaar, Mr. Binns kindly announcing himself as at my service for the day, and seemingly bent on pointing out everything of interest.

One of the most curious sights, and one that is peculiar to Angora, owing to its situation on a hill where little or no water is obtainable, is the bewildering swarms of *su-katirs* (water donkeys) engaged in the transportation of that important necessary up into the city from a stream that flows near the base of the hill. These unhappy animals do nothing from one end of their working lives to the other but toil, with almost machine-like regularity and uneventfulness, up the crooked, stony streets with a dozen large earthen-ware jars of water, and down again with the empty jars. The donkey is sandwiched between two long wooden troughs suspended to a rude pack-saddle, and each trough accommodates six jars, each holding about two gallons of water; one can readily imagine the swarms of these novel and primitive conveyances required to supply a population of thirty-five thousand people. Upon inquiring what they do in case of a fire, I learn that they don't even think of fighting the devouring element with its natural enemy, but, collecting on the adjoining roofs, they smother the flames by pelting the burning building with the soft, crumbly bricks of which Angora is chiefly built; a house on fire, with a swarm of half-naked natives on the neighboring housetops bombarding the leaping flames with bricks, would certainly be an interesting sight.

Angora Water-works.

Near noon we repair to the government house to pay a visit to Sirra Pasha, the Vali or governor of the *vilayet*, who, having heard of my arrival, has expressed a wish to have us call on him. We happen to arrive while he is busily engaged with an important legal decision, but upon our being announced he begs us to wait a few minutes, promising to hurry through with the business.

I have learned during the morning that I have to thank Sirra Pasha's energetic administration for the artificial highway from

Keshtobek, and that he has constructed in the *vilayet* no less than two hundred and fifty miles of this highway, broad and reasonably well made, and actually macadamized in localities where the necessary material is to be obtained. The amount of work done in constructing this road through so mountainous a country is, as before mentioned, plainly out of all proportion to the wealth and population of a second-grade *vilayet* like Angora, and its accomplishment has been possible only by the employment of forced labor. Every man in the whole *vilayet* is ordered out to work at the road-making a certain number of days every year, or provide a substitute; thus, during the present summer there have been as many as twenty thousand men, besides donkeys, working on the roads at one time. Unaccustomed to public improvements of this nature, and, no doubt, failing to see their advantages in a country practically without vehicles, the people have sometimes ventured to grumble at the rather arbitrary proceeding of making them work for nothing, and board themselves; and it has been found expedient to make them believe that they were doing the preliminary grading for a railway that was shortly coming to make them all prosperous and happy; beyond being credulous enough to swallow the latter part of the bait, few of them have the least idea of what sort of a looking thing a railroad would be.

When the Vali hears that the people all along the road have been telling me it was a *chemin de fer*, he fairly shakes in his boots with laughter. Of course I point out that no one can possibly appreciate the road improvements any more than a wheelman, and explain the great difference I have found between the mule-paths of Kodjaili and the broad highways he has made through Angora, and I promise him the universal good opinion of the whole world of 'cyclers. In reply, His Excellency hopes this favorable opinion will not be jeopardized by the journey to Yuzgat, but expresses the fear that I shall find heavier wheeling in that direction, as the road is newly made, and there has been no vehicular traffic to pack it down.

About two hours from Angora I pass through a swampy upland basin, containing several small lakes, and then emerge into a much less mountainous country, passing several mud villages, the inhabitants of which are a dark-skinned people – Turkoman refugees, I think – who look several degrees less particular about their personal cleanliness than the villagers west of Angora. Their wretched mud hovels would seem to indicate the last degree of poverty, but numerous flocks of goats and herds of buffalo grazing near apparently tell a somewhat different story.

Just as darkness is beginning to settle down over the landscape I arrive at one of these unpromising-looking clusters, which, it seems, are now peculiar to the country, and not characteristic of any particular race, for the one I arrive at is a purely Turkish village. After the usual preliminaries of pantomime and *binning*, I am conducted to a capacious flat roof, the common covering of several dwellings and stables bunched up together. This roof is as smooth and hard as a native threshing-floor, and well knowing, from recent experiences, the *modus operandi* of capturing the hearts of these bland and childlike villagers, I mount and straightway secure their universal admiration and applause by riding a few times round the roof. I obtain a supper of fried eggs and *yaort* (milk soured with rennet), eating it on the house-top, surrounded by the whole population of the village, on this and adjoining roofs, who watch my every movement with the most intense curiosity. It is the raggedest audience I have yet been favored with. There are not over half a dozen decently clad people among them all, and two of these are horsemen, simply remaining over night, like myself. Everybody has a fearfully flea-bitten appearance, which augurs ill for a refreshing night's repose.

Here, likewise I am first introduced to a peculiar kind of bread, that I straightway condemn as the most execrable of the many varieties my everchanging experiences bring me in contact with, and which I find myself mentally, and half unconsciously, naming – 'blotting-paper *ekmek*' – a not inappropriate title to convey its appearance to the civilized mind; but the sheets of blotting-paper must be of a wheaten color and in circular sheets about two feet in diameter. This peculiar kind of bread is, we may suppose, the natural result of a great scarcity of fuel, a handful of *tezek*, beneath the large, thin sheet-iron griddle, being sufficient to bake many cakes of this bread. At first I start eating it something like a Shantytown goat would set about consuming a political poster, if it – not the political poster, but the Shantytown goat – had a pair of hands. This outlandish performance creates no small merriment

Genuine Ekmek.

among the watchful on-lookers, who forthwith initiate me into
the mode of eating it *à la Turque*, which is, to roll it up like a
scroll of paper and bite mouthfuls off the end. I afterwards find
this particular variety of *ekmek* quite handy when seated
around a communal bowl of *yaort* with a dozen natives; instead
of taking my turn with the one wooden spoon in common use, I
would form pieces of the thin bread into small handleless
scoops, and, dipping up the *yaort*, eat scoop and all. Besides
sparing me from using the same greasy spoon in common with a
dozen natives, none of them overly squeamish as regards
personal cleanliness, this gave me the appreciable advantage of
dipping into the dish as often as I choose, instead of waiting for
my regular turn at the wooden spoon.

CHAPTER XIV

ACROSS THE KIZIL IRMAK RIVER TO YUZGAT

The country continues much the same as yesterday, with the road indifferent for wheeling. Reaching the expected village about eight o'clock, I breakfast off *ekmek* and new buffalo milk, and at once continue on my way, meeting nothing particularly interesting, save a lively bout occasionally with goat-herds' dogs – the reminiscences of which are doubtless more vividly interesting to myself than they would be to the reader – until high noon, when I arrive at another village, larger, but equally wretched-looking, on the Kizil Irmak River, called Jas-chi-khan. On the west bank of the stream are some ancient ruins of quite massive architecture, and standing on the opposite side of the road, evidently having some time been removed from the ruins with a view to being transported elsewhere, is a couchant lion of heroic proportions, carved out of a solid block of white marble; the head is gone, as though its would-be possessors, having found it beyond their power to transport the whole animal, have made off with what they could. An old and curiously arched bridge of massive rock spans the river near its entrance to a wild, rocky gorge in the mountains; a primitive grist mill occupies a position to the left, near the entrance to the gorge, and a herd of camels are slaking their thirst or grazing near the water's edge to the right – a genuine Eastern picture, surely, and one not to be seen every day, even in the land where to see it occasionally is quite possible.

Riding into Jas-chi-khan, I dismount at a building which, from the presence of several 'do-nothings,' I take to be a *khan* for the accommodation of travellers. In a partially open shed-like apartment are a number of demure looking maidens, industriously employed in weaving carpets by hand on a rude, upright frame, while two others, equally demure-looking, are seated on the ground cracking wheat for *pillau*, wheat being substituted for rice where the latter is not easily obtainable, or is too expensive. Waiving all considerations of whether I am welcome or not, I at once enter this abode of female industry, and after watching the interesting process of carpet-weaving for some minutes, turn my attention to the preparers of cracked wheat. The process is the same primitive one that has been employed among these people from time immemorial, and the same that is referred to in the passage of Scripture which says: 'Two women were grinding corn in the field;' it consists of a small upper and nether millstone, the upper one being turned

A Sketch on the Kizil Irmak.

round by two women sitting facing each other; they both take hold of a perpendicular wooden handle with one hand, employing the other to feed the mill and rake away the cracked grain. These two young women have evidently been very industrious this morning; they have half-buried themselves in the product of their labors, and are still grinding away as though for their very lives, while the constant 'click-clack' of the carpet weavers prove them likewise the embodiment of industry.

They seem rather disconcerted by the abrupt intrusion and scrutinizing attentions of a Frank and a stranger; however, the fascinating search for bits of interesting experience forbids my retirement on that account, but rather urges me to make the most of fleeting opportunities. Picking up a handful of the cracked wheat, I inquire of one of the maidens if it is for *pillau*; the maiden blushes at being thus directly addressed, and with downcast eyes vouchsafes an affirmative nod in reply; at the same time an observant eye happens to discover a little brown big-toe peeping out of the heap of wheat, and belonging to the same demure maiden with the downcast eyes. I know full well that I am stretching a point of Mohammedan etiquette, even by coming among these industrious damsels in the manner I am doing, but the attention of the men is fully concentrated on the bicycle outside, and the temptation of trying the experiment of a little jocularity, just to see what comes of it, is under the circumstances irresistible. Conscious of venturing where angels fear to tread, I stoop down, and take hold of the peeping little brown big-toe, and addressing the demure maiden with the downcast eyes, inquire, 'Is this also for *pillau?*' This proves entirely too much for the risibilities of the industrious *pillau* grinders, and letting go the handle of the mill, they both give themselves up to uncontrollable laughter; the carpet-weavers have been watching me out of the corners of their bright, black eyes, and catching the infection, the click-clack of the carpet-weaving machines instantly ceases, and several of the weavers hurriedly retreat into an adjoining room to avoid the awful and well-nigh unheard-of indiscretion of laughing in the presence of a stranger. Having thus yielded to the temptation and witnessed the results, I discreetly retire, meeting at the entrance a gray-bearded Turk coming to see what the merriment and the unaccountable stop-ping of the carpet-weaving frames is all about.

Ten miles over an indifferent road is traversed next morning; the comfortless reflection that anything like a 'square meal' seems out of the question anywhere between the larger towns scarcely tends to exert a soothing influence on the ravenous attacks of a most awful appetite; and I am beginning to think seriously of making a detour of several miles to reach a mountain village, when I meet a party of three horsemen, a Turkish Bey, with an escort of two *zaptiehs*. I am trundling at the time, and without a moment's hesitancy I make a dead set at the Bey, with the single object of satisfying to some extent my gastronomic requirements.

'Bey Effendi, have you any *ekmek*?' I ask, pointing inquiringly to his saddle-bags on a *zaptieh*'s horse, and at the same time giving him to understand by impressive pantomime the uncontrollable condition of my appetite. With what seems to me, under the circumstances, simply cold-blooded indifference to human suffering, the Bey ignores my inquiry altogether, and concentrating his whole attention on the bicycle, asks, 'What is that?'

'An Americanish *araba*, Effendi; have you any *ekmek*?' toying suggestively with the tell-tale slack of my revolver belt.

'Where have you come from?'

'Stamboul; have you *ekmek* in the saddle-bags, Effendi?' this time boldly beckoning the *zaptieh* with the Bey's effects to approach nearer.

'Where are you going?'

'Yuzgat! *ekmek! ekmek!*' tapping the saddle-bags in quite an imperative manner. This does not make any outward impression upon the Bey's aggravating imperturbability; however; he is not so indifferent to my side of the question as he pretends; aware of his inability to supply my want, and afraid that a negative answer would hasten my departure before he has fully satisfied his curiosity concerning me, he is playing a little game of diplomacy in his own interests.

Never, surely, was the reputation of Dame Fortune for fickleness so completely proved as in her treatment of me this morning – ten o'clock finds me seated on a pile of rugs in a capacious black tent, 'wrassling' with a huge bowl of savory mutton *pillau*, flavored with green herbs, as the guest of a Koordish sheikh; shortly afterwards I meet a man taking a donkey-load of musk-melons to the Koordish camp, who insists on presenting me with the finest melon I have tasted since leaving Constantinople; and high noon finds me the guest of another Koordish sheikh; thus does a morning, which commenced with a fair prospect of no breakfast, following after yesterday's scant supply of unsuitable food, end in more hospitality than I know what to do with.

These nomad tribes of the famous 'black-tents' wander up toward Angora every summer with their flocks, in order to be near a market at shearing time; they are famed far and wide for their hospitality. Upon approaching the great open-faced tent of the Sheikh, there is a hurrying movement among the attendants to prepare a suitable raised seat, for they know at a glance that I am an Englishman, and likewise are aware that an Englishman cannot sit cross-legged like an Asiatic; at first, I am rather surprised at their evident ready recognition of my nationality, but I soon afterwards discover the reason. A huge bowl of *pillau*, and another of excellent *yaort* is placed before me without asking any questions, while the dignified Sheikh fulfils one's idea of a gray-bearded nomad patriarch to perfection, as he sits cross-legged on a rug, solemnly smoking a nargileh, and watching to see that no letter of his generous code of hospitality toward strangers is overlooked by the attendants. These latter seem to be the picked young men of the tribe; fine, strapping fellows, well-dressed, six-footers, and of athletic proportions; perfect specimens of semi-civilized manhood, that would seem better employed in a grenadier regiment than in hovering about the old Sheikh's tent, attending to the filling and lighting of his nargileh, the arranging of his cushions by day and his bed at night, the serving of his food, and the proper reception of his guests; and yet it is an interesting sight to see these splendid young fellows waiting upon their beloved old chieftain, fairly bounding, like great affectionate mastiffs, at his merest look or suggestion.

CHAPTER XV

From the Koordish encampment my route leads over a low mountain spur by easy gradients, and by a winding, unridable trail down into the valley of the eastern fork of the Delijah Irmak. The road improves as this valley is reached, and noon finds me the wonder and admiration of another Koordish camp, where I remain a couple of hours in deference to the powers of the midday sun. One has no scruples about partaking of the hospitality of the nomad Koords, for they are the wealthiest people in the country, their flocks covering the hills in many localities; they are, as a general thing, fairly well dressed, are cleaner in their cooking than the villagers, and hospitable to the last degree. Like the rest of us, however, they have their faults as well as their virtues; they are born freebooters, and in unsettled times, when the Turkish Government, being handicapped by weightier considerations, is compelled to relax its control over them, they seldom fail to promptly respond to their plundering instincts and make no end of trouble. They still retain their hospitableness, but after making a traveller their guest for the night, and allowing him to depart with everything he has, they will intercept him on the road and rob him.

Sunrise on the following morning finds me wheeling eastward from the salt quarry, over a trail well worn by salt caravans, to Yuzgat; the road leads for some distance down a grassy valley, covered with the flocks of the several Koordish camps round about; the wild herdsmen come galloping from all directions across the valley toward me, their uncivilized garb and long swords giving them more the appearance of a ferocious gang of cut-throats advancing to the attack then shepherds. Hitherto, nobody has seemed any way inclined to attack me; I have almost wished somebody would undertake a little devilment of some kind, for the sake of livening things up a little, and making my narrative more stirring; after venturing everything, I have so far nothing to tell but a story of being everywhere treated with the greatest consideration, and much of the time even petted. I have met armed men far away from any habitations, whose appearance was equal to our most ferocious conception of *bashi bazouks*, and merely from a disinclination to be bothered, perhaps being in a hurry at the time, have met their curious inquiries with imperious gestures to be gone; and have been guilty of really inconsiderate conduct on more than one occasion, but under no considerations have I yet found them guilty of anything worse than casting covetous glances at my effects. But there is an apparent churlishness of manner, and an overbearing demeanor, as of men chafing under the restraining influences that prevent them gratifying their natural free-booting instincts, about these Koordish herdsmen whom I encounter this morning, that forms quite a striking contrast to the almost childlike harmlessness and universal respect toward me observed in the disposition of the villagers.

It requires no penetrating scrutiny of these fellows' countenances to ascertain that nothing could be more uncongenial to them than the state of affairs that prevents them stopping me and looting me of everything I possess; a couple of them order me quite imperatively to make a detour from my road to avoid approaching too near their flock of sheep, and their general behavior is pretty much as though seeking to draw me into a quarrel, that would afford them an opportunity of plundering me. Continuing on the even tenor of my way, affecting a lofty unconsciousness of their existence, and wondering whether, in case of being molested, it would be advisable to use my Smith & Wesson in defending my effects, or taking the advice received in Constantinople, offer no resistance whatever, and trust to being able to recover them through the authorities, I finally emerge from their vicinity. Their behaviour simply confirms what I have previously understood of their character; that while they will invariably extend hospitable treatment to a stranger visiting their camps, like unreliable explosives, they require to be handled quite 'gingerly' when encountered on the road, to prevent disagreeable consequences.

Passing through a low, marshy district, peopled with solemn-looking storks and croaking frogs, I meet a young sheikh and his personal attendants returning from a morning's outing at their favorite sport of hawking; they carry their falcons about on small perches, fastened by the leg with a tiny chain. I try to induce them to make a flight, but for some reason or other they refuse; an Osmanli Turk would have accommodated me in a minute. Soon I arrive at another Koordish camp, fording a stream in order to reach their tents, for I have not yet breakfasted, and know full well that no better opportunity of obtaining one will be likely to turn up. Entering the nearest tent, I make no ceremony of calling for refreshments, knowing well enough that a heaping dish of *pillau* will be forthcoming, and that the hospitable Koords will regard the ordering of it as the most natural thing in the world. The *pillau* is of rice, mutton, and green herbs, and is brought in a large pewter dish; and, together with sheet bread and a bowl of excellent *yaort*, is brought on a massive pewter tray, which has possibly belonged to the tribe for centuries. These tents are divided into several compartments; one end is a compartment where the men congregate in the daytime, and the younger men sleep at night, and where guests are received and entertained; the central space is the commissary and female industrial department; the others are female and family sleeping places. Each compartment is partitioned off with a hanging carpet partition; light portable railing of small, upright willow sticks bound closely together protects the central compartment from a horde of dogs hungrily nosing about the camp, and small 'coops' of the same material are usually built inside as a further protection for bowls of milk, *yaort*, butter, cheese, and cooked food; they also obtain fowls from the villagers, which they keep cooped up in a similar manner, until the hapless prisoners are required to fulfil their destiny in chicken *pillau*; the capacious covering over all is strongly woven goats-hair material of a black or smoky brown color. In a wealthy tribe, the tent of their sheikh is often a capacious affair, twenty-five by one hundred feet, containing, among other compartments, stabling and hay-room for the sheikh's horses in winter.

My breakfast is brought in from the culinary department by a young woman of most striking appearance, certainly not less than six feet in height; she is of slender, willowy build, and straight as an arrow; a wealth of auburn hair is surmounted by a small, gay-colored turban; her complexion is fairer than common among Koordish woman, and her features are the queenly features of a Juno; the eyes are brown and lustrous, and, were the expression but of ordinary gentleness, the picture would be perfect; but they are the round, wild-looking orbs of a newly-caged panther – grimalkin-like eyes, that would, most assuredly, turn green and luminous in the dark. Other women come to take a look at the stranger, gathering around and staring at me, while I eat, with all their eyes – and such eyes! I never before saw such an array of 'wild-animal eyes;' no, not even in the Zoo! Many of them are magnificent types of womanhood in every other respect, tall, queenly, and symmetrically perfect; but the eyes – oh, those wild, tigress eyes! Travellers have told queer, queer stories about bands of these wild-eyed Koordish women waylaying and capturing them on the roads through Koordistan, and subjecting them to barbarous treatment. I have smiled, and thought them merely 'travellers' tales;' but I can see plain enough, this morning, that there is no improbability in the stories, for, from a dozen pairs of female eyes, behold, there gleams not one single ray of tenderness: these women are capable of anything that tigresses are capable of, beyond a doubt.

Everybody in Yuzgat knows Youvanaki Effendi Tifticjeeoghlou, to whom I have brought a letter of introduction; and, shortly after reaching town, I find myself comfortably installed on the cushioned divan of honor in that worthy old gentleman's large reception room, while half a dozen serving-men are almost knocking each other over in their anxiety to furnish me coffee, vishner-*su*, cigarettes, etc. They seem determined upon interpreting the slightest motion of my hand or head into some want which I am unable to explain, and, fancying thus, they are constantly bobbing up before me with all sorts of surprising things. Tevfik Bey, general superintendent of the Regie (a company having the monopoly of the tobacco trade in Turkey, for which they pay the government a fixed sum per annum), is also a guest of Tifticjeeoghlou Effendi's hospitable mansion, and he at once despatches a messenger to his Yuzgat agent, Mr. G. O. Tchetchian, a vivacious Greek, who speaks English quite fluently. After that gentleman's arrival, we soon come to a more perfect understanding of each other all round, and a very pleasant evening is spent in receiving crowds of visitors in a ceremonious manner, in which I really seem to be holding a sort of a levee, except that it is evening instead of morning.

The street in front of the Tifticjeeoghlou residence is swarmed with people next morning; keeping open house is, under the circumstances, no longer practicable; the entrance gate has to be guarded, and none permitted to enter but privileged persons. During the forenoon the *Caimacan* and several officials call round and ask me to favor them by riding along a smooth piece of road opposite the municipal *konak*; as I intend remaining over here to-day, I enter no objections, and accompany them forthwith. The rabble becomes wildly excited at seeing me emerge with the bicycle, in company with the *Caimacan* and his staff, for they know that their curiosity is probably on the eve of being gratified. It proves no easy task to traverse the streets, for, like in all Oriental cities, they are narrow, and are now jammed with people. Time and again the *Caimacan* is compelled to supplement the exertions of an inadequate force of *zaptiehs* with his authoritative voice, to keep down the excitement and the wild shouts of '*Bin bacalem! bin bacalem!*' (Ride, so that we can see – an innovation on *bin, bin,* that has made itself manifest since crossing the Kizil Irmak River) that are raised, gradually swelling into the tumultuous howl of a multitude. The uproar is deafening, and, long before reaching the place, the *Caimacan* repents having brought me out. As for myself, I certainly repent having come out, and have still better reasons for doing so before reaching the safe retreat of Tifticjeeoghlou Effendi's house, an hour afterward.

The most that the inadequate squad of *zaptiehs* present can do, when we arrive opposite the municipal *konak*, is to keep the crowd from pressing forward and overwhelming me and the bicycle. They attempt to keep open a narrow passage through the surging sea of humans blocking the street, for me to ride down; but ten yards ahead the lane terminates in a mass of fez-crowned heads. Under the impression that one can mount a bicycle on the stand, like mounting a horse, the *Caimacan* asks me to mount, saying that when the people see me mounted and ready to start, they will themselves yield a passage-way. Seeing the utter futility of attempting explanations under existing conditions, amid the deafening clamor of '*Bin bacalem! bin bacalem!'* I mount and slowly pedal along a crooked 'fissure' in the compact mass of people, which the *zaptiehs* manage to create by frantically flogging right and left before me. Gaining, at length, more open ground, and the smooth road continuing on, I speed away from the multitude, and the *Caimacan* sends one fleet-footed *zaptieh* after me, with instructions to pilot me back to Tifticjeeoghlou's by a roundabout way, so as to avoid returning through the crowds.

The rabble are not to be so easily deceived and shook off as the *Caimacan* thinks, however; by taking various short cuts, they manage to intercept us, and, as though considering the having detected and overtaken us in attempting to elude them, justifies them in taking liberties, their '*Bin bacalem!*' now develops into the imperious cry of a domineering majority, determined upon doing pretty much as they please. It is the worst mob I have seen on the journey, so far; excitement runs high, and their shouts of '*Bin bacalem!*' can, most assuredly, be heard for miles. We are enveloped by clouds of dust, raised by the feet of the multitude; the hot sun glares down savagely upon us; the poor *zaptieh*, in heavy top-boots and a brand new uniform, heavy enough for winter, works like a beaver to protect the bicycle, until, with perspiration and dust, his face is streaked and tattooed like a South Sea Islander's. Unable to proceed, we come to a stand-still, and simply occupy ourselves in protecting the bicycle from the crush, and reasoning with the mob; but the only satisfaction we obtain in reply to anything we say is '*Bin bacalem.*'

One or two pig-headed, obstreperous young men near us, emboldened by our apparent helplessness, persist in handling the bicycle. After being pushed away several times, one of them even assumes a menacing attitude toward me the last time I thrust his meddlesome hand away. Under such circumstances retributive justice, prompt and impressive, is the only politic course to pursue; so, leaving the bicycle to the *zaptieh* a moment, in the absence of a stick, I feel justified in favoring the culprit with a brief, pointed lesson in the noble art of self-defence, the first boxing lesson ever given in Yuzgat. In a Western mob this would have been anything but an act of discretion, probably, but with these people it has a salutary effect; the idea of attempting retaliation is the farthest of anything from their thoughts, and in all the obstreperous crowd there is, perhaps, not one but what is quite delighted at either seeing or hearing of me having thus chastised one of their number, and involuntarily thanks Allah that it didn't happen to be himself.

It would be useless to attempt a description of how we finally managed, by the assistance of two more *zaptiehs*, to get back to Tifticjeeoghlou Effendi's, both myself and the *zaptieh* simply unrecognizable from dust and perspiration. The *zaptieh*, having first washed the streaks and tattooing off his face, now presents himself, with the broad, honest smile of one who knows he well deserves what he is asking for, and says, 'Effendi, backsheesh!'

There is nothing more certain than that the honest fellow merits backsheesh from somebody; it is also equally certain that I am the only person from whom he stands the ghost of a chance of getting any; nevertheless, the idea of being appealed to for backsheesh, after what I have just undergone, merely as an act of accommodation, strikes me as just a trifle ridiculous, and the opportunity of engaging the grinning, good-humoured *zaptieh* in a little banter concerning the abstract preposterousness of his expectations is too good to be lost. So, assuming an air of astonishment, I reply: 'Backsheesh! where is *my* backsheesh? I should think it's *me* that deserves backsheesh if anybody does!' This argument is entirely beyond the *zaptieh*'s child-like comprehension, however; he only understands by my manner that there is a 'hitch' somewhere; and never was there a more broadly good-humored countenance, or a smile more expressive of meritoriousness, nor an utterance more coaxing in its modulations than his 'E-f-fendi, backsheesh!' as he repeats the appeal; the smile and the modulation is well worth the backsheesh.

Early daylight finds me astir on the following morning, for I have found it a desirable thing to escape from town ere the populace is out to crowd about me. Tifticjeeoghlou Effendi's better half has kindly risen at an unusually early hour, to see me off, and provides me with a dozen circular rolls of hard bread – rings the size of rope quoits aboard an Atlantic steamer, which I string on Igali's cerulean waist-scarf, and sling over one shoulder. The good lady lets me out of the gate, and says, '*Bin bacalem,* Effendi.' She hasn't seen me ride yet. She is a motherly old creature, of Greek extraction, and I naturally feel like an ingrate of the meanest type, at my inability to grant her modest request. Stealing along the side streets, I manage to reach ridable ground, gathering by the way only a small following of worthy early risers, and two *katir-jees*, who essay to follow me on their long-eared chargers; but, the road being smooth and level from the beginning, I at once discourage them by a short spurt. A half-hour's trundling up a steep hill, and then comes a coastable descent into lower territory. A conscription party collected from the neighboring Mussulman villages, *en route* to Samsoon, the nearest Black Sea port, is met while riding down this declivity. In anticipation of the Sultan's new uniforms awaiting them at Constantinople, they have provided themselves for the journey with barely enough rags to cover their nakedness. They are in high glee at their departure for Stamboul, and favor me with considerable good-natured chaff as I wheel past. 'Human nature is everywhere pretty much alike the world over,' I think to myself. There is little difference between this regiment of ragamuffins chaffing me this morning and the well-dressed troopers of Kaiser William, bantering me the day I wheeled out of Strassburg.

CHAPTER XVI

THROUGH THE SIVAS VILAYET INTO ARMENIA

The road continues for the most part ridable until about 2 P.M., when I arrive at a mountainous region of rocky ridges, covered chiefly with a growth of scrub-oak. Upon reaching the summit of one of these ridges, I observe some distance ahead what appears to be a tremendous field of large cabbages, stretching away in a northeasterly direction almost to the horizon of one's vision; the view presents the striking appearance of large compact cabbage-heads, thickly dotting a well-cultivated area of clean black loam, surrounded on all sides by rocky, uncultivatable wilds. Fifteen minutes later I am picking my way through this 'cultivated field,' which, upon closer acquaintance, proves to be a smooth lava-bed, and the 'cabbages' are nothing more or less than boulders of singular uniformity; and what is equally curious, they are all covered with a growth of moss, while the volcanic bed they repose on is perfectly naked.

Beyond this singular area, the country continues wild and mountainous, with no habitations near the road; and thus it continues until some time after night-fall, when I emerge upon a few scattering wheat-fields. The baying of dogs in the distance indicates the presence of a village somewhere around; but having plenty of bread on which to sup I once again determine upon studying astronomy behind a wheat-shock. It is a glorious moonlight night, but the altitude of the country hereabouts is not less than six thousand feet, and the chilliness of the atmosphere, already apparent, bodes ill for anything like a comfortable night; but I scarcely anticipate being disturbed by anything save atmospheric conditions. I am rolled up in my tent instead of under it, slumbering as lightly as men are wont to slumber under these unfavorable conditions, when, about eleven o'clock, the unearthly creaking of native *arabas* approaching arouses me from my lethargical condition.

Judging from the sounds, they appear to be making a bee-line for my position; but not caring to voluntarily reveal my presence, I simply remain quiet and listen. It soon becomes evident that they are a party of villagers, coming to load up their buffalo *arabas* by moonlight with these very shocks of wheat. One of the *arabas* now approaches the shock which conceals my recumbent form, and where the pale moonbeams are coquettishly ogling the nickel-plated portions of my wheel, making it conspicuously scintillant by their attentions.

Hoping the *araba* may be going to pass by, and that my presence may escape the driver's notice, I hesitate even yet to reveal myself; but the *araba* stops, and I can observe the driver's frightened expression as he suddenly becomes aware of the presence of strange, supernatural objects. At the same moment I rise up in my winding-sheet-like covering; the man utters a wild yell, and abandoning the *araba*, vanishes like a deer in the direction of his companions. It is an unenviable situation to find one's self in; if I boldly approach them, these people, not being able to ascertain my character in the moonlight, would be quite likely to discharge their fire-arms at me in their fright; if, on the contrary, I remain under cover, they might also try the experiment of a shot before venturing to approach the deserted buffaloes, who are complacently chewing the cud on the spot where their chicken-hearted driver took to his heels.

Under the circumstances I think it best to strike off toward the road, leaving them to draw their own conclusions as to whether I am Sheitan himself, or merely a plain, inoffensive hobgoblin. But while gathering up my effects, one heroic individual ventures to approach part way and open up a shouting inquiry; my answers, though unintelligible to him in the main, satisfy him that I am at all events a human being; there are six of them, and in a few minutes after the ignominious flight of the driver, they are all gathered around me, as much interested and nonplussed at the appearance of myself and bicycle as a party of Nebraska homesteaders might be had they, under similar circumstances, discovered a turbaned old Turk complacently enjoying a nargileh.

No sooner do their apprehensions concerning my probable warlike character and capacity become allayed, than they get altogether too familiar and inquisitive about my packages; and

I detect one venturesome kleptomaniac surreptitiously un-fastening a strap when he fancies I am not noticing. Moreover, laboring under the impression that I don't understand a word they are saying, I observe they are commenting in language smacking unmistakably of covetousness, as to the probable contents of my Whitehouse leather case; some think it is sure to contain *chokh para* (much money), while others suggest that I am a *postaya* (courier), and that it contains letters. Under these alarming circumstances there is only way to manage these overgrown children; that is, to make them afraid of you forthwith; so, shoving the strap-unfastener roughly away, I imperatively order the whole covetous crew to 'haidi!' Without a moment's hesitation they betake themselves off to their work, it being an inborn trait of their character to mechanically obey an authoritative command. Following them to their other *arabas*, I find that they have brought quilts along, intending, after loading up to sleep in the field until daylight. Selecting a good heavy quilt with as little ceremony as though it were my own property, I take it and the bicycle to another shock, and curl myself up warm and comfortable; once or twice the owner of the coverlet approaches quietly, just near enough to ascertain that I am not intending making off with his property, but there is not the slightest danger of being disturbed or molested in any way till morning; thus, in this curious round-about manner, does fortune provide me with the wherewithal to pass a comparatively comfortable night. 'Rather arbitrary proceed-ings to take a quilt without asking permission,' some might think; but the owner thinks nothing of the kind; it is quite customary for travellers of their own nation to help themselves in this way, and the villagers have come to regard it as quite a natural occurrence.

At daylight I am again on the move, and sunrise finds me busy making an outline sketch of the ruins of an ancient castle, that occupies, I should imagine, one of the most impregnable positions in all Asia Minor; a regular Gibraltar. It occupies the summit of a precipitous detached mountain peak, which is accessible only from one point, all the other sides presenting a sheer precipice of rock; it forms a conspicuous feature of the landscape for many miles around, and situated as it is amid a wilderness of rugged brush-covered heights, admirably suited for ambuscades, it was doubtless a very important position at one time. It probably belongs to the Byzantine period, and if the number of old graves scattered among the hills indicate anything, it has in its day been the theatre of stirring tragedy.

Toward sundown the hilly country terminates, and I descend into a broad cultivated valley, through which is a very good wagon-road; and I have the additional satisfaction of learning that it will so continue clear into Sivas, a wagon-road having been made from Sivas into this forest to enable the people to haul wood and building-timber on their *arabas*. Arriving at a good-sized and comparatively well-to-do Mussulman village, I obtain an ample supper of eggs and *pillau*, and, after *binning* over and over again until the most unconscionable Turk among them all can bring himself to importune me no more, I obtain a little peace. Supper for two, together with the tough hill-climbing to-day, and insufficient sleep last night, produces its natural effect; I quietly doze off to sleep while sitting on the divan of a small *khan*, which might very appropriately be called an open shed. Soon I am awakened; they want me to accommodate them by *binning* once more before they retire for the night. As the moon is shining brightly, I offer no objections, knowing that to grant the request will be the quickest way to get rid of their worry. They then provide me with quilts, and I spend the night in the *khan* alone.

About eight o'clock I reach a village situated at the entrance to a rocky defile, with a babbling brook dancing through the space between its two divisions. Upon inquiring for refreshments, a man immediately orders his wife to bring me *pillau*. For some reason or other – perhaps the poor woman has none prepared; who knows? – the woman, instead of obeying the command like a 'guid wifey,' enters upon a wordy demurrer, whereupon her husband borrows a hoe-handle from a bystander and advances to chastise her for daring to thus hesitate about obeying his orders; the woman retreats precipitately into the house, heaping Turkish epithets on her devoted husband's head. This woman is evidently a regular termagant, or she would never have used such violent language to her husband in the presence of a stranger and the whole village; some day, if she doesn't be more reasonable, her husband, instead of satisfying his outraged feelings by chastising her with a hoe-handle, will, in a moment of passion, bid her begone from his house, which in Turkish law constitutes a legal separation; if the command be given in the presence of a competent witness it is irrevocable. Seeing me thus placed, as it were, in an embarrassing situation, another woman – dear, thoughtful creature! – fetches me enough wheat *pillau* to feed a mule, and a nice bowl of *yaort*, off which I make a substantial breakfast.

East of Yennikhan, the road develops into an excellent macadamized highway, on which I find plenty of genuine amusement by electrifying the natives whom I chance to meet or overtake. Creeping noiselessly up behind an unsuspecting donkey-driver, until quite close, I suddenly reveal my presence. Looking round and observing a strange, unearthly combination, apparently swooping down upon him, the affrighted *katir-jee*'s first impulse is to seek refuge in flight, not infrequently bolting clear off the roadway, before venturing upon taking a second look. Sometimes I simply put on a spurt, and whisk past at a fifteen mile pace. Looking back, the *katir-jee* generally seems rooted to the spot with astonishment, and his utter inability to comprehend. These men will have marvellous tales to tell in their respective villages concerning what they saw; unless other bicycles are introduced, the time the 'Ingilisin' went through the country with his wonderful *araba* will become a red-letter event in the memory of the people along my route through Asia Minor. Crossing the Yeldez Irmak River, on a stone bridge, I follow along the valley of the head-waters of our old acquaintance, the Kizil Irmak, and at three o'clock in the afternoon, roll into Sivas, having wheeled nearly fifty miles to-day, the last forty of which will compare favorably in smoothness, though not in levelness, with any forty-mile stretch I know of in the United States. From Angora I have brought a letter of introduction to Mr. Ernest Weakley, a young Englishman, engaged, together with Mr. Rodigas, a Belgian gentleman, for the Ottoman Government, in collecting the Sivas vilayet's proportion of the Russian indemnity; and I am soon installed in hospitable quarters. Sivas artisans enjoy a certain amount of celebrity among their compatriots of other Asia Minor cities for unusual skilfulness, particularly in making filigree silver work. Toward evening myself and Mr. Weakley take a stroll through the silversmith's quarters. The quarters consist of twenty or thirty small wooden shops, surrounding an oblong court; spreading willows and a tiny rivulet running through it give the place a semi-rural appearance. In the little open-front workshops, which might more appropriately be called stalls, Armenian silversmiths are seated cross-legged, some working industriously at their trade, others gossiping and sipping coffee with friends or purchasers.

I am remaining over one day at Sivas, and in the morning we call on the American missionaries. Mr. Perry is at home, and hopes I am going to stay a week, so that they can 'sort of make up for the discomforts of journeying through the country'; Mr. Hubbard and the ladies of the Mission are out of town, but will be back this evening. After dinner we go round to the government *konak* and call on the Vali, Hallil Rifaat Pasha, whom Mr. Weakley describes beforehand as a very practical man, fond of mechanical contrivances; and who would never forgive him if he allowed me to leave Sivas with the bicycle without paying him a visit. The usual rigmarole of salaams, cigarettes, coffee, compliments, and questioning are gone through with; the Vali is a jolly-faced, good-natured man, and is evidently much interested in my companion's description of the bicycle and my journey.

Of course I don't forget to praise the excellence of the road from Yennikhan; I can conscientiously tell him that it is superior to anything I have wheeled over south of the Balkans; the Pasha is delighted at hearing this, and beaming joyously over his spectacles, his fat jolly face a rotund picture of satisfaction, he says to Mr. Weakley: 'You see, he praises up our roads; and he ought to know, he has travelled on wagon roads half way round the world.' The interview ends by the Vali inviting me to ride the bicycle out to his country residence this evening, giving the order for a squad of *zaptiehs* to escort me out of town at the appointed time. 'The Vali is one of the most energetic pashas in Turkey,' says Mr. Weakley, as we take our departure. 'You would scarcely believe that he has established a small weekly newspaper here, and makes it self-supporting into the bargain, would you?'

'I confess I don't see how he manages it among these people,' I reply, quite truthfully, for these are anything but newspaper-supporting people; 'how does he manage to make it self-supporting?'

'Why, he makes every employé of the government subscribe for a certain number of copies, and the subscription price is kept back out of their salaries; for instance, the *mulazim* of *zaptiehs* would have to take half a dozen copies, the *mutaserif* a dozen, etc.; if from any unforeseen cause the current expenses are found to be more than the income, a few additional copies are saddled on each "subscriber".'

Promptly at the hour appointed the squad of *zaptiehs* arrive; Mr. Weakley mounts his servant on a prancing Arab charger, and orders him to manoeuvre the horse so as to clear the way in front; the *zaptiehs* commence their flogging, and in the middle of the cleared space I trundle the bicycle. While making our way through the streets, Mr. Hubbard, who, with the ladies, has just returned to the city, is encountered on the way to invite Mr. Weakley and myself to supper; as he pushes his way through the crowd and reaches my side, he pronounces it the worst rabble he ever saw in the streets of Sivas, and he has been stationed here over twelve years. Once clear of the streets, I mount and soon outdistance the crowd, though still followed by a number of horsemen. Part way out we wait for the Vali's state carriage, in which he daily rides between the city and his residence. While waiting, a terrific squall of wind and dust comes howling from the direction we are going, and while it is still blowing great guns, the Vali and his mounted escort arrive. His Excellency alights and examines the Columbia with much interest, and then requests me to ride on immediately in advance of the carriage. The grade is slightly against me, and the whistling wind seems to be shrieking a defiance; but by superhuman efforts, almost, I pedal ahead and manage to keep in front of his horses all the way. The distance from Sivas is four and a quarter miles by the cyclometer; this is the first time it has ever been measured.

We are ushered into a room quite elegantly furnished, and light refreshments served. Observing my partiality for vishner-*su*, the Governor kindly offers me a flask of the syrup to take along; which I am, however, reluctantly compelled to refuse, owing to my inability to carry it. Here, also, we meet Djaved Bey, the Pasha's son, who has recently returned from

Constantinople, and who says he saw me riding at Prinkipo. The Vali gets down on his hands and knees to examine the route of my journey on a map of the world which he spreads out on the carpet; he grows quite enthusiastic, and exlaims, 'Wonderful!' 'Very wonderful!' says Djaved Bey; 'when you get back to America they will – build you a statue.' Mr. Hubbard has mounted a horse and followed us to the Vali's residence, and at the approach of dusk we take our departure; the wind is favorable for the return, as is also the gradient; ere my two friends have unhitched their horses, I mount and am scudding before the gale half a mile away.

The Vali on Floor with Map.

'Hi hi hi-hi! you'll never overtake him!' the Vali shouts enthusiastically to the two horsemen as they start at full gallop after me, and which they laughingly repeat to me shortly afterward. A very pleasant evening is spent at Mr. Hubbard's house; after supper the ladies sing 'Sweet Bye and Bye,' 'Home, Sweet Home,' and other melodious reminders of the land of liberty and song that gave them birth. Everything looks comfortable and homelike, and they have English ivy inside the dining-room trained up the walls and partly covering the ceiling, which produces a wonderfully pleasant effect. The usual extraordinary rumors of my wonderful speeding ability have circulated about the city during the day and evening, some of which have happened to come to the ears of the missionaries. One story is that I came from the port of Samsoon, a distance of nearly three hundred miles, in six hours, while an imaginative *katir-jee*, whom I whisked past on the road, has been telling the Sivas people an exaggerated story of how a *genii* had ridden past him with lightning-like speed, on a shining wheel; but whether it was a good or an evil *genii* he said he didn't have time to determine, as I went past like a flash and vanished in the distance.

'Come in here a minute,' says Mr. Hubbard, just before our departure for the night, leading the way into an adjoining room; 'here's shirts, under-clothing, socks, handkerchiefs – everything; help yourself to anything you require; I know something about travelling through this country *myself!*' But not caring to impose too much on good nature, I content myself with merely pocketing a strong pair of socks, that I know will come in handy.

Tifticjeeoghlou Effendi was a gentleman of Greek descent. At Zara I have an opportunity of seeing and experiencing something of what hospitality is like among the better class Armenians, for I have brought from Sivas a letter of introduction to Kirkor-agha Vartarian, the most prominent Armenian gentleman in Zara. I have no difficulty whatever in finding the house, and am at once installed in the customary position of honor, while five serving-men hover about, ready to wait on me; some take a hand in the inevitable ceremony of preparing and serving coffee and lighting cigarettes, while others stand watchfully by awaiting word or look from myself or mine host, or from the privileged guests that immediately begin to arrive. The room is of cedar planking throughout, and is absolutely without furniture, save the carpeting and the cushioned divan on which I am seated. Mr. Vartarian sits crossed-legged on the carpet to my left, smoking a nargileh; his younger brother occupies a similar position on my right, rolling and smoking cigarettes; while the guests, as they arrive, squat themselves on the carpet in positions varying in distance from the divan, according to their respective rank and social importance. No one ventures to occupy the cushioned divan alongside myself, although the divan is fifteen feet long, and it makes me feel uncomfortably like the dog in the manger to occupy its whole length alone.

At the supper table mine host and his brother both lavish attentions upon me; knives and forks of course there are none, these things being seldom seen in Asia Minor, and to a cycler who has spent the day in pedalling against a stiff breeze, their absence is a matter of small moment. I am ravenously hungry, and they both win my warmest esteem by transferring choice morsels from their own plates into mine with their fingers. From what I know of strict *haut ton* Zaran etiquette, I think they should really pop these tid-bits in my mouth, and the reason they don't do so is, perhaps, because I fail to open it in the customary *haut ton* manner; however, it is a distasteful thing to be always sticking up for one's individual rights. A pile of quilts and mattresses, three feet thick, and feather pillows galore are prepared for me to sleep on. An attendant presents himself with a wonderful night-shirt, on the ample proportions of which are displayed bewildering colors and figures; and following the custom of the country, shapes himself for undressing me and assisting me into bed. This, however, I prefer to do without assistance, owing to a large stock of native modesty.

I never fell among people more devoted in their attentions; their only thought during my stay is to make me comfortable; but they are very ceremonious and great sticklers for etiquette. I had intended making my usual early start, but mine host receives with open disapproval – I fancy even with a showing of displeasure – my proposition to depart without first partaking of refreshments, and it is nearly eight o'clock before I finally get

At Kirkor-agha Vartarian's.

started. Immediately after rising comes the inevitable coffee and early morning visitors; later an attendant arrives with breakfast for myself on a small wooden tray. Mr. Vartarian occupies precisely the same position, and is engaged in precisely the same occupation as yesterday evening, as is also his brother. No sooner does the hapless attendant make his appearance with the eatables than these two persons spring simultaneously to their feet, apparently in a towering rage, and chase him back out of the room, meanwhile pursuing him with a torrent of angry words; they then return to their respective positions and respective occupations. Ten minutes later the attendant reappears, but this time bringing a larger tray with an ample spread for three persons; this, it afterward appears, is not because mine host and his brother intends partaking of any, but because it is Armenian etiquette to do so, and Armenian etiquette therefore becomes responsible for the spectacle of a solitary feeder seated at breakfast with dishes and everything prepared for three, while of the other two, one is smoking a nargileh, the other cigarettes, and both of them regarding my evident relish of scrambled eggs and cold fowl with intense satisfaction.

Having by this time determined to merely drift with the current of mine host's intentions concerning the time of my departure, I resume my position on the divan after breakfasting, simply hinting that I would like to depart as soon as possible. To this Mr. Vartarian complacently nods assent, and his brother, with equal complacency rolls me a cigarette, after which a good half-hour is consumed in preparing for me a letter of introduction to their friend Mudura Ohana in the village of Kachahurda, which I expect to reach somewhere near noon; mine host dictates while his brother writes. Visitors continue coming in, and I am beginning to get a trifle impatient about starting; am beginning in fact to wish all their nonsensical ceremoniousness at the bottom of the deep blue sea or some equally unfathomable quarter, when, at a signal from Mr. Vartarian himself, his brother and the whole roomful of visitors rise simultaneously to their feet, and equally simultaneously put their hands on their respective stomachs, and, turning toward me, salaam; mine host then comes forward, shakes hands, gives me the letter to Mudura Ohana, and permits me to depart.

The numerous irrigating ditches have retarded my progress to an appreciable extent to-day, so that, notwithstanding the early start and the absence of mountain-climbing, my cyclometer registers but a gain of thirty-seven miles, when, having continued my eastward course for some time after nightfall, and failing to reach a village, I commence looking around for somewhere to spend the night. The valley of the Gevmeili Chai has been left behind, and I am again traversing a narrow, rocky pass between the hills. Among the rocks I discover a small open cave, in which I determine to spend the night. The region is elevated, and the night air chilly; so I gather together some dry weeds and rubbish and kindle a fire. With something to cook and eat, and a pair of blankets, I could have spent a reasonably comfortable night; but a pocketful of pears has to suffice for supper, and when the unsubstantial fuel is burned away, my airy chamber on the bleak mountain-side and the thin cambric tent affords little protection from the insinuating chilliness of the night air. Variety is said to be the spice of life; no doubt it is, under certain conditions, but I think it all depends on the conditions whether it is spicy or not spicy. For instance, the vicissitudes of fortune that favor me with bread and sour milk for dinner, a few pears for supper, and a wakeful night of shivering discomfort in a cave, as the reward of wading fifty irrigating ditches and traversing thirty miles of ditch-bedevilled donkey-trails during the day, may look spicy, and even romantic, from a distance; but when one wakes up in a cold shiver about 1.30 A.M. and realizes that several hours of wretchedness are before him, his waking thoughts are apt to be anything but thoughts complimentary of the spiciness of the situation. Inshallah! fortune will favor me with better dues to-morrow; and if not to-morrow, then the next day, or the next.

CHAPTER XVII

THROUGH ERZINGAN AND ERZEROUM

For mile after mile, off the following morning, my route leads through broad areas strewn with bowlders and masses of rock that appear to have been brought down from the adjacent mountains by the annual spring floods, caused by the melting winter's snows; scattering wheat-fields are observed here and there on the higher patches of ground, which look like small yellow oases amid the desert-like area of loose rocks surrounding them. Squads of diminutive donkeys are seen picking their weary way through the bowlders, toiling from the isolated fields to the village threshing-floors beneath small mountains of wheat-sheaves. Sometimes the donkeys themselves are invisible below the general level of the bowlders, and nothing is to be seen but the head and shoulders of a man, persuading before him several animated heaps of straw. Small lakes of accumulated surface-water are passed in depressions having no outlet; thickets and bulrushes are growing around the edges, and the surfaces of some are fairly black with multitudes of wild-ducks. Soon I reach an Armenian village; after satisfying the popular curiosity by riding around their theshing-floor, they bring me some excellent wheat-bread, thick, oval cakes that are quite acceptable, compared with the wafer-like sheets of the past several days, and five boiled eggs. The people providing these will not accept any direct payment, no doubt thinking my having provided them with the only real entertainment most of them ever saw, a fair equivalent for their breakfast; but it seems too much like robbing paupers to accept anything from these people without returning something, so I give money to the children. These villagers seem utterly destitute of manners, standing around and watching my efforts to eat soft-boiled eggs with a pocket-knife with undisguised merriment. I inquire for a spoon, but they evidently prefer to extract amusement from watching my interesting attempts with the pocket-knife. One of them finally fetches a clumsy wooden ladle, three times broader than an egg, which, of course, is worse than nothing.

About two o'clock I arrive at a road-side *khan*, where an ancient Osmanli dispenses feeds of grain for travellers' animals, and brews coffee for the travellers themselves, besides furnishing them with whatever he happens to possess in the way of eatables to such as are unfortunately obliged to patronize his cuisine or go without anything; among this latter class belongs, unhappily, my hungry self. Upon inquiring for refreshments the *khan-jee* conducts me to a rear apartment and exhibits for my inspection the contents of two jars, one containing the native idea of butter and the other the native conception of a soft variety of cheese; what difference is discoverable between these two kindred products is chiefly a difference in the degree of rancidity and odoriferousness, in which respect the cheese plainly carries off the honors; in fact these venerable and esteemable qualities of the cheese are so remarkably developed that after one cautious peep into its receptacle I forbear to

The Native Idea of Butter.

investigate their comparative excellencies any further; but obtaining some bread and a portion of the comparatively mild and inoffensive butter, I proceed to make the best of circumstances. The old *khan-jee* proves himself a thoughtful, considerate landlord, for as I eat he busies himself picking the most glaringly conspicuous hairs out of my butter with the point of his dagger. One is usually somewhat squeamish regarding hirsute butter, but all such little refinements of civilized life as hairless butter or strained milk have to be winked at to a greater or less extent in Asiatic travelling, especially when depending solely on what happens to turn up from one meal to another.

The narrow, lonely defile continues for some miles eastward from the *khan*, and ere I emerge from it altogether I encounter a couple of ill-starred natives, who venture upon an effort to intimidate me into yielding up my purse. A certain Mahmoud Ali and his band of enterprising freebooters have been terrorizing the villagers and committing highway robberies of late around the country; but from the general appearance of these two, as they approach, I take them to be merely villagers returning home from Erzingan afoot. They are armed with Circassian guardless swords and flint-lock horse-pistols; upon meeting they address some question to me in Turkish, to which I make my customary reply of *Turkchi binmus*; one of them then demands *para* (money) in a manner that leaves something of a doubt whether he means it for begging, or is ordering me to deliver. In order to the better discover their intentions, I pretend not to understand, whereupon the spokesman reveals their meaning plain enough by reiterating the demand in a tone meant to be intimidating, and half unsheaths his sword in a significant manner. Intuitively the precise situation of affairs seems to reveal itself in a moment; they are but ordinarily inoffensive villagers returning from Erzingan, where they have sold and squandered even the donkeys they rode to town; meeting me alone, and, as they think in the absence of outward evidence that I am unarmed, they have become possessed of the idea of retrieving their fortunes by intimidating me out of money.

Never were men more astonished and taken aback at finding me armed, and they both turn pale and fairly shiver with fright

"Stand and Deliver!"

as I produce the Smith & Wesson from its inconspicuous position at my hip, and hold it on a level with the bold spokesman's head; they both look as if they expected their last hour had arrived and both seem incapable either of utterance or of running away; in fact, their embarrassment is so ridiculous that it provokes a smile and it is with anything but a threatening or angry voice that I bid them *haidy!* The bold highwaymen seem only too thankful of a chance to '*haidy*,' and they look quite confused, and I fancy even ashamed of themselves, as they betake themselves off up the ravine.

Since the occupation of Kars by the Russians the military mantle of that important fortress has fallen upon Erzeroum and Erzingan; the booming of cannon fired in honor of the Sultan's birthday is awakening the echoes of the rock-ribbed mountains as I wheel eastward down the valley, and within about three miles of the city I pass the headquarters of the garrison. Long rows of hundreds of white field-tents are ranged about the position on the level greensward; the place presents an animated scene, with the soldiers, some in the ordinary blue, trimmed with red, others in cool, white uniforms especially provided for the summer, but which they are not unlikely to be found also wearing in winter, owing to the ruinous state of the Ottoman exchequer, and one and all wearing the picturesque but uncomfortable fez; cannons are booming, drums beating, and bugles playing.

Upon reaching the city I repair at once to the large custom-house caravanserai and engage a room for the night. The proprietor of the rooms seems a sensible fellow, with nothing of the inordinate inquisitiveness of the average native about him, and instead of throwing the weight of his influence and his persuasive powers on the side of the importuning crowd, he authoritatively bids them '*haidy!*' locks the bicycle in my room, and gives me the key. The Erzingan caravanserai – and all these caravanserais are essentially similar – is a square court-yard surrounded by the four sides of a two-storied brick building; the ground-floor is occupied by the offices of the importers of foreign goods and the custom-house authorities; the upper floor is divided into small rooms for the accommodation of travellers and caravan men arriving with goods from Trebizond. Sallying forth in search of supper, I am taken in tow by a couple of Armenians, who volunteer the welcome information that there is an '*Americanish hakim*' in the city; this intelligence is an agreeable surprise, for Erzeroum is the nearest place in which I have been expecting to find an English-speaking person. While searching about for the *hakim*, we pass near the *zaptieh* headquarters; the officers are enjoying their nargileh in the cool evening air outside the building, and seeing an Englishman, beckon us over. They desire to examine my *teskeri*, the first occasion on which it has been officially demanded since landing at Ismidt, although I have voluntarily produced it on previous occasions, and at Sivas requested the Vali to attach his seal and signature; this is owing to the proximity of Erzingan to the Russian frontier, and the suspicions that any stranger may be a subject of the Czar, visiting the military centres for sinister reasons. They send an officer with me to hunt up the resident pasha; that worthy and enlightened personage is found busily engaged in playing a game of chess with a military officer, and barely takes the trouble to glance at the proffered passport: 'It is *viséd* by the Sivas Vali,' he says, and lackadaisically waves us adieu. Upon returning to the *zaptieh* station, a quiet, unassuming American comes forward and introduces himself as Dr. Van Nordan, a physician formerly connected with the Persian mission.

Nothing in the way of bedding or furniture is provided in the caravanserai rooms, but the proprietor gets me plenty of quilts, and I pass a reasonably comfortable night. In the morning I obtain breakfast and manage to escape from town without attracting a crowd of more than a couple of hundred people; a remarkable occurrence in its way, since Erzingan contains a population of about twenty thousand. The road eastward from Erzingan is level, but heavy with dust, leading through a low portion of the valley that earlier in the season is swampy, and gives the city an unenviable reputation for malarial fevers. To prevent the travellers drinking the unwholesome water in this part of the valley, some benevolent Mussulman or public-spirited pasha has erected at intervals, by the road side, compact mud huts, and placed there in huge earthenware vessels, holding perhaps fifty gallons each; these are kept supplied with pure spring-water and provided with a wooden drinking-scoop.

To-day is the hottest I have experienced in Asia Minor, and soon after leaving the outpost I once more encounter the everlasting mountains, following now the Trebizond and Erzingan caravan trail. Once again I get benighted in the mountains, and push ahead for some time after dark. I am beginning to think of camping out supperless again when I hear the creaking of a buffalo *araba* some distance ahead. Soon I overtake it, and, following it for half a mile off the trail, I find myself before an enclosure of several acres, surrounded by a high stone wall with quite imposing gateways. It is the walled village of Houssenbegkhan, one of those places built especially for the accommodation of the Trebizond caravans in the winter. I am conducted into a large apartment, which appears to be set apart for the hospitable accommodation of travellers. The apartment is found already occupied by three travellers, who, from their outward appearance, might well be taken for cutthroats of the worst description; and the villagers swarming in, I am soon surrounded by the usual ragged, flea-bitten congregation. There are various arms and warlike accoutrements hanging on the wall, enough of one kind or other to arm a small company. They all belong to the three travellers, however; my modest little revolver seems really nothing compared with the warlike display of swords, daggers, pistols and guns hanging around; the place looks like a small armory. The first question is – as is usual of late – 'Russ or Ingilis?' Some of the younger and less experienced men essay to doubt my word, and, on their own supposition that I am a Russian, begin to take unwarrantable liberties with my person; one of them steals up behind and commences playing a tattoo on my helmet with two sticks of wood, by way of bravado, and showing his contempt for a subject of the Czar. Turning round, I take one of the sticks away and chastise him with it until he howls for Allah to protect him, and then, without attempting any sort of explanation to the others, resume my seat; one of the travellers then solemnly places his forefingers together and announces himself as *kardash* (my brother), at the same time pointing significantly to his choice assortment of ancient weapons. I shake hands with

"A Russian, am I?"

him and remind him that I am somewhat hungry; whereupon he orders a villager to forthwith contribute six eggs, another butter to fry them in, and a third bread; a *tezek* fire is already burning, and with his own hands he fries the eggs, and makes my ragged audience stand at a respectful distance while I eat; if I were to ask him, he would probably clear the room of them *instanter*. About ten o'clock my *impromptu* friend and his companion order their horses, and buckle their arms and accoutrements about them to depart; my 'brother' stands before me and loads up his flintlock rifle; it is a fearful and wonderful process; it takes him at least two minutes; he does not seem to know on which particular part of his wonderful paraphernalia to find the slugs, the powder, or the patching, and he finishes by tearing a piece of rag off a by-standing villager to place over the powder in the pan. While he is doing all this, and especially when ramming home the bullet, he looks at me as though expecting me to come and pat him approvingly on the shoulder.

When they are gone, the third traveller, who is going to remain over night, edges up beside me, and pointing to his own imposing armory, likewise announces himself as my brother; thus do I unexpectedly acquire two brothers within the brief space of an evening.

I now encounter the first really great camel caravans, *en route* to Persia with tea and sugar and general European merchandise; they are all camped for the day alongside the road, and the camels scattered about the neighboring hills in search of giant thistles and other outlandish vegetation, for which the patient ship of the desert entertains a partiality. Camel caravans travel entirely at night during the summer. Contrary to what, I think, is a common belief in the Occident, they can endure any amount of cold weather, but are comparatively distressed by the heat; still, this may not characterize all breeds of camels any more than the different breeds of other domesticated animals. During the summer, when the camels are required to find their own sustenance along the road, a large caravan travels but a wretched eight miles a day, the remainder of the time being occupied in filling his capacious thistle and camel-thorn receptacle; this comes of the scarcity of good grazing along the route, compared with the number of camels, and the consequent necessity of wandering far and wide in search of pasturage, rather than because of the camel's absorptive capacity, for he is a comparatively abstemious animal. In the winter they are fed on balls of barley flour, called *nawalla*; on this they keep fat and strong, and travel three times the distance. The average load of a full-grown camel is about seven hundred pounds.

Before reaching Erzeroum I have a narrow escape from what might have proved a serious accident. I meet a buffalo *araba* carrying a long projecting stick of timber; the sleepy buffaloes pay no heed to the bicycle until I arrive opposite their heads, when they give a sudden lurch sidewise, swinging the stick of timber across my path; fortunately the road happens to be of good width, and by a very quick swerve I avoid a collision, but the tail end of the timber just brushes the rear wheel as I wheel past. Soon after noon I roll into Erzeroum, or rather, up to the Trebizond gate, and dismount. Erzeroum is a fortified city of considerable importance, both from a commercial and a military point of view; it is surrounded by earthwork fortifications, from the parapets of which large siege guns frown forth upon the surrounding country, and forts are erected in several commanding positions round about, like watch-dogs stationed outside to guard the city. Patches of snow linger on the Palantokan Mountains, a few miles to the south; the Deve Boyun Hills, a spur of the greater Palantokans, look down on the city from the east; the broad valley of the West Euphrates stretches away westward and northward, terminating at the north in another mountain range.

Having determined upon resting here until Monday, I spend a good part of Friday looking about the city. The population is a mixture of Turks, Armenians, Russians, Persians, and Jews. Here I first make the acquaintance of a Persian *tchai-khan* (tea-drinking shop). With the exception of the difference in the beverages, there is little difference between a *tchai-khan* and a *kahvay-khan*, although in the case of a swell establishment, the *tchai-khan* blossoms forth quite gaudily with scores of coloured lamps. The tea is served scalding hot in tiny glasses, which are first half-filled with loaf-sugar. If the proprietor is desirous of honoring or pleasing a new or distinguished customer, he drops in lumps of sugar until it protrudes above the glass. The tea is made in a samovar – a brass vessel, holding perhaps a gallon of water, with a hollow receptacle in the centre for a charcoal fire. Strong tea is made in an ordinary queen's-ware teapot that fits into the hollow; a small portion of this is poured into the glass, which is then filled up with hot water from a tap in the samovar.

There is a regular Persian quarter in Erzeroum, and I am not suffered to stroll through it without being initiated into the fundamental difference between the character of the Persians and the Turks. When an Osmanli is desirous of seeing me ride the bicycle, he goes honestly and straightforwardly to work at coaxing and worrying; except in very rare instances they have seemed incapable of resorting to deceit or sharp practice to gain their object. Not so childlike and honest, however, are our new acquaintances, the Persians. Several merchants gather round me, and pretty soon they cunningly begin asking me how much I will sell the bicycle for. 'Fifty liras,' I reply, seeing the deep, deep scheme hidden beneath the superficial fairness of their observations, and thinking this will quash all further commercial negotiations. But the wily Persians are not so easily disposed of as this. 'Bring it round and let us see how it is ridden,' they say, 'and if we like it we will purchase it for fifty liras, and perhaps make you a present besides.' A Persian would rather try to gain an end by deceit than by honest and above-board methods, even if the former were more trouble. Lying, cheating, and deception is the universal rule among them; honesty and straightforwardness are unknown virtues. Anyone whom they detect telling the truth or acting honestly they consider a simpleton unfit to transact business.

Two days are spent at the quiet missionary camp, and thoroughly enjoyed. It seems like an oasis of home life in the surrounding desert of uncongenial social conditions. I eagerly devour the contents of several American newspapers, and embrace the opportunities of the occasion, even to the extent of nursing the babies (missionaries seem rare folks for babies), of which there are three in the camp. The altitude of Erzeroum is between six thousand and seven thousand feet; the September nights are delightfully cool, and there are no blood-thirsty mosquitoes. I am assigned a sleeping-tent close alongside a small waterfall, whose splashing music is a soporific that holds me in the bondage of beneficial repose until breakfast is announced both mornings; and on Monday morning I feel as though the hunger, the irregular sleep, and the rough-and-tumble dues generally of the past four weeks were but a troubled dream.

It is nearly 3 P.M., September 7th, when I bid farewell to everybody, and wheel out through the Persian Gate, accompanied by Mr. Chambers on horseback, who rides part way to the Deve Boyun (camel's neck) Pass.

From the pass, my road descends into the broad and cultivated valley of the Passin Su; the road is mostly ridable, though heavy with dust. Part way to Hassen Kaleh I am compelled to use considerable tact to avoid trouble with a gang of riotous *katir-jees* whom I overtake; as I attempt to wheel past, one of them wantonly essays to thrust his stick into the wheel; as I spring from the saddle for sheer self-protection, they think I have dismounted to attack him, and his comrades rush forward to his protection, brandishing their sticks and swords in a menacing manner. Seeing himself reinforced, as it were, the bold aggressor raises his stick as though to strike me, and peremptorily orders me to *bin* and *haidi!* Very naturally I refuse to remount the bicycle while surrounded by this evidently mischievous crew; there are about twenty of them, and it requires much self-control to prevent a conflict, in which, I am persuaded, somebody would have been hurt; however, I finally manage to escape their undesirable company and ride off amid a fusillade of stones.

CHAPTER XVIII

MOUNT ARARAT AND KOORDISTAN

Thin ice covers the still pools of water when I resume my toilsome route over the mountains at daybreak, a raw wind comes whistling from the east, and until the sun begins to warm things up a little, it is necessary to stop and buffet occasionally to prevent benumbed hands. Obtaining some small lumps of wheaten dough cooked crisp in hot grease, like unsweetened doughnuts, from a horseman on the road, I push ahead toward the summit and then down the eastern slope of the mountains; rounding an abutting hill about 9.30, the glorious snow-crowned peak of Ararat suddenly bursts upon my vision; it is a good forty leagues away, but even at this distance it dwarfs everything else in sight. Although surrounded by giant mountain chains that traverse the country at every conceivable angle, Ararat stands alone in its solitary grandeur, a glistening white cone rearing its giant height proudly and conspicuously above surrounding eminences; about mountains that are insignificant only in comparison with the white-robed monarch that has been a beacon-light of sacred history since sacred history has been in existence.

Owing to the disgust engendered by my unsavory quarters in the wretched Dele Baba village last night, I have determined upon seeking the friendly shelter of a wheat-shock again to-night, preferring the chances of being frozen out at midnight to the entomological possibilities of village hovels. Accordingly, near sunset, I repair to a village not far from the road, for the purpose of obtaining something to eat before seeking out a rendezvous for the night. It turns out to be the Koordish village of Malosman, and the people are found to be so immeasurably superior in every particular to their kinsfolk of Dele Baba that I forthwith cancel my determination and accept their proffered hospitality. The Malosmanlis are comparatively clean and comfortable; are reasonably well-dressed, seem well-to-do, and both men and women are, on the average, handsomer than the people of any village I have seen for days past. Almost all possess a conspicuously beautiful set of teeth, pleasant, smiling countenances and good physique; they also seem to have, somehow, acquired easy, agreeable manners.

*   *   *

From this pass I descend into the Aras Plain, and, behold the gigantic form of Ararat rises up before me, seemingly but a few miles away; as a matter of fact it is about twenty miles distant, but with nothing intervening between myself and its tremendous proportions but the level plain, the distance is deceptive. No human habitations are visible save the now familiar black tents of Koordish tribesmen away off to the north, and as I ride along I am overtaken by a sensation of being all alone in the company of an overshadowing and awe-inspiring presence. One's attention seems irresistibly attracted toward the mighty snow-crowned monarch, as though the immutable law of attraction were sensibly exerting itself to draw lesser bodies to it, and all other objects around seemed dwarfed into insignificant proportions. One obtains a most comprehensive idea of Ararat's 17,325 feet when viewing it from the Aras Plain, as it rises sheer from the plain, and not from the shoulders of a range that constitutes of itself the greater part of the height, as do many mountain peaks. A few miles to the eastward is Little Ararat, an independent conical peak of 12,800 feet, without snow, but conspicuous and distinct from surrounding mountains; its proportions are completely dwarfed and over-shadowed by the nearness and bulkiness of its big brother. The Aras Plain is lava-strewn and uncultivated for a number of miles; the spongy, spreading feet of innumerable camels have worn paths in the hard lava deposit that makes the wheeling equal to English roads, except for occasional stationary blocks of lava that the animals have systematically stepped over for centuries, and which not infrequently block the narrow trail and compel a dismount. Evidently Ararat was once a volcano; the lofty peak which now presents a wintry appearance even in the hottest summer weather, formerly belched forth lurid flames that lit up the surrounding country, and poured out fiery torrents of molten lava that stratified the abutting hills, and spread like an overwhelming flood over the Aras Plain. Abutting Ararat on the west are stratiform hills, the strata of which are plainly distinguishable from the Persian trail, and which, were their inclination continued, would strike Ararat at or near the summit. This would seem to indicate the layers to be representations of the mountain's former volcanic over-flowings.

I am sitting on a block of lava making an outline sketch of Ararat, when a peasant happens along with a bullock-load of cucumbers which he is taking to the Koordish camps; he is pretty badly scared at finding himself all alone on the Aras Plain with such a nondescript and dangerous-looking object as a helmeted wheelman, and when I halt him with inquiries concerning the nature of his wares he turns pale and becomes almost speechless with fright. He would empty his sacks as a peace-offering at my feet without venturing upon a remonstrance, were he ordered to do so; and when I relieve him of but one solitary cucumber, and pay him more than he would obtain

Well Guarded at Lunch.

for it among the Koords, he becomes stupefied with astonishment; when he continues on his way he hardly knows whether he is on his head or his feet. An hour later I arrive at Kizil Dizah, the last village in Turkish territory, and an official station of considerable importance, where passports, caravan permits, etc., of everybody passing to or from Persia have to be examined. An officer here provides me with refreshments, and while generously permitting the population to come in and enjoy the extraordinary spectacle of seeing me fed, he thoughtfully stations a man with a stick to keep them at a respectful distance. A later hour in the afternoon finds me trundling up a long acclivity leading to the summit of a low mountain ridge; arriving at the summit I stand on the boundary-line between the dominions of the Sultan and the Shah, and I pause a minute to take a brief, retrospective glance.

The cyclometer, affixed to the bicycle at Constantinople, now registers within a fraction of one thousand miles; it has been on the whole an arduous thousand miles, but those who in the foregoing pages have followed me through the strange and varied experiences of the journey will agree with me when I say that it has proved more interesting than arduous after all. I need not here express any blunt opinions of the different people encountered; it is enough that my observations concerning them have been jotted down as I have mingled with them and their characteristics from day to day; almost without exception, they have treated me the best they knew how; it is only natural that some should know how better than others.

Soon the village of Ovahjik is reached, and some peasants guide me to the residence of the Pasha Khan. The servant who presents my letter of introduction fills the untutored mind of his master with wonderment concerning what the peasants have told him about the bicycle. The Pasha Khan makes his appearance without having taken the trouble to open the envelope. He is a dull-faced, unintellectual-looking personage, and without any preliminary palaver he says: '*Bin bacalem,*' in a dictatorial tone of voice. '*Bacalem yole lazim, bacalem saba,*' I reply, for it is too dark to ride on unknown ground this evening. '*Bin bacalem!*' repeats the Pasha Khan, even more dictatorial than before, ordering a servant to bring a tallow candle, so that I can have no excuse. There appears to be such a total absence of all consideration for myself that I am not disposed to regard very favorably or patiently the obtrusive meddlesomenesss of two younger men – whom I afterward discover to be sons of the Pasha Khan – who seem almost inclined to take the bicycle out of my charge altogether, in their excessive impatience and inordinate inquisitiveness to examine everything about it. One of them, thinking the cyclometer to be a watch, puts his ear down to see if he can hear it tick, and then persists in fingering it about, to the imminent danger of the tally-pin. After telling him

The Persistent Son is Shoved into the Water.

several times not to meddle with it, and receiving overbearing gestures in reply, I deliberately throw him backward into an irrigating ditch. A gleam of intelligence overspreads the stolid countenance of the Pasha Khan at seeing his offspring floundering about on his back in the mud and water, and he gives utterance to a chuckle of delight. The discomfited young man betrays nothing of the spirit of resentment upon recovering himself from the ditch, and the other son involuntarily retreats as though afraid his turn was coming next.

The servant now arrives with the lighted candle, and the Pasha Khan leads the way into his garden, where there is a wide brick-paved walk; the house occupies one side of the garden, the other three sides are inclosed by a high mud wall. After riding a few times along the brick-paved walk, and promising to do better in the morning, I naturally expect to be taken into the house, instead of which the Pasha Khan orders the people to show me the way to the caravanserai. Arriving at the caravanserai, and finding myself thus thrown unexpectedly upon my own resources, I inquire of some bystanders where I can obtain *ekmek*; some of them want to know how many liras I will give for *ekmek!* When it is reflected that a lira is nearly five dollars, one realizes from this something of the unconscionable possibilities of the Persian commercial mind.

While this question is being mooted, a figure appears in the doorway, toward which the people one and all respectfully salaam and give way. It is the great Pasha Khan; he has bethought himself to open my letter of introduction, and having perused it and discovered who it was from and all about me, he now comes and squats down in the most friendly manner by my side for a minute, as though to remove any unfavorable impressions his inhospitable action in sending me here might have made, and then bids me accompany him back to his residence. After permitting him to eat a sufficiency of humble pie in the shape of coaxing, to atone for his former incivility, I agree to his proposal and accompany him back. Tea is at once provided, the now very friendly Pasha Khan putting extra lumps of sugar into my glass with his own hands and stirring it up; bread and cheese comes in with the tea, and under the mistaken impression that this constitutes the Persian evening meal I eat sufficient to satisfy my hunger. While thus partaking freely of the bread and cheese, I do not fail to notice that the others partake very sparingly, and that they seem to be rather astonished because I am not following their example. Being chiefly interested in satisfying my appetite, however, their silent observations have no effect save to further mystify my understanding of the Persian character. The secret of all this soon reveals itself in the form of an ample repast of savory chicken *pillau*, brought in immediately afterward; and while the Pasha Khan and his two sons proceed to do full justice to this highly acceptable dish, I have to content myself with nibbling at a piece of chicken, and ruminating on the unhappy and ludicrous mistake of having satisfied my hunger with dry bread and cheese. Thus does one pay the penalty of being unacquainted with the domestic customs of a country when first entering upon its experiences.

There seems to be no material difference between the social position of the women here and in Turkey; they eat their meals by themselves, and occupy entirely separate apartments, which are unapproachable to members of the opposite sex save their husbands. The Pasha Khan of Ovahjik, however, seems to be a kind, indulgent husband and father, requesting me next morning to ride up and down the brick-paved walk for the benefit of his wives and daughters. In the seclusion of their own

Riding for the Pasha Khan's Ladies.

walled premises the Persian females are evidently not so particular about concealing their features, and I obtained a glimpse of some very pretty faces; oval faces with large dreamy black eyes, and a flush of warm sunset on brownish cheeks. The indoor costume of Persian women is but an inconsiderable improvement upon the costume of our ancestress in the garden of Eden, and over this they hastily don a flimsy shawl-like garment to come out and see me ride. They are always much less concerned about concealing their nether extremities than about their faces, and as they seem but little concerned about anything on this occasion save the bicycle, after riding for them I have to congratulate myself that, so far as sight-seeing is concerned, the ladies leave me rather under obligations than otherwise.

Towards evening I ascend into a more mountainous region, inhabited exclusively by nomad Koords; from points of vantage their tents are observable clustered here and there at the bases of the mountains. Descending into a grassy valley or depression, I find myself in close proximity to several different camps, and eagerly avail myself of the opportunity to pass a night among them. I am now in the heart of Northern Koordistan, which embraces both Persian and Turkish territory, and the occasion is most opportune for seeing something of these wild nomads in their own mountain pastures. The greensward is ridable, and I dismount before the Sheikh's tent in the presence of a highly interested and interesting audience. The half-wild dogs make themselves equally interesting in another and a less desirable sense as I approach, but the men pelt them with stones, and when I dismount they conduct me and the bicycle at once into the tent of their chieftain. The Sheikh's tent is capacious enough to shelter a regiment almost, and it is divided into compartments similar to a previous description; the Sheikh is a big, burly fellow, of about forty-five, wearing a turban the size of a half-bushel measure, and dressed pretty much like a well-to-do Turk; as a matter of fact, the Koords admire the Osmanlis and despise the Persians. The bicycle is reclined against a carpet partition, and after the customary interchange of questions, a splendid fellow, who must be six feet six inches tall, and broad-shouldered in proportion, squats himself cross-legged beside me, and proceeds to make himself agreeable, rolling me cigarettes, asking questions, and curiously investigating anything about me that strikes him as peculiar. I show them, among other things, a cabinet photograph of myself in all the glory of needle-pointed mustache and dress-parade apparel; after a critical examination and a brief conference among themselves they pronounce me an 'English Pasha.' I then hand the Sheikh a set of sketches, but they are not sufficiently civilized to appreciate the sketches; they hold them upside down and sidewise; and not being able to make anything out of them, the

Sheikh holds them in his hand and looks quite embarrassed, like a person in possession of something he doesn't know what to do with.

Shortly after the evening meal, an incident occurs which causes considerable amusement. Everything being unusually quiet, one sharp-eared youth happens to hear the obtrusive ticking of my Waterbury, and strikes a listening attitude, at which everybody else likewise begins listening; the tick, tick is plainly discernible to everybody in the compartment and they become highly interested and amused, and commence looking at me for an explanation. With a view to humoring the spirit of amusement thus awakened, I likewise smile, but affect ignorance and innocence concerning the origin of the mysterious ticking, and strike a listening attitude as well as the others. Presuming upon our interchange of familiarity, our six-foot-sixer then commences searching about my clothing for the watch, but being hidden away in a pantaloon fob, and minus a chain, it proves beyond his power of discovery. Nevertheless, by bending his head down and listening, he ascertains and announces it to be somewhere about my person; the Waterbury is then produced, and the loudness of its ticking awakes the wonder and admiration of the Koords, even to a greater extent than the Turks.

During the evening, the inevitable question of Russ, Osmanli, and English crops up, and I win unanimous murmurs of approval by laying my forefingers together and stating that the English and the Osmanlis are *kardash*. I show them my Turkish *teskeri*, upon which several of them bestow fervent kisses, and when, by means of placing several stones here and there I explained to them how in 1877, the hated Muscov occupied different Mussulman cities one after the other, and was prevented by the English from occupying their dearly beloved Stamboul itself, their admiration knows no bounds.

Quilts are provided for me, and I occupy this same compartment of the tent, in common with several of the younger men. In the morning, before departing, I am regaled with bread and rich, new cream, and when leaving the tent I pause a minute to watch the busy scene in the female department. Some are churning butter in sheep-skin churns which are suspended from poles and jerked back and forth;

Explaining England's Friendly Offices.

others are weaving carpets, preparing curds for cheese, baking bread, and otherwise industriously employed. I depart from the Koordish camp thoroughly satisfied with my experience of their hospitality, but the cerulean waist-scarf bestowed upon me by our Hungarian friend Igali, at Belgrade, no longer adds its embellishments to my personal adornments. Whenever a favorable opportunity presents, certain young men belonging to the noble army of hangers-on about the Sheikh's apartments invariably glide inside, and importune the guest from Frangistan for any article of his clothing that excites the admiration of their semi-civilized minds. This scarf, they were doubtless penetrating enough to observe, formed no necessary part of my wardrobe, and a dozen times in the evening, and again in the morning, I was worried to part with it, so I finally presented it to one of them. He hastily hid it away among his clothes and disappeared, as though fearful, either that the Sheikh might see it and make him return it, or that one of the chieftain's favorites might take a fancy to it and summarily appropriate it to his own use.

CHAPTER XIX

PERSIA AND THE TABREEZ CARAVAN TRAIL

Reaching the suburbs of Khoi, I am initiated into a new departure – new to myself at this time – of Persian sanctimoniousness. Halting at a fountain to obtain a drink, the soldier shapes himself for pouring the water out of the earthenware drinking vessel into my hands; supposing this to be merely an indication of the Persian's own method of drinking, I motion my preference for drinking out of the jar itself. The soldier looks appealingly toward the *moonshi bashi*, who tells him to let me drink, and then orders him to smash the jar. It then dawns upon my unenlightened mind, that being a Ferenghi, I should have known better than to have touched my unhallowed lips to a drinking vessel at a public fountain, defiling it by so doing, so that it must be smashed in order that the sons of the 'true prophet' may not unwittingly drink from it afterward and themselves become defiled. The *moonshi bashi* pilots me to the residence of a certain wealthy citizen outside the city walls; this person, a mild-mannered, purring-voiced man, is seated in a room with a couple of seyuds, or descendants of the prophet; they are helping themselves from a large platter of the finest pears, peaches, and egg plums I ever saw anywhere. The room is carpeted with costly rugs and carpets in which one's feet sink perceptibly at every step; the walls and ceiling are artistically stuccoed, and the doors and windows are gay with stained glass.

Abandoning myself to the guidance of the *moonshi bashi*, I ride around the garden-walks, show them the bicycle, revolver, map of Persia, etc.; like the *moonshi bashi*, they become deeply interested in the map, finding much amusement and satisfaction in having me point out the location of different Persian cities, seemingly regarding my ability to do so as evidence of exceeding cleverness and erudition. The untravelled Persians of the northern provinces regard Teheran as the grand idea of a large and important city; if there is any place in the whole world larger and more important, they think it may perhaps be Stamboul. The fact that Stamboul is not on my map while

Doing the Agreeable.

Teheran is, they regard as conclusive proof of the superiority of their own capital. The *moonshi bashi*'s chief purpose in accompanying me hither has been to introduce me to the attention of the '*hoikim*'; although the pronunciation is a little different from *hakim*, I attribute this to local brogue, and have been surmising this personage to be some doctor, who, perhaps, having graduated at a Frangistan medical college, the *moonshi bashi* thinks will be able to converse with me. After partaking of fruit and tea we continue on our way to the nearest gate-way of the city proper, Khoi being surrounded by a ditch and battlemented mud wall. Arriving at a large, public inclosure, my guide sends in a letter, and shortly afterward delivers me over to some soldiers, who forthwith conduct me into the presence of – not a doctor, but Ali Khan, the Governor of the city, an officer who hereabouts rejoices in the title of the '*hoikim*.'

The Governor proves to be a man of superior intelligence; he has been Persian ambassador to France some time ago, and understands French fairly well; consequently we manage to understand each other after a fashion. Although he has never before seen a bicycle, his knowledge of the mechanical ingenuity of the Ferenghis causes him to regard it with more intelligence than an untravelled native, and to better comprehend my journey and its object. Assisted by a dozen mollahs (priests) and officials in flowing gowns and henna-tinted beards and finger-nails, the Governor is transacting official business, and he invites me to come into the council chamber and be seated. In a few minutes the noon-tide meal is announced; the Governor invites me to dine with them, and then leads the way into the dining-room, followed by his counsellors, who form in line behind him according to their rank. The dining-room is a large, airy apartment, opening into an extensive garden; a bountiful repast is spread on yellow-checkered tablecloths on the carpeted floor; the Governor squats cross-legged at one end, the stately-looking wiseacres in flowing gowns range themselves along each side in a similar attitude, with much solemnity and show of dignity; they – at least so I fancy – evidently are anything but rejoiced at the prospect of eating with an infidel Ferenghi.

After the meal is over the Governor is no longer handicapped by the religious prejudices of the mollahs, and leaving them he invites me into the garden to see his two little boys go through their gymnastic exercises. They are clever little fellows of about seven and nine, respectively, with large black eyes and clear olive complexions; all the time we are watching them the Governor's face is wreathed in a fond, parental smile. The exercises consist chiefly in climbing a thick rope dangling from a cross-beam. After seeing me ride the bicycle the Governor wants me to try my hand at gymnastics, but being nothing of a gymnast I respectfully beg to be excused. While thus enjoying a pleasant hour in the garden, a series of resounding thwacks are heard somewhere near by, and looking around some interven-ing shrubs I observe a couple of *farrashes* bastinadoing a culprit; seeing me more interested in this novel method of administering justice than in looking at the youngsters trying to climb ropes, the Governor leads the way thither. The man, evidently a ryot, is lying on his back, his feet are lashed together and held soles uppermost by means of an horizontal pole, while the *farrashes* briskly belabor them with willow sticks. The soles of the ryot's feet are hard and thick as rhinoceros hide almost from habitually walking barefooted, and under these conditions his punishment is evidently anything but severe. The flagellation goes merrily and uninterruptedly forward until fifty sticks about five feet long and thicker than a person's thumb are broken over his feet without eliciting any signals of distress from the horny-hoofed ryot, except an occasional sorrowful groan of 'A-l-l-ah!' He is then loosed and limps painfully away, but it looks like a rather hypocritical limp, after all; fifty sticks, by the by, is a comparatively light punishment, several hundred sometimes being broken at a single punishment. Upon taking my leave the Governor kindly details a couple of soldiers to show me to the best caravanserai, and to remain and protect me from the worry and annoyance of the crowds until my departure from the city.

A new caravanserai is in process of construction just outside the Tabreez gate, and I become an interested spectator of the Persian mode of building the walls of a house; these of the new

Taking a Drink.

caravanserai are nearly four feet thick. Parallel walls of mud bricks are built up, leaving an interspace of two feet or thereabouts; this is filled with stiff, well-worked mud, which is dumped in by bucketsful and continually tramped by barefooted laborers; harder bricks are used for the doorways and windows. The bricklayer uses mud for mortar and his hands for a trowel; he works without either level or plumb-line, and keeps up a doleful, melancholy chant from morning to night. The mortar is handed to him by an assistant by handsful; every workman is smeared and spattered with mud from head to foot, as though glorying in covering themselves with the trade-mark of their calling.

Strolling away from the busy builders we encounter a man – the 'wather bhoy av the ghang' – bringing a three-gallon pitcher of water from a spring half a mile away. Being thirsty, the soldiers shout for him to bring the pitcher. Scarcely conceiving it possible that these humble mud-daubers would be so wretchedly sanctimonious, I drink from the jar, much to the disgust of the poor water-carrier, who forthwith empties the remainder away and returns with hurried trot to the spring for a fresh supply; he would doubtless have smashed the vessel had it been smaller and of lesser value. Naturally I feel a trifle conscience-stricken at having caused him so much trouble, for he is rather an elderly man, but the soldiers display no sympathy for him whatever, apparently regarding an humble water-carrier as a person of small consequence anyhow, and they laugh heartily at seeing him trotting briskly back half a mile for another load. Had he taken the first water after a Ferenghi had drank from it and allowed his fellow-workmen to unwittingly partake of the same, it would probably have fared badly with the old fellow had they found it out afterward.

Returning cityward we meet our friend, the *moonshi bashi*, looking me up; he is accompanied by a dozen better-class Persians, scattering friends and acquaintances of his, whom he has collected during the day chiefly to show them my map of Persia; the mechanical beauty of the bicycle and the apparent victory over the laws of equilibrium in riding it being, in the opinion of the scholarly *moonshi bashi*, quite overshadowed by a map which shows Teheran and Khoi, and doesn't show Stamboul, and which shows the whole broad expanse of Persia,

The Patriotic Moonshi-Bashi.

and only small portions of other countries. This latter fact seems to have made a very deep impression upon the *moonshi bashi*'s mind; it appears to have filled him with the unalterable conviction that all other countries are insignificant compared with Persia; in his own mind this patriotic person has always believed this to be the case, but he is overjoyed at finding his belief verified – as he fondly imagines – by the map of a Ferenghi.

As though to belie their general reputation of sanctimoniousness, a tall, stately seyud voluntarily poses as my guide and protector *en route* through the awakening bazaar toward the Tabreez gate next morning, cuffing obtrusive youngsters right and left, and chiding grown-up people whenever their inordinate curiosity appeals to him as being aggressive and impolite; one can only account for this strange condescension on the part of this holy man by attributing it to the marvellous civilizing and levelling influence of the bicycle. Arriving outside the gate, the crowd of followers are well repaid for their trouble by watching my progress for a couple of miles down a broad straight roadway admirably kept and shaded with thrifty chenars or plane-trees. Wheeling down this pleasant avenue I encounter mule-trains, the animals festooned with strings of merrily jingling bells, and camels gayly caparisoned, with huge, nodding tassels on their heads and pack-saddles, and deep-toned bells of sheet iron swinging at their throats and sides; likewise the omnipresent donkey heavily laden with all manner of village produce for the Khoi market.

Near midday I make a short circuit to the north, to investigate the edible possibilities of a village nestling in a *cul-de-sac* of the mountain foot-hills. The resident Khan turns out to be a regular jovial blade, sadly partial to the flowing bowl. When I arrive he is perseveringly working himself up to the proper pitch of booziness for enjoying his noontide repast by means of copious potations of arrack; he introduces himself as Hassan Khan, offers me arrack, and cordially invites me to dine with him. After dinner, when examining my revolver, map, etc., the Khan greatly admires a photograph of myself as a peculiar proof of Ferenghi skill in producing a person's physiognomy, and blandly asks me to 'make him one of himself,' doubtless thinking that a person capable of riding on a wheel is likewise possessed of miraculous all 'round abilities. The Khan consumes not less than a pint of raw arrack during the dinner hour, and, not unnaturally, finds himself at the end a trifle funny and venturesome. When preparing to take my departure he proposes that I give him a ride on the bicycle; nothing loath to humor him a little in return for his hospitality, I assist him to mount, and wheel him around for a few minutes, to the unconcealed delight of the whole population, who gather about to see the astonishing spectacle of their Khan riding on the Ferenghi's wonderful *asp-i-awhan*. The Khan being short and pudgy is unable to reach the pedals, and the confidence-inspiring fumes of arrack lead him to announce to the assembled villagers that if his legs were only a little longer he could certainly go it alone, a statement that evidently fills the simple-minded ryots with admiration for the Khan's alleged newly-discovered abilities.

During the forenoon the bicycle is the innocent cause of two people being thrown from the backs of their respective steeds. One is a man carelessly sitting sidewise on his donkey; the meek-eyed jackass suddenly makes a pivot of his hind feet and wheels round, and the rider's legs as suddenly shoot upward. He frantically grips his fiery, untamed steel around the neck as he finds himself over-balanced, and comes up with a broad grin and an irrepressible chuckle of merriment over the unwonted

Hassan Khan takes a Lesson.

spirit displayed by his meek and humble charger, that probably had never scared at anything before in all its life. The other case is unfortunately a lady whose horse literally springs from beneath her, treating her to a clean tumble. The poor lady sings out 'Allah!' rather snappishly at finding herself on the ground, so snappishly that it leaves little room for doubt of its being an imprecation; but her rude, unsympathetic attendants laugh right merrily at seeing her floundering about in the sand; fortunately, she is uninjured. Although Turkish and Persian ladies ride *à la Amazon*, a position that is popularly supposed to be several times more secure than side-saddles, it is a noticeable fact that they seem perfectly helpless, and come to grief the moment their steed shies at anything or commences capering about with anything like violence.

About dusk I fall in with another riotous crowd of homeward-bound fruit-carriers, who, not satisfied at seeing me ride past, want to stop me; one of them rushes up behind, grabs my package attached to the rear baggage-carrier, and nearly causes an overthrow; frightening him off, I spurt ahead, barely escaping two or three donkey cudgels hurled at me in pure wantonness, born of the courage inspired by a majority of twenty to one. There is no remedy for these unpleasant occurrences except travelling under escort, and the avoiding serious trouble or accident becomes a matter for every-day congratulation. At eighteen miles from the last village it becomes too dark to remain in the saddle without danger of headers, and a short trundle brings me, not to Tabreez even now, but to another village eight miles nearer. Here there is a large caravanserai. Near the entrance is a hole-in-the-wall sort of a shop wherein I spy a man presiding over a tempting assortment of cantaloupes, grapes, and pears. The whirligig of fortune has favored me to-day with tea, blotting-paper *ekmek*, and grapes for breakfast; later on two small watermelons, and at 2 P.M. blotting-paper *ekmek* and an infinitesimal quantity of *yaort* (now called *mast*). It is unnecessary to add that I arrive in this village with an appetite that will countenance no unnecessary delay. Two splendid ripe cantaloupes, several fine bunches of grapes, and some pears are devoured immediately, with a reckless disregard of consequences, justifiable only on the grounds of semi-starvation and a temporary barbarism born of surrounding circumstances. After this savage attack on the *maivah-jee*'s stock, I learn that the village contains a small *tchai-khan*; repairing thither I stretch myself on the divan for an hour's repose, and afterward partake of tea, bread, and peaches. At bed-time the *khan-jee* makes me up a couch on the divan, locks the door inside, blows out the light, and then, afraid to occupy the same building with such a dangerous-looking individual as myself, climbs to the roof through a hole in the wall.

Eager villagers carry both myself and wheel across a bridge-less stream upon resuming my journey to Tabreez next morning; the road is level and ridable, though a trifle deep with dust and sand, and in an hour I am threading the suburban lanes of the city. Along these eight miles I certainly pass not less than five hundred pack-donkeys *en route* to the Tabreez market with everything, from baskets of the choicest fruit in the world to huge bundles of prickly camel-thorn and sacks of *tezek* for fuel.

No animals in all the world, I should think, stand in more urgent need of the kindly offices of the Society for the Prevention of Cruelty to Animals than the thousands of miserable donkeys engaged in supplying Tabreez with fuel; their brutal drivers seem utterly callous and indifferent to the pitiful sufferings of these patient toilers. Numbers of instances are observed this morning where the rough, ill-fitting breech-straps and ropes have literally see-sawed their way through the skin and deep into the flesh, and are still rasping deeper and deeper every day, no attempt whatever being made to remedy this evil; on the contrary, their pitiless drivers urge them on by prodding the raw sores with sharpened sticks, and by belaboring them unceasingly with an instrument of torture in the shape of whips with six inches of ordinary trace-chain for a lash.

As is usually the case, a volunteer guide bobs serenely up immediately I enter the city, and I follow confidently along, thinking he is piloting me to the English consulate, as I have requested; instead of this he steers me into the custom-house and turns me over to the officials. These worthy gentlemen, after asking me to ride around the custom-house yard, pretend to become altogether mystified about what they ought to do with the bicycle, and in the absence of any precedent to govern themselves by, finally conclude among themselves that the proper thing would be to confiscate it. Obtaining a guide to show me to the residence of Mr. Abbott, the English consul-general, that energetic representative of Her Majesty's government smiles audibly at the thoughts of their mystification, and then writes them a letter couched in terms of humorous reproachfulness, asking them what in the name of Allah and the Prophet they mean by confiscating a traveller's horse, his carriage, his camel, his everything on legs and wheels consolidated into the beautiful vehicle with which he is journeying to Teheran to see the Shah, and all around the world to see everybody and everything? – ending by telling them that he never in all his consular experiences heard of a proceeding so utterly atrocious. He sends the letter by the consulate dragoman, who accompanies me back to the custom-house. The officers at once see and acknowledge their mistake; but meanwhile they have been examining the bicycle, and some of them appear to have fallen violently in love with it; they yield it up, but it is with apparent reluctance, and one of the leading officials takes me into the stable, and showing me several splendid horses begs me to take my choice from among them and leave the bicycle behind.

Mr. and Mrs. Abbott cordially invite me to become their guest while staying at Tabreez. To-day is Thursday, and although my original purpose was only to remain here a couple of days, the innovation from roughing it on the road, to roast duck for dinner, and breakfast in one's own room of a morning, coupled with warnings against travelling on the Sabbath and invitations to dinner from the American missionaries, proves a sufficient inducement for me to conclude to stay till Monday, satisfied at the prospect of reaching Teheran in good season. It is now something less than four hundred miles to Teheran, with the assurance of better roads than I have yet had in Persia, for the greater portion of the distance; besides this, the route is now a regular post route with *chapar-khanas* (post-houses) at distances of four to five farsakhs apart. On Friday night Tabreez experienced two slight shocks of an earthquake, and in the morning Mr. Abbott points out several fissures in the masonry of the consulate, caused by previous visitations of the same undesirable nature; the earthquakes here seem to resemble the earthquakes of California in that they come reasonably mild and often. The place likewise awakens memories of the Golden State in another and more appreciative particular: nowhere, save perhaps in California, does one find such delicious grapes, peaches, and pears as at ancient Taurus, a specialty for which it has been justly celebrated from time immemorial. On Saturday I take dinner with Mr. Oldfather, one of the missionaries, and in the evening we all pay a visit to Mr. Whipple and family, the consulate link-boy lighting the way before us with a huge cylindrical lantern of transparent oiled muslin called a *farnooze*.

These lanterns are always carried after night before people of wealth or social consequence, varying in size according to the person's idea of their own social importance. The size of the *farnooze* is supposed to be an index of the social position of the person or family, so that one can judge something of what sort of people are coming down the street, even on the darkest night, whenever the attendant link-boy heaves in sight with the *farnooze.* Some of these social indicators are the size of a Portland cement barrel, even in Persia; it is rather a smile-provoking thought to think what tremendous *farnoozes* would be seen lighting up the streets on gloomy evenings, were this same custom prevalent among ourselves; few of us but what could call to memory people whose *farnoozes* would be little smaller than brewery mash-tubs, and which would have to be carried between six-foot link-boys on a pole.

Ameer-i-Nazan, the *Valiat* or heir apparent to the throne, and at present nominal governor of Tabreez, has seen a tricycle in Teheran, one having been imported some time ago by an English gentleman in the Shah's service; but the fame of the bicycle excites his curiosity and he sends an officer around to the consulate to examine and report upon the difference between bicycle and tricycle, and also to discover and explain the *modus operandi* of maintaining one's balance on two wheels. The officer returns with the report that my machine won't even stand up, without somebody holding it, and that nobody but a Ferenghi who is in league with Sheitan, could possibly hope to ride it. Perhaps it is this alarming report, and the fear of exciting the prejudices of the mollahs and fanatics about him, by having anything to do with a person reported on trustworthy authority to be in league with His Satanic Majesty, that prevents the Prince from requesting me to ride before him in Tabreez; but I have the pleasure of meeting him at Hadji Agha on the evening of the first day out. Mr. Whipple kindly makes out an itinerary of the villages and *chapar-khanas* I shall pass on the journey to Teheran; the superintendent of the Tabreez station of the Indo-European Telegraph Company voluntarily telegraphs to the agents at Miana and Zendjan when to expect me, and also to Teheran; Mrs. Abbott fills my coat pockets with roast chicken, and thus equipped and prepared, at nine o'clock on Monday morning I am ready for the home-stretch of the season, before going into winter quarters.

CHAPTER XX

TABREEZ TO TEHERAN

The wheeling improves in the afternoon, and alongside my road runs a bit of civilization in the shape of the splendid iron poles of the Indo-European Telegraph Company. Half a dozen times this afternoon I become the imaginary enemy of a couple of cavalrymen travelling in the same direction as myself; they swoop down upon me from the rear at a charging gallop, valiantly whooping and brandishing their Martini-Henrys; when they arrive within a few yards of my rear wheel they swerve off on either side and rein their fiery chargers up, allowing me to forge ahead; they amuse themselves by repeating this interesting performance over and over again. Being usually a good rider, the dash and courage of the Persian cavalryman is something extraordinary in time of peace; no more brilliant and intrepid cavalry charge on a small scale could be well imagined than I have witnessed several times this afternoon. But upon the outbreak of serious hostilities the average warrior in the Shah's service suddenly becomes filled with a wild, pathetic yearning after the peaceful and honorable calling of a *katir-jee*, an uncontrollable desire to become a humble, contented tiller of the soil, or handy-man about a *tchai-khan*, anything, in fact, of a strictly peaceful character. Were I a hostile trooper with a red jacket, and a general warlike appearance, and the bicycle a machine gun, though our whooping, charging cavalrymen were twenty instead of two, they would only charge once, and that would be with their horses' crimson-dyed tails streaming in the breeze toward me.

About five o'clock I arrive at Hadji Agha, a large village forty miles from Tabreez; here, as soon as it is ascertained that I intend remaining over night, I am actually beset by rival *khan-jees*, who commence jabbering and gesticulating about the merits of their respective establishments, like hotel-runners in

They Swoop Down on Me from the Rear.

the United States; of course they are several degrees less rude and boisterous, and more considerate of one's personal inclinations than their prototypes in America, but they furnish yet another proof that there is nothing new under the sun. Hadji Agha is a village of seyuds, or descendants of the Prophet, these and the mollahs being the most bigoted class in Persia; when I drop into the *tchai-khan* for a glass or two of tea, the sanctimonious old joker with henna-tinted beard and finger-nails, presiding over the samovar, rolls up his eyes in holy horror at the thoughts of waiting upon an unhallowed Ferenghi, and it requires considerable pressure from the younger and less fanatical men to overcome his disinclination; he probably breaks the glass I drank from after my departure.

About dusk the *Valiat* and his courtiers arrive on horseback from Tabreez; the Prince immediately seeks my quarters at the *khan*, and, after examining the bicycle, wants me to take it out and ride; it is getting rather dark, however, so I put him off till morning; he remains and smokes cigarettes with me for half an hour, and then retires to the residence of the local Khan for the night. The Prince seems an amiable, easy-going sort of a person; while in my company his countenance is wreathed in a pleasant smile continually, and I fancy he habitually wears that same expression. His youthful courtiers seem frivolous young bloods, putting in most of the half-hour in showing me their accomplishments in the way of making floating rings of their cigarette smoke. Later in the evening I stroll around to the *tchai-khan* again; it is the gossiping-place of the village, and I find our sanctimonious seyuds indulging in uncomplimentary comments regarding the *Valiat*'s conduct in hobnobbing with the Ferenghi; how bigoted these Persians are, and yet how utterly destitute of principle and moral character!

The road for a short distance east of Hadji Agha is splendid wheeling, and the Prince and his courtiers accompany me for some two miles, finding much amusement in racing with me whenever the road permits of spurting. The country now develops into undulating upland, uncultivated and stone-strewn, except where an occasional stream, affording irrigating facilities, has rendered possible the permanent maintenance of a mud village and a circumscribed area of wheat-fields, melon-gardens, and vineyards.

The country east of Turcomanchai consists of rough, uninteresting upland, with nothing to vary the monotony of the journey, until noon, when after wheeling five farsakhs I reach the town of Miana, celebrated throughout the Shah's dominions for a certain poisonous bug which inhabits the mud walls of the houses, and is reputed to bite the inhabitants while they are sleeping. The bite is said to produce violent and prolonged fever, and to be even dangerous to life. It is customary to warn travellers against remaining over night at Miana, and, of course, I have not by any means been forgotten. Like most of these alleged dreadful things, it is found upon close investigation to be a big bogey with just sufficient truthfulness about it to play upon the imaginative minds of the people. The 'Miana bug-bear' would, I think, be a more appropriate name than Miana bug. The people here seem inclined to be rather rowdyish in their reception of a Ferenghi without an escort.

While trundling through the bazaar toward the telegraph station I become the unhappy target for covertly thrown melon-rinds and other unwelcome missiles, for which there appears no remedy except the friendly shelter of the station. This is just outside the town, and before the gate is reached, stones are exchanged for melon-rinds, but fortunately without any serious damage being done.

Mr. F—, a young German operator, has charge of the control-station here, and welcomes me most cordially to share his comfortable quarters, urging me to remain with him several days. I gladly accept his hospitality till to-morrow morning. Mr. F— has a brother who has recently become a Mussulman, and married a couple of Persian wives; he is also residing temporarily at Miana. He soon comes around to the telegraph station, and turns out to be a wild harum-skarum sort of a person, who regards his transformation into a Mussulman and the setting up of a harem of his own as anything but a serious affair. As a reward for embracing the Mohammedan religion and becoming a Persian subject the Shah has given him a sum of money and a position in the Tabreez mint, besides bestowing upon him the sounding title of Mirza Abdul Kärim Khan. It seems that inducements of a like substantial nature are held out to any Ferenghi of known respectability who formally embraces the Shiite branch of the Mohammedan religion, and becomes a Persian subject – a rare chance for chronic ne'er-do-wells among ourselves, one would think.

This novel and festive convert to Islam readily gives me a mental peep behind the scenes of Persian domestic life, and would unhesitatingly have granted me a peep in person had such a thing been possible. Imagine the ordinary costume of an opera-bouffe artist, shorn of all regard for the difference between real indecency and the suggestiveness of indelicacy permissible behind the footlights, and we have the every-day costume of the Persian harem. In the dreamy eventide the lord of the harem usually betakes himself to that characteristic institution of the East and proceeds to drive dull care away by smoking the kalian and watching an exhibition of the terpsichorean talent of his wives or slaves. This does not consist of dancing, such as we are accustomed to understand the art, but of graceful posturing and bodily contortions, spinning round like a coryphée, with hand aloft, and snapping their fingers or clashing tiny brass cymbals; standing with feet motionless and wriggling the joints, or bending backward until their loose, flowing tresses touch the ground. Persians able to afford the luxury have their womens' apartment walled with mirrors, placed at appropriate angles, so that when enjoying these exhibitions of his wives' abilities he finds himself not merely in the presence of three or six wives, as the case may be, but surrounded on all sides by scores of airy-fairy nymphs, and amid the dreamy fumes and soothing hubble-bubbling of his kalian can imagine himself the happy – or one would naturally think, unhappy – possessor of a hundred. The effect of this mirror-work arrangement can be better imagined than described.

The Bridgeless Streams of Asia.

It seems to have rained heavily in the mountains and not rained at all east of Sercham, for during the next hour I am compelled to disrobe, and ford several freshets coursing down ravines over beds that before the storm were inches deep in dust, the approaching slopes being still dusty; this little diversion causes me to thank fortune that I have been enabled to keep in advance of the regular rainy season, which commences a little later. Striking a Koordish camp adjacent to the trail I trundle toward one of the tents; before reaching it I am overhauled by a shepherd who hands me a handful of dried peaches from a wallet suspended from his waist. The evening air is cool with a suggestion of frostiness, and the occupants of the tent are found crouching around a smoking *tezek* fire; they are ragged and of rather unprepossessing appearance, but being instinctively hospitable, they shuffle around to make me welcome at the fire; at first I almost fancy myself mistaken in thinking them Koords, for there is nothing of the neatness and cleanliness of our late acquaintances about them; on the contrary, they are almost as repulsive as their sedentary relatives of Dele Baba – but a little questioning removes all doubt of their being Koords. They are simply an ill-conditioned tribe, without any idea whether of thrift or good management. They have evidently been to Tabreez or somewhere lately, and invested most of the proceeds of the season's shearing in three-year-old dried peaches that are hard enough to rattle like pebbles; sacksful of these edibles are scattered all over the tent serving for seats, pillows, and general utility articles for the youngsters to roll about on, jump over, and throw around; everybody in the camp seems to be chewing these peaches and throwing them about in sheer wantonness because they are plentiful; every sack contains finger-holes from which one and all help themselves *ad libitum* in wanton disregard of the future.

A few miles from the camp, I am overtaken by four horsemen followed by several dogs and a pig; it proves to be the tardy Sheikh and his retainers, who have galloped several miles to catch me up; the Sheikh is a pleasant, intelligent fellow of thirty or thereabouts, and astonishes me by addressing me as 'Monsieur;' they canter alongside for a mile or so, highly delighted, when the Sheikh cheerily sings out 'Adieu, monsieur!' and they wheel about and return; had their Sheikh been in the camp I stayed at, my treatment would undoubtedly have been different. I am at the time rather puzzled to account for so strange a sight as a pig galloping briskly behind the horses, taking no notice of the dogs which continually gambol about him; but I afterward discover that a pet pig, trained to follow horses, is not an unusual thing among the Persians and Persian Koords; they are thin, wiry animals of a sandy color, and quite capable of following a horse for hours; they live in the stable with their equine companions, finding congenial occupation in rooting around for stray grains of barley; the horses and pig are said to become very much attached to each other; when on the road the pig is wont to signify its disapproval of a too rapid pace, by appealing squeaks and grunts, whereupon the horse responsively slacks its speed to a more accommodating speed for its porcine companion.

Daylight finds me again on the road, determined to make the best of early morning, ere the stiff easterly wind, which seems

Passing a Camel Caravan.

inclined to prevail of late, commences blowing great guns against me. A short distance out, I meet a string of some three hundred laden camels that have not yet halted after the night's march; scores of large camel caravans have been encountered since leaving Erzeroum, but they have invariably been halting for the day; these camels regard the bicycle with a timid reserve, merely swerving a step or two off their course as I wheel past; they all seem about equally startled, so that my progress down the ranks simply causes a sort of a gentle ripple along the line, as though each successive camel were playing a game of follow-my-leader. The road this morning is nearly perfect for wheeling, consisting of well-trodden camel-paths over a hard gravelled surface that of itself naturally makes excellent surface for cycling; there is no wind, and twenty-five miles are daily registered by the cyclometer when I halt to eat the breakfast of bread and a portion of yesterday evening's scrambled eggs which I have brought along.

Three miles of loose sand and stones have to be trundled through before reaching Kasveen; nevertheless my promised sixty miles are overcome, and I enter the city gate at 2 P.M. A trundle through several narrow, crooked streets brings me to an inner gateway emerging upon a broad, smooth avenue; a short ride down this brings me to a large enclosure containing the custom-house offices and a fine brick caravanserai. Yet another prince appears here in the person of a custom-house official; I readily grant the requested privilege of seeing me ride, but the title of a Persian prince is no longer associated in my mind with greatness and importance; princes in Persia are as plentiful as counts in Italy or barons in Germany, yet it rather shocks one's dreams of the splendor of Oriental royalty to find princes manipulating the keys of a one wire telegraph control-station at a salary of about forty dollars a month (25 tomans), or attending to the prosy duties of a small custom-house.

Kasveen is important as being the half-way station between Teheran and the Caspian port of Resht, and on the highway of travel and commerce between Northern Persia and Europe; added importance is likewise derived from its being the terminus of a broad level road from the capital, and where travellers and the mail from Teheran have to be transferred from wheeled vehicles to the backs of horses for the passage over the rugged passes of the Elburz mountains leading to the Caspian slope, or *vice versa* when going the other way.

Among the novel conveyances observed in the courtyard of

the caravanserai is the *takhtrowan*, a large sedan chair provided with shafts at either end, and carried between two mules or horses; another is the before-mentioned *kajaveh*, an arrangement not unlike a pair of canvas-covered dog kennels strapped across the back of an animal; these latter contrivances are chiefly used for carrying women and children.

At seven o'clock on the following morning I pull out toward Teheran, now but six *chapar*-stations distant. Running parallel with the road is the Elburz range of mountains, a lofty chain, separating the elevated plateau of Central Persia from the moist and wooded slopes of the Caspian Sea; south of this great dividing ridge the country is an arid and barren waste, a desert, in fact, save where irrigation redeems here and there a circumscribed area, and the mountain slopes are gray and rocky. Crossing over to the northern side of the divide, one immediately finds himself in a moist climate, and a country green almost as the British Isles, with dense box-wood forests covering the slopes of the mountains and hiding the foot-hills beneath an impenetrable mantle of green. The Elburz Mountains are a portion of the great water-shed of Central Asia, extending from the Himalayas up through Afghanistan and Persia into the Caucasus, and they perform very much the same office for the Caspian slope of Persia, as the Sierra Nevadas do for the Pacific slope of California, inasmuch as they cause the moisture-laden clouds rolling in from the sea to empty their burthens on the seaward slopes instead of penetrating farther into the interior.

Reaching the Shah Abbas caravanserai of Yeng-Imam (all first-class caravanserais are called Shah Abbas caravanserais, in deference to so many having been built throughout Persia by that monarch) about five o'clock, I conclude to remain here over night, having wheeled fifty-three miles. Yeng-Imam is a splendid large brick serai, the finest I have yet seen in Persia; many travellers are putting up here, and the place presents quite a lively appearance. In the centre of the court-yard is a large covered spring; around this is a garden of rose-bushes, pomegranate trees, and flowers; surrounding the garden is a brick walk, and forming yet a larger square is the caravanserai building itself, consisting of a one-storied brick edifice, partitioned off into small rooms.

After the customary programme of riding to allay the curiosity and excitement of the people, I obtain bread, fruit, eggs, butter to cook them in, and charcoal for a fire, the elements of a very good supper for a hungry traveller. Borrowing a handleless frying-pan, I am setting about preparing my own supper, when a respectable-looking Persian steps out from the crowd of curious on-lookers and voluntarily takes this rather onerous duty out of my hands. Readily obtaining my consent, he quickly kindles a fire, and scrambles and fries the eggs.

I am now within fifty miles of Teheran, my destination until spring-time comes around again and enables me to continue on eastward toward the Pacific; the wheeling continues fair, and in the cool of early morning good headway is made for several miles; as the sun peeps over the summit of a mountain spur jutting southward a short distance from the main Elburz Range, a wall of air comes rushing from the east as though the sun were making strenuous exertions to usher in the commencement of another day with a triumphant toot. Multitudes of donkeys are encountered on the road, the omnipresent carriers of the Persian peasantry, taking produce to the Teheran market; the only wheeled vehicle encountered between Kasveen and Teheran is a heavy-wheeled, cumbersome mail wagon, rattling briskly along behind four galloping horses driven abreast, and a newly imported carriage for some notable of the capital being dragged by hand, a distance of two hundred miles from Resht, by a company of soldiers. Pedalling laboriously against a stiff breeze I round the jutting mountain spur about eleven o'clock, and the conical snow-crowned peak of Mount Demavend looms up like a beacon-light from among the lesser heights of the Elburz Range about seventy-five miles ahead.

From the projecting mountain spur the road makes a bee-line across the intervening plain to the capital; a large willow-fringed irrigating ditch now traverses the stony plain for some distance parallel with the road, supplying the caravanserai of Shahabad and several adjacent villages with water. Teheran itself, being situated on the level plain, and without the tall minarets that render Turkish cities conspicuous from a distance, leaves one undecided as to its precise location until within a few miles of the gate; it occupies a position a dozen or more miles south of the base of the Elburz Mountains, and is flanked on the east by another jutting spur; to the southward is an extensive plain sparsely dotted with villages, and the walled gardens of the wealthier Teheranis.

At one o'clock on the afternoon of September 30th, the sentinels at the Kasveen gate of the Shah's capital gaze with unutterable astonishment at the strange spectacle of a lone Ferenghi riding toward them astride an airy wheel that glints and glitters in the bright Persian sunbeams. They look still more wonder-stricken, and half-inclined to think me some supernatural being, as, without dismounting, I ride beneath the gaudily colored archway and down the suburban streets. A ride of a mile between dead mud walls and along an open business street, and I find myself surrounded by wondering soldiers and citizens in the great central *top-maidan*, or artillery square, and shortly afterward am endeavoring to eradicate some of the dust and soil of travel, in a room of a wretched apology for an hotel, kept by a Frenchman, formerly a pastry-cook to the Shah. My cyclometre has registered one thousand five hundred and

Entering the Teheran Gate.

seventy-six miles from Ismidt; from Liverpool to Constantinople, where I had no cyclometre, may be roughly estimated at two thousand five hundred, making a total from Liverpool to Teheran of four thousand and seventy-six miles. In the evening several young Englishmen belonging to the staff of the Indo-European Telegraph Company came round, and re-echoing my own above-mentioned sentiments concerning the hotel, generously invite me to become a member of their comfortable bachelor establishment during my stay in Teheran. 'How far do you reckon it from London to Teheran by your telegraph line?' I inquire of them during our after-supper conversation. 'Somewhere in the neighborhood of four thousand miles,' is the reply. 'What does your cyclometre say?'

CHAPTER XXI

TEHERAN

There is sufficient similarity between the bazaar, the mosques, the residences, the suburban gardens, etc., of one Persian city, and the same features of another, to justify the assertion that the description of one is a description of them all. But the presence of the Shah and his court; the pomp and circumstance of Eastern royalty; the foreign ambassadors; the military; the improvements introduced from Europe; the royal palaces of the present sovereign; the palaces and reminiscences of former kings – all these things combine to effectually elevate Teheran above the somewhat dreary sameness of provincial cities.

The Shah is evidently not indifferent to the fulsome flattery of the courtiers and sycophants about him, nor insensible of the pomp and vanity of his position; nevertheless he is not without a fair share of common-sense. Perhaps the worst that can be said of him is, that he seems content to prostitute his own more enlightened and progressive views to the prejudices of a bigoted and fanatical priesthood. He seems to have a generous desire to see the country opened up to the civilizing improvements of the West, and to give the people an opportunity of emancipating themselves from their present deplorable condition; but the mollahs set their faces firmly against all reform, and the Shah evidently lacks the strength of will to override their opposition. It was owing to this criminal weakness on his part that Baron Reuter's scheme of railways and commercial regeneration for the country proved a failure.

Persia is undoubtedly the worst priest-ridden country in the world; the mollahs influence everything and everybody, from the monarch downward, to such an extent that no progress is possible. Barring outside interference, Persia will remain in its present wretched condition until the advent of a monarch with sufficient force of character to deliver the people from the incubus of their present power and influence: nothing short of a general massacre, however, will be likely to accomplish complete deliverance.

Without compromising his dignity as 'Shah-in-shah,' 'The Asylum of the Universe,' etc., when dealing with his own subjects, Nasr-e-deen Shah has profited by the experiences of his European tour to the extent of recognizing, with becoming toleration, the democratic independence of Ferenghis, whose deportment betrays the fact that they are not dazed by the contemplation of his greatness. The other evening myself and a friend encountered the Shah and his crowd of attendants on one of the streets leading to the winter palace; he was returning to the palace in state after a visit of ceremony to some dignitary. First came a squad of foot-runners in quaint scarlet coats, knee-breeches, white stockings, and low shoes, and with a most fantastic head-dress, not unlike a peacock's tail on dress-parade; each runner carried a silver staff; they were clearing the street and shouting their warning for everybody to hide their faces. Behind them came a portion of the Shah's Khajar body-guard, well mounted, and dressed in a gray uniform, braided with black: each of these also carries a silver staff, and besides sword and dagger, has a gun slung at his back in a red baize case. Next came the royal carriage, containing the Shah: the carriage is somewhat like a sheriff's coach of 'ye olden tyme,' and is drawn by six superb grays; mounted on the off horses are three postilions in gorgeous scarlet liveries. Immediately behind the Shah's carriage came the higher dignitaries on horseback, and lastly a confused crowd of three or four hundred horsemen. As the royal procession approached, the Persians – one and all – either hid themselves, or backed themselves up against the wall, and remained with heads bowed half-way to the ground until it passed. Seeing that we had no intention of striking this very submissive and servile attitude, first the scarlet foot-runners, and then the advance of the Khajar guard, addressed themselves to us personally, shouting appealingly as though very anxious about it: 'Sahib! Sahib!' and motioned for us to do as the natives were doing. These valiant guardians of the Shah's barbaric gloriousness cling tenaciously to the belief that it is the duty of everybody, whether Ferenghi or native, to prostrate themselves in this manner before him, although the monarch himself has long ceased to expect it, and is very well satisfied if the Ferenghi respectfully doffs his hat as he goes past.

The Shah's Foot-runners.

Prominent among the improvements that have been introduced in Teheran of late, may be mentioned gas and the electric light. Were one to make this statement and enter into no further explanations, the impression created would doubtless be illusive; for although the fact remains that these things are in existence here, they could be more appropriately placed under the heading of toys for the gratification of the Shah's desire to gather about him some of the novel and interesting things he had seen in Europe, than improvements made with any idea of benefiting the condition of the city as a whole. Indeed, one might say without exaggeration, that nothing new or beneficial is ever introduced into Persia, except for the personal gratification or glorification of the Shah; hence it is, that, while a few European improvements are to be seen in Teheran, they are found nowhere else in Persia.

Always on the lookout for something to please the Shah, the news of my arrival in Teheran on the bicycle no sooner reaches the ear of the court officials than the monarch hears of it himself. On the seventh day after my arrival an officer of the palace calls on behalf of the Shah, and requests that I favor them all, by following the soldiers who will be sent to-morrow morning, at eight o'clock, Ferenghi time, to conduct me to the palace, where it is appointed that I am to meet the 'Shah-in-shah and King of kings,' and ride with him, on the bicycle, to his summer palace at Doshan Tepe.

Promptly at the hour appointed the soldiers present themselves; and after waiting a few minutes for the horses of two young Englishmen who desire to accompany us part way, I mount the ever-ready bicycle, and together we follow my escort along several fairly ridable streets to the office of the foreign minister. The soldiers clear the way of pedestrians, donkeys, camels, and horses, driving them unceremoniously to the right, to the left, into the ditch – anywhere out of my road; for am I not for the time being under the Shah's special protection? I am as much the Shah's toy and plaything of the moment, as an electric light, a stop-watch, or as the big Krupp gun, the concussion of which nearly scared the soldiers out of their wits, by shaking down the little minars of one of the city gates, close to which they had unwittingly discharged it on first trial.

In company with the interpreter, I now ride out to the Doshan Tepe gate, where we are to await the arrival of the Shah. From the Doshan Tepe gate is some four English miles of fairly good artificial road, leading to one of the royal summer palaces and gardens. His Majesty goes this morning to the mountains beyond Doshan Tepe on a shooting excursion, and wishes me to ride out with his party a few miles, thus giving him a good opportunity of seeing something of what bicycle travelling is like. The tardy monarch keeps myself and a large crowd of attendants waiting a full hour at the gate, ere he puts in an appearance. Among the crowd is the Shah's chief *shikaree* (hunter), a grizzled old veteran, beneath whose rifle many a forest prowler of the Caspian slope of Mazanderan has been laid low. The *shikaree*, upon seeing me ride, and not being able to comprehend how one can possibly maintain the equilibrium, exclaims: 'Oh, ayab Ingilis!' (Oh, the wonderful English!)

Everybody's face is wreathed in smiles at the old *shikaree*'s exclamation of wonderment, and when I jokingly advise him that he ought to do his hunting for the future on a bicycle, and again mount and ride with hands off handles to demonstrate the possibility of shooting from the saddle, the delighted crowd of horsemen burst out in hearty laughter, many of them exclaiming, 'Bravo! bravo!' At length the word goes round that the Shah is coming. Everybody dismounts, and as the royal carriage drives up, every Persian bows his head nearly to the ground, remaining in that highly submissive attitude until the carriage halts and the Shah summons myself and the interpreter to his side.

The Shah impresses one as being more intelligent than the average Persian of the higher class; and although they are, as a nation, inordinately inquisitive, no Persian has taken a more lively interest in the bicycle than His Majesty seems to take, as, through his interpreter, he plys me with all manner of questions. Among other questions he asks if the Koords didn't molest me when coming through Koordistan without an escort; and upon hearing the story of my adventure with the Koordish shepherds between Ovahjik and Khoi, he seems greatly amused. Another large party of horsemen arrived with the Shah, swelling the company to perhaps two hundred attendants.

Pedaling alongside the carriage, in the best position for the Shah to see, we proceed toward Doshan Tepe, the crowd of horsemen following, some behind and others careering over the stony plain through which the Doshan Tepe highway leads. After covering about half a mile, the Shah leaves the carriage and mounts a saddlehorse, in order to the better 'put me through some exercises.' First he requests me to give him an exhibition of speed; then I have to ride a short distance over the rough stone-strewn plain, to demonstrate the possibility of traversing a rough country, after which he desires to see me ride at the slowest pace possible. All this evidently interests him not a

The Shah Escorts Me to Dohan Tepe.

little, and he seems even more amused than interested, laughing quite heartily several times as he rides alongside the bicycle. After awhile he again exchanges for the carriage, and at four miles from the city gate we arrive at the palace garden. Through this garden is a long, smooth walk, and here the Shah again requests an exhibition of my speeding abilities. The garden is traversed with a network of irrigating ditches; but I am assured there is nothing of the kind across the pathway along which he wishes me to ride as fast as possible. Two hundred yards from the spot where this solemn assurance is given, it is only by a lightning-like dismount that I avoid running into the very thing that I was assured did not exist – it was the narrowest possible escape from what might have proved a serious accident.

Riding back toward the advancing party, I point out my good fortune in escaping the tumble. The Shah asks if people ever hurt themselves by falling off bicycles; and the answer that a fall such as I would have experienced by running full speed into the irrigating ditch, might possibly result in broken bones, appeared to strike him as extremely humorous; from the way he laughed I fancy the sending me flying toward the irrigating ditch was one of the practical jokes that he is sometimes not above indulging in. After mounting and forcing my way for a few yards through deep, loose gravel, to satisfy his curiosity as to what could be done in loose ground, I trundle along with him to a small menagerie he keeps at this place. On the way he inquires about the number of wheelmen there are in England and America; whether I am English or American; why they don't use iron tires on bicycles instead of rubber, and many other questions, proving the great interest aroused in him by the advent of the first bicycle to appear in his Capital. The menagerie consists of one cage of monkeys, about a dozen lions, and two or three tigers and leopards. We pass along from cage to cage, and as the keeper coaxes the animals to the bars, the Shah amuses himself by poking them with an umbrella. It was arranged in the original programme that I should accompany them up into their rendezvous in the foot-hills, about a mile beyond the palace, to take breakfast with the party; but seeing the difficulty of getting up there with the bicycle, and not caring to spoil the favorable impression already made, by having to trundle up, I ask permission to take my leave at this point. The request is granted, and the interpreter returns with me to the city – thus ends my memorable bicycle ride with the Shah of Persia.

Scattered here and there about the stony plain between Teheran and the Elburz foot-hills, are many beautiful gardens – beautiful for Persia – where a pleasant hour can be spent wandering beneath the shady avenues and among the fountains. These gardens are simply patches redeemed from the desert plain, supplied with irrigating water, and surrounded with a high mud wall; leading through the garden are gravelled walls, shaded by rows of graceful chenars. The gardens are planted with fig, pomegranate, almond or apricot trees, grape-vines, melons, etc.; they are the property of wealthy Teheranis who derive an income from the sale of the fruit in the Teheran market. The ample space within the city ramparts includes a number of these delightful retreats, some of them presenting the additional charm of historic interest, from having been the property and, peradventure, the favorite summer residence of a former king. Such a one is an extensive garden in the northeast quarter of the city, in which was situated one of the favorite summer palaces of Fatteh-ali-Shah, grandfather of Nasr-e-deen.

That portion of the Teheran bazaar immediately behind the Shah's winter palace, is visited almost daily by Europeans, and their presence excites little comment or attention from the natives; but I had frequently heard the remark that a Ferenghi couldn't walk through the southern, or more exclusive native quarters, without being insulted. Determined to investigate, I sallied forth one afternoon alone, entering the bazaar on the east side of the palace wall, where I had entered it a dozen times before.

The streets outside are sloppy with melting snow, and the roofed passages of the bazaar, being dry underfoot, are crowded with people to an unusual extent; albeit they are pretty well crowded at any time. Most of the dervishes in the city have been driven, by the inclemency of the weather, to seek shelter in the bazaar; these, added to the no small number who make the place their regular foraging ground, render them a greater nuisance than ever. They are encountered in such numbers, that no matter which way I turn, I am confronted by a rag-bedecked mendicant, with a wild, haggard countenance and grotesque costume, thrusting out his gourd alms-receiver, and muttering 'huk yah huk!' each in his own peculiar way.

The mollahs, with their flowing robes, and huge white turbans, likewise form no inconsiderable proportion of the moving throng; they are almost without exception scrupulously neat and clean in appearance, and their priestly costume and Pharisaical deportment gives them a certain air of stateliness. They wear the placid expression of men so utterly puffed up with the notion of their own sanctity, that their self-consciousness verily seems to shine through their skins, and to impart to them a sleek, oily appearance. One finds himself involuntarily speculating on how they all manage to make a living; the mollah 'toils not, neither does he spin,' and almost every other person one meets is a mollah.

As I emerge from the vaulted bazaar the sun is almost setting, and the musicians in the *bala-khanas* of the palace gates are ushering in the close of another day with discordant blasts from ancient Persian trumpets, and belaboring hemispherical kettle-drums. These musicians are dressed in fantastic scarlet uniforms, not unlike the costume of a fifteen century jester, and every evening at sundown they repair to these *bala-khanas*, and for the space of an hour dispense the most unearthly music imaginable. The trumpets are sounding-tubes of brass about five feet long, which respond to the efforts of a strong-winded person, with a diabolical basso-profundo shriek that puts a Newfoundland fog-horn entirely in the shade. When a dozen of these instruments are in full blast, without any attempt at harmony, it seems to shed a depressing shadow of barbarism over the whole city. This sunset music is, I think, a relic of very old times, and it jars on the nerves like the despairing howl of ancient Persia, protesting against the innovation from the pomp and din and glamor of her old pagan glories, to the present miserable era of mollah rule and feeble dependence for national existence on the forbearance or jealousy of other nations. Beneath the musicians' gate, and I emerge into a small square which is half taken up by a square tank of water; near the tank is a large bronze cannon. It is a huge, unwieldy piece, and a muzzle-loader, utterly useless to such a people as the Persians, except for ornament, or perhaps to help impress the masses with an idea of the Shah's unapproachable greatness.

It is the special hour of prayer, and in every direction may be observed men, halting in whatever they may be doing, and kneeling down on some outer garment taken off for the purpose, repeatedly touch their foreheads to the ground, bending in the direction of Mecca. Passing beneath the second musicians' gate, I reach the artillery square just in time to see a company of army buglers formed in line at one end, and a company of musketeers at the other. As these more modern trumpeters proceed to toot, the company of musketeers opposite present arms, and then the music of the new buglers, and the hoarse, fog-horn-like blasts of the fantastic tooters on the *bala-khanas* dies away together in a concerted effort that would do credit to a troop of wild elephants.

When the noisy trumpeting ceases, the ordinary noises round about seem like solemn silence in comparison, and above this comparative silence can be heard the voices of men here and there over the city, calling out 'Al-lah-il-All-ah; Ali Ak-bar!' (God is greatest; there is no god but one God! etc.) with stentorian voices. The men are perched on the roofs of the mosques, and on noblemen's walls and houses; the Shah has a strong-voiced *muezzin* that can be heard above all the others.

The sun has just set; I can see the snowy cone of Mount Demavend, peeping apparently over the high barrack walls; it has just taken on a distinctive roseate tint, as it oftentimes does at sunset; the reason whereof becomes at once apparent upon turning toward the west, for the whole western sky is aglow with a gorgeous sunset – a sunset that paints the horizon a blood red, and spreads a warm, rich glow over half the heavens.

The moon will be full to-night, and a far lovelier picture even than the glorious sunset and the rose-tinted mountain, awaits anyone curious enough to come out-doors and look. The Persian moonlight seems capable of surrounding the most commonplace objects with a halo of beauty, and of blending things that are nothing in themselves, into scenes of such transcendental loveliness that the mere casual contemplation of them sends a thrill of pleasure coursing through the system.

The European lady with her uncovered face is a conundrum and an object of intense curiosity, even in Teheran at the present day; and in provincial cities, the wife of the lone consul or telegraph employé finds it highly convenient to adopt the native costume, face-covering included, when venturing abroad. Here, in the capital, the wives and daughters of foreign ministers, European officers and telegraphists, have made uncovered female faces tolerably familiar to the natives; but they cannot quite understand but that there is something highly indecorous about it, and the more unenlightened Persians doubtless regard them as quite bold and forward creatures. Armenian women conceal their faces almost as completely as do the Persian, when they walk abroad; by so doing they avoid unpleasant criticism, and the rude, inquisitive gaze of the Persian men. Although the Persian readily recognizes the fact that a Sahib's wife or sister must be a superior person to an Armenian female, she is as much an object of interest to him when she appears with her face uncovered on the street, as his own wives in their highly sensational in-door costumes would be to some of us. In order to establish herself in the estimation of the average Persian, as all that a woman ought to be, the European lady would have to conceal her face and cover her shapely, tight-fitting dress with an inelegant, loose mantle, whenever she ventured outside her own doors.

In certain quarters of Teheran one happens across a few

remaining families of *guebres*, or fire-worshippers; remnant representatives of the ancient Parsee religion, whose devotees bestowed their strange devotional offerings upon the fires whose devouring flames they constantly fed, and never allowed to be extinguished. These people are interesting as having kept their heads above the overwhelming flood of Mohammedanism that swept over their country, and clung to their ancient belief through thick and thin – or, at all events, to have steadfastly refused to embrace any other. Little evidence of their religion remains in Persia at the present day, except their 'towers of silence' and the ruins of their old fire-temples. These latter were built chiefly of soft adobe bricks, and after the lapse of centuries, are nothing more than shapeless reminders of the past. A few miles southeast of Teheran, in a desolate, unfrequented spot, is the *guebre* 'tower of silence,' where they dispose of their dead. On top of the tower is a kind of balcony with an open grated floor; on this the naked corpses are placed until the carrion crows and the vultures pick the skeleton perfectly clean; the dry bones are then cast into a common receptacle in the tower. The *guebre* communities of Persia are too impecunious or too indifferent to keep up the ever-burning-fires nowadays; the fires of Zoroaster, which in olden and more prosperous times were fed with fuel night and day, are now extinguished forever, and the scattering survivors of this ancient form of worship form a unique item in the sum total of the population of Persia.

Of the interesting scenes and characters to be seen every day on the streets of Teheran, their name is legion. The peregrinating *tchai*-venders, who, with their little cabinet of tea and sugar in one hand, and samovar with live charcoals in the other, wander about the city picking up stray customers, for whom they are prepared to make a glass of hot tea at one minute's notice; the scores of weird-looking mendicants and dervishes with their highly fantastic costumes, assailing you with 'huk, yah huk!' the barbers shaving the heads of their customers on the public streets – shaving their pates clean, save little tufts to enable Mohammed to pull them up to Paradise; and many others the description and enumeration of which would, of themselves, fill a good-sized volume.

FROM TEHERAN TO YOKOHAMA

Yours Sincerely

Thos Stevens

CHAPTER I

THE START FROM TEHERAN

The season of 1885–86 has been an exceptionally mild winter in the Persian capital. Up to Christmas the weather was clear and bracing, sufficiently cool to be comfortable in the daytime, and with crisp, frosty weather at night. The first snow of the season commenced falling while a portion of the English colony were enjoying a characteristic Christmas dinner of roast-beef and plum-pudding, at the house of the superintendent of the Indo-European Telegraph Station, and during January and February, snow-storms, cold and drizzling rains alternated with brief periods of clearer weather. When the sun shines from a cloudless sky in Teheran, its rays are sometimes uncomfortably warm, even in midwinter; a foot of snow may have clothed the city and the surrounding plain in a soft, white mantle during the night, but, asserting his supremacy on the following morning, he will unveil the gray nakedness of the stony plain again by noon. The steadily retreating snow line will be driven back – back over the undulating foot-hills, and some little distance up the rugged slopes of the Elburz range, hard by, ere he retires from view in the evening, rotund and fiery. This irregular snow line has been steadily losing ground, and retreating higher and higher up the mountain-slopes during the latter half of February, and when March is ushered in, with clear sunny weather, and the mud begins drying up and the various indications of spring begin to put in their appearance, I decide to make a start. Friends residing here who have been mentioning April 15th as the date I should be justified in thinking the unsettled weather at an end and pulling out eastward again, agree, in response to my anxious inquiries, that it is an open spell of weather before the regular spring rains, that may possibly last until I reach Meshed.

During the winter I have examined, as far as circumstances

have permitted, the merits and demerits of the different routes to the Pacific Coast, and have decided upon going through Turkestan and Southern Siberia to the Amoor Valley, and thence either follow down the valley to Vladivostok or strike across Mongolia to Pekin – the latter route by preference, if upon reaching Irkutsk I find it to be practicable; if not practicable, then the Amoor Valley route from necessity. This route I approve of, as it will not only take me through some of the most interesting country in Asia, but will probably be a more straightaway continuous land-journey than any other. The distance from Teheran to Vladivostok is some six thousand miles, and, well aware that six thousand miles with a bicycle over Asiatic roads is a task of no little magnitude, I at once determine upon taking advantage of the fair March weather to accomplish at least the first six hundred miles of the journey between Teheran and Meshed, one of the holy cities of Persia.

The bicycle is in good trim, my own health is splendid, my experience of nearly eight thousand miles of straightaway wheeling over the roads of three continents ought to count for something, and it is with every confidence of accomplishing my undertaking without serious misadventure that I set about making my final preparations to start. The British Chargé d'Affaires gives me a letter to General Melnikoff, the Russian Minister at the Shah's court, explaining the nature and object of my journey, and asking him to render me whatever assistance he can to get through, for most of the proposed route lies through Russian territory. Among my Teheran friends is Mr. M–, a lively, dapper little telegraphist, who knows three or four different languages, and who never seems happier than when called upon to act the part of interpreter for friends about him.

Mr. M–'s linguistic accomplishments include a fair knowledge of Russian, and he readily accompanies me to the Russian Legation to interpret. The Russian Legation is situated down in the old Oriental quarter (birds of a feather, etc.) of the city, and, for us at least, necessitated the employment of a guide to find it. On the way down, Mr. M–, who prides himself on a knowledge of Russian character, impresses upon me his assurance that General Melnikoff will turn out to be a nice, pleasant sort of gentleman.

'Which is Mr. Stevens?' he exclaims, with something akin to

enthusiasm, as he advances almost to the door to meet us, his face fairly beaming with pleasure; and, grasping me warmly by the hand, he proceeds to express his great satisfaction at meeting a person, who had 'made so wonderful a journey,' etc. etc., and etc. Never did Mr. Pickwick beam more pleasantly at the deaf gentleman, or regard more benignantly Master Humphrey's clock, than the Russian Minister regards the form and features of one whom, he says, he feels 'honored to meet.' For several minutes we discuss, through the medium of Mr. M–, my journey from San Francisco to Teheran and its proposed continuation to the Pacific; and during the greater part of the interview General Melnikoff holds me quite affectionately by the hand. 'Wonderful!' he says, 'wonderful! nobody ever made such a remarkable journey; my whole heart will go with you until your journey is completed.'

Mr. M– looks on and interprets between us, with a fixed and confident didn't-I-tell-you-so smile, that forms a side study of no mean quality. 'There will be no trouble about getting permission to go through Turkestan?' I feel constrained to enquire; for such excessive display of affection and bonhommie on the Russian diplomat's part could scarce fail to arouse suspicions. 'Oh dear, no!' he replies. 'Oh dear, no! I will telegraph to General Komaroff, at Askabad, to remove all obstacles, so that nothing shall interfere with your progress.' Having received this positive assurance, we take our leave, Mr. M– reminding me gleefully of what he had said about the Russians being the most agreeable people on earth, and the few remaining clouds of doubt about getting the road through Turkestan happily dissipated by the Russian Minister's assurances of assistance.

Searching through the bazaar, I succeed, after some little trouble, in finding and purchasing a belt-full of Russian gold, sufficient to carry me clear through to Japan; and on the morning of March 10th I bid farewell to the Persian capital, well satisfied at the outlook ahead. While packing up my traps on the evening before starting, it begins raining for the first time in ten days; but it clears off again before midnight, and the morning opens bright and promising as ever. Six members of the telegraph staff have determined to accompany me out to Katoum-abad, the first *chapar*-station on the Meshed pilgrim road, a distance of seven farsakhs. 'Hodge-podge', the cook, and Meshedi Ali, the *gholam*, were sent ahead yesterday with plenty of substantial refreshments and sundry mysterious black bottles – for it is the intention of the party to remain at Katoum-abad over-night, and give me a proper send-off from that point to-morrow morning.

'*Khuda rah pak Kumad!*' (May God sweep your road!), Ali Akbar had exclaimed as I mounted at the door, and as we pass through the city gate the old sentinel, when told that I am at last starting on the promised journey to Meshed on the *asp-i-awhan*, supplements this with '*Padaram daromad!*' (My father has come out!), a Persian metaphorical exclamation, signifying that such wonderful news has had the effect of calling his father from the grave.

Teheran is in semi-obscurity beneath the same hazy veil observed when first approaching it from the west, and which always seems to hover over it. This haziness is not sufficiently pronounced to hide any conspicuous building, and each familiar object in the city is plainly visible from the commanding summit of the pass. The different gates of the city, each with its little cluster of bright-tiled minars, trace at a glance the size and contour of the outer ditch and wall; the large framework of the pavilion beneath which the Shah gives his annual tazzia (representation of the religious tragedy of Hussein and Hassan), denuded of its canvas covering, suggests from this distance the naked ribs of some monster skeleton. The square towers of the royal anderoon – which the Shah professes to believe is the tallest dwelling-house in the world – loom conspicuously skyward above the mass of indefinable mud buildings and walls that characterize the habitations of humbler folk – humbler, but perhaps happier on the whole than the fair occupants of that seven-storied gilded prison.

Hundreds of women – wives, concubines, slaves, and domestics – are understood to be dwelling within these palace walls in charge of sable eunuchs, and the fate of any female whose bump of discretion in an evil moment fails her, is to be hurled headlong from the summit of one of the anderoon towers – such, at least, is the popular belief in Teheran; it may or may not be an exaggeration. Some even assert that the Shah's chief object in building the anderoon so high was to have the

The Start from Teheran.

certainty of this awful doom ever present before its numerous inmates, the more easily to keep them in a submissive frame of mind. Off to the right, below our position, is the Doshan Tepe palace, a memorable spot for me, where I had the satisfaction of first introducing bicycle-riding to the notice of the Persian monarch. Off to the left, the Parsee 'tower of silence' is observed perched among the lonely gray hills far from human habitation or any traversed road; on a grating fixed in the top of this tower, the Guebre population of Teheran deposit their dead, in order that the carrion-crows and the vultures may pick the carcass clean before they deposit the whitened bones in the body of the tower.

A slight drizzling rain is falling when the early riser of the company wakes up and peeps out at daybreak next morning, but it soon ceases, and by seven o'clock the ground is quite dry. The road for a mile or so is too lumpy to admit of mounting, as is frequently the case near a village, and my six companions accompany me to ridable ground. As I mount and wheel away they wave hats and send up three ringing cheers and a 'tiger,' hurrahs that roll across the gray Persian plain to the echoing hills, the strangest sound, perhaps, these grim old hills have ever echoed; certainly, they never before echoed an English cheer.

And now, as my friends of the telegraph staff turn about and wend their way back to Teheran, is as good a time as any to mention briefly the manner in which these genial lightning-jerkers assisted to render my five months' sojourn in the Persian capital agreeable. But a few short hours after my arrival in Teheran, I was sought out by Messrs. Meyrick and North, who no sooner learned of my intention to winter here, than they extended a cordial invitation to join them in their already established bachelors' quarters, where four disconsolate halves of humanity were already messing harmoniously together. With them I took up my quarters, and, under the liberal and wholesome gastronomic arrangements of the establishment, soon acquired my usual semi-embonpoint condition, and recovered from that gaunt, hungry appearance that the hardships and scant fare of the journey from Constantinople had imparted. The house belonged to Mr. North, and he managed to give me a little room to myself for literary work, and, under the influence of a steady stream of letters and papers

from friends and well-wishers in England and America, that
snug little apartment, with a round, moon-like hole in the thick
mud wall for a window, soon acquired the den-like aspect that
seems inseparable from the occupation of distributing ink.

My Teheran "Den."

Three native servants cooked for us, waited on us, turned up
missing when wanted for anything particular, cheated us and
each other, swore eternal honesty and fidelity to our faces,
called us infidel dogs and *pedar sags* behind our backs,
quarrelled daily among themselves over their *modokal*
(legitimate pickings and stealings – ten per cent. on everything
passing through their hands), and meekly bore with any abuse
bestowed gratuitously upon them, for an aggregate of one
hundred and thirty kerans a month – and, of course, their
modokal.

Half an hour after the echoes of the three cheers and the 'tiger'
have died away finds me wet-footed and engaged in fording a
series of aggravating little streams, that obstruct my path so
frequently that to stop and shed one's foot-gear for each soon
becomes an intolerable nuisance. I should think I can lay claim,
without exaggeration, to crossing fifty of these streams inside of
ten miles. A good-sized stream emerges from the Elburz foot-

hills; after reaching the plain it follows no regular channel, but spreads out like an open fan into a gradually widening area of small streams, that play their part in irrigating a few scattering fields and gardens, and are then lost in the sands of the desert to the south. Situated where it can derive the most benefit from these streams is the village of Sherifabad, and beyond Sherifabad stretches a verdureless waste of Aivan-i-Kaif. On this desert, I sit down, for a few minutes, on one of those little mounds of stones piled up at intervals to mark the road when the trail is buried beneath the winter snows; a green-turbaned descendant of the Prophet, bestriding a bay horse, comes from the opposite direction, stops, dismounts, squats down on his hams close by, and proceeds to regale himself with bread and figs, meanwhile casting fugitive glances at the bicycle. Presently he advances closer, gives me a handful of figs, squats down closer to the bicycle, and commences a searching investigation of its several parts.

'Where are you going?' he finally asks. 'Meshed.' 'Where have you come from?' 'Teheran.' With that he hands me another handful of figs, remounts his horse, and rides away without another word. Inquisitiveness is seen almost bristling from the loose sleeves and flowing folds of his sky-blue gown, but his overwhelming sense of his own holiness forbids him holding anything like a lengthly intercourse with an unhallowed Ferenghi, and, much as he would like to know everything about the bicycle, he goes away without asking a single question about it.

There are some stretches of very good road across this desert, and I reach Aivan-i-Kaif near noon. There has been no drinkable water for a long distance, and, being thirsty, my first inquiry is for tea. 'There is a *tchai-khan* at the *umbar* (water-cistern), yonder,' I am told, and straightway proceed to the place pointed out; but '*tchai-khan neis*' is the reply upon inquiring at the umbar. In this manner am I promptly initiated into one peculiarity of the people along this portion of the Meshed pilgrim road, a peculiarity that distinguishes them from the ordinary Persian as fully as the shaking of their heads for an affirmative reply does the people of the Maritza Valley from other people of the Balkan Peninsula.

It is threatening rain as I pick my way through a mile or so of mud ruins, tumble-down walls, and crooked paths, leading from the *umbar* to the house of the Persian telegraph-*jee*, who has been requested, from Teheran, to put me up, and, in view of the threatening aspect of the weather, I conclude to remain till morning. The English Government has taken charge of the Teheran and Meshed telegraph-line, during the delimitation of the Afghan and Turkestan boundary, and, besides guaranteeing the native telegraph-*jees* their regular salary – which is not always forthcoming from the Persian Government – they pay them something extra. In consequence of this, the telegraph-*jees* are at present very favorably disposed toward Englishmen, and Mirza Hassan readily tenders me the hospitality of the little mud office where he amuses himself daily clicking the keys of his instrument, smoking kalians, drinking tea, and entertaining his guests. Mr. McIntire and Mr. Stagno are somewhere between here and Meshed, inspecting and repairing the line for the English Government, for they received it from the Persians in a wretched, tumble-down condition, and Mr. Gray, telegraphist for the Afghan Boundary Commission, is stationed temporarily at Meshed, so that, thanks to the boundary troubles, I am pretty certain of meeting three Europeans on the first six hundred miles of my journey.

Visitors begin dropping in as usual, and, before long, hundreds of villagers are swarming about the telegraph-*khana*, anxious to see me ride. It is coming on to rain, but, in order to rid the telegraph-office of the crowd, I take the bicycle out. Willing men carry both me and the bicycle across a stream that runs through the village, to smooth ground on the opposite side, where I ride back and forth several times, to the wild and boisterous delight of the entire population.

In this manner I succeed in ridding the telegraph-office of the crowd; but there is no getting rid of the visitors. Everybody in the place who thinks himself a little better than the ragamuffin ryots comes and squats on his hams in the little hut-like office, sips the telegraph-*jee*'s sweetened tea, smokes his kalians, and spends the afternoon in staring wonderingly at me and the bicycle. Having picked up a little Pesian during the winter, I am able to talk with them, and understand them, rather better than last season, and, Persian-like, they ply me mercilessly with questions. Often, when some one asks a question of me, Mirza

Hassan, as becomes a telegraph-*jee*, and a person of profound erudition, thoughtfully saves me the trouble of replying by undertaking to furnish the desired information himself. One old mollah wants to know how many farsakhs it is from Aivan-i-Kaif to Yenghi Donia (New World – America); ere I can frame a suitable reply, Mirza Hassan forestalls my intentions by answering, in a decisive tone of voice that admits of no appeal, '*Khylie!*' 'Khylie' is a handy word that the Persians always fall back on when their knowledge of great numbers or long distances is vague and shadowy; it is an indefinite term, equivalent to our word 'many.' Mirza Hassan does not know whether America is two hundred farsakhs away or two thousand, but he knows it to be 'khylie farsakhs,' and that is perfectly satisfactory to himself, and the white-turbaned questioner is perfectly satisfied with 'khylie' for an answer.

After an ample supper of mutton *pillau*, Mirza Hassan proceeds to say his prayers, borrowing my compass to get the proper bearing for Mecca, which I have explained to him during the afternoon. With no little dismay he discovers that, according to my explanation, he has for years been bobbing his head daily several degrees east of the holy city, and, like a sensible fellow, and a person who has become convinced of the infallibility of telegraph instruments, compasses, and kindred aids to the accomplishment of human ends, he now rectifies the mistake.

Everybody along this route uses a praying-stone, a small cake of stone or hardened clay, containing an inscription from the Koran. These praying-stones are obtained from the sacred soil of Meshed, Koom, or Kerbela, and are placed in position on the ground in front of the kneeling devotee during his devotions, so that, instead of touching his forehead to the carpet or the common ground of his native village, he can bring it in contact with the hallowed soil of one of these holy cities. Distance lends enchantment to a holy place, and adds to the efficacy of a prayer-stone in the eyes of its owner, and they are valued highly or lightly according to the distance and the consequent holiness of the city they are brought from. For example, a Meshedi values a prayer-stone from Kerbela, and a Kerbeli values one from Meshed, neither of them having much faith in the efficacy of one from his own city; familiarity with sacred things apparently breeds doubts and indifference. The prayer-stone is reverently touched to lips, cheeks, and forehead at the finish of prayers, and then carefully wrapped and stowed away until praying-time comes round again. To a sceptical and perhaps irreverent observer, these praying-stones would seem to bear about the same relation to a pilgrimage to Meshed or Kerbela as a package of prepared sea-salt does to a season at the sea-side.

CHAPTER II

PERSIA AND THE MESHED PILGRIM ROAD

It rains quite heavily during the night, but clears off again in the early morning, and at eight o'clock I take my departure, Mirza Hassan refusing to allow his son and heir to accept a present in acknowledgement of the hospitality received at his hands. The whole male population of the village is assembled again at the spot where their experience of yesterday has taught them I should probably mount; and the house-tops overlooking the same spot, and commanding a view of the road across the plain to the eastward, are crowded with women and children. The female portion of my farewell audience present quite a picturesque appearance, being arrayed in their holiday garments of red, blue and other bright colors, in honor of Friday, the Mohammedan Sabbath.

Four miles of most excellent camel-path lead across a gravelly plain, affording a smooth, firm, wheeling surface, notwithstanding the heavy rains of the previous night; but beyond the plain the road leads over the pass of the Sardara Kooh, one of the many spurs of the Elburz range that reach out toward the south. This spur consists of saline hills that present a very remarkable appearance in places; the rocks are curiously honey-combed by the action of the salt, and the yellowish earthy portion of the hills are fantastically streaked and seamed with white. A trundle of a couple of miles brings me to the summit, from which point I am able to mount, and, with brake firmly in hand, glide smoothly down the eastern slope. After descending about a mile, I am met by a party of travellers who give me friendly warning of deep water a little farther down the mountain. After leaving them, my road follows down the winding bed of a stream that is probably dry the greater part of the year; but during the spring thaws, and immediately after a rain-storm, a stream of brackish, muddy water a few inches deep trickles down the mountain and forms a most disagreeable area of sticky salt mud at the bottom. The streak this morning can more truthfully be described as yellow liquid mud than as water, and both myself and wheel present anything but a prepossessing appearance in ten minutes after starting down its grimy channel. I am, however, congratulating myself upon finding it so shallow, and begin to think that, in describing the water as nearly over their donkeys' backs, the travellers were but indulging their natural propensity as subjects of the Shah, and worthy followers in the footsteps of Ananias.

About the time I have arrived at this comforting conclusion, I am suddenly confronted by a pond of liquid mud that bars my farther progress down the mountain. A recent slide of land and rock has blocked up the narrow channel of the stream, and backed up the thick yellow liquid into a pool of uncertain depth. There is no way to get around it; perpendicular walls of rock and slippery yellow clay rise sheer from the water on either side. There is evidently nothing for it but to disrobe without more ado and try the depth. Besides being thick with mud, the water is found to be of that icy, cutting temperature peculiar to cold brine, and after wading about in it for fifteen minutes, first finding a fordable place, and then carrying clothes and wheel across, I emerge on to the bank formed by the land-slip looking as woe-begone a specimen of humanity as can well be imagined. Plastered with a coat of thin yellow mud from head to foot, chilled through and through, and shivering like a Texas steer in a norther, feet cut and bleeding in several places from contact with the sharp rocks, and no clean water to wash off the mud! With the assistance of knife, pocket-handkerchief, and sundry theological remarks which need not be reproduced here, I finally succeed in getting off at least the greater portion of the mud, and putting on my clothes.

The weather-clerk inaugurates a regular March zephyr in the east, during the brief halt at Kishlag; and in addition to that doubtful favor blowing against me, the road leading out is lumpy as far as the cultivated area extends, and then it leads across a rough, stony plain that is traversed by a network of small streams similar to those encountered yesterday at Sherifabad. To the left, the abutting front of the Elburz Mountains is streaked and frescoed with salt, that in places vies in whiteness with the lingering patches of snow higher up; to the right extends the gray, level plain, interspersed with small cultivable areas for a farsakh or two, beyond which lies the great *dasht-i-namek* (salt desert) that comprises a large portion of the interior of Persia.

Wild asses abound on the *dasht-i-namek*, and wandering bands of these animals occasionally stray up in this direction. The Persians consider the flesh of the wild donkey as quite a delicacy, and sometimes hunt them for their meat; they are said to be untamable, unless caught when very young, and are then generally too slender-limbed to be of any service in carrying weights. Wild goats abound in the Elburz Mountains; the villagers hunt them also for their meat, but the flesh of the wild goat is said to contribute largely to the prevalence of sore eyes among the people. The Persian will eat wild donkey, wild goat, and the flesh of camels, but only the very poor people – people who cannot afford to be fastidious – ever touch a piece of beef; *gusht-i-goosfang* (mutton) is the staple meat of the country.

In striking and effective contrast to the general aspect of death and desolation that characterizes the desert wastes of Persia – an effect that is heightened by the ruins of caravanserais or villages, that are seldom absent from the landscape – are the cultivated spots around the villages. Wherever there is a permanent supply of water, there also is certain to be found a mud-built village, with fields of wheat and barley, pomegranate orchards, and vineyards. In a country of universal greenness these would count for nothing, but, situated like islands in the sea of sombre gray about them, they often present an appearance of extreme beauty that the wondering observer is somewhat puzzled to account for; it is the beauty of contrast, the great and striking contrast between vegetable life and death.

These impressions are nowhere more strongly brought into notice then when approaching Aradan, a village I reach about five o'clock. Like almost all Persian towns and villages, Aradan has evidently occupied a much larger area at one time than it does at present; and the mournful-looking ruins of mosques, gateways, walls, and houses are scattered here and there over the plain for a mile before reaching the present limits of habitation.

While engaged in fording a stream on the stony plain between the two last-named villages, Mr. Stagno and servant come jogging along from the east, on the hurricane deck of the sorriest-looking pair of *chapar* horses it has been my fortune to meet on a Persian road. The *shagird-chapar* is with them, on a third 'bag of bones,' worse, if possible, than the others. Taking the world over, there is perhaps no class of horses that are subject to so much cruelty and ill-treatment as the *chapar* horses of Persia. With back raw, ribs countable a hundred yards away, spavined, blind of an eye, fistula, and cursed with every ill that horseflesh in the hands of human brutes is subject to, the *chapar* horse is liable to be taken out at any hour of the day or night, regardless of previous services being but just finished. He is goaded on with unsparing lash to the next station, twenty, or perhaps thirty miles away, staggering beneath the weight of the traveller, or his servant, with ponderous saddle-bags.

This *chapar*, or post-service, is established along the great highways of travel between Teheran and Tabreez, Teheran and Meshed, and Teheran and Bushire, with a branch route from the Tabreez trail to the Caspian port of Enzeli; the stations vary from four to eight farsakhs apart. Not all the *chapar* horses are the wretched creatures just described, however, and by engaging beforehand the best horses at each station along the route, certain travellers have made quite remarkable time between points hundreds of miles apart.

Aradan is another telegraph control station, and Mr. Stagno informs me that the telegraph-*jee* is looking forward to my arrival, and is fully prepared to accommodate me over night; and, furthermore, that all along the line the people of the telegraph towns are eagerly anticipating the arrival of the Sahib, with the marvellous vehicle, of which they have heard such strange stories. Aradan is reached about five o'clock; the road leading into the village is found excellent wheeling, enabling me to keep the saddle while following at the heels of a fleet-footed ryot, who voluntarily guides me to the telegraph-*khana*. The telegraph-*jee* is temporarily absent when I arrive, but his *farrash* lets me inside the office yard, spreads a piece of carpet for me to sit on, and with commendable thoughtfulness shuts out the crowd, who, as usual, immediately begin to collect. The quickness with which a crowd collects in a Persian town has to be seen to be fully comprehended. For the space of half an hour,

I sit in solitary state on the carpet, and endure the wondering gaze and the parrot-like chattering of a thin, long row of villagers, sitting astride the high mud wall that encloses three sides of the compound, and during the time find some amusement in watching the scrambling and quarrelling for position. These irrepressible sight-seers commenced climbing the wall from the adjoining walls and houses the moment the *farrash* shut them out of the yard, and in five minutes they are packed close as books on a shelf, while others are quarrelling noisily for places; in addition to this, the roof of every building commanding a glimpse into the *chapar-khana* compound is swarmed with neck-craning, chattering people.

Those Irrepressible Sight-seers.

Soon the telegraph-*jee* puts in an appearance; he proves to be an exceptionally agreeable fellow, and one of the very few

Persians one meets with having blue eyes. He appears to regard it as quite an understood thing that I am going to remain over night with him, and proceeds at once to make the necessary arrangements for my accommodation, without going to the trouble of extending a formal invitation. He also wins my eternal esteem by discouraging, as far as Persian politeness and civility will admit, the intrusion of the inevitable self-sufficients who presume on their 'eminent respectability' as loafers, in contradistinction to the half-naked tillers of the soil, to invade the premises and satisfy their inordinate curiosity, and their weakness for *kalian* smoking and tea-drinking at another's expense. After duly discussing between us a samovar of tea, we take a stroll through the village to see the old castle, and the *umbars* that supply the village with water. The telegraph-*jee* cleared the walls upon his arrival, but the house-tops are out of his jurisdiction, and before starting he wisely suggests putting the bicycle in some conspicuous position, as an inducement for the crowd to remain and concentrate their curiosity upon it, otherwise there would be no keeping them from following us about the village. We set up in plain view of the *bala-khana*, and returning from our walk, are amused to find the old *farrash* delivering a lecture on cycling.

The road into Aradan led me through one populous cemetery, and the road out again leads me through another; beyond the cemetery it follows alongside a meandering streamlet that flows sluggishly along over a bed of deep gray mud. The road is lumpy but ridable, and I am pedalling serenely along, happy in the contemplation of better roads ahead than I had yesterday, when one of those ludicrous incidents happen that have occurred at intervals here and there all along my journey. A party of travellers have been making a night march from the east, and as we approach each other, a wary *kajaveh*-carrying mule, suspicious about the peaceful character of the mysterious object bearing down toward him, pricks up his ears, wheels round, and inaugurates confusion among his fellows, and then proceeds to head them in a determined bolt across the stream. Unfortunately for the women in the *kajavehs*, the mud and water together prove to be deeper than the mule expected to find them, and the additional fright of finding himself in a well-nigh swamped condition, causes him to struggle violently to get out again. In so doing he bursts whatever fastenings may have bound him and his burden together, scrambles ashore, and leaves the *kajavehs* floating on the water!

The women began screaming the moment the mule wheeled round and bolted, and now they find themselves afloat in their queer craft, these characteristic female signals of distress are redoubled in energy; and they may well be excused for this, for the *kajavehs* are gradually filling and sinking; it was never intended that *kajavehs* should be capable of acting in the capacity of a boat. The sight of their companion's difficulties has the effect of causing the other mules to change their minds about crossing the stream, and almost to change their minds about indulging in the mulish luxury of a scare; and fortunately the *charvadars* of the party succeed in rescuing the *kajavehs* before they sink. Nobody is injured, beyond the women getting wet; no damage is done worth mentioning, and as the two heroines of the adventure emerge from their novel craft, their garments dripping with water, their doleful looks are rewarded with unsympathetic merriment from the men. Few have been my wheeling days on Asian roads that have not witnessed something in the shape of an overthrow or runaway; so far, nobody has been seriously injured by them, but I have sometimes wondered whether it will be my good fortune to complete the bicycle journey around the world without some mishap of the kind, resulting in broken limbs for the native and trouble for myself.

After a couple of miles the road and the meandering stream part company, the latter flowing southward and the road traversing a flat, curious, stone-strewn waste; an area across which one could step from one large bowlder to another without touching the ground. Once beyond this, and the road develops into several parallel trails of smooth, hard gravel, that afford as good, or better, wheeling than the finest macadam. While spinning at a highly satisfactory rate of speed along these splendid paths, a small herd of antelopes cross the road some few hundred yards ahead, and pass swiftly southward toward the *dasht-i-namek*. These are the first antelopes, or, for that matter, the first big game I have encountered since leaving the prairies of Western Nebraska. The Persian antelope seems to be a duplicate of his distinguished American relative in a general, all-round sense; he is, if anything, even more nimble-footed than the spring-heeled habitué of the West, possesses the same characteristic jerky jump, and hoists the same conspicuous white signal of retreat. He is a decidedly slimmer-built quadruped, however, than the American antelope; the body is of the same square build, but is sadly lacking in plumpness, and he seems to be an altogether lankier and less well-favored animal. For this constitutional difference, he is probably indebted to the barren and inhospitable character of the country over which he roams, as compared with the splendid feeding-grounds of the Far West. The Persians sometimes hunt the antelope on horseback, with falcons and greyhounds; the

Falconry in Persia.

falcons are taught to fly in advance and attack the fleeing antelopes about the head, and so confuse them and retard their progress in the interest of the pursuing hounds and horsemen.

The road now edges off in a more northeasterly course, and by four o'clock leads me to the base of a low pass over a jutting spur of the mountains. At the base of the spur, a cultivated area, consisting of several wheat-fields and terraced melon-gardens, has been rescued from the unproductive desert by the aid of a bright little mountain stream, whose wild spirit the villagers of Lasgird have curbed and tamed for their own benefit, by turning it from its rocky, precipitous channel, and causing it to descend the hill in a curious serpentine ditch. The contour of the ditch is something like this: ᵕᵕᵕᵕᵕᵕᵕᵕᵕ; it brings the water down a pretty steep gradient, and its serpentine form checks the speed of its descent to an uniform and circumspect pace. The road over the pass leads through a soft limestone formation, and here, as in similar places in Asia Minor, are found those narrow, trench-like trails, worn by the feet of pilgrims and the pack-animal traffic of centuries, several feet deep in the solid rock. On a broad cultivated plain beyond the pass is sighted the village of Lasgird, its huge mud fortress, the most conspicuous object in view, rising a hundred feet above the plain.

CHAPTER III

PERSIA AND THE MESHED PILGRIM ROAD

A mile or so through the cultivated fields brings me to the village just in time to be greeted by the shouts and hand-clapping of a wedding procession that is returning from conducting the bride to the bath. Men and boys are beating rude, home-made tambourines, and women are dancing along before the bride, clicking castanets, while a crowd of at least two hundred villagers, arrayed in whatever finery they can muster for the occasion, are following behind, clapping their hands in measured chorus. This hand-clapping is, I believe, pretty generally practised by the villagers all over Central Asia on festive occasions. As a result of riding for the crowd, I receive an invitation to take supper at the house of the bridegroom's parents.

Squatting on the floor, with their backs to the wall, about fifty villagers form a continuous human line around the room. These all rise simultaneously to their feet as I am announced, bob their heads simultaneously, simultaneously say, 'Sahib salaam,' and after I have been provided with a place, simultaneously resume their seats. Pewter trays are now brought in by volunteer waiters, and set on the floor before the guests, one tray for every two guests, and a separate one for myself. On each tray is a bowl of *mast* (milk soured with rennet – the 'yaort' of Asia Minor), a piece of cheese, one onion, a spoonful or two of pumpkin butter and several flat wheaten cakes. This is the wedding supper. The guests break the bread into the *mast* and scoop the mixture out with their fingers, transferring it to their mouths with the dexterity of Chinese manipulating a pair of chop-sticks; now and then they take a nibble at the piece of cheese or the onion, and they finish up by consuming the pumpkin butter. The groom doesn't appear among the guests; he is under the special care of several female relations in another apartment, and is probably being fed with tid-bits from the henna-stained fingers of old women, who season them with extravagant and lying stories of the bride's beauty, and duly impress upon him his coming matrimonial responsibilities.

Supper eaten and the dishes cleared, an amateur *luti* from among the villagers produces a tambourine and castanets, and, taking the middle of the room, proceeds to amuse the company by singing extempore love songs in praise of the bride and groom to tambourine accompaniment and pendulous swayings of the body. Pretending to be carried away by the melodiousness and sentiment of his own productions, he gradually bends backward with hands outstretched and castanets jingling, until his head almost touches the floor, and maintains that position while keeping his body in a theatrical tremor of delight.

Torchlight processions to the different baths are now made from the house of both bride and groom, for this is the 'hammam night,' devoted to bathing and festivities before the wedding-day. Torches are made with dry camel-thorn, the blaze being kept up by constant renewal; a boy, with a lighted candle, walks immediately ahead of the bridegroom and his female relations, and a man with a *farnooze* brings up the rear. Nobody among the onlookers is permitted to lag behind the man with the *farnooze*, everybody being required to either walk ahead or alongside. The tambourine-beating and shouting and hand-clapping of the afternoon is repeated, and every now and then the procession stops to allow one or two of the women to face the bridegroom and favor him with an exhibition of their skill in the execution of the hip-dance.

The bridal procession is coming down another street, and I stop to try and obtain a glimpse of the bride; but she is completely enveloped in a flaming red shawl, and is supported and led by two women. There seems to be little difference in the two processions, except the preponderance of females in the bride's party; everything is arranged in the same order, and women dance at intervals before the bride as before the groom.

It begins raining before I retire for the night; it rains incessantly all night, and is raining heavily when I awake in the morning. The weather clears up at noon, but it is useless thinking of pushing on, for miles of tenacious mud intervene between the village and the gravelly desert; moreover, the prospect of the fine weather holding out looks anything but reassuring. The villagers are all at home, owing to the saturated condition of their fields, and I come in for no small share of worrying attention during the afternoon. A pilgrim from Teheran turns up and tells the people about my appearance before the Shah; this increases their interest in me to an unappreciated extent, and, with glistening eyes and eagerly rubbing fingers, they ask 'Chand pool Padishah? (How much money did the King give you?) 'I showed the Shah the bicycle, and the Shah showed me the lions, and tigers, and panthers at Doshan Tepe,' I tell them; and a knowing customer, called Meshedi Ali, enlightens then still further by telling them I am not a luti to receive money for letting the Shah-in-Shah see me ride. Still, luti or no luti, the people think I ought to have received a present. I am worried to ride so incessantly that I am forced to seek self-protection in pretending to have sprained my ankle, and in returning to the chapar-khana with a hypocritical limp. I station myself ostensibly for the remainder of the day on the bala-khana front, and busy myself in taking observations of the villagers and their doings.

Returning to the chapar-khana, I get the shagird to pilot me into and round about the fortress. It is rapidly falling to decay, but is still in a sufficiently good state of preservation to show thoroughly its former strength and conformation. The fortress is a decidedly massive building, constructed entirely of mud and adobe bricks, a hundred feet high, of circular form, and some two hundred yards in circumference. The disintegrated walls and débris of former towers form a sloping mound or foundation about fifty feet in height, and from this the perpendicular walls of the castle rise up, huge and ugly, for another hundred feet. Following a foot-trail up the mound-like base, we come to a low, gloomy passage-way leading into the interior of the fort. A door, composed of one massive stone slab, that nothing less than a cannon-shot would shatter, guards the entrance to this passage, which is the only accessible entrance to the place. Following it along for perhaps thirty yards, we emerge upon a scene of almost indescribable squalor – a scene that instantly suggests an overcrowded 'rookery' in the tenement-house slums of New York.

The inhabitants are ragged and picturesque, and meandering about among them, on the most familiar terms, are hundreds of goats. Although everything is in a more or less dilapidated condition, huts or cells still rise above each other in tiers, and the people clamber about from tier to tier, as if in emulation of their venturesome four-footed associates, who are here, we may well imagine, in as perfect a paradise as vagrom goatish nature would care for or expect. At a low estimate, I should place the present population of the old fortress at a thousand people, and about the same number of goats. In the days when the bold Turkoman raiders were wont to make their dreaded *alamans* almost up to the walls of Teheran, and such strongholds as this were the only safeguard of out-lying villagers, the interior of Lasgird fortress resembled a spacious amphitheatre, around which hundreds of huts rose, tier above tier, like the cells of a monster pigeon-house, affording shelter in times of peril to all the inhabitants of Lasgird, and to such refugees as might come in. At the first alarm of the dreaded man-stealers' approach, the outside villagers repaired to the fortress with their portable property; the donkeys and goats were driven inside and occupied the interior space, and the massive stone door was closed and barricaded. The villagers' granaries were inside the fortress, and provisions for obtaining water were not over-looked; so that once inside, the people were quite secure against any force of Turkomans, whose heaviest arms were muskets.

The suggestion of an amphitheatre, as above described, is quite patent at the present day, in something like two or three hundred tiered dwellings; in the days of its usefulness there must have been a thousand. Thanks to the Russian occupation of Turkestan, there is no longer any need of the fortress, and the present population seem to be occupying it at the peril of having it some day tumble down about their ears; for, massive though its walls most certainly are, they are but mud, and the people are indifferent about repairs. Failing to surprise the watchful villagers in their fields or outside dwellings, the baffled marauders would find confronting them fifty feet of solid mud wall without so much as an air-hole in it, rising sheer above the mound-like foundation, and above this, tiers of rooms or cells, from inside which archers or musketeers could make it decidedly interesting for any hostile party attempting to approach. This old fortress of Lasgird is very interesting, as showing the peaceful and unwarlike Persian ryot's method of defending his life and liberty against the savage human hawks that were ever hovering near, ready to swoop down and carry him and his off to the slave markets of Khiva and Bokhara.

*   *   *

Prince Anushirvan Mirza, Governor of Semnoon, Damghan, and Shahrood, is the Shah's cousin, son of Baahman Mirza, uncle of the Shah, and formerly Governor of Tabreez.

During the evening one of the Governor's sons, Prince Sultan Madjid Mirza, comes in with a few leading dignitaries to spend an hour in chatting and smoking. This young prince proves one of the most intelligent Persians I have met in the country; besides being very well informed for a provincial Persian, he is bright and quick-witted. Among the gentlemen he brings in with him is a man who has made the pilgrimage to Mecca *via* 'Iskenderi' (Alexandria) and Suez, and has, consequently, seen and ridden on the Egyptian railway. The Prince has heard his description of this railway, and the light thus gained has not unnaturally had the effect of whetting his curiosity to hear more of the marvellous iron roads of Frangistan; and after exhausting the usual programme of queries concerning cycling, the conversation leads, by easy transition, to the subject of railways.

'Do they have railways in Yenghi Donia?' questioned the Prince.

'Plenty of railways; plenty of everything,' I reply.

'Like the one at Iskenderi and Stamboul?'

'Better and bigger than both these put together a hundred times over; the Iskenderi railroad is very small.'

Nods and smiles of acquiescence from Prince and listeners follow this statement, which show plainly enough that they consider it a pardonable lie, such as every Persian present habitually indulges in himself and thinks favorably of in others.

'Railroads are good things, and Ferenghis are very clever people,' says the Prince, renewing the subject and handing me a handful of salted melon seeds from his pocket, meanwhile nibbling some himself.

'Yes; why don't you have railroads in Iran? You could then go to Teheran in a few hours.'

The Prince smiles amusingly at the thought, as though conscious of railroads in Persia being a dream, altogether too bright to ever materialize, and shaking his head, says: '*Pool neis*' (we have no money).

'The English have money and would build the railroad; but, "Mollah neis" – Baron Reuter? – you know Baron Reuter– "Mollah neis," not "pool neis."'

The Prince smiles, and signifies that he is well enough aware where the trouble lies; but we talk no more of railroads, for he and his father and brothers belong to the party of progress in Persia, and the triumph of priests and old women over the Shah and Baron Reuter's railway is to them a distressful and humiliating subject.

The morning breaks cold and clear, and for some six miles the road is very fair wheeling; after this comes a gradual inclination toward a jutting spur of hills; the following twenty miles being the toughest kind of a trundle through mud, snow-fields, and drifts. This is a most uninviting piece of country to wheel through, and it would seem but little less so to traverse at this time of the year with a caravan of camels, two or three of these animals being found exhausted by the roadside, and a couple of *charvadars* encountered in one place skinning another, while its companion is lying helplessly alongside watching the operation and waiting its own turn to the same treatment. It is said to be characteristic of a camel that, when he once slips down, cold and weary, in the mud, he never again tries to regain his feet. The weather looks squally and unsettled, and I push ahead as rapidly as the condition of the ground will permit, fearing a snow-storm in the hills.

Shelter, and the usual rude accommodation, supplemented on this occasion by a wandering *luti* and his vicious-looking baboon, as also a company of riotous *charvadars*, who insist on singing accompaniments to the *luti*'s soul-harrowing tom-toming till after midnight, are obtained at the caravanserai of Deh Mollah. From Deh Mollah it is only a couple of farsakhs to Shahrood, and after the first three miles, which is slightly upgrade and not particularly smooth, it is down-grade and very fair wheeling the remainder of the distance. The road forks a

Skinning Dead Camels.

couple of miles from Shahrood, and while I am entering by one road, Mr. McIntyre is leaving on horseback by the other to meet me, guessing, from word received from Damghan, that I must have spent last night at Deh Mollah, and would arrive at Shahrood this morning.

Only those who have experienced it know anything of the pleasure of two Europeans meeting and conversing in a country like Persia, where the habits and customs of the natives are so different, and, to most travellers, uncongenial, and only to be tolerated for a time.

I have met Mr. McIntyre in Teheran, so we are not total strangers, which, of course, makes it still more agreeable. After the customary interchange of news, and the discussion of refreshments, Mr. McIntyre hands me a telegram from Teheran, which bears a date several days old. It is from the British Legation, notifying me that permission is refused to go

A Pleasant Anticipation.

through the Turcoman country; an appendage from the Chargé
d'Affaires suggests that I repair to Astrakhan and try the route
through Siberia. And this, then, is the result of General
Melnikoff's genial smiles and ready promises of assistance; after
providing myself with proper money and information for the
Turkestan route, on the strength of the Russian Minister's
promises, I am overtaken, when three hundred miles away, with
a veto against which anything I might say or do would be to no
avail!

Sultan Ahmed Mirza, a son of Prince Anushirvan, is deputy
governor of Shahrood, responsible to his father; and ere I have
arrived an hour the usual request is sent round for a '*tomasha,*'
the word now used by people wanting to see me ride, and which
really means an exhibition. His place is found in a brick
courtyard with the usual central tank, and the airy rooms of the
building all opening upon it, and once again comes the feeling of
playing a rather ridiculous rôle, as I circle awkwardly around
the tank over very uneven bricks, and around short corners
where an upset would precipitate me into the tank – amid, I

can't help thinking, 'roars of laughter.' The Prince is very lavish of his flowery Persian compliments, and says, 'You English have now left nothing more to do but to bring the dead back to life.' In the court-yard my attention is called to a set of bastinado poles and loops, and Mr. McIntyre asks the Prince if he hasn't a prisoner on hand, so that he can give us a *tomasha* in return for the one we are giving him; but it is now the Persian New Year, and the prisoners have all been liberated.

CHAPTER IV

THROUGH KHORASSAN

Shahrood is, or rather was, one of the 'four stations of terror,' Mijamid, Miandasht, and Abassabad being the other three, so called on account of their exposed position and the consequent frequency of Turcoman attacks. Even nowadays they have their little ripples of excitement; rumors of Turcoman raids are heard in the bazaars, and news was brought in and telegraphed to Teheran a week ago that fifteen thousand sheep had been carried off from a district north of the mountains. Word comes back that a regiment of soldiers is on its way to chastise the Turcomans and recover the property; what really will happen, will be a horde of soldiers staying there long enough to devour what few sheep the poor people have left, and then returning without having seen, much less chastised, a Turcoman. The Persian Government will notify the Russian Minister of the misdoings of the Turcomans, and ask to have them punished and the sheep restored; the Russian Minister will reply that these particular Turcomans were Persian subjects, and nothing further will be done.

I accept Mr. McIntyre's invitation to remain and rest up, but only for another day, my experience being that, when on the road, one or two day's rest is preferable to a longer period; one gets rested without getting out of condition. We take a stroll through the bazaar in the morning, and call in at the wine-shop of a Russian-Armenian trader named Makerditch, who keeps arrack and native wine, and sample some of the latter. In his shop is a badly stuffed Mazanderan tiger, and the walls of the private sitting-room are decorated with rude, old-fashioned prints of saints and scriptural scenes. It is now the Persian New Year, and bright new garments and snowy turbans impart a gay appearance to the throngs in the bazaar, for everybody changed his wardrobe from tip to toe on *eid-i-noo-roos* (evening before

New Year's Day), although the 'great unwashed' of Persian society change never a garment for the next twelve months. Considering that the average lower-class Persian puts in a good share of this twelve months in the unprofitable process of scratching himself, one would think it must be an immense relief for him to cast away these old habiliments with all their horrid load of filth and vermin, and don a clean, new outfit; but the new ones soon get as thickly tenanted as the old; and many even put the new garments on over certain of the old ones, caring nothing for comfort and cleanliness, and everything for appearance. The Persian New Year's holiday lasts thirteen days, and on the evening of the thirteenth day everybody goes out into the fields and plucks flowers and grasses to present to his or her friends.

Governors of provinces who retain their position in consequence of having sent satisfactory tribute to the Shah, and ruled with at least a semblance of justice, get presents of new robes on New Year's Day, and those who have been unfortunate enough to lose the royal favor get removed: New Year's Day brings either sorrow or rejoicing to every Persian official's house.

The morning of my departure opens bright and warm after a thunder-storm the previous evening, and Mr. McIntyre accompanies me to the outskirts of the city, to put me on the right road to Mijamid, my objective point for the day, eleven farsakhs distant.

The road has averaged good to-day, and Mijamid is reached at four o'clock. Seeking the shelter of the *chapar-khana*, that devoted building is soon surrounded by a new-dressed and accordingly a good-natured and vociferous crowd shouting – '*Sowar shuk! sowar shuk! tomasha! tomasha!*'

As I survey the grinning, shouting multitude from my retreat on the roof, and note the number of widely-opened mouths, the old wicked thoughts about hot potatoes and dexterity in throwing them persist in coming to the fore. Several scrimmages and quarrels occur between the *chapar-jee* and his *shagirds*, and the crowd, who persist in invading the premises, and the tumult around is something deafening, for it is holiday times and the people feel particularly self-indulgent and disinclined for self-denial. In the midst of the uproar, from out the chaotic mass of rainbow-colored costumes, there forms a little knot of mollahs in huge snowy turbans and flowing gowns of solid blue or green, and at their head the gray-bearded patriarchal-looking old khan of the village in his flowered robe of office from the governor. These gay-looking, but comparatively sober-sided representatives of the village, endeavor to have the crowd cease their clamorous importunities – an attempt, however, that results in signal failure – and they constitute themselves a delegation to approach me in a respectful and decorous manner, and ask me to ride for the satisfaction of themselves and the people.

The profound salaams and good taste of these eminently respectable personages are not to be resisted, and after satisfying them, the khan promises to provide me with supper, which at a later hour turns up in the form of the inevitable dish of *pillau*.

Miandasht is the first place in Khorassan proper, and among the motley gathering of *charvadars*, camel-drivers, pilgrims, travellers, villagers and hangers-on about the serai, are many Khorassanis wearing huge sheepskin busbies, similar to the head-gear of the Roumanians and Tabreez Turks of Ovahjik and the Perso-Turkish border. Most of these busbies are black or brown, but some affect a mixture of black and white, a piebald affair that looks very striking and peculiar.

The *shagird-chapar* here is a man who has been to Askabad and seen the railroad; and when the inevitable question of Russian *versus* English *marifet* (mechanical skill) comes up, he endeavors to impress upon the open-mouthed listeners the marvellous character of the locomotive. 'It is a wonderful *atesh-gharri*' (fire-wagon), he would say, 'and runs on an *awhan rah* (iron road); the *charvadar* puts in *atesh* and *ob*. It goes chu, chu! chu!! ch-ch-ch-chu-ch-u-u-u!!! spits fire and smoke, pulls a long – khylie long – caravan of *forgons* with it, and goes ten farsakhs an hour.' But in order to thoroughly appreciate this travelled and highly enlightened person's narrative, one must have been present in the smoke-permeated room, and by the flickering light of a camel-thorn fire have watched the gesticulations of the speaker and the rapt attention of the listeners; must have heard the exclamations of 'Mashal-l-a-h!' escape honestly and involuntarily from the parted lips of wonder-stricken auditors

At Miandasht.

as they endeavored to comprehend how such things could
possibly be. And yet there is no doubt that, five minutes
afterward, the verdict of each listener, to himself, was that the
shagird-chapar, in describing to them the locomotive, was lying
like a pirate – or a Persian – and, after all, they couldn't conceive
of anything more wonderful than the bicycle and the ability to
ride it, and this they had seen with their own eyes.

Six farsakhs bring me to Abbasabad, the last of the four
stations of terror. A lank villager is on the lookout a couple of
miles west of the place, the people have been apprised of my
coming by some travellers who left Miandasht yesterday
evening. Tucking the legs of his pantaloons in his waistband,
leaving his legs bare and unencumbered, he follows me at a
swinging trot into the village, and pilots me to the caravanserai.
The population of the place are found occupying their
housetops, and whatever points of vantage they can climb to,
awaiting my appearance, their curiosity having been wrought to
the highest pitch by their informant's highly exaggerated
accounts of what they might expect to see. The prevailing color
of the female costume is bright red, and the swarms of these

gaily-dressed people congregated on the housetops, and mingled promiscuously with the dark gray of the mud walls and domes, makes a picture long to be remembered.

And long also to be remembered is the reception awaiting me inside the caravanserai yard – the surging, pushing, struggling, shouting mob, among whom I notice, with some wonderment and speculation, a far larger proportion of blue-eyed people than I have hitherto seen in Persia. Upon inquiry it is learned that Abbasabad is a colony of Georgians, planted and subsidized here by Shah Abbas the Great, as a check on the Turkomans, whose frequent *alamans* rendered the roads hereabout wellnigh impassable for caravans. These warlike mountaineers were brought from the Caucasus and colonized here, with lands, exemption from taxes, and given an annual subsidy. They were found to be of good service as a check on the Turkomans, but were not much of an improvement upon the Turkomans themselves in many respects. As seen in the caravanserai to-day, they seem a turbulent, headstrong crowd of people, accustomed to be petted, and to do pretty much as they please.

Beyond Abbasabad my road skirts Mazinan Lake to the north, passing between the slimy mud-flats of the lake shore and the ever-present Elburz foot-hills, and then through several wholly ruined or partially ruined villages to Mazinan, where I arrive about sunset, my wheel yet again a mass of mud, for the Mazinan lake country is a muddy hole in spring. A drizzling rain ushers in the dusky shades of the evening, as I repair to the *chapar-khana*, a wretched hole, in a most dilapidated condition. The *bala-khana* is little better than being out of doors; the roof leaks like a colander, the windows are mere unglazed holes in the wall, and the doors are but little better than the windows. It promises to be a cold, draughty, comfortless night, and the prospects for supper look gloomy enough in the light of smoky camel-thorn and no samovar to make a cup of tea.

Such is the cheerless prospect confronting me after a hard day's run, when, soon after dark, a man arrives with a thrice-welcome invitation from a Russian officer, who he says is staying at the caravanserai. The officer, he says, has *pillau*, kabobs, wine, plenty of everything, and would be glad if I would bring my machine and come and accept his hospitality for the night. Under the circumstances nothing could be more welcome news than this; and picturing to myself a pleasant evening with a genial, hospitable gentleman, I take the bicycle down the slippery and broken mud stairway, and follow my guide through drizzling rain and darkness, over ditches and through miry byways, to the caravanserai.

The officer is found squatting, Asiatic-like, on his *menzil* floor, his overcoat over his shoulders. He is watching his cook broiling kabobs for his supper. It is a cheery, hopeful prospect, the glowing charcoal fire sparkling in response to the vigorous waving of half a saddle-flap, the savory, sizzling kabobs and the carpeted *menzil*, in comparison with the dreary tumble-down place I have just left. My first impression of the officer himself, however, is scarcely so favorable as my impression of the picture in which he is set – the picture as just described; a sinister leer characterizes the expression of his face, and what appears like a nod, with an altogether unnecessary amount of condescension in it, characterizes his greeting. Hopping down to the ground, lamp in hand, he examines the bicycle minutely, and then indirectly addressing the by-standers, he says, 'Pooh! this thing was made in Tiflis; there's hundreds of them in Tiflis.' Having delivered himself of this lying statement, he hops up on the *menzil* front again and, without paying the slightest attention to me, resumes his squatting position at the fire, and his occupation of watching the preparations of his cook. Nothing is more evident to me than that he had never before seen a bicycle, and astounded at this conduct on the part of an officer who doubtless thinks himself a civilized being, even though he might not understand anything of our own conception of an 'officer and a gentleman,' I begin looking around for an explanation from the fellow who brought me the invitation, thinking there must be some mistake. The man has disappeared and is nowhere to be found.

The *chapar-jee* accompanied us to the caravanserai, and seeing that this man has bolted, and that the Russian officer's intentions toward me are anything but hospitable, he calls the missing man – or the officer, I don't know which – a *pedar suktar* (son of a burnt father), and suggests returning to the cold comfort of the *bala-khana*. My own feelings upon realizing that this wretched, unscrupulous Muscovite has craftily designed and executed this plan for no other purpose but to insult and humiliate one whom he took for granted to be an Englishman, in the eyes of the Persian travellers present, I prefer to pass over and leave to the reader's imagination. After sleeping on it and thinking it over, early next morning I returned to the caravanserai, bent on finding the fellow who brought the invitation, giving him a thrashing, and seeing if the officer would take it up in his behalf. In the morning, the cossacks said he had gone away; whether gone away or hiding somewhere in the caravanserai, he was nowhere to be found; which perhaps was just as well, for the affair might have ended in bloodshed, and in a fight the chances would have been decidedly against myself.

This incident, disagreeable though it be to think of, is instructive as showing the possibilities for mean and contemptible action that may lurk beneath the uniform of a Russian officer. Russian officers as a general thing, however, it is but fair to add, would show up precisely the reverse of this fellow, under similar circumstances, being genial and hospitable to a fault; still, I venture that in no other army in the world, reckoning itself civilized, could be found even one officer capable of displaying just such a spirit as this.

A late luncheon of bread, warm from the oven, is obtained at the village of Lafaram, where I likewise obtain a peep behind the scenes of every-day village life, and see something of their mode of baking bread. The walled village of Lafaram presents a picture of manure heaps, holes of filthy water, mud-hovels, naked, sore eyed youngsters, unkempt, unwashed, bedraggled females, goats, chickens, and all the unsavory elements that enter into the composition of a wretched, semi-civilized community. With bare, uncombed heads, bare-armed, bare-breasted, and bare-limbed, and with their nakedness scarcely hidden beneath a few coarse rags, some of the women are engaged in making and baking bread, and others in the preparation of *tezek* from cow manure and chopped straw. In carrying on these two occupations the women mingle, chat, and help each other with happy-go-lucky indifference to consequences, and with a breezy unconsciousness of there being anything repulsive about the idea of handling hot cakes with one hand and *tezek* with the other. The ovens are huge jars partially sunk in the ground; fire is made inside and the jar heated; flat cakes of dough are then stuck in the inside of the jar, a few minutes sufficing for the baking. The hand and arm the woman inserts inside the heated jar is wrapped with old rags and frequently dipped in a jar of water standing by to keep it cooled; the bread thus baked tastes very good when fresh, but it requires a stomach rendered unsqueamish by dire necessity to relish it after seeing it baked.

The plain beyond Lafaram assumes the character of an acclivity, that in four farsakhs terminates in a pass through a spur of hills. The adverse wind blows furiously all day and shows no signs of abating as the dusk of evening settles down over the landscape. A wayside caravanserai is reached at the entrance to the pass, and I determine to remain till morning. Here I meet with a piece of good fortune in a small way, in the shape of a leg of wild goat, obtained from a native Nimrod; a thin rod of iron, obtained from the *serai-jee*, serves for a skewer, and I spend the evening in roasting and eating wild-goat kabobs, while a youth fans the little charcoal fire for me with the sole of an old geiveh.

CHAPTER V

MESHED THE HOLY

Favored with good roads, I succeed in reaching Gadamgah before dark, where, besides a comfortable and commodious caravanserai, and the pleasure of seeing around a number of fine-spreading cedars, one can obtain the rare luxury of pine-wood to build a fire.

Immediately upon my arrival a knowing and respectable-looking old pilgrim, who calls himself a hadji and a dervish from Mazanderan, rescues me from the annoying importunities of the people and invites me to share the accommodation of his *menzil.* Augmenting his scanty stock of firewood and obtaining eggs and bread, quite a comfortable evening is spent in reclining beside the blazing pine-wood fire, which is itself no trifling luxury in a country of scanty camel-thorn and *tezek.*

It is genuine wintry weather, and with no bedclothes, save a narrow horse-blanket borrowed from my impromptu friend, I spend a cold, uncomfortable night, for a caravanserai *menzil* is but a mere place of shelter after all. The hadji rises early and replenishes the fire, and with his little brass teapot we make and drink a glass of tea together before starting out.

At daybreak the hadji goes outside to take a preliminary peep at the weather, and returns with the unwelcome intelligence that it is snowing.

'Better snow than rain,' I conclude, as I prepare to start, little thinking that I am entering upon the toughest day's experience of the whole journey through Persia.

Before covering three miles, the snow-storm develops into a regular blizzard; a furious, driving storm that would do credit to Dakota. Without gloves, and in summer clothes throughout, I quickly find myself in a most unenviable plight. It is no common snow-storm; every few minutes a halt has to be made, hands buffeted and ears rubbed to prevent these members from freezing; yet foot-gear has to be removed and streams waded in the bitter cold.

The road leads up into a region of broken hills, and the climax of my discomfort is reached, when the blizzard is raging with ever-increasing fury, and the cold has already slightly nipped one finger. While attempting to cross a deep, narrow stream without disrobing, it is my unhappy fate to drop the bicycle into the water, and furthermore to front the necessity of instantly plunging in, armpit deep, to its rescue. When I emerge upon the opposite bank my situation is really quite critical; in a few moments my garments are frozen stiff; everything I have with me is wet; my leathern case, containing the small stock of medicines, matches, writing material, and other small but necessary articles, is full of water, and, with hands benumbed, I am unable to unstrap it.

My only salvation consists in vigorous exercise, and, conscious of this, I splurge ahead through the blinding storm and the fast-deepening snow, fording several other streams, often emerging dripping from the icy water to struggle through waist-deep snow-drifts that are rapidly accumulating under the influence of the driving blast and fast-falling snow. Uncertain of the distance to the next caravanserai, I push determinedly forward in this condition for several hours, making but slow progress. Everything must come to an end, however, and twenty miles from Gadamgah the welcome outlines of a road-side caravanserai become visible through the thickly falling snow-flakes, and the din of many jangling camel-bells proclaims it already occupied.

Leaving the bicycle outside in the snow, I clamber over the humpy forms of kneeling camels, through an intricate maze of mules and over barricades of miscellaneous merchandise, and, making a virtue of dire necessity, invade the *menzil* of a well-to-do looking traveller. Here, waiving all considerations of whether my presence is acceptable or the reverse, I take a seat beside their fire and forthwith proceed to shed my saturated foot-gear. Under ordinary conditions this proceeding would be nothing less than a piece of sublime assurance; but necessity knows no law, and my case is really very urgent. When I explain to the occupants of the *menzil* that this *nolens volens* invasion of their premises is but a temporary arrangement, in the flowery language of polite Persian they tell me that the *menzil*, the fire, and everything they have is mine.

After the inevitable examination of my map, compass, and sundry effects, I begin to fancy my presence something of an embarrassment, and consequently am not a little gratified at hearing the authoritative voice of my friend the hadji shouting loudly at the *charvadars*, telling them that he is a hadji and a Mazanderan dervish, for whom they cannot clear the way too quickly. Looking round, I see him appear at the caravanserai entrance with a party of pilgrims, in whose company he has journeyed from Gadamgah.

Hearing of my arrival, he straightway seeks me out and invites me to share the accommodation of his new-found quarters, not forgetting to explain to the people he finds me with, however, that he is a hadji, a dervish, and that he hails from Mazanderan.

The snow-storm subsides during the night, and a clear, frosty morning breaks upon a wintry landscape, in which nothing is visible but snow. The hadji announces his intention of '*Inshallah Meshed, am roos*' (please God, we will reach Meshed to-day) as he covers up the obtrusive tail of a fish emerging from one of the saddle-bags and prepares to mount. I give him my packages to carry, by way of lightening my burden as much as possible for the struggle through the snow, and promise him a bottle of arrack, upon reaching Meshed, as a reward for thus assisting me through. Arrack is forbidden fruit to a hadji above all things else, so that nothing I could promise him would likely prove more tempting or acceptable, or be better appreciated!

It proves slavish work trundling, tugging, and carrying the bicycle through the deep snow along a half-broken trail made by a few horses, and through deep drifts; but the cold, bracing air is favorable for exertion, and by ten o'clock we reach Shahriffabad, where a halt is made to prepare a cup of tea and to give the hadji's horse a feed of barley.

The sun has by this time become uncomfortably warm, and the narrow trail is fast becoming a miry pathway of mud and slush under the trampling feet of the animals gone ahead, and of villagers' donkeys returning from the city. Mile after mile is devoted to the unhappy task of trundling the bicycle ahead, rear wheel aloft, through mud and slush varying from ankle deep to worse, occasionally varying the programme by fording a stream.

The late storm has been chiefly rain in the lower altitude of the plain, and the day's sunshine has partially dried the surface, but leaving it slippery and treacherous here and there. After leaving the bed of the stream the hadji becomes anxious about reaching Meshed before dark, and advises me to mount and put on the speed.

'*Inshallah, Meshed yek saat*,' he says, and so I mount and bid him follow along behind. By vocal suasion and a liberal application of his cruel, triple-thonged, raw-hide whip, he urges his well-nigh staggering animal into a canter, lifting his forefeet clear of the ground seemingly by the bridle at every jump. Suspicious as to his lank and angular steed's sure-footedness under the strain, I take the very laudable precaution of keeping as far from him as possible, not caring to get mixed up in a catastrophe that seems inevitable every time the horse, goaded by the stinging stimulus of the whip and the threats, makes another jump. Not more than a mile of the six is covered when I have ample reason for congratulating myself on taking this precaution, for the horse stumbles, and, being too far gone to

The Hadji takes a Header.

recover himself, comes down on his nose, and the 'hadji and Mazanderan dervish' is cutting a most ridiculous figure in the mud. His tall lambskin hat flies off and lands in a pool of muddy water some distance ahead; the ponderous saddle-bags, which are merely laid on the saddle, shoot forward athwart the horse's neck, the horse's nose roots quite a furrow in the road, and the horse's owner picks himself up and takes a woeful survey of his own figure. It is needless to say that the survey includes a good deal more real estate than the hadji cares to claim, even though it be the semi sacred soil of the Meshed Plain.

The poor horse is altogether too tired to attempt to recover his legs of his own inclination; but, regarding him as the author of his ignominious misadventure, the hadji surveys him with a wrathful eye for a moment, mutters a few awful imprecations – imported, no doubt, from Mazanderan – and then attacks him savagely about the head with the whip. In his wrath and determination to make a lasting impression of each blow given, the hadji emphasizes each visitation with a very audible grunt; and, to speak correctly, so does the horse.

At length, by adopting a more circumspect pace, we reach the gate of the holy city about sunset without further mishap. The hadji leads the way through a bewildering labyrinth of narrow streets that consist of an open sewage-ditch in the centre, at present full of filth, and a narrow footway of rough, broken, and mud-bespattered cobble-stones on either side. Of course we are followed through these fearful thoroughfares by a surging and vociferous crowd of people such as a Central Asian city alone can produce; but I can this time happily afford to smile at these usually irritating accompaniments to my arrival in a populous city, for ten minutes after entering the gate finds me shaking hands with Mr. Gray, the genial telegraphist of the Afghan Boundary Commission. With a well-guarded gate between our cosey quarters and the shouting mob outside, the evening is spent very pleasantly and quietly, in striking comparison with what it would have been had no one been here to afford me a place of refuge.

Meshed is 'the jumping off place' of telegraphy; the electric spider spins his galvanized web no farther in this direction, and the dirge-like music of civilization's Æolian harp, that, like the roll of England's drum, is heard around the world, approaches the barbarous territory of Afghanistan from two directions, but recoils from entering that fanatical and conservative domain. It approaches from Persia on the one side, and from India on the other; but as yet it only approaches. The drum has already been there; it is only a question of time when the Æolian harp will follow.

Upon receipt of the telegram at Shahrood refusing me permission to go through Turkestan, I telegraphed to Mr. Gray, requesting him to obtain leave for me to go to the Boundary Commission Camp, and accompany them back to India; or reach India from the camp alone. Mr. Gray kindly forwarded my request to the camp, and now urges me to consider myself his guest until the return courier arrives with the answer.

Our most distinguished caller to-day is Mirza Abbas Khan, C. I. E., a Kandahari gentleman, who has been the British political agent at Meshed for many years. He makes a formal call in all the glory of his official garments, a magnificent Cashmere coat lined with Russian sable and profusely trimmed with gold braid; a servant leads his gayly caparisoned horse, and another brings up the rear with a richly mounted kalian.

Abbas Khan is perhaps the handsomest man in Meshed, is in the prime of life, dyes his flowing beard an orthodox red, and possesses most charming manners; in addition to his ample salary he owns the revenue of a village near Meshed, and seems to be altogether the right man in the right place.

Abbas Khan and a friend of his from Herat both agree that the difficulties and dangers of Afghanistan will be likely to prove insurmountable; at the same time promising any assistance they can render me in getting to India, consistent, of course, with Abbas Khan's duties as British Agent.

Meshed is a strange city for a Ferenghi to live in; every day are heard the chanting and singing of newly arriving bands of pilgrims, the strange, wild utterances of dervishes preaching on the streets, and the shouting responses of their auditors. Conspicuous above everything else in the city, as gold is conspicuous from dross, is the golden dome and gold-tipped minarets of the holy edifice that imparts to the city its sacred character. The gold is in thin plates covering the hemispherical roof like sheets of tin; like most Eastern things, its appearance is more impressive from a distance than at close quarters.

The two most important persons in Meshed are the acting Governor-General of Khorassan, and Mardan Khan, Ex-Governor of Sarakhs and Hereditary Chief of the powerful tribe of Timurees. Of course, the Governor sends his salaams, and invites me to come round to the government konak and favor him with an exhibition.

There is nothing particularly interesting about the Governor's apartments, but Mardan Khan's palace is a revelation of barbaric splendor entirely different from anything hitherto seen in the country. In contradistinction to the dazzling, silvery glitter of the mirror-work and stuccoed halls of the Teheran palaces, the home of the wealthy Timurec Chieftain is distinguished by a striking and lavish display of colored glass, gilt, and tinsel.

The scene in this room is an ideal picture of the popular occidental conception of the 'gorgeous East.' Abbas Khan and

The Tomasha at Mardan Khan's.

Mardan Khan sit cross-legged side by side on a rich Turcoman rug, salaaming and exchanging compliments after the customary flowery and extravagant language of the Persian nobility. The marvellous pattern and costly texture of Abbas Khan's coat, the gold braid, the Russian sable lining, and the black Astrakhan cylinder he wears, are precisely matched by the garments of Mardan Khan. Twenty or thirty of the most important dignitaries and mollahs of the city are ranged according to their respective rank or degree of holiness around the room; prominent among them is the Chief Imam of Meshed, a very important and influential person in the holy city.

The Chief Imam is a slim-built, sharp-looking individual of about forty summers, with a face pale, refined, and intellectual; hands white and slender as a lady's, and a foot equally shapely and feminine. He wears a monster green turban, takes his turn regularly at the kalian, and passes it on to the next with the easy gracefulness that comes of good breeding; and by his manners and appearance he creates an impression of being a person rather superior to his surroundings.

Liveried pages pass around little glasses of tea, kalians, cigarettes, and sweetmeats, as well as tiny bottles of lemon-juice and rose-water, a few drops of these two last-named articles being used by some of the guests to impart a fanciful flavor to their tea. Now and then a new guest arrives, steps out of his shoes in the hallway, salaams, and takes his proper position among the people already here. Everybody sits on the carpet except me, for whom a three-legged camp-stool has been thoughtfully provided.

Finally, all the guests having arrived, I ride several times around the brick-walks, the strange audience of turbaned priests and veiled women showing their great approval in murmuring undertones of 'kylie khoob' and involuntary acclamations of 'Mashallah! mash-all-ah!' as they witness with bated breath the strange and incomprehensible scene of a Ferenghi riding a vehicle that will not stand alone.

Altogether, the great tomasha at Mardan Khan's is a decided success. Scarely can this be said, however, of the 'little tomasha' given to the members of Abbas Khan's own family on the way home. Abbas Khan's compound is very small, and the brick-walks very rough and broken; therefore, it is hardly surprising to me, though probably somewhat surprising to him, when, in turning a corner I execute an undignified header into a bunch of rose-bushes.

The third day after my arrival in Meshed, I received a telegram from the British Chargé d'Affaires at Teheran saying: 'You must not attempt to cross the frontier of Afghanistan at any point.' Two days later the expected courier arrives from the Boundary Commission Camp with a letter saying: 'It is useless for you to raise the question of coming to the Commission Camp. In the first place, the Afghans would never allow you to come here; and if you should happen to reach here, you would never be able to get away again.'

These two very encouraging missives from our own people seem at first thought more heartless than even the 'permission refused' of the Russians. It occurs to me that this 'you must not attempt to cross the Afghan frontier' might just as easily have been told me at the Legation at Teheran as when I had travelled six hundred miles to get to it; but the ways of diplomacy are past the comprehension of ordinary mortals.

Mr. Gray, returning from the telegraph office later in the evening, finds me endeavoring to unravel the Gordian knot of the situation through the medium of a brown-study. My geographical ruminations have already resulted in a conviction that there is no possible way to unravel it and reach India with a bicycle; my only chance of doing so is to cut it and abide by the consequences.

'I have just been communicating with Teheran,' says Mr. Gray. 'Everybody wants to know what you propose doing.'

'Tell them I am going down to Beerjand to consult with Heshmet-i-Molk, the Ameer of Seistan, and see if it is possible to get through to Quetta via Beerjand.'

'Ever hear of Dadur?' queries Mr. Gray. 'Ever hear of Dadur, the place of which the Persians tritely say: "Seeing that there is Dadur, why did Allah, then, make the infernal regions?" That is somewhere in Beloochistan. You'll find yourself slowly broiling to death on a geographical gridiron if you attempt to reach India down that way.'

'Never mind; tell them at Teheran I am going that way anyhow.'

Having entered upon this decision, I bid my genial host

farewell on April 7th, and mounting at the door, depart in the presence of a well-behaved crowd of spectators. In my pocket is a general letter from the Governor-General of Khorassan to subordinate officials of the province, ordering them to tender me any assistance I may require, and another from a prominent person in Meshed to his friend Heshmet-i-Molk, the Ameer of Kain and Governor of Seistan, a powerful and influential chief, with his seat of government at Beerjand.

Couched in the sentimental language of the country, one of these letters concludes with the touching remark: 'The Sahib, of his own choice is travelling like a dervish, with no protection but the protection of Allah.'

CHAPTER VI

THE UNBEATEN TRACKS OF KHORASSAN

During the afternoon I traverse a rocky cañon, crossing and recrossing a clear, cold stream that winds its serpentine course from one precipitous wall to another. Mountain trout are observed disporting in this stream, and big, gray lizards scuttle nimbly about among the loose rocks on the bank. The cañon gradually dwindles into a less confined passage between sloping hills of loose rock and bowlders, a wild, desolate region through which the road leads gradually upward to a pass.

Part way up this gorge is a rude stone tower about twenty feet high, on the summit of which is perched a little mud hut, looking almost as though it might be a sentry-box. While yet a couple of hundred yards away, a rough-looking customer emerges from the tower and appears to be awaiting my approach. His head is well-nigh hidden beneath a huge Khorassani busby, and he wears the clothes of an irregular soldier. The long, shaggy wool of the sheepskin head-dress dangling over his eyes imparts a very ferocious appearance, and he is armed with the ordinary Persian sword and one of those antiquated flint-lock muskets that are only to be seen on the deserts of the East or in museums of ancient weapons.

Taken all in all, he presents a very ferocious front; he is, in fact, about the most ruffianly-looking specimen I have seen outside of Asiatic Turkey. As I ride up he motions for me to alight, at the same time retreating a few steps toward his humble stronghold, betraying a spirit of apprehension lest, perchance, he might be unwittingly standing in the way of danger. Greeting him with the customary 'Salaam aleykum' and being similarly greeted in reply, I dismount to ascertain who and what he is. He retreats another step or two in the direction of his strange abode, and eyes the bicycle with evident distrust, edging off to one side as I turn toward him, as though fearful lest it might come whizzing into his sacred person at a moment's notice like a hungry buzz-saw. In response to my inquiries, he points up toward the pass and offers to accompany me thither for the small sum of '*yek keran*;' giving me to understand that without his presence it is highly indiscreet to proceed.

Little penetration is required to understand that this is one of the little black-mailing schemes peculiar to semi-civilization, and which, it is perhaps hardly necessary to explain, comes a

"Motions for me to alight."

trifle too late in the chapter of my Asiatic experiences to influence my movements or replenish the exchequer of the picturesque and enterprising person desirous of shielding me from imaginary harm.

This wily individual is making his living by the novel and ingenious process of trading on the fears and credulity of stray travellers, making them believe the pass is dangerous and charging them a small sum for his services as guard. It is not at all unlikely that he is the present incumbent of an hereditary right to extort black-mail from such travellers along this lonely road as may be prevailed upon without resorting to violence to pay it, and is but humbly following in the footsteps of his worthy sire and still more worthy grandsire.

From the pass the descent is into a picturesque region of huge rocks and splendid streams that come bubbling out from among them, and farther along is a more open space, a few fields of grain, and the little hamlet of Kahmeh. Stopping here an hour for refreshments, the country again becomes rough and hilly for several miles; the road then descends a rocky slope to the plain, where a few miles ahead can be seen the crenelated walls and suburban orchards and villages of Torbet-i-Haiderie.

Remembering my letter from the Governor-General to subordinate officials, I permit a uniformed horseman, who seems anxious to make himself useful in the premises, to pilot me into the city, telling him to lead the way to the Mustapha's office. Guiding me through the narrow, crowded streets into the still more crowded bazaar, he descants, from his commanding position in the saddle, to the listening crowd, on the marvellous nature of my steed and the miraculous ability required to ride it as he had seen me riding it outside the walls. Having accomplished his vain purpose of attracting public attention to himself through me, and by his utterances aroused the popular curiosity to an ungovernable pitch, he rides off and leaves me to extricate myself and find the Mustapha as best I can.

The ignorant, inconsiderate mob at once commence shouting for me to ride. 'Sowar shuk; sowar shuk! tomasha; tomasha!' a thousand people cry in the stuffy, ill-paved bazaar as they struggle and push and surge about me, giving me barely room to squeeze through them. When it is discovered that I am seeking the Mustapha, there is a great rush of the crowd to reach the municipal compound and gain admittance, lest perchance the gates should be closed after I had entered and a tomasha be given without them seeing.

The Mustapha is found seated on the raised floor of his open-fronted office, examining, between whiffs of the kalian, papers brought to him by his subordinates, and I hand him my general letter of recommendation. Taking a cursory glance at the contents, he gives a sweep of his chin toward the bicycle, and says, 'Sowar shuk; tomasha.' Pointing out the utter impossi-bility of complying with his request in a badly-paved compound packed to its utmost capacity with people; he looks wearily at the ragged and unruly multitude before him, as though conscious that it would be useless to try and do anything with them, and then giving some order to an officer resumes his official labors.

The officer summons a couple of *farrashes*, and with long willow switches they flog their way through the crowd, opening a narrow, but instantly filled again, passage for me to follow. Outside the compound the officer practically forsakes me and goes over body and soul to the enemy. Filled with the same dense ignorance and overwhelming desire to see the bicycle ridden, he desires also to gain the approbation of the crowd, and so brings all his powers of persuasion to bear against me. Time and again, while traversing with the greatest difficulty the narrow bazaar in the midst of a surging mob, he faces about and makes the same insane request, shouting like a maniac to make his voice audible above the din of a thousand clamorous appeals to the same purpose. Had I the power to annihilate the whole crazy, maddening multitude with a sweep of the hand, I am afraid they would at this juncture have received but small mercy.

The accommodation provided at the caravanserai consists of doorless *menzils*, elevated three feet above the ground; a walled partition, with an open archway, divides the quarters into a room behind and an open porch in front. Conducting me to one of these free-for-anybody places, which I could just as easily have found and occupied without his assistance, he takes his departure, leaving me to the tender consideration of an overbearing, ragamuffin mob, in whom the spirit of wantonness is already aroused.

I attempt to appeal to the reason of my obstreperous audience by standing on the *menzil* front and delivering a harangue in such Persian as I have at command.

'*Sowar shuk, neis, tomasha caravanserai neis; rah koob neis. Inshalla saba, gitti koob rah Beerjandi, khylie koob tomasha – ky-y-l-ie koob tomasha saba!*' is the burden of this harangue; but eloquent though it be in its simplicity, it fails to accomplish the desired end. Their reply to it all takes the form of howls of disapproval, and the importunities to ride become more clamorous than ever.

An effort to keep them from taking possession of my quarters by shoving them off the front porch, results in my being seized roughly by the throat by one determined assailant and cracked on the head with a stick by another. Ignorant of a Ferenghi's mode of attack, the presumptuous individual, with his hand twisted in my neck-handkerchief, cocks his head in a semi-sidewise attitude, in splendid position to be dropped like a pole-axed steer by a neat tap on the temple. He wears the green *kammerbund* of a seyud, however; and even under the shadow of the legations in Teheran, it is a very serious and risky thing to strike a descendant of the Prophet. For a lone infidel to do so in the presence of two thousand Mussulman fanatics, already imbued with the spirit of wantonness, would be little less than deliberate suicide, so a sense of discretion intervenes to spare him the humiliation of being knocked out of time by an unhallowed first. The stiff, United States army helmet, obtained, it will be remembered, at Fort Sidney, Nebraska, and worn on the road ever since, saves my bump of veneration from actual contact with the stick of number two; and finding me making only a passive resistance, the valiant individual in the green *kammerbund* relaxes both the severity of his scowl and his grip on my neck gear.

After this there is no use trying to keep them from invading my quarters, and I deem it advisable to stand closely by the bicycle, humoring their curiosity and getting along with them as peaceably as possible. The crowd present is constantly augmented by new arrivals from without; at least two thousand people are struggling, pushing and shouting, some coming forward to invade my *menzil*, others endeavoring to escape from the crush. While the rowdiest portion of the crowd struggle and push and shout in the foreground of this remarkable scene, little knots of big-turbaned mollahs and better-class citizens are laying their precious heads together scheming against me in the rear. Now and then a messenger, in the semi-military garb of a *farrash*, pushes his way to the front and delivers a message from these worthies, full of lies and deceit. From the top of their shaved and turbaned heads to the soles of their slip-shod feet they are filled with a pig-headed determination to accomplish their object of seeing the bicycle ridden.

Occasionally a dervish holds aloft the fantastic paraphernalia of his profession, battles his way through the surging human surf, and with his black, ferret-like eyes gleaming with unconscious ferocity through a vision of unkempt hair, thrusts his cocoa-nut alms-receiver under my nose and says, '*Huk yah huk!*' or 'backsheesh!' Shouted at, gesticulated at, intrigued against and solicited for alms all at the same time, and with brain-turning persistency, the classic halls of Bedlam would, in contrast, be a reposeful and calm retreat. Driven by my tormentors almost to the desperate resolve of emptying my six-shooter among them, let the result to myself be what it may, the sun of my persecutions has not reached the meridian even yet. The officer who an hour ago inconsiderately left me to my own resources, now returns with a large party of friends, bent on seeing the same wonderful sight that has seemingly set the whole city in an uproar. He has been about the place collecting friends and acquaintances for the purpose of treating them to an exhibition of my skill on the wheel. The purpose of the officer's return, with his friends, is readily understood by the crowd, and his arrival is announced by a universal roar of '*Sowar shuk! tomasha!*' as though not one of this insatiable mob had yet seen me ride.

Appearing before the elevated porch of the *menzil*, he beckons me to 'come ahead' in quite an authoritative manner. The peculiar beckoning twist of this presumptuous individual's chin and henna-stained beard summoning me to come out and 'perform' reminds me of nothing so much as some tamer of wild animals ordering a trained baboon to spruce himself up and dance for the edification of the circus-going public. Signifying my unwillingness to be thus made a circus of over and over again, the officer beckons even more peremptorily than before, and even makes a feint of coming and fetching me out by force.

As may well be believed, the sum of my patience is no longer equal to the strain, and jerking my revolver around from the obscurity of its hiding-place at my hip to where it can plainly be seen, and laying a hand menacingly on the butt, I warn him to clear off, in a manner that causes him to wilt and turn pale. He leaves the caravanserai at once in high dudgeon. It has been a most humiliating occasion for him, to fall so ignobly from the very high horse on which he just entered with his bosom friends; but it is no more than he rightly deserves.

Shortly after this little incident the part-proprietor of a *tchai-khan* nor far from the caravanserai, proposes that I leave my *menzil* and come with him to his place. Happy in the prospect of any kind of change that will secure me a little peace, I readily agree to the proposal and at once take my departure. A few stones are thrown, fortunately without doing any damage, ere the *tchai-khan* is reached; but once inside, the situation is materially improved.

It soon transpires that the speculative proprietors have conceived the bright idea of utilizing me as an attraction to draw customers to their place of business. Two men are stationed at the door with clubs, and admittance is only granted to likely-looking people who have money to spend on water-pipes and tea. A rival attraction already occupies the field in the person of a Tabreez Turkish *luti* with a performing rib-nosed mandril and a drum. Now and then, when the crowd with no money to spend becomes too clamorous about the doorway, the *luti* goes to the assistance of the guards, and giving the mandril the length of his chain, chases the people away.

The *luti* himself is filled with envy and covetousness at the immense drawing powers of the bicycle; and in a burst of confidence wants to know if I am an 'Inglis *luti*,' at the same time placing his forefingers together as an intimation that if I am we ought by all means to form a combination and travel the country together. About ten o'clock the *khan-jees* make me up quite a comfortable shake-down, and tired out with the tough journey over the mountains and the worrying persecutions of the afternoon, I fall asleep while yet the house is doing a thriving trade; the *luti* singing, the mandril grunting, kalians bubbling, and people talking, all fail to keep me awake.

The mental and physical exhaustion that makes this possible, does not, however, prevent me from falling asleep with a firm determination to leave Torbet-i-Haiderie and its turbulent population too early in the morning for any more crowds to gather. Accordingly, the morning star has scarcely risen above the horizon ere I turn out, waken one of the *khan-jees*, pocket some bread and depart.

Beyond the sand-hills, the villages, and the cultivation is a stony plain extending for sixteen miles, a gradual upward slant to a range of mountains. At the base of the mountains an area of dark-green coloring denotes the presence of fields and orchards and the whereabouts of the important village of Kakh. Beautifully terraced wheat-fields and vineyards, and peach and pomegranate orchards in full bloom, gladden the eyes and present a most striking contrast to the stony plain as the vicinity of Kakh is reached, and another pleasing and conspicuous feature is the dome of a *mesjid* mosaicked with bright-colored tiles.

The good people of Kakh are inquisitive even above their fellows, if such can be possible, but they are well-behaved and mild-mannered with it. After taking the ragged edge off their curiosity by riding up and down the main thoroughfare of the village, the keeper of a mercantile affair locks the bicycle up in his room, and I spend the evening hobnobbing with him and his customers in his little stall-like place of business. Kakh is famous for the production of little seedless raisins like those of Smyrna. Bushels of these are kicking about the place, and our merchant friend becomes filled with a wild idea that I might, perchance, buy the lot. A moment's reflection would convince him that ten bushels of sickly-sweet raisins would be about the last thing he could sell to a person travelling on a bicycle; but his supply of raisins is evidently so outrageously ahead of the demand that his ambition to reduce his stock obscures his better judgment like a cloud, and places him in the position of a drowning man clutching wildly at a straw.

Considerable opium is also grown hereabouts, and the people make it into sticks about the size of a carpenter's pencil; hundreds of these also occupy the merchant's shelves. He seems to have very little that isn't grown in the neighborhood except tea and loaf-sugar.

Ryots, who were absent in their fields when I arrived, come crowding around the store in the evening, bothering me to ride; the shop-keeper bids them wait till my departure in the morning, telling them I am not a *luti*, riding simply to let people see. He provides me with a door that fastens inside, and I am soon in the land of dreams.

Early in the morning I am awakened by people pounding at the door and shouting, '*Aftab*, Sahib – *aftab!*' It is the belated ryots of yesterday eve; thoroughly determined to be on hand and see the start, they are letting me know that it is sunrise.

Beyond Kakh the trail winds its circuitous way through a mountainous region, following one little stream to its source, climbing over the crest of an intervening ridge and down the bed of another stream. It is but an indistinct donkey trail at best, and the toilsome mountain climbing reminds me vividly of the worst parts of Asia Minor. Toward nightfall I wander into the village of Nukhab, a small place perched among the hills, inhabited by kindly-disposed, hospitable folks.

The entire village, as usual, assembles to see me dispose of the eatables so generously provided; and later in the evening there is another highly-expectant assembly waiting around, out of curiosity, to see what sort of a figure a Ferenghi cuts at his evening devotions. Poor benighted followers of the False Prophet, how little they comprehend us Christians! Suddenly it seems to dawn upon the mind of the simple old Khan that, being a stranger in a strange land, I might, perchance, be a trifle mixed about my bearings, and so he kindly indicates the direction of Mecca. When informed that the Ingilis never prostrate themselves toward Mecca and say 'Allah-il-allah!' they evince the greatest astonishment; and then the strange, unnatural impiousness of people who never address themselves to Allah nor prostrate toward the Holy City, impresses their simple minds with something akin to the feeling entertained among certain of ourselves toward extra dare-devil characters, and they seem to take a deeper and kindlier interest in me than ever. The disappointment at not seeing what I look like at prayers is more than offset by the additional novelty imparted to my person by the, to them, strange and sensational omission.

They seem greatly disappointed to learn that I am going away in the morning; they have plenty of *toke-me-morge, pillau, mast,* and *sheerah*, they say – plenty of everything; and they want me to stay with them always.

An enterprising youth is on hand at daybreak making a fire; but it is eight o'clock before I am able to get away; they seem to be mildly scheming among themselves to keep me with them as long as possible.

The trail winds and twists among the mountains, following in the train of a wayward little stream, then leads over a pass and emerges, in the company of another stream, upon a slanting plateau leading down to an extensive plain. Rounding the last spur of the hills, I find myself approaching a crowd numbering at least a hundred people. Hats are waved gleefully, voices are lifted up in joyous shouts of welcome, and the whole company give way to demonstrations of delight at my approach. A minute later I find myself surrounded by the familiar faces of the population of Nukhab – my road has followed a roundabout course of six or seven miles, and our enterprising friends have taken a short cut over the hills to intercept me at this point, where they can watch my progress across the open plain. They have brought along the kind old Kahn's kalian and tobacco-bag, and the wherewithal to make me a parting glass of tea.

CHAPTER VII

BEERJAND AND THE FRONTIER OF AFGHANISTAN

Thirty miles over hill and dale, after leaving the little hamlet, and behold, the city of Beerjand appears before me but a mile or thereabouts away, at the foot of the hills I am descending. One's first impression of Beerjand is a sense of disappointment; the city is a jumbled mass of uninteresting mud buildings, ruined and otherwise, all the same dismal mud-brown hue. Not a tree exists to relieve the eye, nor a solitary green object to break the dreary monotony of the prospect; the impression is that of a place existing under some dread ban of nature that forbids the enlivening presence of a tree, or even the redeeming feature of a bit of greensward.

The Ameer, Heshmet-i-Molk, I quickly learn, is living at his summer-garden at Ali-abad, four farsakhs to the east. Curious to see something of a place so much out of the world, and so little known as Beerjand, I determine upon spending the evening and night here, and continuing on to Ali-abad next morning.

An early start, sixteen miles of road without hills or mountains, but embracing the several qualities of good, bad, and indifferent, and at eight o'clock I dismount in the presence of a little knot of Heshmet-i-Molk's retainers congregated outside his summer-garden, and a goodly share of the population of the adjacent village of Ali-abad. While yet miles away, Ali-abad is easily distinguished as being something out of the ordinary run of Persian villages by the luxuriant foliage of the Ameer's garden.

The village of Ali-abad, consisting of the merest cluster of low mud hovels and a few stony acres wrested from the desert by means of irrigation, the people ragged, dirty, and uncivilized, look anything but an appropriate dwelling-place for a great chieftain. The summer garden itself is enclosed within a high mud wall, and it is only after passing through the gate and shutting out the rude hovels, the rag-bedecked villagers, and the barren desert, that the illusion of unfitness is removed.

My letter is taken in to the Ameer, and in a few minutes is answered in a most practical manner by the appearance of men carrying carpets, tent-poles, and a round tent of blue and white stripes. Winding its silvery course to the summer garden, from a range of hills several miles distant, is a clear, cold stream; although so narrow as to be easily jumped, and nowhere more than knee-deep, the presence of trout betrays the fact that it never runs dry.

The tent is pitched on the banks of this bright little stream, the entrance but a half-dozen paces from its sparkling water, and a couple of guards are stationed near by to keep away intrusive villagers; an abundance of eatables, including sweetmeats, bowls of sherbet, and dried apricots, and pears from Foorg, are provided at once.

A neatly dressed attendant squats himself down on the shady side of the tent outside, and at ridiculously short intervals brings me in a newly primed kalian and a samovar of tea. Everything possible to contribute to my comfort is attended to and nothing overlooked; and the Ameer furthermore proves himself sensible and considerate above the average of his fellow-countrymen by leaving me to rest and refresh myself in the quiet retreat of the tent till four o'clock in the afternoon.

A very agreeable, and, withal, intelligent young man, the incumbent of some office about the Ameer's person, no doubt a mirza, pays me a visit at noon, apparently to supervise the serving up of the more than bountiful repast sent on from his master's table. My attention is at once arrested by the English coat-of-arms on his sword-belt; both belt and clasp have evidently wandered from the ranks of the British army.

'Pollock Sahib,' he says, in reply to my inquiries – it is a relic of the Seistan Boundary Commission.

About four o'clock, this same young man and a companion appear with the announcement that the Ameer is ready to receive me, and requests that I bring the bicycle with me into the garden. The stream flows through a low arch beneath the wall and lends itself to the maintenance of an artificial lake that spreads over a large proportion of the enclosed space. The summer garden is a fabrication of green trees and the cool glimmer of shaded water, rather than the flower-beds, the turf, and shrubbery of the Occidental conception of a garden; the Ameer's quarters consist of an unpretentious one-storied building fronting on the lake.

The Ameer himself is found seated on a plain divan at the open-windowed front, toying with a string of amber beads; a dozen or so retainers are standing about in respectful and expectant attitudes, ready at a moment's notice to obey any command he may give or to anticipate his personal wants. He is a stoutly built, rather ponderous sort of individual, with a full, rotund face and a heavy, unintellectual, but good-natured expression; one's first impression of him is apt to be less flattering to his head than to his heart. He is a person, however, that improves with acquaintance, and is probably more intelligent than he looks. He seems to be living here in a very plain and unpretentious manner; no gaudy stained glass, no tinsel, no mirror-work, no vain gew-gaws of any description

In the Ameer's Garden.

impart a cheap and garish glitter to the place; no gorgeous apparel bedecks his ample proportions. Clad in the ordinary dress of a well-to-do Persian nobleman, Heshmet-i-Molk, happy and contented in the enjoyment of creature comforts and the universal esteem of his people, probably finds his chief pleasure in sitting where we now find him, looking out upon the green trees and glimmering waters of the garden, smoking his kalian, and attending to the affairs of state in a quiet, unostentatious manner.

With a refreshing absence of ceremonial, he discusses with me the prospects of my being able to reach India overland. The conversation on his part, however, almost takes the form of trying to persuade me from my purpose altogether, and particularly not to attempt Afghanistan.

'The Harood is as wide as from here to the other side of the lake yonder (200 yards); *tund* (swift) as a swift-running horse and deep as this house,' he informs me.

'No bridge? no ferry-boat? no means of getting across?'

'*Eitch*' (no), replies the Ameer. '*Pull neis, kishti neis.*'

'Can't it be forded with camels?'

'*Shutor neis.*'

'No village, with people to assist with poles or skins to make a raft?'

'Afghani *dasht-adam* (nomads), no poles; you might perhaps find skins; but the river is tund – t-u-n-d! skins *neis*, poles *neis*; t-u-n-d!!' and the Ameer points to a bird hopping about on the garden walk, intimating that the Harood flows as swiftly as the flight of a bird.

The result of the conference I have been so anxiously looking forward to is anything but an encouraging picture – a picture of insurmountable obstacles on every hand. The deep sand and burning heat of the dreadful Lut Desert intervenes between me and the Mekran coast; the route through Beloochistan, barely passable with camels and guides and skins of water in the winter, is not only impracticable for anything in the summer, but there is the additional obstacle of the spring floods of the Helmund and the Seistan lake.

The region between Beerjand and the Harood is on my map a dismal-looking, blankety-blank stretch of country, marked with the ominous title '*Dasht-i-na-oomid*,' which, being interpreted into English, means Desert of Despair. A gleam of hope that things may not be quite so hopeless as pictured is born of the fact that, in dwelling on the difficulties of the situation, the Ameer makes less capital out of this same Desert of Despair than of the Harood, which has to be crossed on its eastern border.

As regards interference from the Legation of Teheran, thank goodness I am now three hundred miles from the nearest telegraph-pole, and shall enter Afghanistan at a point so much nearer to Quetta than to the Boundary Commission Camp that the chances seem all in favor of reaching the former place if I only succeed in reaching the *Dashti-i-na-oomid* and the Harood.

The result of the foregoing deliberations is a qualified (qualified by the absence of any alternative save turning back) determination to point my nose eastward, and follow its leadership toward the British outpost at Quetta.

'*Khylie koob*' (very well), replies the Ameer, as he listens to my determination; '*khylie koob*;' and he takes a few vigorous whiffs at his kalian as though, conscious of the uselessness of arguing the matter any further with a Ferenghi, he were dismissing the ghost of his own opinions in a cloud of smoke.

Shortly after sunrise on the following morning a couple of well-mounted horsemen appear at the door of my tent, armed and equipped for the road. Their equipment consists of long guns with resting-fork attachement, the prongs of which project above the muzzle like a two-pronged pitchfork; swords, pistols, and the brave but antique display of warlike paraphernalia characteristic of the East. One of them, I am pleased to observe, is the genial young mirza whose snuff-colored roundabout is held in place by the '*dieu et mon droit*' belt of yesterday; his companion is the ordinary sowar, or irregular horseman of the country. They announce themselves as bearers of the Ameer's salaams, and as my escort to Tabbas, a village two marches to the east.

The villages of Darmian and Foorg, looking out upon wild frontier territory, inhabited chiefly by turbulent and lawless tribes – people whose hereditary instincts are diametrically opposed to the sublime ethics of the decalogue – have no doubt often found the grim stronghold towering so picturesquely above them an extremely convenient thing.

The escort points it out and explains that it belongs to the 'Padishah at Teheran,' and not to his own master, the Ameer – a national, as distinct from a provincial, fortification. The cultivated environs of Foorg present a most discouraging front to a wheel-man; walled gardens, rocks, orchards, and ruins, with hundreds of water-ditches winding and twisting among them, the water escaping through broken banks and creating new confusion where confusion already reigns supreme. Among this indescribable jumble of mud, water, rocks, ruins, and cultivation, pitched almost at an angle of forty-five degrees, the natives climb about bare-legged, impressing one very forcibly as so many human goats as they scale the walls, clamber over rocks, or wade through mud and water.

A willing Foogian divests himself of everything but his hat, and carries the bicycle across the stream, while I am taken up behind the mirza. As the mirza's iron-gray gingerly enters the water, an interesting and instructive spectacle is afforded by a hundred or more Foorgians following the shining example of the classic figure carrying the bicycle, for the purpose of being on hand to see me start across the plain toward Tabbas.

Crossing the Stream at Foorg.

Abdurraheim Khan, the chief of several small villages on the Tabbas plain, turns up in the evening. He is the mildest-mannered, kindliest-looking human being I have seen for a long time; he does the agreeable in a manner that leads his guests to think he worships the 'Ingilis' people humbly at a distance, and is highly honored in being able to see and entertain one of those very worshipful individuals. Like nearly all Persians, he is ignorant of the Western custom of shaking hands; the sun-browned paw extended to him as he enters is stared at a moment in embarrassment and then clasped between both his palms.

In reply to my inquiries, I am glad to find that Abdurraheim Khan speaks less discouragingly of the Harood than did the Ameer at Ali-abad; he says it will be fordable for camels, and there will be no difficulty in finding nomads able to provide me an animal to cross over with.

An ancient retainer, without any teeth to speak of, and an annoying habit of shouting 'h-o-i!' at a person, regardless of the fact that one is within hearing of the merest whisper, is detailed to guide me to a few hovels perched among the mountains, four farsakhs to the southeast, from which point the journey across the *Dasht-i-na-oomid* is to begin, with an escort of three sowars, who are to join us there later in the evening.

The little nest of mud huts are found, after a certain amount of hesitation and preliminary going ahead by 'The Aged,' and toward nightfall three picturesque horsemen ride up and dismount; they are the sowars detailed by the Ameer's orders to Abdurraheim, or some other border-land khan, to escort me across the Desert of Despair.

'The Aged' bravely returns to Tabbas in the morning by himself. When on the point of departing, he surveys me wistfully across a few feet of space and shouts 'h-o-i!' He then regards me with a peculiar and indescribable smile. It is not a very hard smile to interpret, however, and I present him with the customary backsheesh. Pocketing the coins, he shouts 'h-o-i!' again, and delivers himself of another smile even more peculiar and indescribable than the other.

'Persian-like, receiving a present of money only excites his cupidity for more,' I think; and so reply by a deprecatory shake of the head. This turns out to be an uncharitable judgment, however, for once; he goes through the pantomime of using a pen and says, 'Abdurraheim Khan.' He saw me write my name, and the date of my appearance at Tabbas, etc., on a piece of paper and give it to Abdurraheim Khan, and he wants me to do the same thing for him.

The three worthies comprising my new escort are most interesting specimens of the genus sowar; the leader and spokesman of the trio says he is a khan; number two is a mirza, and number three a mudbake. Khans are pretty plentiful hereabouts, and it is nothing surprising to happen across one acting in the humble capacity of a sowar; a mirza gets his title from his ability to write letters; the precise social status of a mudbake is more difficult to here determine, but his proper roosting-place is several rungs of the social ladder below either of the others. They are to take me through to the Khan of Ghalakua, the first Afghan chieftain beyond the desert, and to take back to the Ameer a receipt from him for my safe delivery.

'*Pool, pool, pool – keran, keran, keran,*' the probable amount in my possession, the amount they expect to receive as backsheesh, and kindred speculations concerning the financial aspect of the situation, form almost the sole topic of their conversation. Throwing them off their guard, by affecting greater ignorance of their language than I am really guilty of, enables me to size them up pretty thoroughly by their conversation, and thus to adopt a line of policy to counteract the baneful current of their thoughts. Their display of cunning and rascality is ridiculous in the extreme; fancying themselves deep and unfathomable as the shades of Lucifer himself, they are, in reality, almost as transparent and simple as children; their cunning is the cunning of the school-boy. Well aware that the safety of their own precious carcasses depends on their returning to Khorassan with a receipt from the Khan of Ghalakua for my safe delivery, there is little reason to fear actual violence from them, and their childish attempts at extortion by other methods will furnish an amusing and instructive study of barbarian character.

The rain has cleared up, but the weather looks unsettled, as about eight o'clock next morning our little party starts eastward under the guidance of a villager whom I have employed to guide us out of the immediate range of mountains, the sowars betraying a general ignorance of the commencement of the route.

'Inshallah, Ghalakua, Gh-al-a-kua!' exclaims the khan, as he

The Start across the Desert.

swings himself into the saddle. 'Inshallah, Al-lah,' is the response of the mirza and the mudbake, as they carelessly follow his example, and the march across the *Dasht-i-na-oomid* begins.

CHAPTER VIII

ACROSS THE 'DESERT OF DESPAIR'

While traversing this treacherous belt of territory I make the sowars lead the way and perform the office of pathfinder for myself and wheel. Whenever one of them gets stuck in boggy ground, and his horse flounders wildly about, to the imminent risk of unseating its rider, his two hopeful comrades bubble over with merriment at his expense; his own sincere exclamations of 'Allah!' being answered by unsympathetic jeers and sarcastic remarks.

A few minutes later, perchance one of the hilarious twain finds himself unexpectedly in the same predicament; it then becomes his turn to look scared and importune Allah for protection, and also his turn to be the target for the wild hilarity of the others.

And so this lively and eventful afternoon passes away, and about five o'clock we round the base of a conglomerate hill that has been shutting out the prospect ahead, cross a small spring freshet, and emerge upon an extensive gravelly plain stretching away eastward to the horizon. It is the central plain of the *Dasht-i-na-oomid*, the heart of the desert, of which the wild, heterogeneous territory traversed since morning forms the setting. So far as the utility of the bicycle and the horses is concerned, the change is decidedly for the better, even more so for the former than for the latter. The gravelly plain presents very good wheeling surface, and I forge ahead of my escort, following a trail so faint that it is barely distinguishable from the general surface.

Shortly after leaving the mountainous country the three sowars whip their horses into a smart canter to overtake the bicycle. As they come clattering up, the khan shouts loudly for me to stop, and the mirza and mudbake supplement his vocal exertions by gesticulating to the same purpose. Dismounting, and allowing them to approach, in reply to my query of '*Chi mi khoi?*,' the khan's knavish countenance becomes overspread with a ridiculously thin and transparent assumption of seriousness and importance, and pointing to an imaginary boundary-line at his horse's feet he says:

'Bur-raa-ther (brother), Afghanistan.'

'*Khylie koob*, Afghanistan *inja – koob, koob, sowari.*' (Very good, I understand, we are entering Afghanistan; all right, ride on.)

'Sowari neis,' replies the khan; and he tries hard to impress upon me that our crossing the Afghan frontier is a momentous occasion, and not to be lightly regarded. Several times during the day has my delectable escort endeavored to fathom the extent of my courage my impressing upon me the danger to be apprehended in Afghanistan by a Ferenghi. Not less than half a dozen times have they indulged in the grim pantomime of cutting their own throats, and telling me that this is the tragic fate that would await me in Afghanistan without their valuable protection. And now, as we stand on the boundary line, their bronzed and bared throats are again subjected to this highly expressive treatment; and transfixing me with a penetrating stare, as though eager to read in my face some responsive sign of fear or apprehension, the khan repeats with emphasis:

'Bur-raa-ther, Afghanistan.'

Seeing me still inclined to make light of the matter, he turns to his comrades for confirmation.

'O, bur-raa-ther, Afghanistan,' assents the mirza; and the mudbake chimes in with the same words.

'Well, yes, I understand; Afghanistan – what of it?' I inquire, amused at this theatrical display of their childish knavery.

For answer they start to loading up their guns and pistols, which up to now they have neglected to do; and they examine, with a ludicrous show of importance, the edges of their swords and the points of their daggers, staring the while at me to see what kind of an impression all this is making. Their scrutiny of my countenance brings them small satisfaction, methinks, for so ludicrous seems the scene, and so transparent the motives of this warlike movement, that no room is there for aught but a genuine expression of amusement.

Perhaps twenty miles are covered, when we arrive at a pile of dead bush that has been erected for a landmark, and find a dilapidated well containing water. The water is forty feet below the surface, and contains a miscellaneous assortment of dead lizards, the carcasses of various small mammalia, and sundry other unfortunate representatives of animated nature that have fallen in. Beyond this well the country assumes the character of a broad sink or mud-basin, the shiny surface of its mud glistening in the sun like a sheet of muddy water. Sloughs innumerable meander through it, fringed with rank rushes and shrubs. A far heavier down-pour than we were favored with on the plain has drenched a region of stony hills adjacent, and the drainage therefrom has, for the time being, filled and overflowed the winding sloughs.

A dozen or more of these are successfully forded, though not without some difficulty; but we finally arrive at the parent slough, of which the others are but tributaries.

This proves too deep for the sowars' horses to ford, and after surveying the yellow flood some minutes and searching up and down, the khan declares ruefully that we shall have to return to Beerjand. As I remonstrate with him upon his lack of enterprise in turning from so trifling a difficulty, the khan finally orders the mudbake to strip off his purple and fine linen and try the depth. The mudbake proceeds to obey his superior, with many apprehensive glances at the muddy freshet, and wades gingerly in, muttering prayers to Allah the while. Deeper and deeper the yellow waters creep up his shivering form, and when nearly up to his neck, a sudden deepening causes him to bob unexpectedly down almost over his head. Hurriedly retreating, spluttering and whining, he scrambles hastily ashore, where his two companions, lolling lazily on their horses, watching his attempt, are convulsed with merriment over his little misadventure and his fright.

The shivering mudbake, clad chiefly in goose-pimples, now eagerly supplements the khan's proposition for us all to return to Beerjand, and the mirza with equal eagerness murmurs his approval of the same course of action. Making light of their craven determination, I prepare to cross the freshet without their assistance, and announce my intention of proceeding alone. The stream, though deep, is not over thirty yards wide, and a very few minutes suffices for me to swim across with my clothes, my packages, and the saddle of the bicycle; the small, strong rope I have carried from Constantinople is then attached to the bicycle, and, swimming across with the end, the wheel is pulled safely through the water. Neither of the sowars can swim, and they regard the prospect of being left behind with no little consternation. Their guileful souls seem to turn naturally to Allah in their perplexity; and they all prostrate themselves toward Mecca, and pray with the apparent earnestness of deep sincerity. Having duly strengthened and fortified themselves with these devotional exercises, they bravely prepare to resign themselves to kismet and follow my instructions about crossing the stream.

The khan's iron-gray being the best horse of the three, and the khan himself of a more sanguine and hopeful disposition, I make him tie all his clothes and damageable things into a bundle and fasten them on his saddle; the rope is then tied to the bridle and the horse pulled across, his gallant rider clinging to his tail, according to my orders, and praying aloud to Allah on his own account. The gray swims the unfordable middle portion nobly, and the khan comes through with no worse damage than a mouthful or two of muddy water. As the dripping charger scrambles up the bank, the khan allows himself to be hauled up high and dry by its tail; he then looks back at his comrades and favors them with a brief but highly exaggerated account of his sensations.

The mirza and the mudbake deliver themselves of particularly deep-chested acclamations of 'Allah, Allah!' at the prospect of undergoing similar sensations to those described by the khan, whereupon that unsympathetic individual vents his hilarity in a gleeful, heartless peal of laughter, and tells them, with a diabolical chuckle of delight, that they will most likely fare ten times worse than himself on account of the inferiority of their horses compared with the gray. Much threatening, bantering, and persuasion is necessary to induce them to follow the leadership of the khan; but, trusting to kismet, they finally venture, and both come through without noteworthy misadventure. The khan's wild hilarity and ribaldish jeers at the expense of his two subordinates, as he stands on the solid foundation of a feat happily already accomplished and surveys their trepidation, and hears their prayers as they are pulled like human dinghies through the water, is in such ludicrous contrast to his own prayerful utterances under the same circumstances a minute before that my own risibilities are not to be wholly controlled.

This little episode makes a profound impression upon the minds of my escort; they now regard me as a very dare-devil and determined individual, a person entirely without fear, and their deference during the remainder of the afternoon is in marked contrast to their previous attempts to work upon my presumed apprehensions of the dangers of Afghanistan.

Another couple of miles and the eastern edge of the sandy area is reached, after which a compensational proportion of smooth gravel abounds. Shortly after noon another small camp of nomads is reached, some half-dozen inferior tents, pitched on the shelterless edge of an exposed gravelly slope. The afternoon is oppressively hot, and the men are comfortably snoozing in all sorts of outlandish places among the scrubby camel-thorn.

We are not invited into the tents, but bread and *mast* is provided, and, while we eat, four men hold the corners of an ample blue turban sheet over us to shelter us from the sun. Spread out on sheets and on the roofs of the tents are bushels of curds drying in the sun; the curds are compressed into round balls the size of an apple, and when dried into hard balls are excellent things to put in the pocket and nibble along the road. Here we learn that the Harood is only one farsakh distant, and a couple of stalwart young nomads accompany us to assist us across. At Beerjand the Harood was 'deep as a house;' at our last night's camp we were told that it was fordable with camels; here we learn that, though very swift, it is really fordable for men and horses. First we come to a branch less than waist-deep. My nether garments are handed to the khan; in the pocket of my pantaloons is a purse containing a few *kerans*. While engaged in fording this branch the khan ferrets out the purse and extracts something from it, which he deftly slips into the folds of his *kammerbund*. All this I silently observe from the corners of my eyes, but say nothing.

Arriving at the bank of the Harood, I retire behind a clump of reeds, and fold my money-belt, full of gold, up in the middle of my clothes, making a compact bundle, with my gossamer rubber wrapped around the outside. The river is about a hundred and fifty yards wide at the ford, with a sand-bar about mid-stream, and is not above shoulder-deep along the ridge that renders it fordable; the current, however, is frightfully strong. Like the Indians of the West, the Afghan nomads are accustomed from infancy to battling with the elements, and are comparatively fearless in regard to rivers and deserts and storms, etc.

Such, at least, is the impression created by the conduct of the two young men who have come to assist us across. The bicycle, my clothes, and all the effects of the sowars are carried across on their heads, the rushing waters threatening to sweep them off their feet at every step; but nothing is allowed to get wet. When they are carrying across the last bundle, the khan, solicitous for my safety, wants me to hang on to a short rope tied around the waist of the strongest of the nomads. Naturally disdaining any such arrangement as this, however, I declare my intention of crossing without assistance, and wade in forthwith. Ere I have progressed thirty yards, the current fairly sweeps me off my feet and I have to swim for it. Fancying that I am overcome and in a fair way of being drowned, the sowars set up a wild howl of apprehension, and shout excitedly to the nomads to rescue me from a watery grave. The Afghans are not so excited, however, over the outlook; they see that I am swimming all right, and they confine themselves to motioning the direction for me to take. The current carries me some little distance down stream, when I find footing on the lower extremity of the sand-bar, and on it, wade up stream again with some difficulty against swiftly rushing water four feet deep.

The khan thinks I have had the narrowest possible escape, and in tones of desperation he shouts out and begs me not to attempt to cross the other channel without assistance. 'The receipt!' he shouts, 'the receipt! Allah preserve us! the receipt; Heshmet-i-Molk.' The worthy khan is afflicted with a keen consciousness of condign punishment awaiting him at Beerjand, should I happen to come to grief while under his protection, and he, no doubt, suffers an agony of apprehension during the fifteen minutes I am battling with the rapid current of the Harood.

The second channel is found less swift and comparatively easy to ford. The sturdy nomads, having transported all of my escort's damageable effects, those three now stark-naked

Crossing the Harood.

worthies mount with fear and trembling their equally stark-naked steeds – naked all, save for the turbans of the men and the bridles of their horses. Whatever of intrepidity the khan possesses is of a quantity scarcely visible to the naked eye, and it is, therefore, scarcely surprising to find him trying to persuade, first the mudbake and then the mirza, to take the initiative. His efforts prove wholly ineffectual, however, to bring the feebly flowing tide of their courage up to the high-water level of assuming the duties of leadership, and so in the absence of any alternative, he finally screws up his own courage and leads the way. The others allow their horses to follow closely behind. The horses seem to regard the rushing volume of yellow water about them with far less apprehension than do their riders. While dressing myself on the eastern bank, the frightened mutterings of 'Allah' from these gallant horsemen come floating across the water, and, as they reach the sand-bar in the middle of the stream, I can hear their muttered importunities for Providential protection change, like the passing shadow-whims of Nature's children that they are, into gleeful chuckles at their escape.

CHAPTER IX

AFGHANISTAN

Travelling leisurely next morning, we arrive at Ghalakua in the middle of the forenoon; quarters are assigned us by Aminulah Khan, the Chief of the Ghalakua villages and tributary territory. In appearance he is a typical Oriental official, his fluffy, sensuous countenance bearing traces of such excesses as voluptuous Easterns are wont to indulge in, and this morning he is suffering with an attack of 'tab' (fever). Wrapped in a heavy fur-lined overcoat, he is found seated on the front platform of a *menzil* beneath the arched village gateway, smoking cigarettes; in his hand is a bouquet of roses, and numerous others are scattered about his feet. Dancing attendance upon him is a smart-looking little fellow in a sheepskin busby almost as bulky in proportion as his whole body, and which renders his appearance grotesque in the extreme. His keen black eyes sparkle brightly through the long wool of his remarkable headgear, the ends of which dangle over his eyes like an overgrown and wayward bang. The bravery of his attire is measurably enhanced by a cavalry sword, long enough and heavy enough for a six-foot dragoon, a green *kammerbund*, and top-boots of red leather. This person stands by the side of Aminulah Khan, watches keenly everything that is being said and done, receives orders from his master, and transmits them to the various subordinates lounging about. He looks the soul of honesty and watchfulness, his appearance and demeanor naturally conjuring up reflections of faithful servitors about the persons of knights and nobles of old; he is apparently the Khan of Ghalakua's confidential retainer and general supervisor of affairs about his person and headquarters.

Our quarters are in the *bala-khana* of a small half-ruined *konak* outside the village, and shortly after retiring thither the khan's sprightly little retainer brings in tea and fried eggs, besides pomegranates and roses for myself. A new departure makes its appearance in the shape of sugar sprinkled over the eggs.

While we are discussing these refreshments our attendant stands in the doorway and addresses the sowars at some length

We Reach Ghalakua.

in Persian. He is apparently delivering instructions received from his master; whatever it is all about, be delivers it with the air of an orator addressing an audience, and he supplements his remarks with gestures that would do credit to a professional elocutionist. He is as agreeable as he is picturesque; he and I seem to fall *en rapport* at once, as against the untrustworthiness of the remainder of our company. As his keen, honest eyes scrutinize the countenances of the sowars, and then seek my own face, I feel instinctively that he has sized my escort up correctly, and that their innate rascality is as well revealed to him as if he had accompanied us across the desert.

The khan obtains his receipt for my delivery, and by and by Aminulah Khan sends his man to request the favor of a *tomasha*. Leaving my other effects behind in charge of the sowars, I take the bicycle and favor him with a few turns in front of the village gate. Among the various contents of my leathern case is a bag of *kerans*; but, although the case is not locked, it is provided with a peculiar fastening which I fondly imagine to be beyond the ingenuity of the khan to open. So that, while well enough aware of that guileful individual's uncontrollable avarice in general, and his deep, dark designs on my money in particular, I think little of leaving it with him for the few minutes I expect to be absent. It strikes me as a trifle suspicious, however, upon discovering that while everybody else comes to see the *tomasha*, all three of the sowars remain behind.

Instinctively I arrive at the conclusion that with these three worthy kleptomaniacs left alone in a room with some other person's portable property, something is pretty sure to happen to the property; so, excusing myself as quickly as courtesy will permit, I hasten back to our quarters. The mudbake is found posted at the outer gate of the *konak*. He is keeping watch while his delectable comrades search the package in which they sagaciously locate the silver lucre they so much covet. Seeing me approaching, he makes a trumpet of his hands and sings out warningly to his accomplices that I am coming back. Taking no more notice of him than usual, I pass inside and repair at once to the *bala-khana*, to find that the khan and mirza have disappeared.

The mudbake colors up like a guilty school-boy upon seeing me proceed without delay to examine the leathern case. The erstwhile orderly arranged contents are found tumbled about in dire confusion. My bag of about one hundred *kerans* have dwindled to nearly half that number as the result of being in their custody ten minutes.

'Some of you *pedar sags* have stolen my money; who is it? where's the khan?' I inquire, addressing the guilty-looking mudbake. He is now shivering visibly with fright, but makes a ludicrous effort to put a bold face on the matter, and brazenly asks, '*Chand pool?*' (How much is missing?).

'Khylie! where is the khan and the mirza? I will take you all to Aminulah Khan and have you bastinadoed!'

The poor mudbake turns pale at the bare suggestion of the bastinado, and stoutly maintains his own innocence. He would no doubt as stoutly proclaim the guilt of his comrades if by so doing he could escape punishment himself. Nor is this so surprising, when one reflects that either of these worthies would, without a moment's hesitation, perform the same office for him or for each other.

Without wasting time in bandying arguments with the mudbake, I sally forth in search of the others, and meet them just outside the gate; they are returning from hiding the money in the ruins. The crimson flood of guilt overspreads their faces as I raise my finger and shake it at them by way of admonition. With them following behind with all the meekness of discovered guilt, I lead the way back up into the *bala-khana*. Arriving there, both of them wilt so utterly and completely, and proceed to plead for mercy with such ludicrous promptness, that my sense of the ridiculous outweighs all other considerations, and I regard their demonstrations of remorse with a broad smile of amusement. It is anything but a laughing matter from their own standpoint, however; the mudbake warns them forthwith that I have threatened to have them bastinadoed, and they fairly writhe and groan in an agony of apprehension.

It is a ludicrous and yet a strangely touching spectacle to see these three poor devils grovelling and pleading before me, and at the same time praying to Allah for protection in the little *bala-khana*, hoping thereby to save themselves from cruel mutilation and life-long disgrace. A watchful eye is kept outside by the mirza, who does his groaning and praying near the door, and the sight of an Afghan approaching is the signal for a mute appeal for mercy from all three, and a transformation to ordinary attitudes and vocations, the completeness of which would do credit to professional comedians.

When a favorable opportunity presents, with much peering about to make sure of being unobserved, his comrades lower the khan down over the rear wall of the *bala-khana*, and a minute later they hoist him up again with the same show of caution.

Producing from his *kammerbund* a red handkerchief containing the stolen *kerans*, he advances and humbly lays it at my feet, at the same time kneeling down and implanting yet another osculatory favor on my geivehs. Joyful at seeing my readiness to second them in keeping the matter hidden from stray Afghans that come dropping in, the guilty sowars are still fearful lest they have not yet secured my complete forgiveness.

The sharp-eyed wearer of the big busby, the cavalry sword, and red jack-boots turns up early next morning. He dropped in once or twice yesterday, and being possessed of more brains than the three sowars put together, he gathered from appearances, and his general estimation of their character, that all is not right. These suspicions he promptly communicated to his master. Aminulah Khan is only too well acquainted with the weakest side of the Persian character, and at once jumps to the conclusion that the sowars have stolen my money. Sending for me and summoning the sowars to his presence, without preliminary palaver he accuses them of robbing me of '*pool*.' Addressing himself to me, he inquires: '*Sahib, Parsee namifami?*' (Do you understand Persian?)

'*Kam Kam*' (a little), I reply.

'*Sowari pool? pool koob;* rupee – rupee *koob?*'

'*O, O, pool koob; rupee koob; sowari neis, sowari khylie koob adam.*'

In this brief interchange of disconnected Persian the khan has asked me whether the sowars have stolen money from me, and I have answered that they have not, but that, on the contrary, they are most excellent men, both 'trustie and true.' May the recording angel enter my answer down with a recommendation for mercy! During this examination the little busby-wearer stands and closely scrutinizes the changeful countenances of the accused. He thoroughly understands that I am mercifully shielding them from what he considers their just deserts, and he chips in a word occasionally to Aminulah Khan, aside, like a sharp lawyer watching the progress of a cross-examination.

The chief himself, though ostensibly accepting my statement, has his own suspicions to the same purpose, and before dismissing them he shakes his finger menacingly at the sowars and significantly touches the hilt of his sword. The three culprits look guilty enough to satisfy the most merciful of judges, but, relying on my co-operation to shield them, they stoutly maintain their innocence.

Some little delay occurs about starting for Furrah, my next objective point on the road to India; the khan explains that all of his sowars have been sent off to help garrison Herat; that the best he can provide in the form of a mounted escort is an elderly little man, whom he points out, with an evident doubt as to my probable appreciation.

The man looks more like a Persian than an Afghan, which he probably is, as the population of these border-land districts is much mixed. Nothing would have pleased me better than to have had Aminulah Khan bid me go ahead without any escort whatever, but next to nobody at all, the most satisfactory arrangement is the harmless-looking old fellow in the Persian lamb's-wool hat. Telling him that he has done well in sending his sowars to Herat, and that the old fellow will answer very well as guide, I prepare to take my departure.

My guide disappears, and shortly returns mounted on a powerful and spirited gray. Aminulah Khan gives him a letter, and after mutual salaams, and 'good ahfis,' the old sowar leads the way at a pace which shows him to be filled with exaggerated ideas about my speediness.

The Furrah Rood, at the ferry, is about two hundred yards wide, and with a current of perhaps five miles an hour. A dozen stalwart men with rude, heavy sweeps propel the boat across; but at every passage the swift current takes it down-stream twice as far as the river's width. After disembarking the passengers, the boatmen have to tow it this distance up-stream again before making the next crossing. The boatmen wear a single garment of blue cotton that in shape resembles a plain loose shirt. When nearing the shore, three or four of them deftly slip their arms out of the sleeves, bunch the whole garment up around their necks, and spring overboard. Swimming to shallow water with a rope, they brace themselves to stay the down-stream career of the boat.

The people regard me with a deep and peculiar interest; very few remarks are made among themselves, and no one puts a single question to me or ventures upon any remarks. All this is in strange contrast to the everlasting gabble and the noisy and persistent importunities of the Persians. The Afghans are plainly full of speculations concerning my mission, who I am, and what I am doing in their country; although they regard the bicycle with great curiosity, the machine is evidently a matter of secondary importance.

Riding part way to the city gate, I send the guide ahead to notify the governor of my arrival, and to present the letter from Aminulah Khan. He is absent what appears to me an unnecessarily long time, and I determine to follow him in and take my chances on the tide of circumstances, as in the cities of Persia. It is not without certain lively apprehensions of possible adventure, however, that I approach the little arched gateway of this gray-walled Afghan city, conscious of its being filled with the most fanatical population in the world. In addition to this knowledge is the disquieting reflection of being a trespasser on forbidden territory, and therefore outside the pale of governmental sympathy should I get into trouble.

The fascination of penetrating the strange little world within those high walls, however, ill brooks these retrospective reflections, or thoughts of unpleasant consequences, and I make no hesitation about riding up to the gate. A sharp, short turn and abrupt rise in the road occurs at the gate, necessitating a dismount and a trundle of about thirty yards, when I suddenly find myself confronting a couple of sentries beneath the archway of the gate. The sensation of surprise seems quite in order of late, and these sentries furnish yet another sensation, for they are wearing the red jackets of British infantrymen and the natty peaked caps of the Royal Artillery. The same crimson flush of embarrassment – or whatever it may be – that was observed in the countenance of the Eimuck chief, overspreads their faces, and they seem overcome with confusion and astonishment; but they both salute mechanically as I pass in. Fifty yards of open waste ground enables me to mount and ride into the entrance of the principal street. I have precious little time to look about me, and no opportunity to discover what the result of my temerity would be after the people had recovered from their amazement, for hardly have I gotten fairly into the street when I am met by my old guide, conducting a guard of twelve soldiers who have been sent to bring me in.

CHAPTER X

ARRESTED AT FURRAH

Perhaps no stranger occurrence in the field of personal adventure in Central Asia has happened for many a year than my entrance into Furrah on a bicycle. Only those who know Afghanistan and the Afghans can fully realize the ticklish character of this little piece of adventure.

My soldier-escort are fine-looking fellows, wearing the well-known red jackets of the British Army, evidently the uniform of some sepoy regiment. Forming around me, they conduct me through the gate of an inner enclosure near by, and usher me into a small compound where Mahmoud Yusuph Khan, the commander-in-chief of the garrison, is engaged in holding a morning reception of his subordinate chiefs and officers. The spectacle that greets my astonished eyes is a revelation indeed; the whole compound is filled with soldiers wearing the regimentals of the Anglo-Indian army. As I enter the compound and trundle the bicycle between long files of soldiers toward Mahmoud Yusuph Khan and his officers, five hundred pairs of eyes are fixed on me with intense curiosity. These are Cabooli soldiers sent here to garrison Furrah, where they will be handy to march to the relief of Herat, in case of demonstrations against that city by the Russians. The tension over the Penjdeh incident has not yet (April, 1886) wholly relaxed, and I feel instinctively that I am suspected of being a Russian spy.

In the centre of the compound is a large bungalow, surrounded by a slightly raised porch. Seated on a mat at one end of this is Mahmoud Yusuph Khan, and ranged in two long rows down the porch are his chiefs and officers. They are all seated cross-legged on a strip of carpet, and attendants are serving them with tea in little porcelain cups. They are the most martial-looking assembly of humans I ever set eyes on. They are fairly bristling with quite serviceable looking weapons, besides many of the highly ornamented, but less dangerous, 'gewgaws of war' dear to the heart of the brave but conservative warriors of Islam. Prominent among the peculiarities observed are strips of chain mail attached to portions of their clothing as guards against sword-cuts, noticeably on the sleeves. Some are wearing steel helmets, some huge turbans, and others the regular Afghan military hat, this latter a rakish-looking head-piece something like the hat of a Chinese Tartar general.

Mahmoud Yusuph Khan himself is wearing one of these hats, and is attired in a tight-fitting suit of buckran, pipe-clayed from head to foot; in his hat glitters a handsome rosette of nine diamonds, which I have an opportunity of counting while seated beside him. He is a stoutish person, full-faced, slightly above middle age, less striking in appearance than many of his subordinates. When I have walked up between the two rows of seated chieftains and gained his side, he forthwith displays his knowledge of the English mode of greeting by shaking hands. He orders an attendant to fetch a couple of camp chairs, and setting one for me, he rises from the carpet and occupies the other one himself. Tea is brought in small cups instead of glasses, and is highly sweetened after the manner of the Persians; sweetmeats are handed round at the same time. After ascertaining that I understand something of Persian, he expresses his astonishment at my appearance in Furrah. At first it is painfully evident that he suspects me of being a Russian spy; but after several minutes of questions and answers, he is apparently satisfied that I am not a Muscovite, and he explains to his officers that I am an 'Ingilis *nockshi*' (correspondent). He is greatly astonished to hear of the route by which I entered the country, as no traveller ever entered Afghanistan across the *Dasht-i-no-oomid* before. I tell him that I am going to Kandahar and Quetta, and suggest that he send a sowar with me to guide the way. He smiles amusedly at this suggestion, and shaking his head vigorously, he says, 'Kandahar *neis*; Afghanistan's bad; *khylie* bad;' and he furthermore explains that I would be sure to get killed.

'*Khylie koob*; I don't want any sowar, I will go alone; if I get killed, then nobody will be blamable but myself.'

'Kandahar *neis*,' he replies, shaking his finger and head, and looking very serious; 'Kandahar *neis; beest* (20) sowars couldn't see you safely through to Kandahar; Afghanistan's bad; a Ferenghi would be sure to get killed before reaching Kandahar.'

Pretending to be greatly amused at this, I reply, '*koob*; if I get killed, all right, I don't want any sowars; I will go alone.'

At hearing this, he grows still more serious, and enters into quite an eloquent and lengthy explanation, to dissuade me from the idea of going. He explains that the Ameer has little control over the fanatical tribes in Zemindavar, and that although the Boundary Commission had a whole regiment of sepoys, the Ameer couldn't guarantee their safety if they came to Furrah. He furthermore expresses his surprise that I wasn't killed before getting this far. The officer of the guard who brought me in, and who is standing against the porch close by, speaks up at this stage of the interview and tells with much animation of how I was riding down the street, and of the people all speechless with astonishment.

Mahmoud Yusuph Khan repeats this to his officers, with comments of his own, and they look at one another and smile and shake their heads, evidently deeply impressed at what they consider the dare-devil recklessness of a Ferenghi in venturing alone into the streets of Furrah. The warlike Afghans have great admiration for personal courage, and they evidently regard my arrival here without escort as a proof that I am possessed of a commendable share of that desirable quality.

Mahmoud Yusuph Khan now attempts to explain at length sundry reasons why it is necessary to place me, for the time being, under guard. He seems very anxious to convey this unpleasant piece of information in the flowery *langue diplomatique* of the Orient, or in other words, to coat the bitter pill of my detention with a sugary coating of Eastern politeness.

After the interview the twelve red-jackets that appear to constitute the Governor's body-guard are detailed to conduct me to a walled garden outside the city. Before departing, however, I give the strange assembly of Afghan warriors an exhibition of riding around the compound. The guard, under the leadership of the officer with the bull-dog phiz, fix bayonets and form into a file on either side of me as I trundle back through the same street traversed upon my arrival. Accompanying us is a man on a gray horse whom everybody addresses respectfully as 'Kiftan Sahib' (Captain), and another individual afoot in a bottle-green roundabout, a broad leathern belt, a striped turban, white baggy pantalettes, and pointed red shoes.

Outside the gate, at the suggestion of the young man in the bottle-green roundabout, I mount and ride, wheeling slowly along between the little files of soldiers. The soldiers are delighted at the novelty of their duty, and they swing briskly along as I pedal a little faster. They smile at the exertion necessary to keep up, and falling in with their spirit of amusement, I gradually increase my speed, and finally shoot ahead of them entirely.

Kiftan Sahib comes galloping after me on the gray, and with good-humored anxiety motions for me to stop and let the soldiers catch up. He it is upon whom the commander-in-chief has saddled the responsibility for my safe-keeping, and this little display of levity and my ability to so easily out-distance the soldiers, awakens in him the spirit of apprehension at once. One can see that he breathes easier as soon as we are safely inside the garden gate.

About four o'clock I am visited by a fatherly old khan in a sky-blue gown, and an interesting Cabooli cavalry colonel, with pieces of chain mail distributed about his uniform, and a fierce-looking moustache that stands straight out from his upper lip. Sweetmeats enough to start a small candy shop have been sent me during the afternoon, and setting them out before my guests, we are soon on the most familiar terms.

The mission of these two officers is apparently to prepare me gradually for the intelligence that I am to be taken back to Herat. So skilfully and diplomatically does the old khan in the cerulean gown acquit himself of this mission, that I thoroughly understand what is to be my disposition, although Herat is never mentioned. He talks volubly about the Ameer, the Wali, the Padishah, the dowleh, Cabool, Allah, and a host of other subjects, out of which I readily evolve my fate; but, as yet, he breathes nothing but diplomatic hints, and these are clothed in the most pleasant and reassuring smiles, and given in tones of paternal solicitude.

Mahmoud Yusuph Khan himself comes to the garden in the cool of the evening, and for half an hour occupies bungalow No. 2.

His remarks during our second interview are largely

composed of furtive queries, intended to penetrate what he evidently, even as yet, suspects to be the secret object of my mysterious appearance in the heart of the country. Your Afghan official is nothing if not suspicious, and although he professed his own conviction, in the morning, of my being an English 'nokshi,' his constitutionally suspicious nature forbids him accepting this impression as final.

Understanding thoroughly by this time that I am not to be allowed to go through by way of Giriskh and Kandahar, and dreading the probability of being taken back into Persia, I ask permission to travel south to Jowain and the frontier of Beloochistan. The Afghan-Beloochi boundary is not more than fifty or sixty miles south of Furrah, and while it would be difficult to say what advantage would be gained by reaching there, it would at all events be some consolation to find myself at liberty.

The interview ends, however, without much additional light being shed on their intentions; but the advent of more sweetmeats shortly after the Governor's departure, and the unexpected luxury of a bottle of Shiraz wine, heightens the conviction that my own wishes in the matter are to be politely ignored.

During the forenoon the blue-gowned old khan and his major-domo, the mail-clad colonel, again present themselves at my bungalow. They are gracious and friendly to a painful degree, and sugar would scarcely melt in the mouth of the paternal old khan as he delivers the 'Wali's salaams to the Sahib.' Tea and sweetmeats are handed around, and Kiftan Sahib and Bottle Green join our company.

Nothing but the formal salaams has yet been said; but intuition is a faithful forerunner, and ere another word is spoken, I know well enough that the khan and the colonel have been sent to break the disagreeable news that I am to be taken to Herat, and that Kiftan Sahib and Bottle Green have dropped in out of curiosity to see how I take it.

The kindly old khan finds his task of awakening the spirit of disappointment anything but congenial, and he seems very loath to deliver the message. When he finally unburdens himself, it is with averted eyes and roundabout language.

He dwells piously and at considerable length upon our

obligations to submit to the will of Allah, not forgetting a liberal use of the Oriental fatalist's favorite expression: 'kismet.'

For the sake of argument, rather than with any hope of influencing things in my favor, I reply:

'All right, I don't ask the Ameer's protection; I will go to Kandahar and Quetta alone, on my own responsibility; then if I get murdered by the Ghilzais, nobody but myself will be to blame.'

'The Wali has his orders from the Padishah, the Ameer Abdur Rahman Khan, that no Ferenghi is to come in the country.'

'Tell the Wali that Afghanistan is Allah's country first and Abdur Rahman's country second. Inshallah, Allah gives everybody the road.'

The old khan is evidently at a loss how to meet so logical an argument, and the colonel, Kiftan Sahib, and Bottle Green are deeply impressed at what they consider my unanswerable wisdom. They look at one another and shake their heads and smile.

Late in the afternoon of the second day my scarlet guard marshal themselves in front of the bungalow, and Kiftan Sahib and Bottle Green bid me prepare for departure to Herat. The old khan and the colonel, and several other horsemen, appear at the gate; the soldiers form themselves into two files, and between them, I trundle from my circumscribed quarters. The rude ferry-boat is awaiting our coming, and in a few minutes the khan and the colonel bid me quite an affectionate farewell on the river-bank, gazing eagerly into my face as though regretful at the necessity of parting so soon.

Several horsemen have already crossed and are awaiting us on the opposite shore. Kiftan Sahib and another officer with a henna-tinted beard are in charge of the party taking me back. Besides myself and these two, the party consists of eleven horsemen; with sundry modifications, their general appearance, arms, and dress resemble the make-up of a Persian sowar rather than the regular Afghan soldier. The sun is just setting behind those western mountains I passed three days ago as we reach the western shore, the boatmen are unloading the saddles and accoutrements of our party, and I sit down on the bank and survey the strange scene just across the river.

The steep bluff opposite is occupied by people who accompanied us to the river. Many of them are seizing this opportune moment to prostrate themselves toward the Holy City, the geographical position of which is happily indicated by the setting sun.

Prominent among the worshippers are seen side by side the cerulean figure of the khan, and the colonel in all the bravery of his military trappings, his chain armor glistening brightly in the waning sunlight. A little removed from the crowd, the twelve red-coats are ranged in a row, performing the same pious ceremony; as their bared heads bob up and down one after another, the scarlet figures outlined in a row against the eastern sky are strangely suggestive of a small flock of flamingoes engaged in fishing.

CHAPTER XI

UNDER ESCORT TO HERAT

The plain, heretofore hard, now changes into loose sand and gravel, and the trail becomes quite obliterated. In addition to these undesirable changes, the wind commences blowing furiously from the north, making it absolutely impossible to ride. Rounding the base of an abutting mountain, we emerge upon the grassy lowlands of the Harood in the vicinity of Subzowar. Subzowar is a sort of way-station between Furrah and Herat, the only inhabited place, except tents, on the whole journey. It is on the west side of the Harood and the broad, swift stream is full to overflowing, a turgid torrent rushing along at a dangerous pace.

After much shouting and firing of guns, a score of villagers appear on the opposite bank, and several of them come wading and swimming across. They seem veritable amphibians, capable of stemming the tide that wellnigh sweeps strong horses off their feet. The river is fordable by following a zigzag course well known to the local watermen. One of them carries the bicycle safely across on his head, and others lead the sowars' horses by the bridle.

When all the Afghans but Kiftan Sahib have been assisted over, the strongest horse of the party is brought back for my own passage. A dozen natives are made to form a close cordon about me to rescue me in case of misadventure, while one leads the horse by his bridle and another steadies him by holding on to his tail. Kiftan Sahib himself brings up the rear, and, as the rushing waters deepen around us, he abjures me to keep a steady seat and, in a voice that almost degenerates into an apprehensive whine, he mutters: 'The receipt, Sahib, the receipt.'

Whether from their knowledge of the unsuitableness of the country ahead, or from a new spasm of apprehension concerning their responsibility, does not appear; but in the morning Kiftan Sahib and the chief of the sowars insist upon me mounting a horse and handing the bicycle over to the tender mercies of the person in charge of the nummud pack-horse. They point in the direction of Herat, and deliver themselves of a marvellous quantity of deprecatory pantomime. My own impression is that, having recrossed the Harood, the only great obstacle in the path of a wheelman between Furrah and Herat, their abnormally suspicious minds imagine that there is now nothing to prevent me taking wings and outdistancing them to the latter place.

Finding them determined, and, moreover, nothing loath to try a horse for a change, on the back-stretch, I take the wheel apart and distribute fork, backbone, and large wheel among the sowars. The only fit place for the latter is on the top of the nummuds and blankets on the spare pack-horse, and, before starting, I see to fastening it securely on top of the load. This pack-horse is a powerful black stallion that puts in a good share of his time trying to attack the other horses. Owing to this uncontrollable pugnacity, he is habitually led along at some considerable distance from the party, generally to the rear.

The person in charge of him is a young negro as black, and proportionately powerful, as himself. Wild and ferocious as is the stallion, he is a civilized and mild-mannered animal compared with his manager. In the matter of facial expression and intellectual development this uncivilized descendant of Ham is first cousin to a wild gorilla, and it is not without certain misgivings that I leave the web-like bicycle-wheel in his charge. He has been a very interesting study of uncivilization all along, and his bump of destructiveness is as large as an orange.

The sun goes down and dusk settles over our trail, and still the chief of the sowars and Kiftan Sahib lead the way. Many of the horses are pretty badly fagged, they have had nothing to eat all day and next to nothing to drink, and the party are straggling along the trail for a couple of miles back. At length lights are observed twinkling in the darkness ahead. Half an hour later we dismount in a nomad camp, and one after another the remainder of the party come straggling in, some of them leading their horses. Both men and animals are well-nigh overcome with fatigue.

The shrill neighing of the ferocious and spirited black stallion is heard as he approaches and realizes that he is coming into camp; he is a glorious specimen of a horse, neither hunger nor thirst can curb his spirit. He is carrying far the heaviest load of the party, yet he comes into camp at ten o'clock, after hustling along over stones and sand since before day-light, without food or water; neighing loudly and ready to fight all the horses within reach.

The chief of the sowars goes out to superintend the unloading of the black stallion; and soon I hear him addressing the negro in angry tones, supplementing his reproachful words with several resounding blows of his riding-whip. The wild darkey's disapproval of these proceedings finds expression in a roar of pain and fear that would do justice to a yearling bull being dragged into the shambles.

The cause of this turmoil shortly turns up in the shape of my wheel, with no less than eleven spokes broken, and the rim considerably twisted out of shape. Kiftan Sahib surveys the damaged wheel a moment, draws his own rawhide from his *kammerbund*, and rises to his feet. With a hoarse cry of alarm the negro vanishes into the surrounding gloom; the next moment is heard his eager chuckling laugh, the spontaneous result of his lucky escape from Kiftan Sahib's vengeful rawhide.

The explanation of the negro is that the black horse laid down with his load. The wheel presents a well-nigh ruined appearance, and I retire to my couch in a most unenviable frame of mind; lying awake for hours, pondering over the probability of being able to fix it up again at Herat.

The wind blows raw and chilly from the north as we depart at early dawn, and the men muffle themselves up in whatever wraps they happen to have. Unwilling to trust the wheel further in the charge of the negro, I carry it myself, resting it on one stirrup, and securing it with a rope over my shoulder. It is a most awkward thing to carry on horseback; but, unhandy though it be, I regret not having so carried it the whole way from Subzowar.

From the busy nomad camp, the trail seems to make a gradual ascent until, on the morning of April 30th, we arrive at the bluff-like termination of a rolling upland country, and behold! spread out below is the famous valley of Herat. Like a

"The famous Valley of Herat."

panorama suddenly opened up before me is the charmed stretch of country that has time and again created such a stir in the political and military circles of England and Russia, the famous 'gate to India' about which the two greatest empires of the world have sometimes almost come to blows. Several populous villages are scattered about the valley within easy range of human vision; the Heri Rood, now bursting its natural boundaries under the stimulus of the spring floods, glistens broadly at intervals like a chain of small lakes. The fortress of Herat is dimly discernible in the distance beyond the river, probably about twenty miles from our position; it is rendered distinguishable from other masses of mud-brown habitations by a cluster of tall minarets, reminding one of a group of factory chimneys. The whole scene, as viewed from the commanding view of our ridge, embraces perhaps four hundred square miles of territory; about one-tenth of this appears to be under cultivation, the remainder being of the same stony, desert-like character as the average camel-thorn *dasht*.

Letters are forwarded to the city immediately upon our arrival, and on the following morning an officer and several soldiers make their appearance, to receive me from Kiftan Sahib and duly receipt for my transfer. The officer announces himself as having once been to Bombay, and proceeds to question me in a mixture of Persian and Hindostani.

Finding me ignorant of the latter language, he openly accuses me of being a Russian, raising his finger and wagging his head in a deprecatory manner.

'Merg Sahib,' the political agent of the Boundary Commission, he says is at Murghab, and 'Ridgeway Sahib' at Maimene. Learning that a courier is to be sent at once to them with letters in regard to myself, I quickly embrace the opportunity of sending a letter to each by the same messenger, explaining the situation, and asking Colonel Ridgeway to try and render me some assistance in getting through to India.

The transfer having been duly made, I am conducted, a mile or so, to the garden of a gentleman named Mohammed Ahzim Khan, my quarters there being an open bungalow just large enough to stretch out in. Here is provided everything necessary for the rude personal comfort of the country, and such additional luxuries as raisins and pomegranates are at once brought.

The second day in the garden is remembered as the anniversary of my start from Liverpool, and I have plenty of time for retrospection. It is unnecessary to say that the year has been crowded with strange experiences. Not the least strange of all, perhaps, is my present predicament as a prisoner in the Herat Valley.

In the afternoon there arrives from Herat a Peshawari gentleman named Mirza Gholam Ahmed, who is stationed here in the capacity of native agent for the Indian government. He is an individual possessed of considerable Asiatic astuteness, and his particular mission is very plainly to discover for the governor of Herat whether I am English or Russian. He is a somewhat fleshy, well-favored person, and withal of pre-possessing manners. He introduces himself by shaking hands and telling me his name, and forthwith indulges in a pinch of snuff preparatory to his task of interrogation. Accompanying him is the officer who received me from Kiftan Sahib in the apricot garden, and whose suspicions of my being a Russian spy are anything but allayed.

During the interview he squats down on the threshold of the little bungalow, and concentrates his curiosity and suspicion into a protracted penetrating stare, focused steadily at my devoted countenance. Mohammed Ahzim Khan imitates him to perfection, except that *his* stare contains more curiosity and less suspicion. Mirza Gholam Ahmed proceeds upon his mission of fathoming the secret of my nationality with extreme wariness, as becomes an Oriental official engaged in a task of significant import, and at first confines himself to the use of Persian and Hindostani. It does not take me long, however, to satisfy the trustworthy old Peshawari that I am not a Muscov, and fifteen minutes after his preliminary pinch of snuff, he is unbosoming himself to me to the extent of letting me know that he served with General Pollock on the Seistan Boundary Commission, that he went with General Pollock to London, and moreover rejoices in the titular distinction of C.I.E. (Companion Indian Empire), bestowed upon him for long and faithful civil and political services.

He understands English sufficiently well to comprehend the meaning of my remarks and queries, and even knows a few words himself. From him I learn that I will not be permitted to visit Herat, and that I am to be kept under guard until Faramorz

Khan's courier returns from the Boundary Commission Camp with Colonel Ridgeway's answer. He tells me that the fame of the bicycle has long ago been brought to Herat by pilgrims returning from Meshed, and the marvellous stories of my accomplishments are current in the bazaars. Fourteen farsakhs (fifty-six miles) an hour, and nothing said about the condition of the roads, is the average Herati's understanding of it; and many a grave, turbaned merchant in the bazaar, and wild warrior on the ramparts, indulges in day-dreams of an iron horse little less miraculous in its deeds than the winged steed of the air we read of in the Arabian Nights.

The direct results of Mirza Gholam Ahmed's visit and favorable report to the Governor of Herat, are made manifest on the following day by the appearance of his companion of yesterday in charge of two attendants, bringing me boxes of sweetmeats, almonds, raisins, and salted nuts, together with a package of tea and a fifteen-pound cone of loaf-sugar; all backsheesh from the Governor of Herat. Mirza Gholam Ahmed himself contributes a cake of toilet soap, a few envelopes and sheets of paper, and Huntley & Palmer's Reading biscuits. Upon stumbling upon these latter acceptable articles, one naturally falls to wondering whether this world-famed form of biscuit-makers suspect that their wares sometimes penetrate even inside the battlemented walls of Herat. With them come also three gunsmiths, charged with the duty of assisting in the reparation of the bicycle, badly damaged by the horse, it is remembered, on the way from Furrah.

The whole of the fifth and sixth days are consumed in the task of repairing the damages to the bicycle, the result being highly satisfactory, considering everything. Six new spokes that I have with me have been inserted, and sundry others stretched and the ends newly threaded. The gunsmiths are quite expert workmen, considering the tools they have to work with, and when they happen to drill a hole a trifle crooked, they are full of apologies, and remind me that this is Afghanistan and not Frangistan. They know and appreciate good material when they see it, and during the process of heating and stretching the spokes, loud and profuse are the praises bestowed upon the quality of the iron. '*Koob awhan*,' they say, '*Khylie koob awhan; Ferenghi awhan koob.*' As artisans, interested in mechanical affairs, the ball-bearings of the pedals, one of which I take apart to show them, excites their profound admiration as evidence of the marvellous skill of the Ferenghis. Much careful work is required to spring the rim of the wheel back into a true circle, every spoke having to be loosened and the whole wheel newly adjusted. Except for the handy little spoke-vice which I very fortunately brought with me, this work of adjustment would have been impossible.

Day after day passes wearily along; wearily, notwithstanding the kindly efforts of my guardians to make things pleasant and comfortable. From an Asiatic's standpoint, nothing could be more desirable than my present circumstances; with nothing to do but lay around and be waited on, generous meals three times daily, sweetmeats to nibble and tea to drink the whole livelong day; conscious of requiring rest and generous diet – all this, however, is anything but satisfactory in view of the reflection that the fine spring weather is rapidly passing away, and that every day ought to see me forty or fifty miles nearer the Pacific Coast.

Thus the days of my detention pass away, until the ninth day after my arrival here. On the evening of May 8th, the officer who first interviewed me in the apricot orchard comes to my bungalow, and brings salaams from Faramorz Khan. He and Mohammed Ahzim Khan, after a brief discussion between themselves, commence telling me, in the same roundabout manner as the blue-gowned Khan at Furrah, that the Ameer at Cabool has no control over the fanatical nomads of Zemindavar. Mohammed Ahzim Khan draws his finger across his throat, and the officer repeats 'Afghan badmash, badmash, b-a-d-m-a-s-h!' (desperado).

This parrot-like repetition is uttered in accents so pleaful, and is, withal, accompanied by such a searching stare into my face, that its comicality for the minute overcomes any sense of disappointment at the fall of my hopes. For my experience at Furrah teaches me that this is really the object of their visit.

Another ingenious argument of these polite and, after a certain childish fashion, astute Asiatics, is a direct appeal to my magnamity. 'We know you are brave, and to accomplish your object would even allow the Ghilzais to cut your throat; but the Wali begs you to sacrifice yourself for the reputation of his country, by keeping out of danger,' they plead. 'If you get killed, Afghanistan will get a bad name.'

They are in dead earnest about converting me by argument and pleadings to their view of the case. I point out that, so far as the reputation of Afghanistan is concerned, there can be little difference between forbidding travellers to go through for fear of their getting murdered, and their actual killing. I remind them, too, that I am a 'nokshi,' and can let the people of Frangistan understand this if I am turned back.

These arguments, of course, avail me nothing; the upshot of instructions received from the Boundary Commission camp, is that I am to be conducted at once back into Persia.

CHAPTER XII

TAKEN BACK TO PERSIA

The Governor of Herat sends '*khylie* salaams' and permission for me to ride the bicycle, stipulating that I keep near the escort. So, with many an injunction to me about *dasht-adam, kooh, dagh,* etc., by way of warning me against venturing too far ahead, we bid farewell to the garden, with its strange associations, in the early morning. Beside Mohammed Ahzim Khan and myself are three sowars, mounted on splendid horses.

Over a country that consists chiefly of trailless hills and intervening strips of desert, we wend our weary way, the bicycle often proving more of a drag than a benefit. The weather gets insufferably hot; in places the rocks fairly shimmer with heat, and are so hot that one can scarce hold the hand to them. We camp for the first night at a village, and on the second at an *umbar* that suggests our approach to Persia, and in the morning we make an early start with the object of reaching Karize before evening.

The day grows warm apace, and, at ten miles, the khan calls a halt for the discussion of what simple refreshments we have with us. Our larder embraces dry bread and cold goat-meat and a few handfuls of raisins. It ought also to include water in the leathern bottle swinging from the stirrup of one of the sowars; but when we halt, it is to discover that this worthy has forgotten to fill his bottle. The way has been heavy for a bicycle, trundling wearily through sand mainly, with no riding to speak of; and young as is the day, I am well-nigh overcome with thirst and weariness. I am too thirsty to eat, and, miserably tired and disgusted, one gets an instructive lesson in the control of the mind over the body. Much of my fatigue comes of low spirits, born of disappointment at being conducted back into Persia.

One of the sowars is despatched ahead to fill his bottle with water at a well known to be some five miles farther ahead, and to meet us with it on the way. On through the sand and heat we plod wearily, myself almost sick with thirst, fatigue, and disgust. Mohammed Ahzim Khan, observing my wretched condition, insists upon me letting one of the sowars try his hand at trundling the wheel, whilst I rest myself by riding his horse. Both the sowars bravely try their best to relieve me, but they cut ridiculous figures, toppling over every little while. At length one of them upsets the bicycle into a little gully, and falling on it, snaps asunder two spokes. The khan gives him a good tongue-lashing for his carelessness; but one can hardly blame the fellow, and I take it under my own protection again, before it goes farther and fares worse.

About 2 P.M. the sowar sent forward meets us with water; but it is almost undrinkable. Far better luck awaits us, however, farther along. Sighting an Eimuck camel-rider in the distance, one of the sowars gives chase and halts him until we can come up. Slung across his camel he has a skin of *doke*, the most welcome thing one can wish for under the circumstances. Everybody helps himself liberally of the refreshing beverage, shrinking the Eimuck's supply very perceptibly. The Eimuck joins heartily with our party in laughing at the altered contour of the pliant skin, as pointed out jocularly by Mohammed Ahzim Khan, bids us 'salaam *aleykum*,' and pursues his way across country.

Some time in the night I am awakened. A strange horseman has arrived in camp with a letter for me. He wears the uniform of a military courier. The sowars make a blaze of brushwood for me to read by. It is a letter from Mr. Merk, the political agent of the Boundary Commission. It is a long letter, full of considerate language, but no instructions affecting the orders of my escort. Mr. Merk explains why Mahmoud Yusuph Khan could not take the responsibility of allowing me to proceed to Kandahar. The population of Zemindavar, he points out, are particularly fanatical and turbulent, and I should very probably have been murdered; etc.

The march toward Karize is resumed in good season in the morning. 'What was that? a cuckoo?' At first I can scarcely believe my own senses, the idea of cuckoos calling in the jungles of Afghanistan being about the last thing I should have expected to hear, never having heard of travellers hearing them anywhere in Central Asia, nor yet having heard them myself before. But there is no mistake; for ere we pass Kafir Kaleh, I hear the familiar notes again and again.

The road is a decided improvement over anything we have struck since leaving Herat, and by noon we arrive at Karize. For some inexplicable reason the Sooltan of Karize receives our party with very ill grace. He looks sick, and is probably suffering from fever, which may account for the evident sourness of his disposition.

Mohammed Ahzim Khan is anything but pleased at our reception, and as soon as he receives the receipt for my delivery makes his preparations to return. I don't think the Sooltan even tendered my escort a feed of grain for their horses, a piece of inhospitality wholly out of place in this wild country.

As for myself, he simply orders a villager to supply me with food and quarters, and charge me for it. Mohammed Ahzim Khan comes to my quarters to bid me good-by, and he takes the opportunity to explain 'this is Iran, not Afghanistan. Iran, *pool*; Afghanistan, *pool neis*.' There is no need of explanation, however; the people rubbing their fingers eagerly together and crying, '*pool, pool*,' when I ask for something to eat, tells me plainer than any explanations that I am back again among our pool-loving friends, the subjects of the Shah. As I bid Mohammed Ahzim Khan farewell, I feel almost like parting from a friend; he is a good fellow, and with nine-tenths of his inquisitiveness suppressed, would make a very agreeable companion.

And so, here I am within a hundred and sixty miles of Meshed again. More than a month has flown past since I last looked back upon its golden dome; it has been an eventful month. My experiences have been exceptional and instructive, but I ought now to be enjoying the comforts of the English camp at Quetta, instead of halting over-night in the mud huts of the surly Sooltan of Karize.

A camel runs away and unseats his rider in deference to his timidity at my strange appearance as I bowl briskly across the Meshed plain at noon. By one o'clock I am circling around the moat of the city, and by two am snugly ensconced in my old quarters, relating the adventures of the last five weeks to Gray, and receiving from him in exchange the latest scraps of

European news. I have made the one hundred and sixty miles from Karize in two days and a half – not a bad showing with a bicycle that has been tinkered up by Herati gunsmiths.

Since my departure from Meshed, southward bound, another wandering correspondent has invaded the Holy City. Mr. R—, 'special' of a great London daily paper, whom I had the pleasure of meeting once or twice in Teheran, has come eastward in an effort to enter Afghanistan. He has been halted by peremptory orders at Meshed. Disgusted with his ill-luck at not being permitted to carry out his plans, he is on the eve of returning to Constantinople. As I am heading for the same point myself, we arrange to travel there in company. Being somewhat under the weather from a recent attack of fever, he has contracted for a Russian *fourgon* to carry him as far as Shahrood, the farthest point on our route to which vehicular conveyance is practicable. Our purpose is to reach the Caspian port of Bunder Guz, thence embark on a Russian steamer to Baku, over the Caucasus Railway to Batoum, thence by Black Sea steamer to Constantinople.

Accordingly, soon after sunrise on the morrow, the road around the outer moat of Meshed is circled once again. A middle-aged descendant of the Prophet, riding a graceful dapple-gray mare, spurs his steed into a swinging gallop for about five miles across the level plain in an effort to bear me company. Three miles farther, and for miles over the steep and unridable gradients of the Shahriffabad hills, I may anticipate the delights of having his horse's nose at my shoulder, and my heels in constant jeopardy. To avoid this, I spurt ahead, and ere long have the satisfaction of seeing him give it up.

In the foot-hills I encounter, for the first time, one of those characteristics of Mohammedan countries, and more especially of Persia, a caravan of the dead. Thousands of bodies are carried every year, on horseback or on camels, from various parts of Persia, to be buried in holy ground at Meshed, Kerbella, or Mecca. The corpses are bound about with canvas, and slung, like bales of merchandise, one on either side of the horse. The stench from one of these corpse-caravans is something fearful, nothing more nor less than the horrible stench of putrid human bodies. And yet the drivers seem to mind it very little indeed. One stout horse in the party I meet this morning carries two corpses; and in the saddle between them rides a woman! 'Mashallah!' perchance those very bodies, between which she sits perched so indifferently, are the remains of small-pox victims. But, what cares the woman? – she is not a Mohammedan, and a female one at that ? – and does she not believe in kismet? What cares she for Ferenghi 'sanitary fads?' – if it is her kismet to take the small-pox, she will take it; if it is her kismet not to, she won't. One would think, however, that common sense and common prudence would instruct these people to imitate the excellent example of the Chinese, in taking measures to dispose of the flesh before transporting the bones to distant burial-places. Many of the epidemics of disease that decimate the populations of Eastern countries, and sometimes travel into the West, originate from these abominable caravans of the dead and kindred irrationalities of the illogical and childlike Oriental.

A new surprise awaits us at Mijamid, something that we are totally unprepared for. As we reach the *chapar-khana* there, a voice from the roof greets us with 'Sprechen sie Deutsch?' Looking up in astonishment, we behold Colonel G—, a German officer in the Shah's army, whom both of us are familiarly acquainted with by sight, from seeing him so often at the morning reviews in the military maidan at Teheran. But this is not all, for with him are his wife and daughter. This is the first time European ladies have traversed the Meshed-Teheran road, Teheran being the farthest point eastward in Persia that lady travellers have heretofore penetrated to. Colonel G— has been appointed to the staff of the new Governor-General of Khorassan, and is on his way to Meshed. The appearance of Ferenghi ladies in the Holy City will be an innovation that will fairly eclipse the introduction of the bicycle. All Meshed will be wild with curiosity, and the poor ladies will never be able to venture into the streets without disguise.

There is furor enough over them in Mijamid; the whole population is assembled *en masse* before the *chapar-khana*. The combination of the bicycle, three Ferenghis, and, above all, two Ferenghi ladies, is an event that will form a red-letter mark in the history of Mijamid for generations of unborn Persian ryots to talk about and wonder over.

The colonel produces a bottle of excellent Shiraz wine and a box of Russian cigarettes. The ladies have become sufficiently Orientalized to number among their accomplishments the smoking of cigarettes. They are delighted at meeting us, and are already acquainted with the main circumstances of my misadventure in Afghanistan. Camp-stools are brought out, and we spend a most pleasant hour together, before continuing on our opposite courses. The wondering natives are almost speechless with astonishment at the spectacle of the two ladies sitting out there, faces all uncovered, smoking cigarettes, sipping claret, and chatting freely with the men. It is a regular circus-day for these poor, unenlightened mortals. The ladies are charming, and the charm of female society loses nothing, the reader may be sure, from one's having been deprived of it for a matter of months.

Our way leads up fearful rocky paths, where the horses have to be led, and at times assisted; up, up, until our elevation is nearly ten thousand feet, and we are among a chaotic wilderness of precipitous rocks and scrub pines. A false step in some places, and our horses would roll down among the craggy rocks for hundreds of feet. It is a toilsome march, but we cross the Tash Pass, and camp for the night in a little inter-mountain valley, beside a stream at the foot of a pine-covered mountain. The change from the dry interior plains is already novel and refreshing. Grass abounds in abundance, and the prospect is the greenest I have seen for nine months.

A march of a dozen miles from this valley over a tortuous mountain trail brings us into a country the existence of which one could never, by any stretch of the imagination, dream of in connection with Persia, as one sees it in its desert-like character south of the mountains. The transformation is from one extreme of vegetable nature to the other. We camp for lunch on velvety greensward beneath a grove of oak and cherry trees. Cuckoos are heard calling round about, singing birds make melody, and among them we both recognize the cheery clickety-click of my raisin-loving Herati friends, the bul-buls. Flowers, too, are here at our feet in abundance, forget-me-nots and other familiar varieties.

An hour after our arrival, Abdul goes out and discovers a Persian gentleman named Mahmoud Turki Aghi, who presents himself in the capacity of British agent here. As we were in ignorance of the presence of any such official being in Asterabad, he comes as a pleasant surprise, and still more pleasant comes an invitation to accept his hospitality.

From him we learn that the steamer we expect to take at Bunder Guz, the port of Asterabad, eight farsakhs distant, will not sail until six days later. Mindful of the fever, from which he is still a sufferer to an uncomfortable extent, R— looks a trifle glum at this announcement, and, after our traps are unpacked at Mahmoud Turki Aghi's, he ferrets out a book of travels that I had often heard him refer to as an authority on sundry subjects. Turning over the leaves, he finds a reference to Bunder Guz, and reads out the story of a certain 'gimlet-tailed fly' that makes life a burden to the unwary traveller who elects to linger there on the Caspian shore. Between this gimlet-tailed pest, however, and the mosquitoes of Asterabad we decide that there can be very little to choose, and so make up our minds to accept our host's hospitality for a day and then push on.

During the day we call on the Russian consul to get our passports *viséd*. As between English and Russian *prestige*, the latter are decidedly to the fore in Asterabad. The bear has his big paw firmly planted on this fruitful province – it is more Russian than Persian now; before long it will be Russian altogether.

Our road from Asterabad leads through jungle nearly the whole distance to Bunder Guz. In the woods are clearings consisting of rice-fields, orchards, and villages. The villages are picturesque clusters of wattle houses with peaked thatch roofs that descend to within a few feet of the ground. Groves of English walnut-trees abound, and plenty of these trees are also scattered through the jungle.

We reach our destination by the middle of the afternoon, and find the place a wretched village, right on the shore of the Caspian. We repair to the caravanserai, but find the rooms so evil-smelling that we decide upon camping out and risking the fever rather than court acquaintance with possible cholera, providing no better place can be found elsewhere.

R— and Abdul go ahead to try and secure better quarters, and shortly the latter returns, and announces that they have been successful. So I, and the *charvadars*, with the horses, follow him through a crooked street of thatched houses, at the end of which we find R— seated beneath the veranda of a rude hotel kept by an Armenian Jew. As we approach I observe that my companion looks happier than I have seen him look for days. He is pretty thoroughly disgusted with Persia and everything in it, and this, together with his fever, has kept him in anything but an amiable frame of mind. But now his face is actually illumined with a smile.

On the little table before him stand a half-dozen black bottles, imperial pints, bearing labels inscribed with outlandish Russian words.

'This is civilization, my boy – civilization reached at last,' says R—, as he sees me coming.

'What, this wretched tumble-down hole?' I exclaim, waving my hand at the village.

'No, not that,' replies R—; 'this – this is civilization,' and he holds up to the light a glass of amber Russian beer.

On the evening of June 3rd we put off, together with a number of native passengers, in a lighter, for the vessel which is loading up with bales of cotton at the floating dock. Most of the night is spent in sitting on deck and watching the Persian roustabouts carry the cargo aboard, for the shouting, the inevitable noisy squabbling, and the thud of bales dumped into the hold render sleep out of the question.

The steamer starts at sunrise, and the captain comes round to pay his respects. He is more of a German than a Russian, and seems pleased to welcome aboard his ship the first English or American passengers he has had for years. He makes himself agreeable, and takes a good deal of interest in explaining anything about the burning of petroleum residue on the Caspian steamers instead of coal. He takes us down below and shows us the furnaces, and explains the *modus operandi*. We are delighted at the evident superiority of this fuel over coal, and the economy and ease of supplying the furnaces. Seven copecks the forty pouds, the captain says, is the cost of the fuel, and two and a half roubles the expense of running the vessel at full speed an hour.

The ménu of these Caspian steamers is very good, based on the French school of cookery rather than English. No early breakfast is provided, however; breakfast at eleven and dinner at six are the only refreshments provided by the ship's regular service – anything else has to be paid for as extras. At eleven o'clock we descend to the dining saloon, where we find the table spread with caviare, cheese, little raw salt fishes, pickles, vodka, and the unapproachable bread of Russia. The captain and passengers are congregated about this table, some sitting, others standing, and all reaching here and there, everybody helping himself and eating with his fingers. Now and then each one tosses off a little tumbler of vodka. We proceed to the table and do our best to imitate the Russians in their apparent determination to clean off the table. The edibles before us comprise the elements of a first-class cold luncheon, and we sit down prepared to do it ample justice. By and by the Russians leave this table one by one, and betake themselves to another, on the opposite side of the saloon. As they sit down, waiters come in bearing smoking hot roasts and vegetables, wine and dessert.

A gleam of intelligence dawns upon my companion as he realizes that we are making a mistake, and pausing in the act of transferring bread and caviare to his mouth, he says to me, impressively:

'This is only sukuski, you know, on this table.'

'Why, of course! Didn't you know that? Your ignorance surprises me; I thought you knew.' And then we follow the example of everybody else and pass over to the other side.

The sukuski is taken before the regular meal in Russia. The tidbits and the vodka are partaken of to prepare and stimulate the appetite for the regular meal.

Early in the morning we moor our ship to the dock at Krasnovodsk, and load and unload merchandise till noon.

Except for the sea, and the raggedness and abject servility of the poor class of people, one might imagine Krasnovodsk some Far Western fort. Scarcely a female is seen on the streets, soldiers are everywhere, and in the commercial quarter every other place is a vodka-shop. We visit one of these and find men in red shirts and cowhide boots playing billiards and drinking, others drinking and playing cards. Rough and sturdy men they look – frontiersmen; but there is no spirit, no independence, in their expression; they look like curs that have been chastised and bullied until the spirit is completely broken. This peculiar and resigned expression is observable on the faces of the common people from one end of Russia to the other. It is quite extraordinary for a common Russian to look one in the eye. Nor is this at all deceptive; a social superior might step up and strike one of these men brutally in the face without the slightest provocation, and, though the victim of the outrage might be strong as an ox, no remonstrance whatever would be made. It is difficult for us to comprehend how human beings can possibly become so abjectly servile and spiritless as the lower-class Russians. But the terrors of the knout and Siberia are ever present before them. Cheap chromo-lithographs of Georgian saints hang on the walls of the saloon, and with them are mingled fancy pictures of Tiflis and Baku *café-chantant* belles. Long rows of vodka-bottles are the chief stock-in-trade of the place, but 'peevo' (beer) can be obtained from the cellar.

Another night of drenching dew, and by six o'clock next morning we are drawing near to the great petroleum port of Baku. From Krasnovodsk we have crossed the Caspian from east to west right on the line of latitude 40°.

CHAPTER XIII

ROUNDABOUT TO INDIA

Our steamer moves up alongside a stout wooden wharf, the gang-plank is run out, and the passengers permitted to file ashore. A cordon of police prevents them passing down the wharf, while custom-house officers examine their baggage. We are, of course, merely in transit through the country; more than that, the Russian authorities seem anxious, for some reason, to make a very favorable impression upon us two Central Asian travellers; so a special officer comes aboard, takes our passports, and with an excessive show of politeness refuses to take more than a mere formal glance at our traps. A horde of ragamuffin porters struggle desperately for the privilege of carrying the passengers' baggage. Poor, half-starved wretches they seem, reminding me, in their rags and struggles, of desperate curs quarrelling savagely over a bone. American porters strive for passengers' baggage for the sake of making money; with these Russians, it seems more like a fierce resolve to obtain the wherewithal to keep away starvation. Burly policemen, armed with swords, like the gendarmerie of France, and in blue uniforms, assail the wretched porters and strike them brutally in the face, or kick them in the stomach, showing no more consideration than if they were maltreating the merest curs. Such brutality on the one hand, and abject servility and human degradation on the other is to be seen only in the land of the Czar. Servility, it is true, exists everywhere in Asia, but only in Russia does one find the other extreme of coarse brutality constantly gloating over it and abusing it.

Everywhere, everywhere, hovers the shadow of the police. One seems to breathe dark suspicion and mistrust in the very air. The people in the civil walks of life all look like whipped curs. They wear the expression of people brooding over some deep sorrow. The crape of dead liberty seems to be hanging on every door-knob. Nobody seems capable of smiling; one would think the shadow of some great calamity is hanging gloomily over the city. Nihilism and discontent run riot in the cities of the Caucasus; government spies and secret police are everywhere, and the people on the streets betray their knowledge of the fact by talking little and always in guarded tones.

The speed of our train is about twenty miles an hour, and it starts from Baku an hour behind the advertised time. For the first few miles unfenced fields of ripe wheat characterize the landscape, and a total absence of trees gives the country a dreary aspect. The day is Sunday, but peasants, ragged and more wretched-looking than any seen in Persia, are harvesting grain. The carts they use are most peculiar vehicles, with wheels eight or ten feet in diameter. The tremendous size of the wheels is understood to materially lighten their draught. After a dozen miles the country develops into barren wastes, as dreary and verdureless as the deserts of Seistan. At intervals of a mile the train whirls past a solitary stone hut occupied by the family of the watchman or section-hand. Sometimes a man stands out and waves a little flag, and sometimes a woman. Whether male or female, the flag-signaller is invariably an uncouth bundle of rags.

We have been promising ourselves a day in Tiflis, the old Georgian capital, and now the head-quarters of the Russian army of the Caucasus.

We find it both pleasant and interesting, for here are all modern improvements of hotel and street, as well as English telegraph officers, one a former acquaintance at Teheran. Tiflis now claims about one hundred and sixty thousand inhabitants, and is situated quite picturesquely in the narrow valley of the Kur. The old Georgian quarters still retain their Oriental appearance – gabled houses, narrow, crooked streets, and filth. The modernized, or European, portion of the city contains broad streets, rows of shops in which is displayed everything that could be found in any city in Europe, and street-railways.

The station is crowded with people going away themselves or seeing friends off. As usual, the military overshadows and predominates everything. Between civilians and the wearers of military uniforms one plainly observes in a Russian Caucasus crowd that no love is lost. The strained relationship between the native population and the military aliens from the north is generally made the more conspicuous by the comparative sociability of the Georgians among themselves and kindred people of the Caucasus. Circassian officers in their picturesque uniforms and beautifully chased swords and pistols mingle sociably with the civilians, and are evidently great favorites; but that the blue-coated, white-capped Russians are hated with a bitter, sullen hatred requires no penetrating eye to see. The military brutality that crushed the brave and warlike people of Georgia, Circassia, and Mingrelia, and well-nigh depopulated the country, has left sore wounds that will take the wine and oil of time many a generation to heal completely up.

East of Tiflis, the Caucasus Railway may, roughly speaking, be said to traverse the dreary wastes of an Asiatic country; west of it, to wind around among the green hills and forest-clad heights of Europe's southeastern extremity. Lovelier and more beautifully green grows the country, and more interesting, too, grow the people and the towns, as our train speeds westward toward Batoum and the Black Sea coast. Everything about the railway, also, seems to be more prosperous, and better equipped. The improvised telegraph poles of worn-out lengths of rail seen east of Tiflis give place to something more becoming. Sometimes we speed for miles past ordinary cedar poles, procured, no doubt, from the mountain forests near at hand. Occasionally are stretches of iron poles imported from England, and then poles composed of two iron railway-rails clamped together. For much of the way we see the splendidly equipped Indo-European Telegraph Company's line, the finest telegraph line in the world. Equipped with substantial iron poles throughout, and with every insulator covered with an iron cap in countries where the half-civilized natives are wont to do them damage, this line runs through the various countries of Europe and Asia to Teheran, Persia, where it joins hands with the British Government line to India.

We double our engines – our compact, tenderless, petroleum-burning engines – at the foot of the Suran Pass. At its base, a stream disappears in an arched cave at the foot of a towering rocky cliff, and I have bethought me since of whether, like Allan Quatermain's subterranean stream, it would, if followed, reveal things heretofore unseen. And so we climb the lovely Suran

Pass, rattle down the western slope upon the Black Sea coast, and reach Batoum at 11 P.M.

A pleasant day in Batoum, and we take passage aboard a Messageries Maritimes steamer for Constantinople. Late at night we depart, amid the glare and music of a violent thunderstorm, and in the morning wake up in the roadstead of Trebizond.

The scenery along the Anatolian coast is striking and lovely in the extreme as we steam along in full view of it all next day. It is mountainous the whole distance, but the prospect is charmingly variable. Sometimes the mountains are heavily wooded down to the water's edge, and sometimes the slopes are prettily chequered with clearings and cultivation.

More and more lovely it grows next day, as we pass Samsoon, celebrated throughout the East for chibouque tobacco; Sinope, memorable as the place where the first blow of the Crimean War was delivered; and on the morning of the third day, Ineboli, the 'town of wines.'

On the evening of the third day we lay off the entrance to the Bosphorus till morning, when we steam down that charming strait to Constantinople. It is almost a year since I took, in company with our friend Shelton Bey, a pleasure trip up the Bosphorus and gazed for the first time on its wondrous beauties. I have seen considerable since, but the Bosphorus looks as fresh and lovely as ever.

Several very pleasant days are spent in Constantinople, talking over my Central Asian adventures with former acquaintances and seeing the city. But as these were pretty thoroughly described in Volume I., there is no need for repetition here. With many regrets I part company with R—, who has proved a very pleasant companion indeed, amd set sail for India.

We touch at Smyrna and the Piræus, and at the latter place a number of recently disbanded Greek soldiers come aboard; some are Albanian Greeks whose costume is sufficiently fantastic to merit description. Beginning at the feet, these extremities are incased in moccasins of red leather, with pointed toes that turn upward and inward and terminate in a black worsted ball. The legs look comfortable and active in tights of coarse gray cloth, but the *pièce de résistance* of the costume is the kilt. This extends from the hips to the middle of the thighs, and instead of being a simple plaited cloth, like the kilt of the Scotch Highlanders, it consists of many folds of airy white material that protrude in the fanciful manner of the stage costume of a *coryphée*. A jacket of the same material as the tights covers the body, and is embellished with black braid; this jacket is provided with open sleeves that usually dangle behind like immature wings, but which can be buttoned around the wrists so as to cover the back of the arm. The head-gear is a red fez, something like the national Turkish head-dress, but with a huge black tassel that hangs half-way down the back, and which seems ever on the point of pulling the fez off the wearer's head with its weight. At noon of the fifth day out we arrive in Alexandria Harbor, to find the shipping gayly decorated with flags and the cannon booming in honor of the anniversary of Her Majesty Queen Victoria's coronation.

Alexandria is the most flourishing and Europeanized city I have thus far seen in the East. That portion of the city destroyed by the incendiary torches of Arabi Pasha is either built up again or in process of rebuilding. Like all large city fires, the burning would almost seem to have been more of a benefit than otherwise, in the long-run, for imposing blocks of substantial stone buildings, many with magnificent marble fronts, have risen, Phoenix-like, from the ashes of the inferior structures destroyed by the fire. After seeing Constantinople, Teheran, or even Tiflis, one cannot but be surprised at Alexandria – surprised at finding its streets well paved with massive stone blocks, smoothly laid, and elevated in the middle, after the most approved methods; surprised at the long row of really splendid shops, in which is displayed everything that can be found in a European city; surprised at the swell turn-outs on the Khediveal Boulevard of an evening; surprised at the many evidences of wealth and European enterprise. In the yet unfinished quarters of the city, houses are going up everywhere, the large gangs of laborers, both men and women, engaged in their erection, create an impression of beehive-like activity, and everybody looks happy and contented. After so many surprises comes a feeling of regret that this commercial and industrial rose, that looks so bright and flourishing under the stimulating influence of the English occupation, should ever again be exposed to the blighting influence of an Oriental administration.

My route to India takes me along the Egyptian Railway to

Suez, thence by steamer down the Red Sea to Aden and Karachi. A passenger train on this railway consists of carriages divided into classes as they are in England, the first and second class cars being modelled on the same lines as the English. The third-class cars, however, are mere boxes provided with seats, and with iron bars instead of windows. Nice airy vehicles these, where the conditions of climate render airiness desirable, but it must be extremely interesting to ride in one of them through an Egyptian sand-storm.

Very curious it looks as we approach Suez to see the spars and masts of big steamers moving along the ship-canal, close at hand, without seeing anything of the water. The high dumps, representing the excavations from the canal, conceal everything but the masts and the top of the funnels even when one is close by.

Several days are spent at Suez, waiting for the steamer which we will call the Mandarin, on which I am to take passage to Karachi. Suez is a wretched hole, although there is a passably good English hotel facing the water-front. It is the month of Bairam, however, and there is consequently a good deal of picturesque life in the native quarters.

The Mandarin comes along on July 7th, and a decidely stably smell is wafted over the waters toward us as we follow behind her with the little launch that is to put me aboard when the steamer condescends to ease up and allow us to approach. The Mandarin, owing to the quarantine, has kept me waiting several days at Suez, and when at last she steams out of the canal and we give chase with the little launch, and finally range alongside, the whole length of the deck is observed to be bristling with ears. Some particularly hopeful agent of the Indian Government has been sanguine enough to ship one hundred and forty mules from Italy to Karachi during the monsoon season, on the deck of a notoriously rolling ship, and with nothing but temporary plank fittings to confine the mules. The mules are ranged along either side of the deck, seventy mules on each side, heads facing inward, and with posts and a two-inch plank separating them from the remainder of the deck, and into stalls of six mules each. Cocoanut matting is provided for them to stand on, and a plank nailed along the deck for them to brace their feet against when the vessel rolls. Nothing could be more happily arranged than this, providing the mules were unanimously agreed about remaining inside the railed-off space, and providing the monsoons had agreed not to roll the Mandarin violently about. With unpardonable short-sightedness, however, it seems that neither of these important factors in the case has been seriously considered or consulted, and, as an additional insult to the mules, the plank in front of them is elevated but four feet six above the deck.

They are a choice lot of four-year-old mules, unbroken and wild, harum-skarum and skittish. Well-fed four-year-old mules are skinfull of deviltry under any circumstances, and ranged like so many red herrings in their boxes, with no exercise, and every motion of the ship jostling them against one another, they very quickly developed a capacity for simon-pure cussedness that caused the officers of the ship no little anxiety from day to day, and a good deal more anxiety when they reflected on the weather that would be encountered on the Indian Ocean.

All goes well with them, however, as we glide along the placid bosom of the Red Sea; the oppressive heat has a wilting effect even on the riotous spirits of the young mules. They still exhibit their mulish contempt for the barriers reared so confidingly around them, and develop new and startling traits of devilment every day; but it is not until we leave Aden, and the long swells come rolling up from the monsoon region, that the real fun begins.

Now and then a mule will be caught off his guard and be flung violently to the deck, but the look of astonishment dies away as it nimbly regains its feet, and gives place to angry attack on its neighbor and a half-reproachful, half-apprehensive look at the sea. So far, however, the mules seem to more than hold their own, and, all oblivious of what is before them, they are comparatively happy and mischievous. But on the night of the third day out from Aden, the full force of the monsoon swells strikes the Mandarin, and, true to her character, she responds by rolling and pitching about in the trough of the sea in a manner that fills the mules with consternation, and ends in their utter collapse and demoralization. Planks break and give way as the whole body of mules are flung violently and simultaneously forward, and before midnight the mules are piled up in promiscuous and struggling heaps, while tons of water come on deck and wash and tumble them about in all imaginable shapes and forms.

All hands are piped up and kept busy tying the mules' legs, to prevent them regaining their feet only to be flung violently down again in the midst of a struggling heap of their fellows. There is ony one mule actually dead in the morning, but the others are the worst used up, discouraged lot of mules I ever saw. Mules that but the day before would nearly jump out of their skins if one attempted to pat their noses, now seem anxious to court human attention and to atone for past sins. Many of them are pretty badly skinned up and bruised, and a few of them are well-nigh flayed alive from being see-sawed back and forth about the deck. It is not a pleasant picture to dwell upon, and it would be much pleasanter to have to record that the mules proved too much for the monsoon, but truth will prevail, and before we reach Karachi the monsoon has scored fourteen mules dead and pretty much all the others more or less wounded. But this is no discredit to the mules; in fact, I have greater respect for the staying qualities of a mule than ever before, since the monsoon only secured ten per cent of them for the sharks after all.

A week from Aden, and fourteen days from Suez we reach Karachi. The tide happens to be out at the time, and so we have to lay to till the following morning, when the Mandarin crosses the bar and drops anchor preparatory to unloading the now badly demoralized mules into lighters.

Thus far my precise plans have been held in abeyance until my arrival on Indian soil. Whether I would find it practicable to start on the wheel again from Karachi, or whether it would be necessary to proceed to the northeast, I had not yet been able to find out.

The result of my investigations at once proves the impossibility, even were it desirable, of starting from Karachi. The Indus River is at flood, inundating the country, which is also jungly and wild and without roads. The heat throughout Scinde in July is something terrific; and to endeavor to force a way through flooded jungle with a bicycle at such a time would be little short of madness.

Under these conditions I decide to proceed by rail to Lahore, the capital of the Punjab, whence, I am told, there will be a good road all the way to Calcutta. As the crow files, Lahore is nearer to Furrah than Karachi is, so that my purpose of making a continuous trail will be better served from that point anyhow.

It is July 28th when I at length find myself in Lahore. The heat is not only wellnigh unbearable, but dangerous. Prickly heat has seized hold upon me with a promptness that is anything but agreeable; the thermometer in my room at Clarke's Hotel registers 108° at midnight! A punkah-wallah is indispensable night and day.

CHAPTER XIV

THROUGH INDIA

The heat is intense, being the end of the heated term at the commencement of the earliest monsoons. It is certainly not less than 130° Fahr., in the sun, when at 3 P.M. I mount and shape my course toward Amritza, some thirty-five miles down the Grand Trunk Road.

In such a temperature and beneath such a sun it behooves the discreet Caucasian to dress as carefully for protection against the heat as he would against the frost of an Arctic winter. The United States army helmet which I have constantly worn since obtaining it at Fort Sydney, Neb., has now to be discarded in favor of a huge pith solar topee an inch thick and but little smaller than an umbrella. This overshadowing head-dress imparts a cheerful, mushroom-like aspect to my person, and casts a shadow on the smooth whitish surface of the road, as I ride along, that wellnigh obliterates the shadow of the wheel and its rider.

Thus sheltered from the rays of the Indian sun, I wheel through the beautifully shaded suburban streets of Lahore, past dense thickets of fruitful plantains, across the broad switch-yard of the Scinde, Delhi & Punjab Railway, and out on to the smooth, level surface of the Grand Trunk Road. This road is, beyond a doubt, the finest highway in the whole world. It extends for nearly sixteen hundred miles, an unbroken highway of marvellous perfection, from Peshawur on the Afghan frontier to Calcutta. It is metalled for much of its length with a substance peculiar to the country, known as kunkah. Kunkah is obtained almost anywhere throughout the Land of the Five Rivers, underlying the surface soil. It is a sort of loose nodular limestone, which when wetted and rolled cements together and forms a road-surface smooth and compact as an asphaltum pavement, and of excellent wearing quality. It is a magnificent road to bicycle over; not only is it broad, level, and smooth, but for much of the way it is converted into a veritable avenue by spreading shade-trees on either side. Far and near the rich Indian vegetation, stimulated to wear its loveliest garb by the early monsoon rains, is intensely green and luxuriant; and through the richly verdant landscape stretches the wide, straight belt of the road, far as eye can reach, a whitish streak, glaring and quivering with reflected heat.

Splendid wheeling though it be, it soon becomes distressingly apparent that propelling a bicycle has now to be considered in connection with the overpowering heat. Half the distance to Amritza is hardly covered, and the riding time scarcely two hours, yet it finds me reclining beneath the shade of a roadside tree more used up than five times the distance would warrant in a less enervating climate. The greensward around me as I recline in the shade is teeming with busy insects, and the trees are swarming with the beautiful winged life of the tropical air. Flocks of paroquets with most gorgeous plumage – blue, red, green, gold, and every conceivable hue – flit hither and thither, or sweep past in whirring flight.

Some of the native pedestrians pause for a moment and cast a wondering look at the unaccustomed spectacle of a Sahib and a bicycle reclining alone beneath a wayside tree. All salaam deferentially as they pass by, but there is a refreshing absence of the spirit of obtrusion that sometimes made life a burden among the Turks and Persians.

No sort of accommodation is to be obtained this side of Amritza, however, so, waiting until the dreadful power of the sun is tempered somewhat by his retirement beneath the trees, I resume my journey, making several brief halts in deference to an overwhelming sense of lassitude ere completing the thirty-five miles. Owing to these frequent halts, it is after dark when I arrive at Amritza – a thoroughly wilted individual, and suffering agonies from the prickly heat aggravated by the feverish temperature superinduced by the exertion of the afternoon ride.

A willing native guides me to a hotel where a smooth-mannered Parsee Boniface accommodates Sahibs with supper, charpoy, and *chota-hazari* for the small sum of Rs4; punkah-wallahs, pahnee-wallahs, sweepers, etc., extra. A cooling douche with water kept at a low temperature in the celebrated porous bottles, a change of underclothing, and a punkah-wallah vigorously engaged in creating an artificial breeze, soon change things for the better. All these refreshing and renovating appliances, however, barely suffice to stimulate one's energy up to the duty of jotting down in one's diary a brief summary of the day's happenings.

The punkah of India is a long, narrow fan, suspended by cords from the ceiling; attached to it is another cord which finds its way outside through a convenient hole in the wall or window frame. For the magnificent sum of three annas (six cents) the hopeful punkah-wallah sits outside and fills the room with soothing, sleep-inducing breezes for the space of a day or night, by a constant seesawing motion of the string. Few Europeans are able to sleep at night or exist during the day without the punkah-wallah's services, for at least nine months of the year. The slightest negligence on his part at night is sufficient to summon the sleeper instanter from the land of dreams to the stern reality that the dusky imp outside has himself dropped off to sleep.

One needs only to traverse the Grand Trunk Road for a few days in order to obtain a comprehensive idea of India's teeming population. Vehicles and pedestrians throng the road again this morning, pouring into Amritza as though to attend some great festival. The impression of some festive occasion obtains additional color from parties of musicians who keep up a perpetual tom-toming on their drums as they trudge along; the object of their noisiness is apparently to gratify their own love of the sounding rattle of the drums.

At the police-chowkee of Ghundeala, ten miles from Amritza, a halt is made for rest and a drink of water. To avoid trampling on the caste prejudices, or the sanctimonious religious feelings of the natives, everybody drinks from his hands, or from a cheap earthenware dish that may afterward be smashed. The Sikhs and Mohammedans of the Punjab are far more reasonable in this matter than are the Brahmans and other ultra-holy idolaters of the country farther south. Among the Hindoos, where caste prejudices exist throughout all the strata of society, to avoid the awful consequences of touching their lips to a vessel out of which some unworthy wretch a shade less holy has previously drunk, the fastidious worshipper of Krishna, Vishnu, or Kamadeva always drinks from his hands, unless possessed of a private drinking vessel of his own. The hands are held in position to form a trough leading to the mouth; while an assistant pours water in at one end, the recipient receives it at the other. No little skill and care is required to prevent the water running down one's sleeve: the average native seems to think the human throat a gutter down which the water will flow as fast as he can pour it into the hands.

Seesum or banyan trees, shading twenty yards' width of luxuriant greensward on either side of the road, and each and every tree sheltering groups of natives, resting, idling, washing their clothes in some silent pool, or tending a few grazing buffaloes, form a truly Arcadian scene for mile after mile next day. These buffaloes are huge, unwieldy animals with black, hairless hides, strong and heavy almost as rhinoceroses. In striking contrast to them are the aristocratic little cream-colored Brahmani cows, with the curious big 'camel-hump' on their withers. These latter animals are pampered and revered and made much of among the Brahmans; mythology has it that Brahma created cows and Brahmans at the same time, and the cow is therefore an object of worship and veneration.

Taken all in all, the worship of the Hindoos has something eminently rational about it; their worship is frequently bestowed upon some tangible object that contributes directly to their material enjoyment. It is very much like going back to the first principles of gratitude for direct blessings received to worship 'Mother Ganga,' the noble stream that brings down the moisture from the Himalayas to water their plains and quicken into life their needy crops, or to worship the gentle bovine that provides them daily with milk and cheese and ghee.

Above the trees, not far away, is observed the weathercock of a chapel-spire, plainly indicating the location of the European quarter. Taking a branch road leading in that direction, I discover a party of English and native gentlemen playing a game of lawn-tennis. Arriving on the scene just as the game is breaking up, I am cordially invited to 'come in and take a peg.' To the uninitiated a 'peg' is a rather ambiguous term, but to the Anglo-Indian its interpretation takes the seductive form of a big tumbler of brandy and soda, a 'long drink,' than which nothing could be more acceptable in my present fagged-out condition. No hesitation is therefore made in accepting; and, under the stimulating influence of the generous brandy and soda, exhausted nature is quickly recuperated. While not an advocate of indiscriminate indulgence in alcoholic stimulants, after an enervating ride through the wilting heat of an Indian day I am convinced that nothing is more beneficial than what Anglo-Indians laconically describe as a 'peg.'

This very opportune meeting results, naturally enough, in a pressing invitation to stay over and recruit up for a day, a programme to which I offer no objections, feeling rather overdone and in need of rest and recuperation.

The day's rest does me a world of good, and upon resuming my journey the voice of my own experience is augmented by the advice of my entertainers, in warning me against overexertion and fatigue in so trying a climate as India. It has rained during the night, and the early morning is signalled by cooler weather than has yet been experienced from Lahore. Companies of tall Sikhs, magnificent-looking fellows, in their trim karki uniforms and monster turbans, are drilling within the native infantry lines as I wheel through the broad avenues of one of the finest cantonments in all India, and English officers and their wives are taking the morning air on horseback.

Travelling leisurely, and resting often, for thirty miles, the afternoon brings me to the small town of Peepli, where a dâk bungalow provides food and shelter of a certain kind. The sleeping-accommodation of the dâk bungalow may hardly be described as luxurious; ants and other insects swarm in myriads, and lizards drag their slimy length about the timber of the walls and ceiling. The wild jungle encroaches on the village, and the dâk bungalow occupies an isolated position at one end. The jungle resounds with the strange noises of animals and birds, and a friendly native, who speaks a little English, confides the joyful information that the deadly cobra everywhere abounds.

For the first time it is cool enough to sleep without the services of the punkah-wallah, and not a soul remains about the dâk bungalow after nightfall. The night is dark and cloudy, but not by any means silent, for the 'noises of the night' are multitudinous and varied, ranging from the tuneful croaking of innumerable frogs to the yelping chorus of the jackals – the weird nocturnal concert of the Indian jungle, a musical *mélange* far easier to imagine than describe. About ten o'clock, out from the gloomy depths of the jungle near by is suddenly heard the unmistakable caterwauling of a panther, followed by that cunning arch-dissembler's inimitable imitation of a child in distress. As though awed and paralyzed by this revelation of the panther's dread presence, the chirping and juggling and p-r-r-r-ring and yelping of inferior creatures cease as if by mutual impulse moved, and the pitter-patter of little feet are heard on the clay floor of my bungalow. The cry of the forest prowler is repeated, nearer than before to my quarters, and presently something hops up on the foot of the charpoy on which my recumbent form is stretched; and still continues the pattering of feet on the floor. It is pitch dark within the bungalow, and, uncertain of the nature of my strange visitant, I kick and 'qu-e-e-k' at him and scare him off; but, evidently terrorized by the appearance of the panther, the next minute he again invades my couch.

To have one's room turned *nolens volens* into a place of refuge for timid animals, hiding from a prowling panther which is not unlikely to follow them inside, is anything but a desirable experience in the dark. Should his panthership come nosing inside the bungalow, in his eagerness to secure something for supper he might not pause to discriminate between brute and human; and as his awe-inspiring voice is heard again, apparently quite near by, I deem it expedient to warn him off. So reaching my Smith & Wesson from under the pillow, I fire a shot up into the thatched roof. The little intruders, whatever they may be, scamper out of the bungalow, nor wait upon the order of their going, and a loud scream some distance away a moment later tells of the panther's rapid retreat into the depths of the jungle.

Soon a courageous bull-frog gives utterance to a subdued, hesitative croak; his excellent example is quickly followed by others; answering noises spring up in every direction, and ere long the midnight concert of the jungle is again in full melody.

South of Paniput the trees alongside the road are literally swarming with monkeys; they file in long strings across the road, looking anxiously behind, evidently frightened at the strange appearance of the bicycle. Shinnying up the toddy-palms, they ensconce themselves among the foliage and peer curiously down at me as I wheel past, giving vent to their perturbation in excited cries. Twenty-five miles down the road, an hour is spent beneath a grove of shady peepuls, watching the amusing antics of a troop of monkeys in the branches. Their marvellous activity among the trees is here displayed to perfection, as they quarrel and chase one another from tree to tree. The old ones seem passively irritable and decidedly averse to being bothered by the antics and mischievous activity of the youngsters. Taking possession of some particular branch, they warn away all would-be intruders with threatening grimaces and feints. The youthful members of the party are skinful of pranks and didoes, carried on to the great annoyance of their more aged and sedate relatives, who, in revenge, put in no small portion of their time punishing or pursuing them with angry cries for their deeds of wanton annoyance.

Peacocks, too, are strutting majestically about the green-sward beneath the trees, their gorgeous tails expanded, or, perched on some horizontal branch, they awake the screaming echoes in reply to others of their kindred calling in the jungle. In the same way that monkeys are regarded and worshipped as the representatives of the great mythological monkey-king Hanumān, who assisted Rāma in his war with Rāvana for the possession of Sita, so is the peacock revered and held sacred as the bird upon which rode Kartikeya the god of war and commander-in-chief of the armies of the Puranic gods. Thus do both these denizens of the jungle obtain immunity from harm at the hands of the natives, by reason of mythological association. English sportsmen shoot them, however, except in certain specified districts where the government has made their killing prohibitory, in deference to the religious prejudices of the Hindoos. The Rajput warriors of Ulwar used to march to battle with a peacock's feather in their turbans; they believe that the reason why this fine-plumaged bird screams so loudly when it thunders is because it mistakes the noise for the roll of war-drums.

CHAPTER XV

DELHI AND AGRA

From the police-thana of Rai, where the night is spent, to Delhi, the character of the road changes to a mixture of clay and rock, altogether inferior to kunkah. The twenty-one miles are covered, however, by 8.30 A.M.., that hour finding me wheeling down the broad suburban road to the Lahore Gate amid throngs of country people carrying baskets of mangoes, plantains, pomegranates, and other indigenous products into the markets of the old Mogul capital. Massive archways, ruined forts and serais, placid water-tanks, lovely gardens, feathery toddy-palms, plantain-hedges, and throngs of picturesque people make the approach to historic Delhi a scene long to be remembered.

Entering the Lahore Gate, suitable accommmodation is found at Northbrook Hotel, a comfortable hostelry under native management near the Moree Gate, and overlooking from its roof the scenes of the most memorable events connected with the siege of Delhi in 1857. Letters are found at the post-office apprising me of a bicycle-camera and paper negatives awaiting my orders at the American Consulate at Calcutta, and it behooves me to linger here for a few days until its arrival in reply to a telegram. No more charming spot could possibly be found to linger in than the old Mogul capital, with its wondrous wealth of historical associations, both remotely antique and comparatively modern, its glorious monuments of imperial Oriental splendor and its reminiscences of heroic deeds in battle.

It has been my good fortune, I find, to arrive at the old Mogul capital the day before the commencement of an annual merrymaking, picnicking, and general holiday at the celebrated Kootub Minar. The Kootub Minar is about eleven miles out of Delhi, situated amid the ruins of ancient Dilli (Delhi), the old

Hindoo city from which the more modern city takes its name. It is conceded to be the most beautiful minar monument in the world, and ranks with the Taj Mahal at Agra as one of the beautiful architectural triumphs peculiar to the splendid era of Mohammedan rule in India, and which are not to be matched elsewhere. The day following my arrival I conclude to take a spin out on my bicycle as far as the Kootub, and see something of it, the ruins amid which it stands, and the Hindoos in holiday attire. I choose the comparative coolness of early morning for the ride out; but early though it be, the road thither is already swarming with gayly dressed people bent on holiday-making.

The Kootub Minar is found to be a beautifully fluted column, two hundred and forty feet high, and it soars grandly above the mournful ruins of old Dilli, its hoary wealth of crumbled idol temples, tombs, and forts. The minar is supposed to have been erected in the latter part of the twelfth centry to celebrate the victory of the Mohammmedans over the Hindoos of Dilli. The general effect of the tall, stately Mohammedan monument among the Hindoo ruins is that of a proud gladiator standing erect and triumphant amid fallen foes. At least, that is how it looks to me, as I view it in connection with the ruins at its base and ponder upon its history. A spiral stairway of three hundred and seventy-five steps leads to the summit. A group of natives are already up there, enjoying the cool breezes and the prospect below. In the comprehensive view from the summit one can read an instructive sermon of centuries of stirring Indian history in the gray stone-work of ruined mosques and tombs and fortresses and pagan temples that dot the valley of the Jumna hereabout almost as thickly as the trees.

While watching the interesting performances of the Hindoo conjurers I have left the bicycle at a little dâk bungalow near the old entrance-gate. From the commanding height of the Kootub one could see that the Delhi road is a solid mass of vehicles and pedestrians (how the people in teeming India do swarm on these festive occasions!). It looks impossible to make one's way with a bicycle against that winding stream of human beings, and so, after wandering about a while among the striking and peculiar colonnades of the ancient pagan temples, paying the regulation tribute of curiosity to the enigmatic iron column, and doing the place in general, I return to the bungalow, thinking of starting

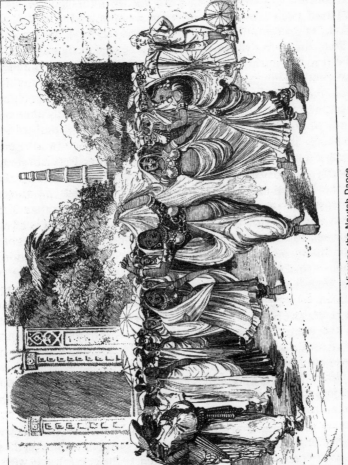

Viewing the Nautch Dance.

back to Delhi, when I find that my 'cycle of strange experiences' has attracted to itself a no less interesting gathering than a troupe of Nautch girls and their chaperone. The troupe numbers about a dozen girls, and they have come to the merry-making at the Kootub to gather honest shekels by giving exhibitions of their terpsichorean talents in the Nautch dance.

I had been wondering whether an opportunity to see this famous dance would occur during my trip through India; and so when four or five of the prettiest of these dusky damsels gather about me, smile at me winsomely, ogle me with their big black eyes, smile again, smile separately, smile unanimously, smile all over their semi-mahogany but nevertheless not unhandsome faces, and every time displaying sets of pearly teeth, what could I do, what could anyone have done, but smile in return?

There is no language more eloquent or more easily understood than the language of facial expression. No verbal question or answer is necessary. I interpret the winsome smiles of the Nautchnees aright, and they interpret very quickly the permission to go ahead that reveals itself in the smile they force from me. Eight of the twelve are commonplace girls of from fourteen to eighteen, and the other four are 'dark but comely' – quite handsome, as handsomeness goes among the Hindoos. Their arms are bare of everything save an abundance of bracelets, and the upper portion of the body is rather scantily draped, after the manner and custom of all Hindoo females; but an ample skirt of red calico reaches to the ankle. Rings are worn on every toe, and massive silver anklets with tiny bells attached make music when they walk or dance. They wear a profusion of bracelets, necklaces of rupees, head-ornaments, ear-rings, and pendent charms, and a massive gold or brass ring in the left nostril. The nostril is relieved of its burden by a string that descends from a head-ornament and takes up the weight.

The Nautch girls arrange themselves into a half-circle, their scarlet costumes forming a bright crescent, terminating in a mass of spectators, whose half-naked bodies, varying in color from pale olive to mahogany, are arrayed in costumes scarcely less showy than the dancers. The chaperone and eight outside girls tom-tom an appropriate Nautch accompaniment on drums with their fingers, the four prettiest girls advance, and favoring me with sundry smiles, and coquettish glances from their bright black eyes, they commence to dance.

An idea seems to prevail in many Occidental minds that the Nautch dance is a very naughty thing; but nothing is further from the truth. Of course it can be made naughty, and no doubt often is; but then so can many another form of innocent amusement. The Nautch dance is a decorous and artistic performance when properly danced; the graceful motions and elegant proportions of the human form, as revealed by lithe and graceful dancers, are to be viewed with an eye as purely artistic and critical as that with which one regards a Venus or other production of the sculptor's studio.

The four dancers take the lower hem of their red garment daintily between thumb and finger of the right hand, spreading its ample folds into the figure of an opened fan, by bringing the outstretched arm almost on a level with the shoulder. A mantle of transparent muslin, fringed with silver spangles, is worn about the head and shoulders in the same indescribably graceful manner as the mantilla of the Spanish señorita. Raising a portion of this aloft in the left hand, and keeping the 'fan' intact with the right, the dancers twirl around and change positions with one another, their supple figures meanwhile assuming a variety of graceful motions and postures from time to time. Now they imitate the spiral movement of a serpent climbing around and upward on an imaginary pole; again they assume an attitude of gracefulness, their dusky countenances half hidden in seeming coquetry behind the muslin mantle, the large red fan waving gently to and fro, the feet unmoving, but the undulating motions of the body and the tremor of the limbs sufficing to jingle the tiny ankle-bells. On the whole, the Nautch dance would be disappointing to most people witnessing it; its fame leads one to expect more than it really amounts to.

Several days are passed at Delhi, waiting the arrival of a small bicycle-camera from Calcutta, which has been forwarded from America. Most of this time is spent in the pleasant occupation of reclining in an arm-chair beneath the punkah, the only comfortable situation in Delhi at this season of the year. Nevertheless, I manage to spin around the city mornings and evenings, and visit the famous fort and palace of Shah Jehan.

My camera having duly arrived, together with a package of letters, which are always doubly welcome to a wanderer in distant lands, I prepare to resume my southward journey. The few days' rest has enabled me to recover from the wilting effects of riding in the terrific heat, and I have seen something of one of the most interesting points in all Asia. Delhi is sometimes called the 'Rome of Asia,' which, it seems to me, is a very appropriate name to give it.

Neatly clad and modest-looking females, native converts to Christianity, are walking in orderly procession to church, testaments in hand, as I wheel through the streets of Delhi on Sunday morning toward the Agra road. Very interesting is it to see these dusky daughters of heathendom arrayed in modest white muslin gowns, their lithe and graceful forms freed from the barbarous jewellery that distinguishes the persons of their unconverted sisters. Very charming do they look in their Christianized simplicity and self-contained demeanor as they walk quietly, and at a becoming Sabbath-day pace, two by two, down the Chandni Chouk. They present an instructive comparison to the straggling groups of heathen damsels who watch them curiously as they walk past and then proceed to chant idolatrous songs, apparently in a spirit of wanton raillery at the Christian maidens and their simple, unornamented attire. The fair heathens of Delhi have a sort of naughty, Parisian reputation throughout the surrounding country, and so there is nothing surprising in this exhibition of wanton hilarity directed at these more strait-laced converts to the religion of the Ferenghis. The heathen damsels, arrayed in very worldly costumes, consisting of flaring red, yellow, and blue garments, the whole barbaric and ostentatious array of nose-rings, earrings, armlets, anklets, rupee necklaces, and pendents, and the multifarious gewgaws of Hindoo womankind, look surpassingly wicked and saucy in comparison with their converted sisters. The gentle converts try hard to regard their heathen songs with indifference, and to show by their very correct deportment the superiority of meekness, virtue, and Christianity over gaudy clothes, vulgar silver jewellery, and heathenism. The whole scene reminds one very forcibly of a gang of wicked street-boys at home, poking fun at a Sunday-school procession or a platoon of Salvation Army soldiers parading the streets.

It is but thirty-five miles from Muttra to Agra, and notwithstanding showers and heat, the distance is covered by half-past ten. Wheeling at this pace, however, is an indiscretion, and the completion of the stretch is signalized by a determination to seek shade and quiet for the remainder of the day. Once again the sociable officers of the garrison tender me the hospitality of their quarters, and the ensuing day is spent in visiting that wonder of the world, the Taj Mahal, Akbar's fort, and other wonderful monuments of the palmy days of the Mogul Empire.

From the fort we drive in a native gharri to the Taj, a mile-drive through suburban scenery, plantain-gardens, groves, and ruins. In approaching the garden of the Taj, one passes through a bazaar, where the skilful Hindoo artisans are busy making beautiful inlaid tables, inkstands, plates, and similar fancies, as well as models of the Taj, out of white Jeypore marble. These are the hereditary descendants and successors of the men who in the palmy days of the Mogul power spent their lives in decorating the royal palaces and tombs with mosaics and tracery. Nowadays their skill is expended on mere articles of *virtù*, to be sold to European tourists and English officers. Some of them are occasionally employed by the Indian Government to repair the work desecrated by vandals during the mutiny, and under the purely commercial government of the East India Company. One curious phase of this work is, that the men employed to replace with imitations the original stones that have been stolen receive several times higher pay than the men in Akbar's time, who did such splendid work that it is not to be approached, these days. Several months' imprisonment is now the penalty of prying out stones from the mosaic-work of the Taj.

This lovely structure has been described so often by travellers that one can scarce venture upon a description without seeming to repeat what has already been said by others. One of the best descriptions of its situation and surroundings is given by Bayard Taylor. He says: 'The Taj stands on the bank of the Jumna, rather more than a mile to the eastward of the Fort of Agra. It is approached by a handsome road cut through the mounds left by the ruins of ancient palaces. It stands in a large garden, inclosed by a lofty wall of red sandstone, with arched galleries around the interior, and entered by a superb gateway of sandstone, inlaid with ornaments and inscriptions from the Koran in white marble. Outside this grand portal, however, is a spacious quadrangle of solid masonry, with an elegant structure, intended as a caravanserai, on the opposite side. Whatever may be the visitor's impatience, he cannot help pausing to notice the fine proportions of these structures, and the massive style of their construction. Passing under the open demi-vault, whose arch hangs high above you, an avenue of dark Italian cypress appears before you. Down its centre sparkles a long row of fountains, each casting up a single slender jet. On both sides, the palm, the banyan, and feathery bamboo mingle their foliage; the song of birds meets your ears, and the odor of roses and lemon-flowers sweetens the air. Down such a vista, and over such a foreground, rises the Taj.'

Of the Taj itself, fault has been found with its proportions by severe critics, like the party who regards the Moti Mesjid 'nun' as faulty because she wears a point-lace collar; but the ordinary visitor will find room for nothing but admiration and wonder. It is hard to believe that there is any defect, even in its proportions, for so perfect do these latter appear, that one is astonished to learn that it is a taller building than the Kootub Minar. One would never guess it to be anywhere near so tall as 243 feet. The building rests on a plinth of white marble, eighteen feet high and a hundred yards square. At each corner of the plinth stands a minaret, also of white marble, and 137 feet high. The mausoleum itself occupies the central space, measuring in depth and width 186 feet. The entire affair is of white Jeypore marble, resting upon a lower platform of sandstone: 'A thing of perfect beauty and of absolute finish in every detail, it might pass for the work of a genii, who knew naught of the weaknesses and ills with which mankind are beset. It is not a great national temple erected by a free and united people, it owes its creation to the whim of an absolute ruler who was free to squander the resources of the State in commemorating his personal sorrows or his vanity.'

Another distinguished visitor, commenting on the criticisms of those who profess to have discovered defects, says: 'The Taj is like a lovely woman; abuse her as you please, but the moment you come into her presence, you submit to its fascination.'

The next morning I bid farewell to Agra, more than satisfied with my visit to the Taj. It stand unique and distinct from anything else one sees the whole world round. Nothing one could say about it can give the satisfaction derived from a visit, and no word-painting can do it justice.

At the Taj Mahal.

CHAPTER XVI

FROM AGRA TO SINGAPORE

On the street leading out of Miran Serai is a very handsome and elaborately ornamented temple. Passing by early in the morning, I pay it a brief, unceremonious visit of inspection, kneeling on the steps and thrusting my helmeted head in to look about, not caring to go to the trouble of removing my shoes. Inside is an ancient Brahman, engaged in sweeping out the floral offerings of the previous day; he favors me with the first indignant glance I have yet received in India. When I have satisfied my curiosity and withdrawn from the door-way, he comes out himself and shuts the beautifully chased brazen door with quite an angry slam. The day previous was the anniversary of Krishna's birth, and the blood of sacrificial goats and bullocks is smeared profusely about the altar. It is, probably, the enormity of an unhallowed unbeliever in one god, thrusting his infidel head inside the temple at this unseemly hour of the morning, while the blood of the mighty Krishna's sacrificial victims is scarcely dry on the walls, that arouses the righteous wrath of the old heathen priest – as well, indeed, it might.

The evening hour brings me into Cawnpore, down a fine broad street divided in the centre by a canal, with flights of stone steps for banks and a double row of trees – a street far broader and finer than the Chandni Chouk – and into an hotel kept by a Parsee gentleman named Byramjee. Life at this hostelry is made of more than passing interest by the familiar manner in which frogs, lizards, and birds invade the privacy of one's apartments. Not one of these is harmful, but one naturally grows curious about whether a cobra or some other less desirable member of the reptile world is not likely at any time to join their interesting company. The lizards scale the walls and ceiling in search of flies, frogs hop sociably about the floor, and a sparrow now and then twitters in and out.

A two weeks' drought has filled the farmers of the Cawnpore

district with grave apprehensions concerning their crops; but enough rain falls to-night to gladden all their hearts, and also to leak badly through the roof of my bedroom

Impatient to be getting along, I misinterpret a gleam of illusory sunshine at noon on the third day of the rain-storm and pull out, taking a cursory glance at the Memorial Church as I go. A drenching shower overtakes me in the native military lines, compelling me to seek shelter for an hour beneath the portico of their barracks. The road is perfectly level and smooth, and well rounded, so that the water drains off and leaves it better wheeling than ever; and with alternate showers and sunshine I have no difficulty in covering thirty-four miles before sunset. This brings me to a caravanserai, consisting of a quadrangular enclosure with long rows of cell-like rooms. The whole structure is much inferior to a Persian caravanserai, but there is probably no need of the big brick structures of Shah Abbas in a winterless country like India.

Interesting subjects are not wanting for my camera through the day; but the greatest difficulty is experienced about changing the negatives at night. A small lantern with a very feeble light, made still more feeble by interposing red paper, suffices for my own purpose; but the too attentive chowkee-dar, observing that my room is in darkness, and fancying that my light has gone out accidentally, comes flaring in with a torch, threatening the sensitive negatives with destruction.

Soon I overtake an individual doing penance for his sins by crawling on his stomach all the way to Benares, the Mecca of the Hindoo religion. In addition to crawling, he is dragging a truck containing his personal effects by a rope tied about his waist. Every fifty yards or so he stands up and stretches himself; then he lies prostrate again and worms his wearisome way along the road like a snake. Benares is still about a hundred miles distant, and not unlikely this determined devotee has already been crawling in this manner for weeks. This painful sort of penance was formerly indulged in by Hindoo fanatics very largely; but the English Government has now all but abolished the practice by mild methods of discouragement. The priests of the different idols in Benares annually send out thousands of missionaries to travel throughout the length and breadth of India to persuade people to make pilgrimages to that city. Each missionary proclaims the great benefits to be derived by going to worship the particular idol he represents; in this manner are the priests enriched by the offerings presented. Not long since one of these zealous pilgrim-hunters persuaded a wealthy rajah into journeying five hundred miles in the same manner as the poor wretch passed on the road to-day. The infatuated rajah completed the task, after months of torture, on all-fours, accompanied the whole distance by a crowd of servants and priests, all living on his bounty.

The sacred river is at its highest flood, and hereabout not less than a mile and half wide. The ferry service is rude and inefficient, being under the management of natives, who reck little of the flight of time or modern improvements. The superintendent will bestir himself, however, in behalf of the Sahib who is riding the Ferenghi gharri around the world: instead of putting me aboard the big slow ferry, he will man a smaller and swifter boat to ferry me over. The 'small boat' is accordingly produced, and turns out to be a rude flat-boat sort of craft, capable of carrying fully twenty tons, and it is manned by eight oarsmen.

Much of the Ganges' present width is mere overflow, shallow enough for the men to wade and tow the boat. It is tugged a considerable distance up-stream, to take advantage of the swift current in crossing the main channel. The oars are plied vigorously to a weird refrain of 'deelah, sahlah – deelah, sahlah!' the stroke oarsman shouting 'deelah' and the others replying 'sahlah' in chorus. Two hours are consumed in crossing the river, but once across the road is perfection itself, right from the river's brink.

Through the valley of the sacred river, the splendid kunkah road leads onward to Benares, the great centre of Hindoo idolatry, a city that is more to the Hindoo than is Mecca to the Mohammedans or Jerusalem to the early Christians. Shrines and idols multiply by the roadside, and tanks innumerable afford bathing and purifying facilities for the far-travelled pilgrims who swarm the road in thousands. As the heathen devotee approaches nearer and nearer to Benares he feels more and more devotionally inclined, and these tanks of the semi-sacred water of the Ganges Valley happily afford him opportunity to soften up the crust of his accumulated trangressions, preparatory to washing them away entirely by a plunge off the Ramnāgar ghaut at Benares. Many of the people are trudging their way homeward again, happy in the possession of bottles of sacred water obtained from the river at the holy city. Precious liquid this, that they are carrying in earthenware bottles hundreds of weary miles to gladden the hearts of stay-at-home friends and relations.

Thirty miles from Allahabad, I pause at a wayside well to obtain a drink. It is high noon, and the well is on unshaded ground. For a brief moment my broad-brimmed helmet is removed so that a native can pour water into my hands while I hold them to my mouth. Momentary as is the experience, it is followed by an ominous throbbing and ringing in the ears – the voice of the sun's insinuating power. But a very short distance is covered when I am compelled to seek the shelter of a little road-overseer's chowkee, the symptoms of fever making their appearance with alarming severity.

The quinine that I provided myself with at Constantinople is brought into requisition for the first time; it is found to be ruined from not being kept in an air-tight vessel. A burning fever keeps me wide awake till 2 A.M., and in the absence of a punkah, prickly heat prevents my slumbering afterward. This wakeful night by the roadside enlightens me to the interesting fact that the road is teeming with people all night as well as all day, many preferring to sleep in the shade during the day and travel at night.

It is fifty miles from my chowkee to Benares, and the dread of being overtaken with serious illness away from medical assistance urges upon me the advisability of reaching there to-day, if possible. The morning is ushered in with a stiff head-wind, and the fever leaves me feeling anything but equal to pedalling against it when I mount my wheel at early daybreak. By sheer strength of will I reel off mile after mile, stopping to rest frequently at villages and under the trees.

Of all the cities of the East, Benares is perhaps the most interesting at the present day to the European tourist. Its fourteen hundred shivalas or idol temples, and two hundred and eighty mosques, its wonderful bathing ghauts swarming with pilgrims washing away their sins, the burning bodies, the sacred Ganges, the hideous idols at every corner of the streets, and its strange idolatrous population, make up a scene that awakens one to a keen appreciation of its novelty. One realizes fully that here the idolatry, the 'bowing down before images' that in our Sunday-school days used to seem so unutterably wicked and perverse, so monstrous, and so far, far away, is a tangible fact. To keep up their outward appearance on a par with the holiness of their city, men streak their faces and women mark the parting in their hair with red. Sacred bulls are allowed to roam the streets at will, and the chief business of a large proportion of the population seems to be the keeping of religious observances and paying devotion to the multitudinous idols scattered about the city.

Conspicuous above all other buildings in the city is the mosque of Aurungzebe, with its two shapely minarets towering high above everything else. The view from the summit of the minarets is comprehensive and magnificently lovely; the wonderful beauty of the trees and shivalas, the green foliage, and the gilt and red temples, so beautifully carved and gracefully tapering; the broad, flowing Ganges, the busy people, the moving boats, the rajahs' palaces along the water-front, make up a truly beautiful panorama of the Sacred City of the Hindoos. From here we take a native boat and traverse the water-front to see the celebrated bathing ghauts and the strange, animated scene of pilgrims bathing, bodies burning, and swarms of people ascending and descending the broad flights of steps. How intensely eager do these dusky believers in the efficacy of 'Mother Ganga' as a purifier of sin dip themselves beneath the yellow water, rinse out their mouths, scrape their tongues, rub, duck, splash, and disport; they fairly revel in the sacred water; happy, thrice happy they look, as well indeed they might, for now are they certain of future happiness. What the 'fountain filled with blood' is to the Christian, so is the precious water of dear Ganga to the sinful Hindoo: all sins, past, present, and future, are washed away.

Next to washing in the sacred stream during life, the Hindoo's ambition is to yield up the ghost on its bank, and then to be burned on the Burning Ghaut and have his ashes cast adrift on the waters. On the Manikarnika ghaut the Hindoos burn their dead. To the unbelieving Ferenghi tourist there seems to be a 'nigger in the fence' about all these heathen ceremonies, and in

The Burning-ghauts at Benares.

the burning of the dead the wily priesthood has managed to obtain a valuable monopoly on firewood, by which they have accumulated immense wealth. No Hindoo, no matter how pious he has been through life, how many offerings he has made to the gods, or how thoroughly he has scoured his yellow hide in the Ganges, can ever hope to reach Baikunt (heaven) unless the wood employed at his funeral pyre come from a *domra*. *Domras* are the lowest and most despised caste in India, a caste which no Hindoo would, under any consideration, allow himself to touch during life, or administer food to him if starving to death; but after his holier brethren have yielded up the ghost, then the despised *domra* has his innings. Then it is that the relatives of the deceased have to humble themselves before the *domra* to obtain firing to burn the body. Realizing that they now have the pull, the wily *domras* sometimes bleed their mournful patrons unmercifully. As many as a thousand rupees have been paid for a fire by wealthy rajahs. The *domra* who holds the monopoly at the Manikarnika ghaut is one of the richest men in Benares.

A rest of two days and a few doses of quinine subdue the fever and put me in condition to resume my journey. Twelve miles from Benares, on the East Indian Railway, is Mogul Serai, to which I deem it advisable to wheel in the evening, by way of getting started without over-exertion at first.

A few miles south of Shergotti the bridge spanning a tributary of the Sone is broken down, and no ferry is in operation. The stream, however, is fordable, and four stalwart Bengalis carry me across on a charpoy, hoisted on their shoulders; they stem the torrent bravely, and keep up their strength and courage by singing a refrain. From this point the road becomes undulating, and of indifferent surface; the macadam is badly washed by the soaking monsoon rains, and the low, level country is gradually merging into the jungle-covered hills of Bengal.

The character of the people has undergone a decided change since leaving Delhi and Agra, and the Bengalis impress one decidedly unfavorably in comparison with the more manly and warlike races of the Punjab. Abject servility marks the demeanor of many, and utter uselessness for any purpose whatsoever, characterizes one's intuitive opinion of a large percentage of the population of the villages. Except for the pressing nature of one's needs, the look of unutterable perplexity that comes over the face of a Bengali villager, to-day, when I ask him to obtain me something to eat, would be laughable in the extreme. 'N-a-y, Sahib, n-a-y!' he replies, with a show of mental distraction as great as though ordered to fetch me the moon. An appeal for rice, milk, dhal, chuppatties, at several stalls results in the same failure; everybody seems utterly bewildered at the appearance of a Sahib among them searching for something to eat.

The country becomes hillier, and the wild, jungle-covered hills and dark ravines alongside the road are highly suggestive of royal Bengal tigers. The striped monsters infest these jungles in plenty; during the afternoon I pass through a village where a depredatory man-eater has been carrying off women and children within the last few days.

It is all but a sub-aqueous performance pedalling along the road next morning; the air is laden with a penetrating drizzle, the watery clouds fairly hover on the tree-tops and roll in dark masses among the hills, while the soaked and saturated earth reeks with steam. The road is macadamized with white granite, and after one of those tremendous downpourings that occur every hour or so the wheel-worn depressions on either side become narrow streams, divided by the white central ridge. Down the long, straight slopes these twin rivulets course right merrily, the whirling wheels of the bicycle flinging the water up higher than my head. The ravines are roaring, muddy torrents, but they are all well bridged, and although the road is lumpy, an unridable spot is very rarely encountered. For days I have not had a really dry thread of clothing, from the impossibility of drying anything by hanging it out. Under these trying conditions, a relapse of the fever is matter for daily and hourly apprehension.

Mount Parisnath, four thousand five hundred and thirty feet high, the highest peak of the Bengal hills, overlooks my dâk bungalow at Doomree, and also a region of splendid tropical scenery, dark wooded ridges, deep ravines, and rolling masses of dark-green vegetation.

During the night the weather actually grows chilly, a raw wind laden with moisture driving me off the porch into the shelter of the bungalow. No portion of Parisnath is visible in the morning but the base, nine-tenths of its proportions being above the line of the cloud-masses that roll along just above the trees. Another day through the hilly country and, a hundred and fifty miles from Calcutta, the flourishing coal-mining district of Asansol brings me again to the East India Railway and semi-European society and accommodation. Instead of doughy chuppatties, throat-blistering curry, and octogenarian chicken, I this morning breakfast off a welcome bottle of Bass's ale, baker's bread, and American cheese.

By nine o'clock the bicycle is threading its way among the moving throngs on the pontoon bridge that spans the Hooghli between Howrah and Calccutta, and half an hour later I am enjoying a refreshing bath in Cook's Adelphi Hotel.

I have no hestiation in saying that, except for the heat, my tour down the Grand Trunk Road of India has been the most enjoyable part of the whole journey, thus far. What a delightful trip a-wheel it would be, to be sure, were the temperature only milder!

My reception in Calcutta is very gratifying. A banquet by the Dalhousie Athletic Club is set on foot the moment my arrival is announced. With such enthusiasm do the members respond that the banquet takes place the very next day, and over forty applicants for cards have to be refused for want of room. For genuine, hearty hospitality, and thoroughness in carrying out the interpretation of the term as understood in its real home, the East, I unhesitatingly yield the palm to Anglo-Indians. Time and again, on my ride through India, have I experienced Anglo-Indian hospitality broad and generous as that of an Arab chief, enriched and rendered more acceptable by a feast of good-fellowship as well as creature considerations.

The City of Palaces is hardly to be seen at its best in September, for the Viceregal Court is now at Simla, and with it all the government officials and high life. Two months later and Calcutta is more brilliant, in at least one particular, than any city in the world. Every evening in 'the season' there is a turn-out of splendid equipages on the bund road known as the Strand, the like of which is not to be seen elsewhere, East or West. It is the Rotten Row of Calcutta embellished with the gorgeousness of India. Wealthy natives display their luxuriousness in vying with one another and with the government officials in the splendor of their carriages, horses, and liveries.

On the 18th sails the opium steamer Wing-sang to Hong-kong, aboard which I have been intending to take passage, and whose date of departure has somewhat influenced my speed in coming toward Calcutta. To cross overland from India to China with a bicycle is not to be thought of. This I was not long in finding out after reaching India. Fearful as the task would be to reach the Chinese frontier, with at least nine chances out of ten against being able to reach it, the difficulties would then have only commenced.

The day before sailing, the bicycle branch of the Dalhousie Athletic Club turns out for a club run around the Maidan, to the number of seventeen. It is in the evening; the long rows of electric lamps stretching across the immense square shed a moon-like light over our ride, and the smooth, broad roads are well worthy the metropolitan terminus of the Grand Trunk.

My stay of five days in the City of Palaces has been very enjoyable, and it is with real regret that I bid farewell to those who come down to the shipping ghaut to see me off.

The voyage to the Andamans is characterized by fine weather enough; but from that onward we steam through a succession of heavy rain-storms; and down in the Strait of Malacca it can pour quite as heavily as on the Gangetic plains. At Penang it keeps up such an incessant downpour that the beauties of that lovely port are viewed only from beneath the ship's awning. But it is lovely enough even as seen through the drenching rain. Dense groves of cocoa-nut palms line the shores, seemingly hugging the very sands of the beach. Solid cliffs of vegetation they look, almost, so tall, dark, and straight, and withal so lovely, are these forests of palms. Cocoa-nut palms flourish best, I am told, close to the sea, a certain amount of salt being necessary for their healthful growth.

The weather is more propitious as we steam into Singapore, at which point we remain for half a day, on the tenth day out from Calcutta. Singapore is indeed a lovely port. Within a stone's-throw of where the Wing-sang ties up to discharge freight the dark-green mangrove bushes are bathing in the salt waves. Very seldom does one see green vegetation mingling familiarly with the blue water of the sea – there is usually a strip of sand or other verdureless shore – but one sees it at lovely Singapore.

CHAPTER XVII

THROUGH CHINA

Daily rains characterize our voyage from Singapore through the China Sea – rather unseasonable weather, the captain says; and for the second time in his long experience as a navigator of the China Sea, St. Elmo's lights impart a weird appearance to the spars and masts of his vessel. The rain changes into misty weather as we approach the Ladrone Islands, and, emerging completely from the wide track of the typhoon's moisture-laden winds on the following morning, we learn later, upon landing at Hong-kong, that they have been without rain there for several weeks.

The consuls and others express grave doubts about the wisdom of my undertaking in journeying alone through China, and endeavor to dissuade me from making the attempt. Opinion, too, is freely expressed that the Viceroy will refuse his permission, or, at all events, place obstacles in my way. The passport is forthcoming on October 12th, however, and I lose no time in making a start.

After a few miles the hitherto dead level of the valley is broken by low hills of reddish clay, and here the stone paths merge into well-beaten trails that on reasonably level soil afford excellent wheeling. The hillsides are crowded with graves, which, instead of the sugar-loaf 'ant hillocks' of the paddy-fields, assume the traditional horseshoe shape of the Chinese ancestral grave. On the barren, gravelly hills, unfit for cultivation, the thrifty and economical Celestial inters the remains of his departed friends. Although in making this choice he is supposed to be chiefly interested in securing repose for his ancestors' souls, he at the same time secures the double advantage of a well-drained cemetery, and the preservation of his cultivable lands intact. Everything, indeed, would seem to be made subservient to this latter end; every foot of productive soil seems to be held as of paramount importance in the teeming delta of the Choo-kiang.

Beyond the first of these cemetery hills, peopled so thickly with the dead, rise the tall pawn-towers of the large village of Chun-Kong-hoi. The natural dirt-paths enable me to ride right up to the entrance-gate of the main street. Good-natured crowds follow me through the street; and outside the gate of departure I favor them with a few turns on the smooth flags of a rice-winnowing floor. The performance is hailed with shouts of surprise and delight, and they urge me to remain in Chun-Kong-hoi all night.

An official in big tortoise-shell spectacles examines my passport, reading it slowly and deliberately aloud in peculiar sing-song tones to the crowd, who listen with all-absorbing attention. He then orders the people to direct me to a certain inn. This inn blossoms forth upon my as yet unaccustomed vision as a peculiarly vile and dingy little hovel, smoke-blackened and untidy as a village smithy. Half a dozen rude benches covered with reed mats and provided with uncomfortable wooden pillows represent what sleeping accommodations the place affords. The place is so forbidding that I occupy a bench outside in preference to the evil-smelling atmosphere within.

As it grows dark the people wonder why I don't prefer the interior of the dimly lighted *hittim*. My preference for the outside bench is not unattended with hopes that, as they can no longer see my face, my greasy-looking, half-naked audience would give me a moment's peace and quiet. Nothing, however, is further from their thoughts; on the contrary, they gather closer and closer about me, sticking their yellow faces close to mine and examining my features as critically as though searching the face of an image. By and by it grows too dark even for this, and then some enterprising individual brings a couple of red wax tapers, placing one on either side of me on the bench.

By the dim religious light of these two candles, hundreds of people come and peer curiously into my face, and occasionally some ultra-inquisitive mortal picks up one of the tapers and by its aid makes a searching examination of my face, figure, and clothes. Mischievous youngsters, with irreligious abandon,

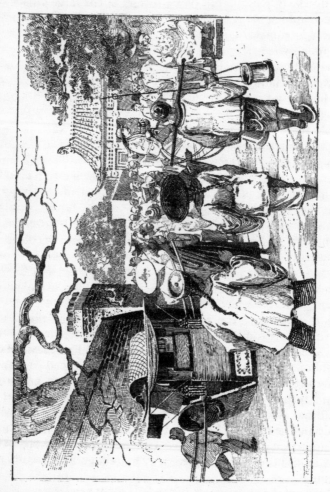

"I favor them with a few turns."

attempt to make the scene comical by lighting joss-sticks and waving bits of burning paper.

The tapers on either side, and the youngsters' irreverent antics, with the evil-spirit-dispersing joss-sticks, make my situation so ridiculously suggestive of an idol that I am perforce compelled to smile. The crowd have been too deeply absorbed in the contemplation of my face to notice this side-show; but they quickly see the point, and follow my lead with a general round of merriment. About ten o'clock I retire inside; the irrepressible inquisitives come pouring in the door behind me, but the *hittim*-keeper angrily drives them out and bars the door.

Several other lodgers occupy the room in common with myself; some are smoking tobacco, and others are industriously 'hitting the pipe.' The combined fumes of opium and tobacco are well-nigh unbearable, but there is no alternative. The next bench to mine is occupied by a peripatetic vender of drugs and medicines. Most of his time is consumed in smoking opium in dreamy oblivion to all else save the sensuous delights embodied in that operation itself. Occasionally, however, when preparing for another smoke, he addresses me at length in about one word of pidgin-English to a dozen of simon-pure Cantonese. In a spirit of friendliness he tenders me the freedom of his pipe and little box of opium, which is, of course, 'declined with thanks.'

Long into the midnight hours my garrulous companions sit around and talk, and smoke, and eat peanuts. Mosquitoes likewise contribute to the general inducement to keep awake; and after the others have finally lain down, my ancient next neighbor produces a small mortar and pestle and busies himself pounding drugs. For this operation he assumes a pair of large, round spectacles, that in the dimly lighted apartment and its nocturnal associations are highly suggestive of owls and owlish wisdom. The old quack works away at his mortar, regardless of the approach of daybreak, now and then pausing to adjust the wick in his little saucer of grease, or to indulge in the luxury of a peanut.

Such are the experiences of my first night at a Chinese village *hittim*; they will not soon be forgotten.

*   *   *

During the day I have sprained my right knee, and it becomes painful in the night and wakes me up. In the morning my way is made through the waking city with a painful limp, that gives rise to much unsympathetic giggling among the crowd at my heels. Perhaps they think all Fankwaes thus hobble along; their giggling, however, is doubtless evidence of the well-known pitiless disposition of the Chinese. The sentiments of pity and consideration for the sufferings of others, are a well-nigh invisible quality of John Chinaman's character, and as I limp slowly along, I mentally picture myself with a broken leg or serious illness, alone among these people. A Fankwae with his leg broken! a Fankwae lying at the point of death! why, the whole city would want to witness such an extraordinary sight; there would be no keeping them out; one would be the centre of a tumultuous rabble day and night!

Across the creeks which occasionally join issue with the river, are erected frail and wabbly bamboo foot-rails; some of these are evidently private enterprises, as an ancient Celestial is usually on hand for the collection of tiny toll. Narrow bridges, rude steps cut in the face of the cliffs, trails along narrow ledges, over rocky ridges, down across gulches, and anon through loose shale on ticklishly sloping banks, characterize the passage through the cañon. The sun is broiling hot, and my knee swollen and painful. It is barely possible to crawl along at a snail's pace by keeping my game leg stiff; bending the knee is attended with agony. Frequent rests are necessary, and an examination reveals my knee badly inflamed.

It is almost dark when I arrive at the next village, prepared to seek such accommodations for the night as the place affords, if any. The people, however, seem decidedly inclined to give me the cold shoulder, eying me suspiciously from a respectful distance, instead of clustering, as usual, close about me. Being pretty tired and hungry, and knowing absolutely nothing of the distance to the next place, I endeavor to cultivate their friendship by smiles, and by addressing the nearest youngster in polite greetings of 'chin-chin.'

All this proves of no avail; they seem one and all to be laboring under the impression that my appearance is of evil portent to themselves. Perchance some social calamity they have just been visited with, is attributed in their superstitious minds to the fell influence of the foreign devil, who has so suddenly bobbed up in their midst just at this unhappy, inauspicious moment. Peradventure some stray and highly exaggerated bit of news in regard to Fankwae aggression in Tonquin (the French Tonquin expedition) has happened to reach the little interior village this very day, and the excited people see in me an emissary of destruction, here for the diabolical purpose of spying out their country. A dozen reasons, however, might be here advanced, and all be far wide of the truth.

It is now getting pretty dark, and considering the unfortunate condition of my knee, the situation is, to say the least, annoying. It is not without apprehensions of being followed that I leave the village; and ere I am two hundred yards away, torches are observed moving rapidly about, and soon loud shouts of 'Fankwae, Fankwae!' tell me that a number of men are in pursuit.

Darkness favors my retreat, and scrambling down the river bank, I shape my course across the sand and shallow side-channels to a small island, thickly covered with bamboo, the location of which is now barely outlined against the lingering streaks of daylight in the western sky. Half an hour is consumed in reaching this; but no small satisfaction is derived from seeing the flaming torches of my pursuers continue on up the bank. The dense bamboo thickets afford an excellent hiding-place, providing my divergence is not suspected. A little farther up-stream, on the bank, are the lights of another village; and as I crouch here in the darkness I can see the torches of the pursuing party entering this village, and can hear them making shouting inquiries of their neighbors about the foreign devil.

The thicket is alive with ravenous mosquitoes that issue immediately their peculiar policy of assurance against falling asleep. Unappeased hunger, mosquitoes, and the perilousness of the situation occupy my attention for some hours, when, seeing nothing further of the vengeful aspirants for my gore, I drag my weary way up-stream, through sand and shallow water. Keeping in the river-bed for several miles, I finally regain the bank, and, although my inflamed knee treats me to a twinge of agony at every step, I steadily persevere till morning.

An hour or two of morning light brings me to the town of Quang-shi, after an awful tugging through sand-hills, unbridged ravines and water. Hardly able to stand from fatigue and the pain of my knee, the desperate nature of the road, or, more correctly, the entire absence of anything of the kind, and the disquieting incident of the night, awaken me to a realizing sense of my helplessness should the people of Quang-shi prove to be hostile. Conscious of my inability to run or ride, savagely hungry, and desperately tired, I enter Quang-shi with the spirit of a hunted animal at bay. With revolver pulled round to the front ready to hand, and half expecting occasion to use it in defence of my life, I grimly speculate on the number of my cartridges and the probabilty of each one bagging a sore-eyed Celestial ere my own lonely and reluctant ghost is yielded up.

All this, fortunately, is found to be superfluous speculation, for the good people of Quang-shi prove, at least, passively friendly; a handful of *tsin* divided among the youngsters, and a general spend-thrift scatterment of ten cents' worth of the same base currency among the stall-keepers for *chow-chow* heightens their friendly interest in me to an appreciable extent.

Chao-choo-foo is the next city marked on my itinerary, but as Quang-shi is not on my map I have no means of judging whether Chao-choo-foo is four *li* up-stream or forty. All attempts to obtain some idea of the distance from the natives result in the utter bewilderment of both questioned and querist.

Far easier, however, is it to make them understand that I want to go to that city by boat. The loquacious owner of a twenty-foot sampan puts in his appearance as soon as my want is ascertained, and favors me with an unpunctuated speech of some five minutes' duration. For fear I shouldn't quite understand the tenor of his remarks, he insists on thrusting his yellow Mongolian phiz within an inch or two of mine own. At the end of five minutes I thrust my fingers in my ears out of sheer consideration for his vocal organs, and turn away; but the next moment he is fronting me again, and repeating himself with ever-increasing volubility. Finding my dulness quite impenetrable, he searches out another loquacious mortal, and by the aid of the tiny beam-scales every Chinaman carries for weighing broken silver, they finally make it understood that for six big rounds (dollars) he will convey me in his boat to Chao-choo-foo. Understanding this, I promptly engage his services.

Bundles of joss-sticks, rice, fish, pork, and a jar of samshoo (rice arrack) are taken aboard, and by ten o'clock we are underway. Two men, named respectively Ah Sum and Yung Po, a woman, and a baby of eighteen months comprise the company aboard. Ah Sum, being but an inconsequential wage-worker, at once assumes the onerous duties of towman; Yung Po, husband, father, and sole proprietor of the sampan, manipulates the rudder, which is in front, and occasionally assists Ah Sum by poling.

Much of the scenery along the river is lovely in the extreme, and at dark we cast anchor in a smooth, silent reach of the river just within the frowning gateway of a rocky cañon. Dark masses of rock tower skyward five hundred feet in a perpendicular wall, casting a dark shadow over the twilight shimmer of the water. In the north, the darksome prospect is invested with a lurid glow, apparently from some large fire; the cañon immediately about our anchoring place is alive with moving torches, representing the restless population of the river, and on the banks clustering points of light here and there denote the locality of a village.

The last few miles has been severe work for poor Ah Sum, clambering among rocks fit only for the footsteps of a goat. He sticks to the tow-line manfully to the end, but wading out to the boat when over-heated, causes him to be seized with violent cramps all over; in his agony he rolls about the deck and implores Yung Po to put him out of his misery forthwith. His case is evidently urgent, and Yung Po and his wife proceed to administer the most heroic treatment. Hot samshoo is first poured down his throat and rubbed on his joints, then he is rolled over on his stomach; Yung Po then industriously flagellates him in the bend of the knees with a flat bamboo, and his wife scrapes him vigorously down the spine with the sharp edge of a porcelain bowl.

Ah Sum groans and winces under this barbarous treatment, but with solicitous upbraidings they hold him down until they have scraped and pounded him black and blue, almost from head to foot. Then they turn him over on his back for a change of programme. A thick joint of bamboo, resembling a quart measure, is planted against his stomach; lighted paper is then inserted beneath, and the 'cup' held firmly for a moment, when it adheres of its own accord.

This latter instrument is the Chinese equivalent of our

cupping-glass; like many other inventions, it was probably in use among them ages before anything of the kind was known to us. Its application to the stomach for the relief of cramps would seem to indicate the possession of drawing powers; I take it to be a substitute for mustard plasters. While the wife attends to this, Yung Po pinches him severely all over the throat and breast, converting all that portion of his anatomy into little blue ridges. By the time they get through with him, his last estate seems a good deal worse than his first, but the change may have saved his life.

Before retiring for the night lighted joss-sticks are stuck in the bow of the sampan, and lighted paper is waved about to propitiate the spirit of the waters and of the night; small saucers of rice, boiled turnip, and peanut-oil are also solemnly presented to the tutelary gods, to enlist their active sympathies as an offset against the fell designs of mischievous spirits. Falling asleep under the soothing influence of these extra-ordinary precautions for our safety and a supper of rice, ginger, and fresh fish, I slumber peacefully until well under way next morning. Ah Sum is stiff and sore all over, but he bravely returns to his post, and under the combined efforts of pole and tow-line we speed along against a swift current at a pace that is almost visible to the naked eye.

A few miles from No-foo-gong and a rocky precipice towers up on the west shore, something like a thousand feet high. The crackling of fire-crackers innumerable and the report of larger and noisier explosions attract my attention as we gradually crawl up toward it; and coming nearer, flocks of pigeons are observed flying uneasily in and out of caves in the lower levels of the cliff.

In the course of time our sampan arrives opposite and reveals a curious two-storied cave temple, with many gayly dressed people, pleasure sampans, and bamboo rafts. This is the Kum-yam-ngan, a Chinese Buddhist temple dedicated to the Goddess of Mercy. It is the home of flocks of sacred pigeons, and the shrine to which many pilgrims yearly come; the pilgrims manage to keep their feathered friends in a chronic state of trepidation by the agency of fire-crackers and miniature bombs. Outside, under the shelter of the towering cliffs to the right, are more temples or dwellings of the priests; they present a curious mixture of blue porcelain, rock, and brick which is intensely characteristic of China.

Yung Po now summons his entire pantomimic ability, to inform me that Chao-choo-foo is still some distance up the river, at all events that is my interpretation of his words and gestures. On this supposition I enter no objections when he bids me accompany him to the market and purchase a new supply of provisions for the remainder of the journey.

Impatient to proceed to Chao-choo-foo I now motion for them to make a start. Yung Po points to the frowning walls of the city we have just visited, and blandly says, 'Chao-choo-foo.' Having accomplished his purpose of bamboozling me into replenishing his larder, by making me believe our destination is yet farther upstream, he now turns round and tells me that we have already arrived. The neat little advantage he has just been taking of my ignorance with such brilliant results to the larder of the boat, has visibly stimulated his cupidity, and he now brazenly demands the payment of filthy lucre, making a circular hole with his thumb and finger to intimate big rounds in contradistinction to mere *tsin*.

The assumption of dense ignorance has not been without its advantages at various times on my journey around the world, and regarding Yung Po's gestures with a blankety blank stare, I order him to proceed up stream to Chao-choo-foo. The result of my refusal to be further bamboozled by the wily Yung Po, without knowing something of what I am doing, is that I am shortly threading the mazy alleyways of Chao-choo-foo with Ah Sum and Yung Po for escort. What the object of this visit may be I haven't the remotest idea, unless we are proceeding to the quarters of some official to have my passport seen to, or to try and enlighten my understanding in regard to Yung Po's claims for battered Mexican dollars.

Vague apprehensions arise that, peradventure, the six dollars paid at Quang-shi was only a small advance on the cost of my passage up, and that Yung Po is now piloting me to an official to establish his just claims upon pretty much all the money I have with me. Ignorant of the proper rate of boat hire, disquieting visions of having to retreat to Canton for the lack of money to pay the expenses of the journey through to Kui-kiang are flitting through my mind as I follow the pendulous motions of

Yung Po's pig-tail along the streets. The office that I have been conjuring up in my mind is reached at last, and found to be a neat room provided with forms and a pulpit-like desk.

A pleasant-faced little Chinaman in a blue silk gown is examining a sheet of written characters through the medium of a pair of tortoise-shell spectacles. On the wall I am agreeably astonished to see a chromo of Her Majesty Queen Victoria, with an inscription in Chinese characters. The little man chin-chins (salaams) heartily, removes his spectacles and addresses me in a musical tone of voice.

Yung Po explains obsequiously that my understanding of Chinese is conspicuously unequal to the occasion, a fact that at once becomes apparent to the man in blue silk; whereupon he quickly substitutes written words for spoken ones and presents me the paper. Finding me equally foggy in regard to these, he excuses my ignorance with a courteous smile and bow, and summons a gray-queued underling to whom he gives certain directions. This person leads the way out and motions for me to follow. Yung Po and Ah Sum bring up behind, keeping in order such irrepressibles as endeavor to peer too obtrusively into my face.

Soon we arrive at a quarter with big monstrous dragons painted on the walls, and other indications of an official residence; palanquin-bearers in red jackets and hats with tassels of red horse-hair flit past at a fox-trot with a covered palanquin, preceded by noisy gong-beaters and a gayly comparisoned pony. This is evidently the yamen or mandarin's quarter, and here we halt before a door, while our guide enters another one, and disappears. The door before us is opened cautiously by a Celestial who looks out and bestows upon me a friendly smile. A curly black dog emerges from between his legs and presents himself with much wagging of tail and other manifestations of canine delight.

All this occurs to me as very strange; but not for a moment does it prepare me for the agreeable surprise that now presents itself in the appearance of a young Englishman at the door. It would be difficult to say which of us is the most surprised at the other's appearance. Mutual explanations follow, and then I learn that, all unsuspected by me, two missionaries of the English Presbyterian mission are stationed at Chao-choo-foo.

At Canton I was told that I wouldn't see a European face nor hear an English word between that city and Kui-kiang. On their part, they have read in English papers of my intended tour through China, but never expected to see me coming through Chao-choo-foo.

I am, of course, overjoyed at the opportunity presented by their knowledge of the language to arrange for the continuation of my journey in a manner to know something about what I am doing. They are starting down the river for Canton to-morrow, so that I am very fortunate in having arrived to-day. As their guest for the day I obtain an agreeable change of diet from the swashy preparations aboard the sampan, and learn much valuable information about the nature of the country ahead from their servants. They have never been higher up the river than Chao-choo-foo themselves, and rather surprise me by giving the distances to Canton as two hundred and eighty miles.

By their kind offices I am able to make arrangements for a couple of coolies to carry the bicycle over the Mae-ling Mountains as far as the city of Nam-ngan on the head waters of the Kan-kiang, whence, if necessary, I can descend into the Yang-tsi-kiang by river. The route leads through a mountainous country up to the Mae-ling Pass, thence down to the head waters of Kan-kiang.

All is ready by eight o'clock on the morning of October 22nd; the coolies have lashed the bicycle to parallel bamboo poles, as also a tin of lunch biscuits, a tin of salmon, and of corned beef, articles kindly presented by the missionaries.

Nam-ngan is said to be two hundred miles distant, but subsequent experience would lessen the distance by about fifty miles. Our way leads first through the cemeteries of Chao-choo-foo, and along little winding stone-ways through the fields leading, in a general sense, along the right bank of the Pi-kiang.

The villagers in the upper districts of Quang-tung are peculiarly wanting in facial attractiveness; in some of the villages on the Upper Pi-kiang the entire population, from puling infants to decrepit old stagers whose hoary cues are real pig-tails in respect to size, are hideously ugly. They seem to be simple, primitive people, bent on satisfying their curiosity; but in the pursuit of this they are, if anything, somewhat more considerate or more conservative than the Persians.

A three-storied pagoda on a prominent hill to the right marks the approach to Nam-hung, and another of nine stories marks the entrance. Swarms of people follow us through the streets, rushing with eager curiosity to obtain a glimpse of my face. Sometimes the surging masses of people, struggling and pushing and dodging, separate me from the coolies, and the din of the shouting and laughing is so great that my shouts to them to stop are unheard. A shout, or a wave of the hand results only in a quickening of the people's curiosity and an increase in the volume of their own noisiness. Thus hemmed in among a compact mass of apparently well-meaning, but highly inflammable Chinese, hooting, calling, laughing, and gesticulating, I follow the lead of Ching-We and Wong-Yup through a mile of streets to the *hittim*.

At the *hittim*, with much angry expostulation and firmness of decision, the following mob are barred entrance to our room. They are not by any means satisfied, however; they quickly smash in a little closed panel so they can look in, and every crack between the boards betrays a row of peering eyes. Ching-We is a hollow-eyed victim of the drug, and yearns for peace and quiet so that he can pass away the evening amid the seductive pleasures of the opium-smoker's heaven. The rattle and racket of the determined sight-seers outside, clamorously demanding to come in and see the Fankwae, annoy him to the verge of desperation under the circumstances.

He patiently endeavors to forget it all, however, and to banish the whole troublesome world from his thoughts, by producing his opium-pipe and lamp and attempting to smoke. But just as he is getting comfortably settled down to rolling the little knob of opium on the needle and has puckered his lips for a good pull, a decayed turnip comes sailing through the open panel and hits him on the back. The people looking in add insult to injury by indulging in an audible snicker, as Ching-We springs up and glares savagely into their faces. This indiscreet expression of their levity at once seals their doom, for Ching-We grabs a pole and hits the boards such a resounding whack, and advances upon them so savagely, that only a few undaunted youngsters remain at their post; the panel is repaired, and comparative peace and quiet restored for a short time. No sooner, however, has Ching-We mounted to the first story of heavenly beatitude

Hardly a Cycling Country.

from the effects of the first pipe of opium, than loud howls of 'Fankwae! Fankwae!' are heard outside, and a shower of stones comes rattling against the boards. Ching-We goes to the partition door and indulges in an angry and reproachful attack upon the unoffending head of the establishment. The unoffending head of the establishment goes immediately to the other door and indulges in an angry and reproachful attack upon the shouters and stone-throwers outside. The Chinese are peculiar in many things, and in nothing, perhaps, more than their respect for words of reproach. Whether the long-suffering inn-keeper hurled at their heads one of the moral maxims of Confucius, or an original production of his own brain, is outside the pale of my comprehension; but whatever it is, there is no more disturbance outside.

It must be about midnight when I am awakened from a deep sleep by the gabble of many people in the room. Transparent lanterns adorned with big red characters held close to my face cause me to blink like a cat upon opening my wondering eyes. These lanterns are held by yameni-runners in semi-military garb, to light up my features for the inspection of an officer wearing a rakish Tartar hat with a brass button and a red horse-hair tassel. The yameni-runners wear the same general style of head-dress, but with a loop instead of the brass button. The officer is possessed of a wonderfully soft, musical voice, and holds forth at great length concerning me, with Ching-We.

The officer takes my passport to the yamen, and ere leaving the room, pantomimically advises me to go to sleep again. In the morning Ching-We returns the two-foot square document with the Viceregal seal, and winks mysteriously to signify that everything is lovely, and that the goose of permission to go ahead to Nam-ngan hangs auspiciously high.

The morning opens up cool and cloudy, the pebble pathway is wider and better than yesterday, for it is now the thoroughfare along which thousands of coolies stagger daily with heavy loads of merchandise to the commencement of river navigation at Nam-hung. The district is populous and productive; bales of paper, bags of rice and peanuts, bales of tobacco, bamboo ware, and all sorts of things are conveyed by muscular coolies to Nam-hung to be sent down the river.

Gradually have we been ascending since leaving Nam-hung,

and now is presented the astonishing spectacle of a broad flight of stone steps, certainly not less than a mile in length, leading up, up, up, to the summit of the Mae-ling Pass. Up and down this wonderful stairway hundreds of coolies are toiling with their burdens, scores of travellers in holiday attire and several palanquins bearing persons of wealth or official station. The stairway winds and zigzags up the narrow defile, averaging in width about twenty feet. Refreshment houses are perched here and there along the side, sometimes forming a bridge over the steps.

The stairway terminates at the summit in a broad stone archway of ancient build, over which are several rooms; this is evidently an office for the collection of revenue from the merchandise carried over the pass. Standing beneath this arch one obtains a comprehensive view of the country below to the north; a pretty picture is presented of gabled villages and temples, green hills, and pale-gold ripening rice-fields. The little silvery contributaries of the Kan-kiang ramify the picture like veins in the human palm, and the brown, cobbled pathways are seen leading from village to village, disappearing from view at short intervals beneath a cluster of tiled houses.

Steeper but somewhat shorter steps lead down from the pass, and the pathway follows along the bank of a tiny stream, leading through an almost continuous string of villages to the walls of Nam-ngan.

CHAPTER XVIII

DOWN THE KAN-KIANG VALLEY

The country is still nothing but river and mountains, and a sampan is engaged to float me down the Kan-kiang as far as Kan-tchou-foo, from whence I hope to be able to resume my journey a-wheel. The water is very low in the upper reaches of the river, and the sampan has to be abandoned a few miles from where it started. I then get two of the boatmen to carry the wheel, intending to employ them as far as Kan-tchou-foo.

From the stories current at Canton, the reputation of Kan-tchou-foo is rather calculated to inspire a lone Fankwae with sundry misgivings. Some time ago an English traveller, named Cameron, had in that city an unpleasantly narrow escape from being burned alive. The Celestials conceived the diabolical notion of wrapping him in cotton, saturating him with peanut-oil, and setting him on fire. The authorities rescued him not a moment too soon.

Ere we are five miles from the sampan these festive mariners of the Kan-kiang have developed into shuffling, shirking gormandizers, who peer longingly into every eating-house we pass by and evince a decided tendency to convert their task into a picnic. Finding me uncomplaining in footing their respective 'bills of lading' at the frequent places where they rest and indulge their appetites for tid-bits, they advance, in the brief space of four hours, from a simple diet of peanuts and bubbles of greasy pastry to such epicurean dishes as pickled duck, salted eggs, and fricasseed kitten!

The liberality of my purse for a short day and a half, with its concomitant luxurious living, has so thoroughly demoralized the unaccustomed river-men, that they encroach still further upon my bounty and forbearance by revelling all night in the sensuous delights of opium, at my expense, and turning up in the morning in anything but fit condition for the road. Putting this and that together, I conclude that we have not yet reached Kan-tchou-foo; but the carriers have developed into an insufferable nuisance, a hinderance to progress, rather than a help, so I determine to take them no farther.

I tell them nothing of my intentions until we reach a lonely spot a mile from the city. Here I tender them suitable payment for their services and the customary present, attach my loose effects to the bicycle and about my person, and motion them to return. As I anticipated, they make a clamorous demand for more money, even seizing hold of the bicycle and shouting angrily in my face. This I had easily foreseen, and wisely preferred to have their angry demonstrations all to myself, rather than in a crowded city where they could perhaps have excited the mob against me.

For the first time in China I have to appeal to my Smith & Wesson in the interests of peace; without its terrifying possession I should on this occasion undoubtedly have been under the necessity of 'wiping up a small section of Kiang-se' with these two worthies in self-defence. In the affairs of individuals, as of nations, it sometimes operates to the preservation of peace to be well prepared for war. How many times has this been the case with myself on this journey around the world!

The barometer of satisfaction at the prospect of reaching Kui-kiang before the appearance of old age rises from zero-level to a quite flattering height, as I find the pathways more than half ridable after delivering myself of the dead weight of native 'assistance.' Twelve miles farther and I am approaching the grim high walls of a large city that instinctively impresses me as being Kan-tchou-foo. The confused babel of noises within the teeming wall-encompassed city reaches my ears in the form of an 'ominous buzz,' highly suggestive of a hive of bees, into the interior of which it would be extremely ticklish work for a Fankwae to enter. 'Half an hour hence,' I mentally speculate, 'the pitying angels may be weeping over the spectacle of my seal-brown roasted remains being dragged about the streets by the ribald and exultant rag, tag, and bobtail of Kan-tchou-foo.'

The city probably contains two hundred thousand people, judging from the length of this street and the wonderful quantity and richness of the goods displayed in the shops.

Along this street I see a more lavish display of rich silks, furs, tiger-skins, and other evidences of opulence than was shown me at Canton. The pressure of the crowds reduces me at once to the necessity of drifting helplessly along, whithersoever the seething human tide may lead. Sometimes I fancy the few officiously interested persons about me, whom I endeavor to question in regard to the hoped-for Jesuit mission, have interpreted my queries aright and are piloting me thither; only to conclude by their actions, the next minute, that they have not the remotest conception of my wants, beyond reaching the other side of the city.

A dozen times during this trying trundle of a mile along the chief business thoroughfare of Kan-tchou-foo, the swelling whoops and yells of 'Fankwae' seem to portend the immediate bursting of the anticipated storm, and a dozen times I breathe easier at the subsidence of its volume. The while I am still hoping faintly for a repetition in part of my delightful surprise at Chao-choo-foo, we arrive at a gate leading out on to a broad paved quay of the Kan-kiang, which flows close by the walls.

Here I first realize the presence of Imperial troops, and awaken to the probability that I am indebted to their known proximity for the self-restraint of the mob, and their comparatively mild behavior. These Celestial warriors would make excellent characters on the spectacular stage; their uniforms are such marvels of color and pattern that it is difficult to disassociate them from things theatrical. Some are uniformed in sky blue, and others in the gayest of scarlet gowns, blue aprons with little green pockets, and blue turbans or Tartar hats with red tassels. Their gowns and aprons are patterned so as to spread out to a ridiculous width at bottom, imparting to the gay warrior an appearance not unlike an opened fan, his head constituting the handle.

As a matter of fact, the soldiers of the Imperial army are the biggest dandies in the country; when on the march coolies are provided to carry their muskets and accoutrements. As seen to-day, beneath the walls of Kan-tchou-foo, they impress me far more favorably as dandies than as soldiers equal to the demand of modern warfare.

Like soldiers the whole world round, however, they seem to be a good-natured, superior class of men; no sooner does my

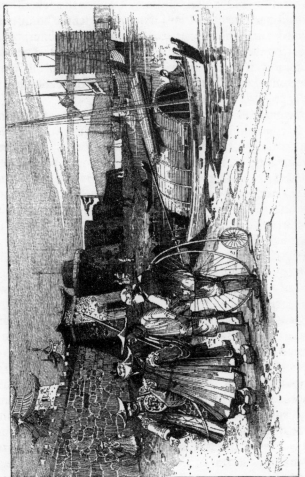

Beneath the Walls of Kan-tchou-foo.

presence become known than several of them interest themselves in checking the aggressive crowding of the people about me. Some of them even accompany me down to the ferry and order the ancient ferryman to take me across for nothing. This worthy individual, however, enters such a wordy protestation against this that I hand him a whole handful of the picayunish *tsin*. The soldiers make him give me back the overpayment, to the last *tsin*. The sordid money-making methods of the commercial world seem to be regarded with more or less contempt by the gallant sons of Mars everywhere, not excepting even the soldiers of the Chinese army.

The wonderful industry of these people is more apparent in this mountain-country than anywhere else. The valleys are very narrow, often little more than mere ravines between the mountains, and wherever a square yard of productive soil is to be found it is cultivated to its utmost capacity. In places the mountain-ravines are terraced to their very topmost limits, tier after tier of substantial rock wall banking up a few square yards of soil that have been gathered with infinite labor and patience from the ledges and crevices of the rocky hills. The uppermost terrace is usually a pond of water, gathered by the artificial drainage of still higher levels, and reserved for the irrigation of the score or more descending 'steps' of the rice-growing stairway beneath it.

The people hereabout seem unusually timid and alarmed at my strange appearance; it is both laughable and painful to see the women hobble off across the fields, frightened almost out of their wits. At times I can look about me and, within a radius of five hundred yards, see twenty or thirty females, all with deformed feet, scuttling off toward the villages with painful efforts at speed. One might well imagine them to be a colony of crippled rabbits, alarmed at the approach of a dog, endeavoring to hobble away from his destructive presence.

About four o'clock in the afternoon my road once again brings me to a ferry across the Kan-kiang. Just previous to reaching the river, I meet on the road eight men, carrying a sedan containing a hideous black idol about twice as large as a man. A mile back from the ferry is another large walled city with a magnificent pagoda; this city I fondly imagine to be Lin-kiang, next on my map and itinerary to Ki-ngan-foo, and I mentally congratulate myself on the excellent time I have been making for the last two days.

Across the ferry are several official sampans with a number of boys gayly dressed in red and carrying old battle-axes; also a small squad of soldiers with bows and arrows. No sooner does the ferryman land me than the officer in charge of the party, with a wave of his hand in my direction, orders a couple of soldiers to conduct me into the city; his order is given in an off-hand manner peculiarly Chinese, as though I were a mere unimportant cipher in the matter, whose wishes it really was not worth while to consult. The soldiers conduct me to the city and into the yamen or official quarter, where I am greeted with extreme courtesy by a pleasant little officer in cloth top-boots and a pigtail that touches his heels. He is one of the nicest little fellows I have met in China, all smiles and bustling politeness and condescension; a trifle too much of the latter, perhaps, were we at all on an equality; but quite excusable under the conditions of Celestial refinement and civilization on one side, and untutored barbarism on the other.

Having duly copied my passport (apropos of the Chinese doing almost everything in a precisely opposite way to ourselves may be pointed out the fact that, instead of attaching visés to the traveller's passport, like European nations, each official copies off the entire document), the little officer with much bowing and scraping leads the way back to the ferry. My explanation that I am bound in the other direction elicits sundry additional bobbings of the head and soothing utterances and smiles, but he points reassuringly to the ferry. Arriving at the river, the little officer is dumbfounded to discover that I have no sampan – that I am not travelling by boat, but overland on the bicycle. Such a possibility had never entered his head; nor is it wonderful that it should not, considering the likelihood that nobody, in all his experience, had ever travelled to Kui-kiang from here except by boat. Least of all would he imagine that a stray Fankwae should be travelling otherwise.

It is a drizzly, disagreeable morning as I trundle out of the city gate over cobble-stones, made slippery by the rain. Walking before me is a slim young yameni-runner with a short bamboo-spear, and on his back a white bull's eye eighteen inches in diameter; he is bare-footed and bare-headed and bare-legged.

In striking contrast to him is the dandified individual who brings up the rear, about ten paces behind the bicycle. He likewise is a yameni-runner, but of higher degree than his compatriot of the advance; instead of a vulgar and rusty spear, he is armed with an oiled paper parasol, a flaming red article ornamented with blue characters and gilt women. Besides this gay mark of distinction and social superiority, he owns both shoes and hat, carrying the former, however, chiefly in his hand; when fairly away from town, he deliberately turns his red-braided jacket inside out to prevent it getting dirty. This transformation brings about a change from the two white bull's-eyes, to big rings of stitching by which these distinguishing appendages are attached.

A substantial meal of yams and pork is obtained at a way-side eating-house, after which yet another evidence of the sybaritic tastes of the rear-guard comes to light, in the form of a beautiful jade-stone opium pipe, with which he regales himself after *chow-chow*. He is, withal, possessed of more than average intelligence; it is from questioning him that I learn the rather startling fact that, instead of having reached Lin-kiang, I have not yet even come to Ki-ngan-foo! Ta-ho is the name of the city we have just left, and Ki-ngan-foo is whither we are now directly bound.

The fastidious gentleman at the rear has betrayed symptoms of a very uneasy state of mind during the afternoon, and now, as he halts the procession a moment to turn the bull's-eye side of his coat outward, and to put on his shoes, he gives me a puzzled, sorrowful look and shakes his head dolefully. The trickiness of former acquaintances causes me to misinterpret this display of emotion into an hypocritical assumption of sorrow at the near prospect of our parting company, with ulterior designs on the nice long strings of *tsin* he knows to be in my leathern case. It soon becomes evident, however, that trouble of some kind is anticipated in Ki-ngan-foo, for he points to my revolver and then to the city and solemnly shakes his head.

As we proceed down the street my appearance seems to stir the population up to a pitch of wild excitement. Merchants dart in and out of their shops, people in rags, people in tags, and people in gorgeous apparel, buzz all about me and flit hither and thither like a nest of stirred-up wasps. If curiosity has seemed to be rampant in other cities it passes all the limits of Occidental imagination in Ki-ngan-foo. Upon seeing me everybody gives utterance to a peculiar spontaneous squeak of surprise, reminding me very much of the monkeys' notes of alarm in the tree-tops along the Grand Trunk road, India.

By the time we are half-way along the street the whole city seems in wild tumult. Men rush ahead, peer into my face, deliver themselves of the above-mentioned peculiar squeak, and run hastily down some convergent alley-way. Stall-keepers quickly gather up their wares, and shop-keepers frantically snatch their goods inside as they hear the tumult and see the mob coming down the street. The excitement grows apace, and the same wanton cries of 'Fankwae! Fankwae!' that followed me through Kan-tchou-foo are here repeated with wild whoops and exultant cries. One would sometimes think that all the devils of Dante's 'Inferno' had gotten into the crowd and set them wild with the spirit of mischief.

By this time the yameni-runners are quaking with fear; he of the paper parasol and jade-stone pipe walks beside me, convulsively clutching my arm, and with whiningly anxious voice shouts out orders to his subordinate. In response to these orders the advance-guard now and then hurries forward and peeps around certain corners, as though expecting some hidden assailants.

Thus far, although the symptoms of trouble have been gradually assuming more and more alarming proportions, there has been nothing worse than demoniacal howls. The chief reason of this, however, it now appears, has been the absence of loose stones, for no sooner do we enter an inferior quarter where loose stones and bricks are scattered about, than they come whistling about our ears. The poor yameni-runners shout deprecatingly at the mob; in return the mob loudly announce their intention of working destruction upon my unoffending head. Fortunately for me that head is pretty thoroughly hidden beneath the thick pith thatchwork of my Indian solar topee, otherwise I should have succumbed to the first fusillade of stones at the instance of a cracked pate.

Things begin to look pretty desperate as we approach the gate of the Manchu quarter; an immense crowd of people have hurried down back streets and collected at this gate; fancying they are there for the hostile purpose of heading us off, I come very near dodging into an open door-way with a view of defending myself till the yameni-runners could summon the authorities. There is no time for second thought, however; previous little time, in fact, for anything but to keep my helmet in its place and hurry along with the bicycle. The yameni-runners repeatedly warn the crowd that I am armed with a *top-fanchee* (revolver); this, doubtless, prevents them from closing in on us, and keeps their aggressive spirit within certain limits.

A moment's respite is happily obtained at the Manchu gate; the crowd gathered there in advance are comparatively peaceful, and the mob, for a moment, seem to hesitate about following us inside. Making the most of this opportunity, we hurry forward toward the yamen, which, I afterward learn, is still two or three hundred yards distant. Ere fifty yards are covered the mob come pouring through the gate, yelling like demons and picking up stones as they hurry after us. 'A horse, a horse, my kingdom for a horse!' or, what would suit me equally as well, a short piece of smooth road in lieu of break-neck cobble-stones.

Again are we overtaken and bombarded vigorously; ignorant of the distance to the yamen, I again begin looking about for some place in which to retreat for defensive purposes, unwilling to abandon the bicycle to destruction and seek doubtful safety in flight. At this juncture a brick strikes the unfortunate rear-guard on the arm, injuring that member severely, and quickening the already badly frightened yameni-runners to the urgent necessity of bringing matters to an ending somehow.

Pointing forward, they persist in dragging me into a run. Thus far I have been very careful to preserve outward composure, feeling sure that any demonstration of weakness on my part would surely operate to my disadvantage. The runners' appealing cries of 'Yameni! yameni!' however, prove that we are almost there, and for fifty or seventy-five yards we scurry along before the vengeful storm of stones and pursuing mob.

As I anticipated, our running only increases the exultation of the mob, and ere we get inside the yamen gate the foremost of them are upon us. Two or three of the boldest spirits seize the bicycle, though the majority are evidently afraid I might turn loose on them with the *top-fanchee*. We are struggling to get loose from these few determined ruffians when the officials of the yamen, hearing the tumult, come hurrying to our rescue.

The only damage done is a couple of spokes broken out of the bicycle, a number of trifling bruises about my body, a badly dented helmet, and the yameni-runner's arm rather severely hurt. When fairly inside and away from danger the pent-up feelings of the advance-guard escape in silent tears, and his superior of the jade-stone pipe sits down and mournfully bemoans his wounded arm. This arm is really badly hurt, probably has sustained a slight fracture of the bone, judging from its unfortunate owner's complaints.

The Che-hsein, as I believe the chief magistrate is titled, greets me while running out with his subordinates, with reassuring cries of 'S-s-o, s-s-o, s-s-o, s-s-o,' repeated with extraordinary rapidity between shouts of deprecation to the mob. The mob seem half inclined to pursue us even inside the precincts of the yamen, but the authoritative voice of the Che-hsein restrains their aggressiveness within partly governable measure; nevertheless, in spite of his presence, showers of stones are hurled into the yamen so long as I remain in sight.

As quickly as possible the Che-hsein ushers me into his own office, where he quickly proves himself a comparatively enlightened individual by arching his eyebrows and propounding the query, 'French?' 'Ying-yun,' I reply, feeling the advantage of being English or American, rather than French, more appreciably perhaps than I have ever done before or since.

It must be near about midnight when the excitement has finally subsided, and the mob disperse to their homes. Six yameni-runners then file into the room, paper umbrellas slung at their backs in green cloth cases, and stout bamboo quarter-staves in hand. The Che-hsein gives them their orders and delivers a letter into the hands of the officer in charge; he then bids me prepare to depart, bidding me farewell with much polite bowing and scraping, and sundry memorable 'chin-chins.'

A closely covered palanquin is waiting outside the door; into this I am conducted and the blinds carefully drawn. A squad of men with flaming torches, the Che-hsein, and several officials lead the way, maintaining great secrecy and quiet; stout carriers hoist the palanquin to their shoulders and follow on behind; others bring up the rear carrying the bicycle.

Back through the Manchu quarter and out of the gate again our little cavalcade wends its way, the officials immediately about the palanquin addressing one another in undertones; back, part way along the same street which but a few short hours ago resounded with the hoots and yells of the mischievous mob, down a long flight of steps, and the palanquin is resting at the end of a gang-plank leading aboard a little passenger sampan. The worthy Che-hsein bows and scrapes and chin-chins me along the gang-plank, the bicycle is brought aboard, the six yameni-runners follow suit, and the boat is poled out into the river.

It now becomes apparent that my bicycling experiences in China are about ending, and that the authorities have determined upon passing me down the Kan-kiang by boat to the Yang-tsi-kiang. I am to be passed on from city to city like a bale of merchandise, delivered and receipted for from day to day.

At early morn we land and pursue our way for a few miles across country to Lin-kiang, which is situated on a big tributary stream a few miles above its junction with the Kan-kiang. Our way leads through a rich strip of low country, sheltered and protected from inundations by an extensive system of dykes. Here we pass through orchards of orange-trees bristling with the small blood-red mandarin oranges; we help ourselves freely from the trees, for their great plenteousness makes them of very little value. On the stalls they can be purchased six for one cent; like the people in the great peanut producing country below Nam-hung, the cheapness and abundance of oranges here seems an inducement for the people to almost subsist thereon.

Everybody is either buying, stealing, selling, packing, gathering, carrying, or eating oranges; coolies are staggering Lin-kiang-ward beneath big baskets of newly plucked fruit, and others are conveying them in wheelbarrows; boats are being loaded for conveyance along the river. Every orange-tree is distinguished by white characters painted on its trunk, big enough so that those who run may read the rightful owner's name and take warning accordingly.

At length the river-voyage comes to an end at Wu-chang, on the Poyang Hoo, when I am permitted to proceed overland with an escort to Kui-kiang.

The paths improve, and soon I see the smoke of a steamer on

the Yang-tsi-kiang; than which, it is needless to say, no more welcome sight has greeted my vision the whole world round. Only the smoke is seen, rising above the city; it cannot be a steamer, it is too good to be possible! this isn't Kui-kiang; this is another wretched disappointment, the smoke is some Chinese house on fire! Not until I get near enough to distinguish flags on the consulates, and the crosses on the mission churches, do I permit myself fully to believe that I am at last actually looking at Kui-kiang, the city that I have begun to think a delusion and a snare, an *ignis fatuus* that was dancing away faster than I was approaching.

The sight of all these unmistakable proofs that I am at last bidding farewell to the hardship, the horrible filth, the soul-harrowing crowds, the abominable paths, and the ever-present danger and want of consideration; that in a little while all these will be a dream of the past, gives wings to my wheel wherever it can be mounted and ridden. The yameni-runner is left far behind, and I have already engaged a row-boat to cross the little lake in the rear of the city, and the boatman is already pulling me to the 'Ying-yun,' when the poor yameni-runner comes hurrying up and shouts frantically for me to come back and fetch him.

Knowing that the man has to take back his receipt I yield to his request, follow him first to the Kui-kiang yamen, and from thence proceed to the English consulate. Captain McQuinn, of the China Steam Navigation Company's steamer Peking, and the consulate doctor see me riding down the smooth gravelled bund, followed by a crowd of delighted Celestials. 'Hello! are you from Canton?' they sing out in chorus. 'Well, well, well! nobody expected to ever see anything of you again; and so you got through all safe, eh?'

'What's the matter? you look bad about the eyes,' says the observant doctor, upon shaking hands; 'you look haggard and fagged out.'

Upon surveying myself in a mirror at the consulate I can see that the doctor is quite justified in his apprehensions. Hair long, face unshaven for five weeks, thin and gaunt-looking from daily hunger, worry, and hard dues generally, I look worse than a hunted greyhound. I look far worse, however, than I feel; a few days' rest and wholesome fare will work wonders.

An appetizing lunch of cold duck, cheese, and Bass's ale is quickly provided by Mr. Everard, the consul, who seems very pleased that the affair at Ki-ngan-foo ended without serious injury to anybody.

The Peking starts for Shanghai in an hour after my arrival; a warm bath, a shave, and a suit of clothes, kindly provided by pilot King, brings about something of a transformation in my appearance. Bountiful meals, clean, springy beds, and elegantly fitted cabins, form an impressive contrast to my life aboard the sampans on the Kan-kiang. The genii of Aladdin's lamp could scarcely execute any more marvellous change than that from my quarters and fare and surroundings at the village *hittim*, where my last night on the road from Canton was spent, and my first night aboard the elegant and luxurious Peking, only a day later.

A pleasant run down the Yang-tsi-kiang to Shanghai, and I arrive at that city just twenty-four hours before the Japanese steamer, Yokohama Maru, sails for Nagasaki.

CHAPTER XIX

THROUGH JAPAN

Nagasaki lies at the shoreward base of a range of hills, over a pass called the Himi-toge, which my road climbs immediately upon leaving the city. A good road is maintained over the pass, and an office established there to collect toll from travellers and people bringing produce into Nagasaki. The aged and polite toll-collector smiles and bows at me as I trundle innocently past his sentry-box-like office up the steep incline, hoping that I may take the hint and spare him the necessity of telling me the nature of his duty. My inexperience of Japanese tolls and roads, however, renders his politeness inoperative, and, after allowing me to get past, duty compels him to issue forth and explain. A wooden ticket containing Japanese characters is given me in exchange for a few tiny coins. This I fancy to be a passport for another toll-place higher up. Subsequently, however, I learn it to be a return ticket, the old toll-keeper very naturally thinking I would return, by and by, to Nagasaki.

About sunset I roll into the smooth, clean streets of Omura, a good-sized town, and seek the accommodation of a charming *yadoya* (inn) pointed out by a youth in semi-European clothes, who seems bubbling over with pleasure at the opportunity of rendering me this slight assistance. A room is assigned me upstairs, a mat spread for me to recline on, by a polite damsel, who touches her forehead to the floor both when she makes her appearance and her exit. Having got me comfortably settled down with the customary service of tea, sweets, little boxed brazier of live charcoal, spittoon, etc., the proprietor, his wife, and daughter, all come up and prostrate themselves after the most approved fashion.

After all the salaaming and deferentiality experienced in other Eastern countries, one still cannot help being impressed with the spectacle of several grotesque Japs bowing before one's

The Himi-toge Toll-house.

seated figure like Hindoos prostrating themselves before some idol. With any other people than the Japs this lowly attitude would seem offensively servile; but these inimitable people leave not the slightest room for thinking their actions obsequious. The Japs are a wonderful race; they seem to be the happiest people going, always smiling and good-natured, always polite and gentle, always bowing and scraping.

After a bountiful supper of several fishy preparations and rice, the landlord bobs his head to the floor, sucks his breath through the teeth after the peculiar manner of the Japs when desirous of being excessively polite, and extends his hands for my passport. This the *yadoya* proprietor is required to take and have examined at the police station, provided no policeman calls for it at the house.

The Japanese Government, in its efforts to improve the institutions of the country, has introduced systems of reform from various countries. Commisssions were sent to the different Western countries to examine and report upon the methods of education, police, army, navy, postal matters, judiciary, etc. What was believed to be the best of the various systems was then selected as the model of Japan's new departure and adoption of Western civilization. Thus the police service is modelled from the French, the judiciary from the English, the schools after the American methods, etc. Having inaugurated these improvements, the Japs seem determined to follow their models with the same minute scrupulosity they exhibit in copying material things. There is probably as little use for elaborate police regulations in Japan as in any country under the sun; but having chosen the splendid police service of France to pattern by, they can now boast of having a service that lacks nothing in effectiveness.

A very good road, with an avenue of fine spreading conifers of some kind, leads out of Omura. To the left is the bay of Omura, closely skirted at times by the road. At one place is observed an inland temple, connected with the mainland by a causeway of rough rock. The little island is covered with dark pines and jagged rocks, amid which the Japs have perched their shrine and erected a temple. Both the Chinese and Japs seem fond of selecting the most romantic spots for their worship and the erection of religious edifices.

The gravelly hills about Ureshino are devoted to the cultivation of tea; the green tea-gardens, with the undulating, even rows of thick shrubs, looking very beautiful where they slope to the foot of the bare rocky cliffs. Ureshino and the baths are some little distance off the main road to Shimonoseki; so, not caring particularly to go there, I continue on to the village of Takio, where rainy weather compels a halt of several hours. Everything is so delightfully superior, as compared with China, that the Japanese village *yadoya* seems a veritable paradise during these first days of my acquaintance with them. Life at a Chinese village *hittim* for a week would wellnigh unseat the average Anglo-Saxon's reason, whereas he might spend the same time very pleasantly in a Japanese country inn. The region immediately around Takio is not only naturally lovely, but is embellished by little artificial lakes, islands, grottoes, and various landscape novelties such as the Japs alone excel in.

In every town and village one is struck with the various imitations of European goods. Ludicrous mistakes are everywhere met with, where this serio-comical people have attempted to imitate name, trade-mark, and everything complete. In one portion of the eating-house where lunch is obtained to-day are a number of umbrella-makers manufacturing gingham umbrellas; on every umbrella is stamped the firm-name 'John Douglas, Manchester.'

The happiest state of affairs seems to exist among all classes and conditions of people in Japan. One passes school-houses and sees the classes out on the well-kept grounds, going through various exercises, such as one would never expect to see in the East. To-day I pause a while before the public-school in Nakabairu, watching the interesting exercises going on. Under the supervision of teachers in black frock-coats and Derby hats, a class of girls are ranged in two rows, throwing and catching pillows, altogether – back and forth at the word of command. Classes of boys are manipulating wooden dumb-bells and exercising their muscles by various systematic exercises. The youngsters are enjoying it hugely, and the whole affair looks so thoroughly suggestive of the best elements of Occidental school-life that it is difficult to believe the evidence of one's own eyes. I suspect the Japanese children are about the only children in the wide, wide world who really enjoy studying their lessons and going to school. One of the teachers comes to the gate and greets me with a polite bow. I address him in English, but he doesn't know a word.

Following for some distance along the bank of a large canal I reach the village of Hakama for the night. The *yadoya* here is simply spotless from top to bottom; however the Japanese hotel-keeper manages to transact business and preserve such immaculate apartments is more of a puzzle every day. The regulation custom at a *yadoya* is for the newly arrived guest to take a scalding hot bath, and then squat beside a little brazier of coals, and smoke and chat till supper-time. The Japanese are more addicted to hot-water bathing than the people of any other country. They souse themselves in water that has been heated to 140° Fahr., a temperature that is quite unbearable to the 'Ingurisu-zin' or 'Amerika-zin' until he becomes gradually hardened and accustomed to it. Both men and women bathe regularly in hot water every evening. The Japs have not yet imbibed any great quantity of *mauvaise honte* from their association with Europeans, so the sexes frequent the bath-tub indiscriminately, taking no more notice of one another than if they were all little children. 'Venus disporting in the waves' – of a bath-tub – is a regular feature of life at a Japanese inn. Nor can they quite understand why the European tourist should object to the proprietor, his wife and children, chambermaid, tea-girls, guests and visitors crowding around to see him undress and waltz into the tub. Bless their innocent Japanese souls! why *should* he object? They are only attracted out of curiosity to see the whiteness of his skin, to note his peculiar manner of undressing, and to satisfy a general inquisitiveness concerning his corporeal possibilities. They have no squeamishness whatever about his watching their own natatorial duties; why, then, should he shrink within himself and wave them off?

From Hakamatsu to Kokura the country is hilly and broken; from Kokura one can look across the narrow strait and see Shimonoseki, on the mainland of Japan. Thus far we have been traversing the island of Kiū-Shiū, separated from the main island by a strait but a few hundred yards wide at Shimonoseki. From Kokura the jinrikisha road leads a couple of *ri* farther to Dairi; thence footpaths traverse hills and wax-tree groves for another two miles (a *ri* is something over two English miles) to the village of Moji. Here I obtain passage on a little ferry-boat across to Shimonoseki, arriving there about two o'clock in the afternoon.

A big Shinto temple occupies the crest of a little hill near by, and flights of stone steps lead up to the entrance. At the foot of the steps, and repeated at several stages up the slope, are the peculiar *torii*, or 'bird-perches,' that form the distinctive mark of a Shinto temple. Numerous shrines occupy the court-yard of the temple; the shrines are built of wood mostly, and contain representations of the various gods to whose particular worship they are dedicated. Before each shrine is a barred receptacle for coins. The Japanese devotee poses for a minute before the shrine, bowing his head and smiting together the palms of his hands; he then tosses a diminutive coin or two into the barred treasury, and passes on round to the next shrine he wishes to pay his respects to.

The architecture of the villages above Shimonoseki is strikingly artistic. The quaint gabled houses are painted a snowy white, and are roofed with brown glazed tiles of curious pattern, also rimmed with white. About the houses are hedges grotesquely clipped and trained in imitation of storks, animals, or fishes, miniature orange and persimmon trees, pretty flower-gardens and little landscape vanities peculiar to the Japanese. Circling around through little valleys, over small promontories and along smooth, gravelly stretches of sea-shore road, for thirty miles, brings me to anchor for the night in a good-sized village.

Most farm-houses are now thatched with straw; one need hardly add that they are prettily and neatly thatched, and that they are embellished by various unique contrivances. Some of them, I notice, are surrounded by a broad, thick hedge of dark-green shubbery. The hedge is trimmed so that the upper edge appears to be a continuation of the brown thatch, which merely changes its color and slopes at the same steep gradient to the ground. This device produces a very charming effect, particularly when a few neatly trimmed young pines soar above the hedge like green sentinels about the dwelling. One inimitable piece of 'botanical architecture' observed to-day is a thick shrub trimmed into an imitation of a mountain, with trees growing on the slopes, and a temple standing in a grove. Before

many of the houses one sees curious tree-roots or rocks, that have been brought many a mile down from the mountains, and preserved on account of some fanciful resemblance to bird, reptile, or animal. Artificial lakes, islands, waterfalls, bridges, temples, and groves abound; and at occasional intervals a large figure of the Buddha squats serenely on a pedestal, smiling in happy contemplation of the peace, happiness, prosperity, and beauty of everything and everybody around. Happy people! happy country! Are the Japs acting wisely or are they acting foolishly in permitting European notions of life to creep in and revolutionize it all? Who can tell? Time alone will prove. They will get richer, more powerful, and more enterprising, because of the necessity of waking themselves up to keep abreast of the times; but wealth and power, and the buzz and rattle of machinery and commerce do not always mean happiness.

CHAPTER XX

THE HOME STRETCH

The following morning is frosty, and low, scudding clouds denote unsettled weather, as I resume my journey. Much of the time my road practically follows the shore, and sometimes simply follows the windings and curvatures of the gravelly beach. Most of the low land near the shore appears to be reclaimed from the sea – low, flat-looking mud-fields, protected from overflow by miles and miles of stout dikes and rock-ribbed walls. Fishing villages abound along the shore, and for long distances a recent typhoon has driven the sea inland and washed away the road. Thousands of men and women are engaged in repairing the damages with the abundance of material ready to hand on the sloping granite-shale hills around the foot of which the roadway winds.

Fish are cheaper and more plentiful here than anything else, and the old dame at the *yadoya* of a fishing village cooks me a big skate for supper, which makes first-rate eating, in spite of the black, malodorous sauce she uses so liberally in the cooking.

In this room is a wonderful brass-bound cabinet, suggestive of soul-satisfying household idols and comfortable private worship. During the evening I venture to open and take a peep in this cabinet to satisfy a pardonable curiosity as to its contents. My trespass reveals a little wax idol seated amid a wealth of cheap tinsel ornaments, and bits of inscribed paper. Before him sets an offering of rice, *saké*, and dried fish in tiny porcelain bowls.

Clear and frosty opens the following morning; the road is good, the country gradually improves, and by nine o'clock I am engaged in looking at the military exercises of troops quartered in the populous city of Hiroshima. The exercises are conducted within a large square, enclosed with a low bank of earth and a ditch. Crowds of curious civilians are watching the efforts of

I pull up at a village Yadoya.

raw cavalry recruits to ride stout little horses, that buck, kick, bite, and paw the air. Every time a soldier gets thrown the on-lookers chuckle with delight. Both men and horses are undersized, but look stocky and serviceable withal. The uniform of the cavalry is blue, with yellow trimmings. The artillery looks trim and efficient, and the horses, although rather small, are powerful and wiry, just the horses one would select for the rough work of a campaign.

Everybody in Japan smokes, both men and women. The universal pipe of the country is a small brass tube about six inches long, with the end turned up and widened to form the bowl. This bowl holds the merest pinch of tobacco; a couple of whiffs, a smart rap on the edge of the brazier to knock out the residue, and the pipe is filled again and again, until the smoker feels satisfied. The girls that wait on one at the *yadoyas* and tea-houses carry their tobacco in the capacious sleeve-pockets of their dress, and their pipes sometimes thrust in the sash or girdle, and sometimes stuck in the back of the hair.

The important city of Okoyama provides abundant food for observation – the clean, smooth streets, the wealth of European goods in the shops, and the swarms of ever-interesting people, as I wheel leisurely through it on Saturday, December 4th. No human being save Japs has so far crossed my path since leaving Nagasaki, nor am I expecting to meet anybody here. An agreeable surprise, however, awaits me, for at the corner of one of the principal business thoroughfares a couple of American missionaries appear upon the scene. Introducing themselves as Mr. Carey and Mr. Rowland, they inform me that three families of missionaries reside together here, and extend a cordial invitation to remain over Sunday. I am very glad indeed to accept their hospitality for to-morrow, as well as to avail myself of an opportunity to get my proper bearings. Nothing in the way of a reliable map or itinerary of the road I have been traversing from Shimonoseki was to be obtained at Nagasaki, and I have travelled with but the vaguest idea of my whereabouts from day to day. Only from them do I learn that the city we meet in is Okoyama, and that I am now within a hundred miles of Kobe, north of which place 'Murray's Handbook' will prove of material assistance in guiding me aright.

Pleasant days are spent at Kobe and Ozaka. Twenty-seven

miles of level road from the latter city, following the course of the Yodo-gawa, a broad shallow stream that flows from Lake Biwa to the sea, brings me to Kioto. From the eighth century until 1868 Kioto was the capital of the Japanese empire, and is generally referred to as the old capital of the country. The present population is about a quarter of a million, about half of what it was supposed to be in the heyday of its ancient glory as the seat of empire.

Living at Kioto is Mr. B—, an Amercian ex-naval officer, who several years ago forsook old Neptune's service to embark in the more peaceful pursuit of teaching the ideas of youthful Japs to shoot. The occasion was auspicious, for the whole country was fired with enthusiasm for learning English. English was introduced into the public schools as a regular study. Mr. B— is settled at Kioto, and now instructs a large and interesting class of boys in the mysteries of his mother tongue. Taking a letter of introduction he makes me comfortable for the afternoon and night at his pleasant residence on the banks of the Yodo-gawa. Under the pilotage of his private jinrikisha-man, I spend a portion of the afternoon in making a flying visit to various places of interest.

At Kioto begins the Tokaido, the most famous highway of Japan, a road that is said to have been the same great highway of travel, that it is to-day, for many centuries. It extends from Kioto to Tokio, a distance of three hundred and twenty-five miles.

Another road, called the Nakasendo, the 'Road of the Central Mountains,' in contradistinction to the Tokaido, the 'Road of the Eastern Sea,' also connects the old capital with the new; but, besides being somewhat longer, the Nakasendo is a hillier road, and less interesting than the Tokaido. After leaving the city the Tokaido leads over a low pass through the hills to Otsu, on the lovely sheet of water known as Biwa Lake.

This lake is of about the same dimensions as Lake Geneva, and fairly rivals that Switzer gem in transcendental beauty. The Japs, with all their keen appreciation of the beauties of nature, go into raptures over Biwa Lake. Much talk is made of the 'eight beauties of Biwa.' These eight beauties are: The Autumn Moon from Ishi-yama, the Evening Snow on Hira-yama, the Blaze of Evening at Seta, the Evening Bell of Mii-dera, the Boats sailing back from Yabase, a Bright Sky with a Breeze at Awadzu, Rain by Night at Karasaki, and the Wild Geese alighting at Katada. All the places mentioned are points about the lake. All sorts of legends and romantic stories are associated with the waters of Lake Biwa. Its origin is said to be due to an earthquake that took place several centuries before the Christian era; the legend states that Fuji rose to its majestic height from the plain of Suruga at the same moment the lake was formed. Temples and shrines abound, and pilgrims galore come from far-off places to worship and see its beauties.

A *ri* beyond Okabe and the pass of Utsunoya necessitates a mile or two of trundling. Here occurs a tunnel some six hundred feet in length and twelve wide; a glimmer of sunshine or daylight is cast into the tunnel by a system of simple reflectors at either entrance. These are merely glass mirrors, set at an angle to reflect the rays of light into the tunnel.

Descending this little pass the Tokaido traverses a level rice-field plain, crosses the Abe-kawa, and approaches the sea-coast of Shidzuoka, a city of thirty thousand inhabitants. The view of Fuji, now but a short distance ahead, is extremely beautiful; the smooth road sweeps around the gravelly beach, almost licked by the waves. The breakers approach and recede, keeping time to the inimitable music of the surf; vessels are dotting the blue expanse; villages and tea-houses are seen resting along the crescent-sweep of the shore for many a mile ahead, where Fuji slopes so gracefully down from its majestic snow-crowned summit to the sea.

It is indeed a glorious ride around the crescent bay, through the sea-shore villages of Okitsu, Yui, Kambara, and Iwabuchi to Yoshiwara, a little town on the footstool of the big, gracefully sweeping cone. The stretch of shore hereabout is celebrated in Japanese poetry as Taga-no-ura, from the peculiarly beautiful view of Fuji obtained from it.

This remarkable mountain is the highest in Japan, and is probably the finest specimen of a conical mountain in existence. Native legends surround it with a halo of romance. Its origin is reputed to be simultaneous with the formation of Biwa Lake, near Kioto, both mountain and lake being formed in a single night – one rising from the plain twelve thousand eight hundred feet, the other sinking till its bed reached the level of the sea.

The summit of Fuji is a place of pilgrimage for Japanese ascetics who are desirous of attaining 'perfect peace' by imitating Shitta-Tai-shi, the Japanese Buddha, who climbed to the summit of a mountain in search of *nirvana* (calm). Orthodox Japs believe that the grains of sand brought down on the sandals of the pilgrims ascend to the summit again of their own accord during the night.

Down the street near my *yadoya*, within a boarded enclosure, a dozen wrestlers are giving an entertainment for a crowd of people who have paid two *sen* apiece entrance-fee. The wrestlers of Japan form a distinct class or caste, separated from the ordinary society of the country by long custom, that prejudices them against marrying other than the daughter of one of their own profession. As the biggest and more muscular men have always been numbered in the ranks of the wrestlers, the result of this exclusiveness and non-admixture with physical inferiors is a class of people as distinct from their fellows as if of another race. The Japanese wrestler stands head and shoulders above the average of his countrymen, and weighs half as much more. As a class they form an interesting illustration of what might be accomplished in the physical improvement of mankind by certain Malthusian schemes that have been at times advocated.

Within a twelve-foot arena the sturdy athletes struggle for the mastery, bringing to bear all their strength and skill. No 'hippodroming' here: stripped to the skin, the muscles on their brown bodies standing out in irregular knots, they fling one another about in the liveliest manner. The master of ceremonies, stiff and important, in a faultless gray garment bearing a samurai crest, stands by and wields the fiddle-shaped lacquered insignia of his high office, and utter his orders and decisions in an authoritative voice.

The country observed from the elevation of the Hakone Pass is extremely beautiful, the white-tipped cone of the magnificent Fuji towering over all, like a presiding genius. Near the hamlet of Yamanaka is a famous point, called Fuji-mi-taira (terrace for looking at Fuji). Big cryptomerias shade the broad stony path along much of its southern slope to Hakone village and lake.

Hakone is a very lovely and interesting region, nowadays a favorite summer resort of the European residents of Tokio and Yokohama. From the latter place Hakone Lake is but about fifty miles distant, and by jinrikisha and kago may be reached in one day. The lake is a most charming little body of water, a regular mountain-gem, reflecting in its clear, crystal depths the pine-clad slopes that encompass it round about, as though its surface were a mirror. Japanese mythology peopled the region round with supernatural beings in the early days of the country's history, when all about were impenetrable thickets and pathless woods. Until the revolution of 1868, when all these old feudal customs were ruthlessly swept away, the Tokaido here was obstructed with one of the 'barriers,' past which nobody might go without a passport. These barriers were established on the boundaries of feudal territories, usually at points where the traveller had no alternate route to choose.

Gangs of men are dragging stout hand-carts, loaded with material for the construction of the Tokaido railway, now rapidly being pushed forward. Every mile of the road is swarming with life – the strangely interesting life of Japan. Thirty miles from Yomoto, and Totsuka provides me a comfortable *yadoya*, where the people quickly show their knowledge of the foreigner's requirements by cooking a beefsteak with onions, also in the morning by charging the first really exorbitant price I have been confronted with along the Tokaido. Totsuka is within the treaty limits of Yokohama. A mile or so toward Yokohama I pass, in the morning, the 'White Horse Tavern,' kept in European style as a sort of road-house for foreigners driving out from that city or Tokio.

A fierce wind, blowing from the south, fairly wafts me along the last eleven miles of the Tokaido, from Totsuka to Yokohama.

Kanagawa is practically a suburban part of Yokohama: one Japanese-owned clock observed here points to the hour of eight, another to eleven, and a third to half past-nine, but the clock at the Club Hotel, on the Yokohama bund, is owned by an Englishman, and is just about striking ten, when the last vault from the saddle of the bicycle that has carried me through so many countries is made. And so the bicycle part of the tour around the world, which was begun April 22, 1884, at San Francisco, California, ends December 17, 1886, at Yokohama.

At this port I board the Pacific mail steamer City of Peking, which in seventeen days lands me in San Francisco. Of the enthusiastic reception accorded me by the San Francisco Bicycle Club, the Bay City Wheelmen, and by various clubs throughout the United States, the daily press of the time contains ample record. Here, I beg leave to hope that the courtesies then so warmly extended may find an echoing response in this long record of the adventures that had their beginning and ending at the Golden Gate.

ITINERARY:

GIVING THE NAME AND DATE OF EACH SLEEPING-POINT ON THE BICYCLE TOUR AROUND THE WORLD

VOLUME I

UNITED STATES

CALIFORNIA

1884		
April	22	San Francisco
	23	House in the tuiles
	24	Elmira
	25	Sacramento
	26	Near Rocklin
	27–28	Clipper Gap
	29	Blue Cañon
	30	Summit House

NEVADA

May	1	Verdi
	2	Ranch on Truckee River
	3	Hot Springs
	4	Lovelocks
	5	Mill City
	6	Winnemucca
	7	Stone House
	8	Ranch on Humboldt
	9	Palisade
	10	Carlin
	11	Halleck
	12	C P Section House

UTAH

	13	Tacoma
	14	Matlin
	15	Salt House
	16	Near Corrinne
	17	Willard City
	18	Ogden
	19	Echo City
	20	Castle Rocks

WYOMING TERRITORY

May	21	Evanston
	22	Hilliard
	23	In abandoned freight wagon
	24	Carter Station
	25	Near Granger
	26	Rocks Springs
	27	Ranch
	28–29	Rawlins
	30	Carbon
	31	Lookout
June	1–2	Laramie City
	3	Cheyenne

NEBRASKA

	4	Pine Bluffs
	5	Potter Station
	6	Lodge Pole
	7	Ranch on Platte
	8	Ogallala
	9	In a 'dug-out'
	10	Brady Island
	11	Plum Creek

	12	Kearney Junction
	13	Grand Island
	14	Duncan
	15	North Bend
	16	Fremont
	17–18	Omaha

IOWA

	19	Farm near Nishnebotene
	20	Farm near Griswold
June	21	Farm near Menlo
	22	Farm near De Soto
	23	Altoona
	24	Kellogg
	25	Victor
	26	Tiffin
	27	Moscow

ILLINOIS

	28	Rock Island
	29	Atkinson
	30	La Moile
July	1	Yorkville
	2	Naperville
	3	Lyons
	4–11	Chicago

INDIANA

	12	Miller Station
	13	Beneath a wheat shock
	14	Goshen
	15	Farm

OHIO

	16	Ridgeville
	17	Empire House
	18	Bellevue
	19	Village near Cleveland
	20	Madison

PENNSYLVANIA

| | 21 | Roadside Hotel near Erie |

NEW YORK

	22	Angola
	23	Buffalo
	24	Leroy
	25	Farm near Canandaigua
	26	Marcellus
	27	East Syracuse
	28	Erie Canal Inn
	29	Indian Castle
	30	Crane's Village
	31	Westfalls Inn

MASSACHUSETTS

Aug.	1	Otis
	2	Palmer
	3	Worcester
	4	Boston

EUROPE

ENGLAND

1885		Liverpool
May	2	Warrington
	3	Stone
	4	Coventry
	5	Fenny Stratford
	6	Great Berkhamstead
	7–8	London
	9	Croydon
	10	British Channel Steamer

FRANCE

Via		Dieppe
	11	Elbeuf
	12	Mantes
	13–15	Paris
	16	Sezanne
	17	Bar le Duc
	18	Tronville
	19	Nancy

GERMANY

| | 20 | Phalzburg |

21	Strasburg			**ASIA**

21 Strasburg
22 Oberkirch
23 Rottenburg
24 Blauburen
25–26 Munich
27 Alt Otting

AUSTRIA – HUNGARY

28 Hoag
29 Strenberg
30 Neu Lengbach
31 Vienna
June 1–3 Vienna
4 Altenburg
5 Neszmely
6–7 Budapest
8 Duna Pentele
9 Szegazard
10 Duna Szekeso
11–12 Eszek
13 Sarengrad
14 Neusatz
15 Batanitz

SERVIA, BULGARIA, AND TURKEY

16–17 Belgrade
18 Jagodina
19 Nisch
June 20–21 Bela Palanka
22 Sofia
23 Ichtiman
24 Near Tartar Bazardjic
25 Cauheme
26 Near Adrianople
27–28 Eski Baba
29 Small Village
30 Tchorlu
July 1 Camped out
2 Constantinople

6,000 miles wheeled from San
Francisco.

ASIA

ASIA MINOR

Aug. 10 Ismidt
11 Geiveh
12 Terekli
13 Beyond Torbali
14 Nalikhan
15 Bey Bazaar
16–17 Angora
18 Village
19 Camped out
20 Koordish Camp
21 Yuzgat
22 Camped out
23 Village
24–25 Sivas
26 Zara
27 Armenian Village
28 Camp in a cave
29 Merriserriff
30 Erzingan
31 Houssenbeg Khan
Sept. 1 Village in Euphrates
Valley
2–6 Erzeroum
7 Hassan Kaleh
8 Dela Baba
9 Malosman
10 Sup Ogwanis Monas-
tery

PERSIA

11 Ovahjik
12 Koordish Camp
13 Peri
14 Khoi
15 Village near Lake
Ooroomiah
16 Village near Tabreez
17–20 Tabreez
21 Hadji Agha
22 Turcomanchai
23 Miana

24	Koordish Camp	28	Kasveen
25–26	Zendjan	29	Yeng Imam
27	Heeya	30	Teheran

VOLUME II

1886

Mar.	10	Katoum-abad
	11	Aivan-i-Kaif
	12	Aradan
	13–15	Lasgird
	16	Semnoon
	17	Gusheh
	18	Deh Mollah
	19–20	Shahrood
	21	Mijamid
	22	Miandasht
	23–24	Mazinan
	25	Subzowar
	26	Wayside caravanserai
	27	Shurab
	28	Gadamgah
Mar.	29	Wayside caravanserai
	30–	
Ap.	6	Meshed
April	7	Shahriffabad
	8	Caravanserai
	9	Torbet-i-Haiderai
	10	Camp on Goonabad Desert
	11	Kakh
	12	Nukhab
	13	Small hamlet
	14	Beerjand
	15	Ali-abad
	16	Darmian
	17	Tabbas
	18	Huts on desert edge

AFGHANISTAN

April	19	Camp on Desert of Despair
	20	Nomad camp

	21	Village on Harud
	22	Ghalakua
	23	Nomad camp
	24–25	Furrah (arrested by Afghans)
	26	Nomad camp
	27	Subzowar
	28	Nomad camp
	29	Camp out
	30–	
May	9	Herat
May	10	Village
	11	Roadside *umbar*
	12	Camp in Heri-rood jungle

PERSIA

	13	Karize (released by Afghans
	14	Nomad camp
	15	Furriman
	16–18	Meshed
	19	Caravanserai
	20	Near Nishapoor
	21	Lafaram
	22	Wayside *umbar*
	23	Mazinan
	24	Near caravanserai
	25	Camp out
	26–27	Shahrood
	28	Camp out
	29	Asterabad
	30	Bunder Guz

Russian steamer to Baku; rail to Batoum; steamer to Constantinople and India. Renewed bicycle tour:

INDIA

Aug.		Lahore
	1	Amritza
	2	Beas River
	3	Jullunder
	4	Police chowkee
	5–6	Umballa
	7	Peepli
	8	Paniput
	9	Police chowkee
	10–14	Delhi
	15	Dàk bungalow
	16	Bungalow
	17	Muttra
Aug.	18–19	Agra
	20	Mainipoor
	21	Miran-serai
	22–26	Cawnpore
	27	Caravanserai
	28	Caravanserai
	29–30	Roadside hut
Sept.	1–2	Benares
	3	Mogul-serai
	4	Caravanserai
	5	Dilli
	6	Shergotti
	7	Dàk bungalow
	8	Dàk bungalow
	9	Burwah
	10	Rannegunj
	11	Burdwan
	12	Hooghli
	13–17	Calcutta

Steamer to Canton –

CHINA

Oct.	7–12	Canton
	13	Chun-kong-hi
	14	Low-pow
	15	Chin-yuen
	16	Bamboo thicket
	17–20	Aboard sampan
	21	Schou-chou-foo
	22	Small village
	23	Do.
	24	Nam-hung
	25–28	Nam-ngan
	29	Aboard sampan
	30	Large village
	31	Large village near Kan-tchou-foo
Nov.	1	Small mountain hamlet
	2	Walled garrison city
	3	Ta-ho
	4	Ki-ngan foo (under arrest)
	5–15	Under arrest on sampan
	16	Inn near Kui-Kiang
	17	Yangtsi-Kiang steamer
	18	Shanghai
	19–20	Japanese steamer

JAPAN

	21–22	Nagasaki
	23	Omura
	24	Ushidza
	25–26	Futshishi
	27	Hakama
	28	Shemonoseki
	29	Village
	30	Do.
Dec.	1	A small fishing hamlet
	2	Do.
	3	Do.
	4–5	Okoyama
Dec.	6	Himeji
	7–8	Kobe
	9	Ozaka
	10	Kioto
	11	Saka-no-shita
	12	Miya
	13	Hamamatsu
	14	Roadside inn
	15	Mishima
	16	Totsuka
	17	Yokohama

DISTANCE ACTUALLY WHEELED, ABOUT 13,500 MILES.